*Ay, in the catalogue ye go for men;*
*As hounds and greyhounds, mongrels, spaniels, curs,*
*Shoughs, water-rugs and demi-wolves, are clept*
*All by the name of dogs: the valued file*
*Distinguishes the swift, the slow, the subtle,*
*The housekeeper, the hunter, every one*
*According to the gift which bounteous nature*
*Hath in him closed, whereby he does receive*
*Particular addition, from the bill*
*That writes them all alike: and so of men.*

— William Shakespeare, *Macbeth*,
Act III, Scene 1

*here princes paupers criminals and saints are all the same*
*no more or less than god's beloved child aboard this train*

— Julie Miller, "Orphan Train," 1999

# Conceiving Parenthood

American Protestantism
and the Spirit of Reproduction

*Amy Laura Hall*

WILLIAM B. EERDMANS PUBLISHING COMPANY
GRAND RAPIDS, MICHIGAN / CAMBRIDGE, U.K.

Published 2008 by
Wm. B. Eerdmans Publishing Co.
2140 Oak Industrial Drive N.E., Grand Rapids, Michigan 49505 /
P.O. Box 163, Cambridge CB3 9PU U.K.

Printed in the United States of America

12  11  10  09  08        7  6  5  4  3  2  1


Library of Congress Cataloging-in-Publication Data

Hall, Amy Laura.
    Conceiving parenthood: American Protestantism and the
  spirit of reproduction / Amy Laura Hall.
          p.      cm.
    Includes bibliographical references and index.
    ISBN  978-0-8028-3936-7 (cloth: alk. paper)
  1. Family — Religious aspects — Christianity. 2. Parenting —
  Religious aspects — Christianity. 3. Child rearing — Religious aspects —
  Christianity. 4. Human reproduction — religious aspects —
  Protestant churches. 5. Family — United States. 6. Parenting —
  United States. 7. Child rearing — United States.
  8. Human reproduction — United States.    I. Title.

  BV4526.3.H35    2008
  261.8′358740973 — dc22

                                            2007039265

www.eerdmans.com

This book is dedicated to my grandparents

*Ethel Mae Elliston Hall*
*Robert McConnell Hall*

*Agnes Louise Alagood Tisdale*
*Francis Ray Tisdale*

to my parents

*Robert Edward Hall*
*Carol Azalee Tisdale Hall*

and to my daughters

*Rachel Hall Utz*
*Emily Hall Utz*

# Contents

# INTRODUCTION:
## Conceiving Parenthood

American Protestantism
and the Spirit of Reproduction

*Hope of the world, thou Christ of great compassion,*
*speak to our fearful hearts by conflict rent.*
*Save us, thy people, from consuming passion,*
*who by our own false hopes and aims are spent.*

*Hope of the world, God's gift from highest heaven,*
*bringing to hungry souls the bread of life,*
*still let thy spirit unto us be given,*
*to heal earth's wounds and end all bitter strife.*

*Hope of the world, afoot on dusty highways,*
*showing to wandering souls the path of light,*
*walk thou beside us lest the tempting byways*
*lure us away from thee to endless Night.*

*Hope of the world, who by thy cross didst save us*
*from death and dark despair, from sin and guilt,*
*we render back the love thy mercy gave us;*
*take thou our lives, and use them as thou wilt.*

*Hope of the world, O Christ o'er death victorious,*
*who by this sign didst conquer grief and pain,*
*we would be faithful to thy gospel glorious;*
*thou art our Lord! Thou dost forever reign.*[1]

Georgia Harkness, 1954

1. "HOPE OF THE WORLD," Words: Georgia Harkness, Words © 1954, ren. 1982 The

1

Figure 0.1. Advertisement for birthing center at Duke Health Raleigh Hospital. The ad copy reads: "In the world of hospital birthing centers, consider us the smart little boutique where you always find the latest thing (exactly in your size.) . . . Just the place to find something perfect to take home with you."

This advertisement ran inside the front cover of *Carolina Parent,* a free monthly magazine for parents in "the Triangle," the region of North Carolina encompassing Raleigh, Durham, and Chapel Hill that considers itself the epicenter of the New South.

I picked up a copy outside our favorite, kid-friendly diner in Durham. Much to my family's chagrin (I was supposed to be off-duty, reading the magazine as a lark with the kiddos), I became quickly absorbed by the advertisement. The ad touts the attractions of the "boutique" birthing center at Duke Health Raleigh Hospital, a place where new mothers can "find something perfect to take home with" them. I found a chilling question left hanging there among the posh frocks. What if a woman partook of Duke's boutique services and ended up with a baby who was, well . . . common, or *unique* in a way some might not consider quite the *right sort of unique?*

That question hangs over many medically governed pregnancies in the twenty-first century. What if a woman's baby turns out to be not quite what she expected when she was expecting? What if the creature that was to be "exactly in [her] size" turns out not to be the "perfect" "something" to take home? Consider the woman who has kept religiously to the rules of the "Best Odds Diet" from this generation's best-selling pregnancy guide, *What to Expect When You're Expecting*. What if she finds herself faced with the news that she is carrying a distinctly *unexpected* fetus? Did she fail? Or, what if she is called to welcome someone else's infant, child, or even teenager into her home, perhaps one whose needs are not at all what she expected when she dreamed someday of expecting?

In many civic conversations in the United States about genetic manipulation and so-called designer babies, commentators express moral disgust with the would-be mother who might choose to design her family. "What kind of monster-mom would be drawn to such discriminating technology?" This seems to be the rhetorical punch behind many comments on the biotechnological future of mothering. But American critics of designer babies seldom grapple with the pressures bearing down on many middle-class to upper-class women when they set out to determine precisely *when* to expect and *whom* to expect. Critics consider even less the pressures bearing down on the working-class women who face unemployment if they fail to reproduce according to their boss's schedule for production.

Many of the white, middle-class women I have corresponded with while writing this book have told me they feel a responsibility to be discriminating. They have deemed it their task to be choosy for the sake of their family's future, or even their nation's future. Women have explained (at times in excruciatingly painful detail) the pressure they feel under to conceive of parenthood in ways that involve meticulous timing and intense quality control. A woman described the pressure to time her pregnancies *just so* for the sake of optimal sibling relationships and college financing. A colleague described the importance of conceiving on time to maximize limited maternity leave, and to schedule a medically nonnecessary cesarean to minimize interruption from work. Another beloved friend described the pressure that led her to terminate one twin with Down syndrome for the sake of the other, "normal" twin sharing the womb. Another told of the pressure she felt to achieve what has come to be called "gender balancing" through selective in vitro fertilization. Many mothers related the pressure they felt to watch for even a week's delay in the *to-be-expected* timing for the first recognizable smile, bowel movement, full night's sleep, for weight gain (for baby) and weight loss (for mother); the pressure to find the optimal preschool, elementary teacher, and gifted program; the pressure, in sum, to give birth to and then form a child who will cohere to the expectations of her family, friends, and neighbors.

I have also heard in painful detail the stories of parents on the *other* side. I have heard story after story of parents who have children deemed as those-to-be-avoided, whether through prenatal screening, standardized testing and school tracking, private schooling, neighborhood selection, or the careful race segregation that attends much of American life. These are what Laurie Zoloth, in lament, has called "Wal-Mart children," children who are the opposite of the boutique pregnancies Duke Health Raleigh Hospital refers to in the advertisement above. As one mother in a Roman Catholic parish in Durham put it, "My kid is the one that other mothers hope won't be in *their* child's class, pulling them down; and that totally stinks. There are fewer and fewer Down syndrome kids around, because of abortion, and I think that it is going to be harder and harder for parents like me to find schools to help our kids learn." These are children who, by the same logic of choosiness pressuring many white, upper-middle-class pregnancies, seem inadequately *planned*, whether due to disability, spacing, maternal age, race, or some combination of these.

The stories of parents whose kids do not fit or who are considered woefully "at risk" propelled me to write this book. These stories taught me not to discount as merely pathetic the anxieties of parents with "normal children." Such stories from parents on the margins played in my mind throughout this project, jangling in strange concord yet discord with the stories of mothers struggling to find the very best piano teacher for their budding musical genius.

Are these stories new? Do they represent a shift in parenthood itself? Well, yes and no. Early during my time on the faculty at Duke University I was asked to serve as the only woman and the only nonscientist on a panel discussing a new, characteristically ambitious genomics program. The title of the panel was "Does Genomics Pose *New* Ethical Questions?" It was in sweating over my preparation for that panel that I came to suspect that the new era of reproductive biotechnology actually poses many of the same *old* ethical questions. "Who is my neighbor?" and "Am I my brother's keeper?" both came to mind. Also, I kept wondering, "Who do you say that I am?"

We proceeded that night with the standard academic dog and pony show, during which everyone politely agreed to disagree without calling one another shocking names. Afterward I was packing up my bag to leave, hoping that somehow God had spoken through my awkward testimony in that sterile academic space. The sound technician came forward to pick up the microphones. As he was winding up the electrical cords, he leaned over to me and said quietly, "You know, my son has autism. If we had known while my wife was pregnant that he had that, we probably would not have him today. I am glad we didn't know. I love him. Thanks for what you said."

Such unexpected testimonies arrived as a complicated blessing and summons throughout this project. Just when I thought I was only blowing hot air into the already overinflated discipline that is "medical ethics," I would be approached by an unwed mother who was proud to have resisted her social worker's pressure to use Norplant; by a couple who had refused prenatal testing and was then scolded by medical professionals when their child was born with a disability; by a grandfather who had lost his job with a Christian firm when he had embraced as a gift his supposedly "illegitimate" grandchild; by a minister whose Latino parishioners were being pressured to give up their children for foster care because they couldn't answer fully the social worker's questions in English. I do not expect this book to give any clear answers to any radically new ethical questions posed by new technologies. But our look back into American history may help us note the ways some very old questions reverberate in our families and our neighborhoods. The supposedly brave new world of biotechnology overlays an old world of fear, shame, and class aspiration.

I also came to understand that some ideal, inchoate group of people called "the church" was not going to work as the easy answer to the old questions. One friend related a story from a faculty meeting, during which senior scholars known for extolling the importance of hospitality refused to give up their primo parking spaces for a few months to a colleague greatly pregnant with twins. I have been privy to stories about faculty who refused to designate child-care space in amply situated seminary buildings. My idealism about "the church" and something called "Christian community" dissipated during my first years as a "Christian ethicist." Any institution on the make, much like an aspiring family, is likely to be tempted to seek primarily approval from the world of quantified value.

Yet there are indeed real churches and faithful institutions testifying otherwise. Many colleagues and my wonderful students at Duke Divinity School consistently brought me stories of hope writ small. The same students and faculty navigating the high-pressure aspirations of the academy brought to me, like manna, stories of incarnate, forgiving, and complicated care in their rural North Carolina parishes in the middle of "nowhere," in their ministries with downtown parishes that had been supposedly forsaken by God, and in their daily work in underfunded social service agencies with children who were viewed as beyond help. The stories were not grand — not showcases of quantifiable pastoral leadership, but stories of quiet transformation. The blessed, daily banality of grace in real congregations, as told by my pastor-students and pastor-colleagues, has seemed at least as palpable as the frustrating hypocrisy of organized mainline Protestantism.

One pastor's story narrates well the intertwining of blessing and struggle in congregational life. The pastor got a call that a young couple, after several years of hoping and nine months of embodied longing, had received their long-awaited baby. But the grandparent calling the pastor wanted to make clear that the baby's mother did not want the pastor to visit them in the hospital. Understanding from the tone that more than mere modesty was involved in the request, the pastor gently asked if he could be of help in some way. Yes, through prayer, the caller responded, for the baby girl had been born with a cleft palate. Perhaps because he prayerfully respected the mother's wishes, the pastor was eventually invited to the hospital to pray with the couple and their baby. He told me later that he was able simply to say to the mother that her baby was beautiful. For she was, he explained to me, "beautiful." The young couple went on to struggle with their news, and the spreading of their news throughout the relatively small community. They did not bring the baby to church, so reluctant were they, perhaps, to deal with the awkward comments of others. And, somewhat to the pastor's confusion, they waited until the baby was well past the usual time to have her baptized. They waited until the series of reconstructive surgeries to erase the mark of disability was complete before they brought the child to be liturgically marked as God's own.

When I asked the pastor if he could explain the couple's reaction, he said he thought they were probably troubled by a sense of shame. On further reflection, he wondered whether this young, professional couple had not felt a bit afraid of being perceived as poor white people, given that many white people in that region seem even now to associate cleft palate with families living in white poverty.

Yet the pastor had also been, through grace, capable of the holy patience that could indeed wait for this baptism. Rather than heaping another level of shame onto the young couple, admonishing them for their fear, he waited for them to be ready to bring their beloved child to the font. It is also no small feat of holy courage that the young mother did not count her child to be marked indelibly as a mistake, as a sign that she had failed as a mother or as proof that God was powerless to transform. The story is one of delayed baptism, but the baby was baptized in God's time. She was received in the midst of a congregation that had waited until the couple was ready to come back to church.

The shame, blessing, and grace intertwined in this simple story may give the reader hope to resist the narratives of shame. It is my prayer that stories like this one will emerge as people read and discuss the book. For, indeed, the material covered in this book begs for hopeful resistance.

## A Story of Two Families

This is a story of two families. One of them happy, one of them sad. One of them clean, the other careless. One of them healthy, and one of them sick. Suppose we call them the clean family and the careless family. Now how does it happen that the careless family is sick while the clean family is not?[2]

We begin our journey into the realm of science, faith, and children with America's grand storyteller himself. The Walt Disney film *Cleanliness Brings Health* was part of the Health for the Americas campaign of 1945, produced for the Office of Inter-American Affairs. The film begins and ends with the image shown in figure 0.2. The frame depicts two easels; two families, two worlds apart. Throughout the film a bronzed man's hand reaches into the frame to paint the images, to switch the scenes on either side of the dichotomy, and, on one occasion, to pull a wandering, cross-eyed pig out of the careless family's home. The ostensible message of the film is fairly simple. Build a latrine; wash your hands and clothes regularly with "plenty of good soap"; cook your food in a raised oven and protect it from flies; sweep your yard and house; etc.

I was referred to this film by a graduate student, Jennifer MacKenzie, who found it while researching postwar Disney shorts. When I brought it home, my daughters (who can spot a cartoon a mile away) begged to watch it with me. So all of us — Mom, Dad, and kids — watched the movie several times so that I could take my scholarly notes. Knowing the basic nature of my research, the girls were a flurry of helpful observation: "But, Mom, you tell us to wash our hands all the time!"; "But, Mom, shouldn't we sweep our house?"; and "Ooh! That is so gross! They should wash their hands!" My husband asked me about my maternal prudence. Should we show this film as a

---

2. *Cleanliness Brings Health*, Walt Disney Productions, 1945. Available on DVD *Walt Disney Treasures — on the Front Lines* (2004).

**Figure 0.2. Scene from *Cleanliness Brings Health***

source of ironic cultural reading when, after all, we *do* want our daughters to wash their hands, not poop in the yard, and not eat feces-infested dirt?

Good point. I am not *anti*-soap. (Although no farm-lard soap would produce the suds supposedly necessary for cleanliness in the film.) But the Disney film uses a clear didactic of *shame*. Rather than using one easel, with one family going about their day washing with soap, penning their happy pigs, and using the latrine, the film employs another family's indignity to reinforce its message. Quite apart from the ridiculously whiter whites of the clean family's clothing and the outrageous lathering quality of the white soap they have so prudently procured, the film sets up a working dichotomy between one family and the other. Beginning with the two easels, the cartoon narrative toggles back and forth between clean and careless, between the industrious and idle. The careless family enters their predicament in sickness, midstream in their predicament of laziness. Even before the father inadvertently eats fecal matter and thus cannot work, the family is drawn as slouching, scratching, half-dressed, and devoid of countenance. Their faces are continually hidden from the viewer, as the disembodied hand drawing their fate has left them without real personhood. Selling the clean family depends on shaming the dirty family, and linking the latter to unhappiness, poverty, irresponsibility, and illness. Selling the clean family depends on instilling in viewers the fear that they too might be perceived by the all-seeing universal viewer as irresponsible and dirty. The viewers must, therefore, take a particular kind of hygienic care — with their dishes, their kitchens, their yards, and their children — lest they be mistaken as idle. The careless family's suffering is due to their own careless ways.

The film gives a compelling answer to the opening question — "Now how does it happen that the careless family is sick while the clean family is not?" The cinematic form of the answer is rhetorically powerful. Now that *you* have seen the film, how will *you be seen?* If indeed the theologian is right, that mercy is a virtue cultivated in the knowledge that we are like kin with those who suffer, this Walt Disney film offers the case against mercy.

Some readers may find my rhetoric here overblown. But I will be delighted indeed if readers find their lives marked by embodied kinship with those whose families are considered dirty, careless, profligate, and idle. I will be delighted to hear from mainstream white Americans who are eager to teach their children solidarity with *those* children counted subtly as mistaken or beyond help. The chapters that follow represent merely one plausible narration of the period and technologies covered. Nothing I present here is beyond dispute, and nothing will give me greater pleasure than to prompt among congregations and families the stories of *otherwise.*

I do suggest, however, that this material have a sobering effect on those who care for children, whether in the home, congregation, neighborhood, or nation-state. It can help us note the ways that stories like this tale of two families work their way into how we perceive our own children, our own kitchens, our own neighbors, and the neighbors we carefully try not to see. This book may help readers perceive the vicious *comparison* that seems to creep into so many conversations about family life in the United States. Tracing the thread of social Darwinism implicit in much of American culture, we may note that many conversations about families and children in the United States presume an economics of scarcity. Mainline Protestant conversations — that is, the default way of speaking for those in the decision-making classes — denote the fear of being perceived as ill-fitted for a struggle to survive and flourish in an economy with not enough to go around.

As a white, Methodist clergywoman in a church considered by many historians to be the most characteristically American, I have a vested interest in this wake-up call. The irony beneath this book involves my belief that the very Protestant tradition that should have emphasized a sense of divine gratuity, human contingency, sufficient abundance, and the radical giftedness of all life came in twentieth-century America instead to epitomize *justification by meticulously planned procreation.* To put this point in its starkest possible form: a tradition that had within it the possibility of leveling all believers as orphaned and gratuitously adopted kin came instead to baptize a culture of carefully delineated, racially encoded domesticity.

By doing so, mainline middle-class Protestantism sold out in at least two ways. First, by downplaying the gratuity of grace, middle-class Protestants endorsed a particular configuration of domesticity as a means to do no less than "save the world." My own tradition, American Methodism, had become increasingly enamored with "the allure of respectability" by the beginning of the twentieth century.[3] What had happened to New England Methodists in the mid–nineteenth century became paradigmatic for Methodism throughout the nation. The movement's "original fire" became "tempered with virtues of middle-class propriety and urbane congeniality." What began as a "populist movement" eventually "doubled back," as historian Nathan Hatch words it, "toward learning, decorum, professionalism, and social standing."[4] Accomplishing the proper model of family life came to be the way an American couple could prove themselves providentially fit.

Second, in American mainline Protestantism this culturally loaded conception of kinship subtly distinguished *us* from *them,* reinforcing race as a dividing line in American religion, and not just in the South. The relatively self-sufficient, middle-class, white, Protestant nuclear family of two parents and two or perhaps three aptly gender-balanced children came to be the model by which all other configurations, colors, and classes of domesticity were viewed as, at best, unusual. Thus, through various outward signs of an invisible grace, mainline Protestantism became the default mode of Americana — what Margaret Lamberts Bendroth calls the "neutral backing to the ethnic crazy quilt of American diversity."[5] Those whose lives did not fit were all too often conceived not so much as markers of "diversity" (a conception that is itself theologically suspect) but as *ill-begotten.*

This pressure toward respectability involved a didactic of aspiration and shame, subtly and sometimes overtly depicting families who were not up to the "mythical standard" of "white, middle-class mainline Protestants" as "other," to quote again Lamberts Bendroth. The rhetoric of domestic hygiene

---

3. Nathan Hatch, *The Democratization of American Christianity* (New Haven: Yale University Press, 1989), pp. 201-6.

4. Hatch, *Democratization of American Christianity,* p. 202.

5. Margaret Lamberts Bendroth, *Growing Up Protestant: Parents, Children, and Mainline Churches* (New Brunswick, N.J.: Rutgers University Press, 2002), p. 1.

and health in the Disney film depends on a set of questions posed to the viewer. In a raw way, the caricature of poor hygiene and poverty encourages what seems to be at play in much that I will cover in this book: envy upward, disdain downward, and assessing, horizontal comparison. How, then, is a society to deal with sickness? How is a country's leadership to deal with human suffering? By one plausible reading of the American family in the twentieth century, the language of health, domestic hygiene, human responsibility, and divine providence intertwines so that there arises a fear of being associated with suffering, together with a responsibility, whenever possible, to distance one's family from those mothers who seem, in contrast to the "clean family," careless.

While this will be explicit in chapter 1, "Holy Hygiene," the pattern will continue as we move through the marketing of infant formula and "scientific motherhood" in chapter 2, the various attempts to "form a more perfect union" through eugenics as covered in chapter 3, and the ways that the atomic-powered utopia of the future is marketed in the Atomic Age, as narrated in chapter 4. It is my argument that the rhetoric at play in this Disney short is still at play in the pursuit of domestic hygiene, the appeal of pediatric psychopharmaceuticals, and the allure of planning with precision in "the genomic revolution."

## "The More Valuable Types of People"

The implications of the divide between planned and ill-begotten reverberate throughout debates on public school funding, immigration, and regional family planning. A eugenics essay from 1931 has a title that reverberates in the Duke Health Raleigh Hospital advertisement from 2004 and the Disney short of 1945: "Wanted: Better Babies: How Shall We Get Them?" The editors of *People* explain: "President Hoover says progress is the margin by which the next generation excels this. *People* here offers a discussion by four experts on how to widen the margin."[6] Interspersed with photographs of naked babies playing with blocks and small children engaged in industrious role-playing, the article aims to answer the live question (then, as now) of social spending on families with children.

Ellsworth Huntington, noted as "co-author of *The Builders of Amer-*

---

6. Ellsworth Huntington, Eugene Robinson, Ray Erwin Baber, and Maurice R. Davie, "Wanted: Better Babies: How Shall We Get Them?" *People,* April 1931, pp. 2, 3. Courtesy of Cold Spring Harbor Eugenics Archive.

*ica*," begins the piece by explaining the basic criteria by which social spending on parents and children must be judged. First, does the social spending raise "the number of children in families where both parents rise well above the average in intelligence, strength of character, and general value as members of society"?[7] This is a basic argument of eugenics, to which we will return in chapter 3. But the second criterion gives significant pause. It says the spending should help ensure that the right sorts of families do not have to intermingle with the wrong sorts: "how fully does [the scheme] satisfy the economic requirement of insuring the selected families against the decline in the standard of living which is often the penalty of having children?" Huntington elaborates:

> Insurance against a decline in the standard of living means more than relief of the sudden financial strain which often accompanies the birth of a child. It means also that as the number of children increases up to reasonable limits, the family is not obliged to economize to a degree that is painful or humiliating, but can live essentially as before. Some sacrifice on the part of the parents for the sake of children is doubtless desirable, but it is obviously too much to ask ordinary human beings to step down to a lower economic level and build a new set of social relationships because they have three or four children.[8]

To put Huntington's point simply, the "finest of our middle classes" (as he names the sector at which eugenic social spending should aim) should not have to step down and intermingle with those beneath them. The effort to "build a new set of social relationships" is more than leaders should expect from those they wish to encourage toward propitious procreating. Moving on to assess various forms of such schemes, Huntington argues that those whom eugenicists deem to be "the more valuable types of people" can best be encouraged to procreate if they know they will not have to become *associated with* those who are "obviously incompetent or weak."[9] Indeed, Huntington worries that any scheme will be too easily hijacked by people who wish to make all social insurance "apply to all classes alike." Better to wait, he suggests, for a cultural consensus about who should and should not have babies. In this way, in the future, society can be assured that the right sort of mother will be prepared to devote "her life to the bringing up of healthy, happy, hearty children who will be real contributors to human progress."

7. Huntington et al., "Wanted," p. 2.
8. Huntington et al., "Wanted," p. 2.
9. Huntington et al., "Wanted," p. 48 (continued from p. 2).

### "Morally Obligated to Plan"

In this book we will focus at various points on the Methodist church in America, a church that may be more or less epitomized by the May 1958 cover of *Together: The Midmonth Magazine for Methodist Families* (fig. 0.3). A father and mother, their son, and their daughter ride in a motorboat that sports an American flag flying jauntily behind. The little girl points upward, and the entire family looks off to their left, our right. The article title at the top right of the cover is characteristic of many articles in this postwar venture toward what Dan Wakefield (in a review of *Together* for the *Nation*) called "slick-paper Christianity."[10] "Who Should Own the Moon?" the title asks. Beneath this title runs a promise that "The Christian Family" will appear "in color" in the pages that follow. This combination of patriotism, the balanced family of four, the assumption of proprietary leadership, and the depiction of "The Christian Family" is compelling. The sense that it was Methodists like those pictured here in full color that should determine through careful discernment just "who should own the moon" says much. In a 1967-68 Gallup poll, Methodists were named the religious group "most liked" by members of other denominations.[11] As this friendly form of neighborly leadership hit home, it did so with a powerful rhetoric of "responsible parenthood."

In 1954 the Methodist church held a national conference on family life right on the heels of the World Council of Churches assembly in Evanston, Illinois. The theme of the World Council gathering was "Christ the Hope of the World." The Methodist theme? "The Christian Family — the Hope of the World" (fig. 0.4).

"There is no contradiction in these themes," Bishop G. Bromley Oxnam explained, for the Christian family must serve as that "unifying force" to bring together "the community, the nation, and eventually the world."[12] In the face of "expanding imperialism" and the serious threat of atomic warfare, it was the nuclear family that would unite all peoples, as pictured in the banner unfurled across the globe.

In his address to the gathering, Bishop Oxnam delineated the particulars of a Christian home and family. Salient for our purposes are two remarks, one

10. Dan Wakefield, "Slick-Paper Christianity," *Nation*, January 19, 1957, pp. 56-57. Thanks to Andy Keck for this reference.

11. Peter Williams, *America's Religions: From Their Origins to the Twenty-First Century* (Urbana: University of Illinois Press, 2002), p. 365.

12. Bishop G. Bromley Oxnam, "The Christian Family, the Hope of the World," in *Report: The Christian Home — the Hope of the World,* pp. 3-6. Bishop Oxnam's title reflects that of the conference; the title of the report has slightly different wording.

**Figure 0.3. Cover of *Together: The Midmonth Magazine for Methodist Families*, May 1958**

Figure 0.4. Banner for Methodist conference on family life, 1954

on segregation and the other on "the proper spacing of children." It makes no sense, the bishop explained, to set apart "a child because it is the least bit darker in complexion than the other members of the family." The way Bishop Oxnam explicated the meaning of integration, however, is notable: "Every child of God is entitled to that place in society which he has won by his industry and character." It is contrary to "democracy" and "true religion" to keep someone from a "position of honor" because of the color of his skin. "Surely a man has the unsegregated right to earn his living in terms of his capacity and his character." In this summary Oxnam effectively expanded the meritocracy of the previous generation toward the possible inclusion of those with "darker" skin. This impulse represented a broadening of the purview of one perceiving from above, assessing the possible contributions to be made in a civic society. Such an impulse is insufficiently probing theologically, and is insufficiently radical when faced with the Methodist configuration of parenthood.

The bishop also spoke of procreation. "Christian parents are morally obligated to plan for the coming of their children. The proper spacing of children is an expression of love and therefore a religious obligation." If the Christian family is the "hope of the world," the form of its faith can easily become a version of domesticity. If the iconic definition of the Christian family is the nuclear family, the future of humanity may reside at the comfortable suburban kitchen table. If this salvific, nuclear family is configured within an American meritocracy, it takes but one more slight step to suggest that family planning for human "capacity" is the means through which a nation will redeem the world. Thus, Christian parents are not only *permitted* to space their children, but family planning, by Bishop Oxnam's reading, is "a religious obligation."

No small part of my motivation for this project derives from a fear that my own church has been responsible for baptizing the divide between children perceived as chosen and children perceived as just occurring through default. This has had implications in civic conversations about both selective termination and immigration from Latino-Catholic countries. The national obligation to plan one's family for quality and quantity control has become an assumption of twenty-first-century life. Those who believe and practice otherwise are coming to be seen as threats to national cohesion. A recent book by Harvard historian Samuel P. Huntington says the question, Who are we? poses a challenge to America's national identity. Huntington says the "Anglo-Protestant culture" that has held America together may be under threat of invasion by others who do not accept the assumptions of the "American civil religion,"[13] which is a

13. Samuel P. Huntington, *Who Are We? The Challenges to America's National Identity* (New York: Simon and Schuster, 2004), p. 38 and foreword.

form of "Christianity without Christ."[14] I will suggest as a haunting refrain throughout this book that mainline Protestants need to remember not who we are, but Whose we are, not for the sake of shoring up national identity, but for the sake of remembering the One on whom our life and hope depend.

In her groundbreaking *American Literature* essay, "Manifest Domesticity," Amy Kaplan says "the conceptual border between the domestic and the foreign" is at issue both in the "imperial project of civilizing" the globe and in the configuration of life within the middle-class homes in mid-nineteenth-century America.[15] The cover image of the Methodist family conference report represents the dynamics of domesticity and what might count as a properly situated family in the global mission of the Methodist church in the mid–twentieth century. Through a responsible process of democratization and global science, Methodism would bring to the other families elsewhere on the map a new order.

Perhaps nowhere was this dynamic more at play in print than in an article Margaret Sanger wrote for *Together* in September 1957. "History's greatest race is speeding to its climax: Population vs. world food supplies. And the way it looks now, there may soon be *Too Many People!*"[16] With a stock photograph of turbaned, brown-skinned men in a gathering, the essay, in image and word, calls on Methodist readers to endorse the exportation of family planning. "The World is exploding at the seams," Sanger warns. "From the Orient to South America, from Eastern Europe to the U.S., soaring birth rates are posing future problems potentially more dangerous than the H-bomb." Sanger thus begins her article by portraying a world beset by a danger even greater than the ever-present Cold War fear of nuclear annihilation. In characteristic style she goes on to name "teeming Asia" in tones of infestation: "Have-not nations, with millions more mouths to feed each year, must spill over their borders in unending aggressions, searching for more and more food-producing areas."[17] As we proceed, we will consider how mainline Protestants in the United States came to see themselves as the forgers of a new worldwide domestic order through the promotion of properly calibrated, usefully capable children.

If planned domesticity is the hope of the world, and the United States is the world superpower, then aptly ordered domesticity is arguably the salvation of the planet. One of Ellsworth Huntington's greatest concerns in his an-

---

14. Huntington, *Who Are We?* p. 106.
15. Amy Kaplan, "Manifest Domesticity," *American Literature* 70 (1998): 581-606.
16. Margaret Sanger, "Too Many People," *Together*, September 1957, p. 16.
17. Sanger, "Too Many People," p. 16.

swer to President Hoover's charge in 1931 was that the American people would accept a social insurance plan that was "haphazard." This fear that the nation would insufficiently order itself against social devolution drove much in the eugenics movement. But, by one reading, this intent to plan the reproduction of the species for the sake of national betterment ran well beyond its explicitly eugenic forms. The call to order the world — whether through the summons to designate just who would own the moon or through the call to address the problem of "teeming Asia" — reverberated through mainline Protestant literature in the twentieth century. We were, to coin a phrase now associated with a United Methodist in the White House, the "deciders." The sense that American Methodists were to be the ones called to justify the margins of the political world was pervasive during the periods covered in this book. We were to get a view of the terrain from well above the fray. Having secured this view, we were to plan, plant, and procreate accordingly.

## The Protestant Spirit of Reproduction?

I hope to prompt a different sort of vision, encouraging my own mainline Protestant tradition to rearticulate the grace that should have recognized *other people's* children as blood kin and as of incalculable worth. The same Protestant tradition that sociologist Max Weber read as leading to a thoroughly mercantilist vision of humanity must now articulate that no life may be simultaneously loved and critically assessed. If mainline Protestants in North America have to a large extent lived Weber's prediction, so may mainline Protestants now challenge the dominant paradigm by choosing life.

Jonathan Kozol put this point beautifully in an article for the *Nation* called "The Details of Life." In this essay Kozol brings together the gratuity of each life, the blessed and difficult details of a neighborhood considered to be outside God's reach, and death-dealing calculation. His defense of children living in poverty at the dawn of the twenty-first century may be read as a frontal challenge to the economic computation diagnosed in Weber's *Protestant Ethic and the Spirit of Capitalism,* written at the dawn of the twentieth century. As Weber read the American version of Protestantism, "this asceticism turned with all its force against one thing: the spontaneous enjoyment of life and all it had to offer."[18] He saw American culture on the verge of requiring the economic calculation of every moment and every life. In an-

18. Max Weber, *The Protestant Ethic and the Spirit of Capitalism,* trans. Talcott Parsons (1930; reprint, London: Routledge, 1992), p. 166.

swer, Kozol is here worth quoting at length on the problem with the language of "investment":

> Advocates for children, most of whom dislike this ethos, nonetheless play into it in efforts to obtain financial backing from the world of business. "A dollar spent on Head Start," they repeat time and again, "will save our government six dollars over twenty years" in lowered costs for juvenile detention and adult incarceration. It's a point worth making if it's true, although it's hard to prove; and, still, it is a pretty dreadful way to have to think about 4-year-olds. . . .
>
> . . . Sometimes it seems that "having fun" is seen as a luxurious entitlement that cannot be accorded to the child of a woman who relies on welfare lest it make dependent status too enjoyable. It seems at times that happiness itself is viewed as an extravagance and that our sole concerns in dealing with such children must be discipline, efficiency and future worth.[19]

By describing the complex but still hopeful work of St. Ann's Episcopal Church in the Bronx, Kozol summarizes the theological engine propelling this book: "Childhood ought to have at least a few entitlements that aren't entangled with utilitarian considerations. One of them should be the right to a degree of unencumbered satisfaction in the sheer delight and goodness of existence in itself. *Another ought to be the confidence of knowing that one's presence on this earth is taken as an unconditional blessing that is not contaminated by the economic uses that a nation does or does not have for you.*"[20]

I fear that a toxic calculus of worth exists on the extreme ends of the economic spectrum — in the focus on genius and "children of promise," as narrated in a *New York Times Magazine* cover article entitled "The Prodigy Puzzle," and in the "malign neglect" of the children Jonathan Kozol will not let his readers ignore.[21] The affirmation of life to which Christians are called eschews this entire schema of appraisal, even at the risk of seeming to be "filled with new wine."

---

19. Jonathan Kozol, "The Details of Life," *Nation*, May 22, 2000, pp. 16, 18.

20. Kozol, "The Details of Life," p. 19, emphasis added.

21. Ann Hulbert, "The Prodigy Puzzle," *New York Times Magazine*, November 20, 2005, pp. 64-71, 78, 104, 107-8, 120. The term "malign neglect" echoes the title of another Kozol essay in the *Nation* (June 10, 2002, pp. 20, 22-23).

### God's Beloved Child Aboard This Train . . .

In *The Souls of Black Folk,* the noted sociologist and civil rights activist W. E. B. Du Bois begins each chapter by placing together a quotation from what would clearly be considered "high culture" and a line of music taken from the life of the African American church. In what may be read as an employment of philosopher G. W. F. Hegel, Du Bois melds each quotation and each line into a synthesis for the future of the race.

As I move in this book from "Holy Hygiene" to the "Corporate Breast" to the impulse to "Form a More Perfect Union" and achieve "Domestic Security" through the "Genomic Revolution," I offer more of a juxtaposition on race and identity than a synthesis of the two. At the beginning of each chapter I quote a hymn that may helpfully sound as a refrain throughout the chapter. In earlier times Methodists could be characterized by our willingness to sing the Lord's song as though we were people in a strange land.[22] The optimal way to read this book is to read first through the hymn that opens each chapter and then return to the hymn periodically while reading the chapter. The words of each hymn may thus prompt you to consider and contrast the messages running through congregations and homes in the periods covered. Rather than seeking a Du Boisian–Hegelian synthesis of hymnody and American culture, I let the hymns sit as a historical testimony to *otherwise.*

The hymns may also prompt stories between generations about resistance. I do not intend this book to serve as a relentless interrogation of those who failed to choose life. Nor do I mean to focus attention on any particular company, administration, advertising campaign, family, individual, or congregation. The individual writers and corporations I have chosen to discuss were, in complicated ways, representative of their time, but their representation has relevance today. The most helpful way to use this material is through the telling of stories, amidst people who were privy to the hype and hymns of the last century. At least this has been my experience in relating the material in this book orally. Many of the men and women explicitly named here have so much more to their story than my story can tell; they tell stories of faithful acts of quiet peacemaking and hospitality in churches that sing the hymns interspersed.

The grandmothers who sang the hymns may be prompted to remember also the advertisements in the chapters, and to tell stories about how they negotiated the pressures of proper motherhood and the germ-free home. They

---

22. See in particular Karen B. Westerfield Tucker, *American Methodist Worship* (New York: Oxford University Press, 2001).

may laugh about the girdle advertisements even while remembering aloud the ways their bodies came under scrutiny. They may remember the pressure to have their children's heads and limbs measured, but remember also the ways they affirmed each life at the church picnic. Grandfathers who sang the hymns while at war may also tell stories about their difficult reentry as men with disabilities in congregations that were now, postwar, "on the move." Grandfathers who find themselves now unexpectedly grandfathering children in foster care or through adoption may tell how the ideas they received decades prior regarding who counts as kin have been bent and expanded.

It is my hope that the interplay of hymnody with the images and narratives of mainstream American culture may prompt families of faith and kinship to tell narratives of grace as well as struggle as they work their way through the book. For the images and advertisements and national campaigns that appear here as representative are merely part of the story from the past three generations. It is my hope that stories will emerge about life with those who could not or would not be ordered, with those who slip through the screens, appear haphazard, and have not been judged as calculatedly capable. It is my expectation that such stories are available, after digging, in even the most picture-perfect family. Through faith in the one that will come again to conquer grief and pain, we may have the courage to dig truthfully.

# 1 Holy Hygiene

## *Parents'*, Protestantism,
## and the Germ-Free Home

*He's got the whole world in His hands.*
*He's got the whole world in His hands.*
*He's got the whole world in His hands.*

*He's got the wind and the rain in His hands.*
*He's got the wind and the rain in His hands.*
*He's got the whole world in His hands.*

*He's got the tiny little baby in His hands.*
*He's got the tiny little baby in His hands.*
*He's got the whole world in His hands.*

*He's got you and me, brother, in His hands.*
*He's got you and me, sister, in His hands.*
*He's got the whole world in His hands.*

*He's got everybody here in His hands.*
*He's got everybody here in His hands.*
*He's got the whole world in His hands.*

African American spiritual, popularized 1958

Figure 1.1. "The Baby." American Social Hygiene Association, "Youth and Life" poster series, 1922.

The last paragraph reads: "The human mother can bring more than the simple animal instincts to the aid of her new-born child. Real motherhood develops by the addition of knowledge and understanding to the mother's instinctive love."

No. 22

The Baby

Human beings, too, are mammals, and fertilization and development take place within the mother. The period of development or pregnancy is nine months

At birth the muscles contract and push the child through the birth canal (vagina) into the outer world

The human mother can bring more than the simple animal instincts to the aid of her new-born child. Real motherhood develops by the addition of knowledge and understanding to the mother's instinctive love

T he baby portrait seems commonplace, a simple facet of family life in the twenty-first-century United States. Yet the poster from a 1922 series entitled "Youth and Life" may be read within a particular historical context. "The Baby" as an object of focused attention, study, and medical expertise was, in an important sense, a new concept at the turn of the twentieth century. The technology to capture her isolated, precise, black-and-white image had materialized only in the closing decades of the nineteenth century.

The place of this poster in history also involves the particular story science had to tell about "the baby." The scientific story about the infant's place within the "origin of species" had emerged at roughly the same time as did the technology needed to take her isolated image. Concomitant with both photography and Darwinism was a growing sense that "the baby" should become an object of scientific and medical study. With the hope of improving the state of maternal proficiency, various national, regional, and local organizations gained the expertise to display in article, pamphlet, and poster the idea that "the baby" was due the "addition of knowledge and understanding" offered by research medicine. By bringing into conceptual range "the baby" as a target of attention, social workers, civic planners, and physicians sought to provide what was deemed an indispensable and novel supplement to "mother's instinctive love."

This poster is characteristic of a shift that unquestionably enabled notable gains in infant health through public-awareness campaigns for domestic hygiene. But the hygiene came at a cost, for the benefits were socially, economically, and racially encoded. "The baby" on which the domestic hygiene effort focused was too often a specific baby — a baby the logic of the day judged to be worth the effort. At the same time that social and medical scientists focused on "the baby," they established what were touted as objective, factual, indisputable tools for determining just which babies were worth the effort. The same language system by which mothers, social workers, and physicians could measure gains lent scientific legitimacy to a calculus of human life. This calculus reflected a growing sense that the individual baby was a precious but fragile commodity to be quantifiably evaluated, carefully habituated, and hygienically safeguarded from those humans and households on the *other* side of a divide.

At the same time, what I call "the Lysol habit," or "the germ-free home," named the female body — as it stood even on the right side of the divide — as a source of potential disorder and contamination. Put simply, a woman's body required careful cleaning and meticulous control. The baby poster, from a cooperative venture between the American Social Hygiene Association (ASHA) and the U.S. Public Health Service, focused on the individual infant as an instantiation of the human species. From it, aspiring young women were to glean appropriate facts regarding procreation.

The need for scientific experts to give young women the facts about the proper functioning and control of their own bodies was newly established. We can consider the cost of this expertise on the women themselves by reading the poster closely. The text describes the process within the mother's body: "Human beings, too, are mammals, and fertilization and development take place within the mother. The period of development or pregnancy is nine months. At birth the muscles contract and push the child through the birth canal (vagina) into the outer world." The technical language used for birth is not merely distanced from the fully "human" mother; it is as if "the muscles" are under a microscope, as if "the mother" is conceptually dissected for examination. The language of mammalian science reinforces the notion that the breeding female needs scientifically informed husbandry — which is of course problematic for a series meant to emphasize that the female reader was more than a specimen of nature to be observed, described, and controlled. She was "more than the simple animal" whose "instincts" would be sufficient to raise her child. The *ideal* mother would be capable of internalizing the "addition of knowledge and understanding" conveyed by the sort of team of experts represented by ASHA and other such newly forming organizations. The internalization of their knowledge would also be a key component in her habituation of domestic hygiene. The simpler, maternal love presumably present in non-Western cultures and among other, non-Western mothers was a mark of the simple, instinctive "primitive."

This tension between the instinctual and the learned would run throughout the rise of what historian Rima Apple has termed "scientific motherhood." The interwoven language of natural maternal instinct and medical proficiency portrayed some mothers and some households as less than fully developed or civilized. Mothers not privy to the set of practices for raising "The Baby" seemed somehow more primal and, in an often vague but still powerful sense, less evolved. Women who still held to their grandmothers' wisdom on infant feeding, pregnancy prevention, family sleep patterns, and the like became projects for reform or, too often, fell outside the purview of American progress altogether.

After the war the particular set of practices for domesticity was joined by tools requisite for achieving the optimal home for "The Baby." One needed the proper formula, the proper contraceptive, the proper kitchen appliances, the proper disinfectant, the proper infant clothing, infant shoes, baby powder, hair detangler, toothpaste . . . the list goes on and on — toward the Baby Einstein video and the Fisher-Price Peaceful Planet Aquarium advertised in *Parents'* magazine at the beginning of the twenty-first century. The features on this battery-operated crib accoutrement "all combine to ease baby into a deep blue sleep. . . . And what could be more *natural* than that?"[1] It is possible to interpret the marketability of a sterile, plastic aquarium (with fuchsia fish and simulated wave sounds) as the apex of the new, safely evolved "natural." The articles in the magazine discuss the growing array of products to protect one's children from the germs of other mothers' children. A mother who wants to raise a baby who will be OneStepAhead will do well to purchase, for example, a Clean 'n Comfy Shopping Cart Cover: "Unlike others, our smarter cover shields the entire area, *offering 360 degrees of germ-free protection.*"[2] (The OneStepAhead Web site also recommends the Clean 'n Comfy Restaurant Highchair Cover, just to be safe.)

It is plausible that the emergence of such products runs along a historic

---

1. Fisher-Price, a division of Mattel, 2000, in *Parents'*; emphasis in original.
2. Accessed 2006: www.onestepahead.com; emphasis added.

trajectory — a trajectory of "The Baby" and all the scientific research and product development needed to keep her safe during the twentieth century.

## "Not a Germ in the Universe"

An Evaporated Milk Association advertisement from the June 1929 issue of *Parents'* magazine trumpets in bold headings: "Science Discovers," "Specialists Confirm," and "Think of This Astonishing Result!"[3] After an opening quotation of praise for evaporated milk, the advertisement explains: "That is the declaration of one of the leading pediatricians (baby specialists) of the country in an article recently published in The Journal of the American Medical Association, reporting the result of an experiment with Evaporated Milk for babies." The parenthetical explanation of pediatrics indicates that this medical specialty was gaining broader prominence as the mark of respectability. At the bottom of the advertisement is an offer for a booklet entitled *A Safer World for Babies*. In such a world, effected in part by evaporated milk, there may be "complete *freedom* from anything that can endanger health," a goal "for which the world has struggled for half a century" and "for which the world so long has sought." Scientists had been working and "the world" had been longing for this product, providing a "surely safe and wholesome milk supply." The portrayal of evaporated milk as an accomplishment of global importance, the promise of "complete freedom" from danger, the noted expertise of the "baby specialist" — all combine to suggest that evaporated milk is the clearly proper choice of a mother reading *Parents'*. The need for a "safer world" takes as given that the world is less than optimally safe. The wording assumes a kind of pressure and anxiety about the dangers of infant care and the need for medical research to help move toward that safety. Most important for this chapter is the claim that "sterilization makes it free from anything that could endanger health," for the "sealed, air-tight container brings it to you as safe as if there were not a germ in the universe."

What the research team working on evaporated milk would bring to the mother reading *Parents'* was a product sealed off from any menace that might lurk between laboratory and kitchen. The scientists working for "half a century" had brought baby a "safer world," a world crafted to exist "as if there were not a germ in the universe."

3. Evaporated Milk Association, in *Parents'*, June 1929, p. 45. *Children: The Parents' Magazine,* launched in 1926, became simply *The Parents' Magazine,* or *Parents',* with the August 1929 issue. I will use the name *Parents'* throughout the book.

We will pay specific attention in this chapter to the ways *other* children and *other* mothers fared in the marketing of a safer, more sterile world for babies. In her attempt to establish herself as a proper mother in a world free from all germs, the aspiring young woman was encouraged to distinguish herself and her children from the bodies and beds and clothes and daily bread of *other* women's children. *The baby* on whom *the mother* was to focus was a specifically construed baby — a baby whose lineage and environment signaled his safe, providential heritage. This conception of parenting reinforced a divide between *our* children and children considered to be on the *other* side of a variously named boundary. The implied assessment of safety and risk to *the baby* in the material I will cover involved an effort to keep one's own children in a protected world away from the contamination posed by *other* people and their children. This was a bitter gift to the mothers whose circumstances allowed them to prove their families' worth. For by my reading of "the germ-free home," the aspiration to craft families of providential promise teetered on the knife edge of maternal self-loathing, whereby a woman's own body became a site of potentially hidden menace.[4] The pressure and anxiety of perfect hygiene were significant in themselves. No baby and no mother should be burdened with the level of domestic aspiration recommended in the advertisements and articles considered here. Yet I wish in this chapter to amplify the relation of hygiene to race in the last century. The gift of a "safer world for babies" was bitter in a different way for women whose children were markedly *other*. There were infants, children, and families whose identity as mistaken was essential to the marketing of products to aspiring mothers. The protected "baby" as an isolate of the human family was a particular baby, and much of the marketing to her mother played upon and encouraged her desire to keep her household on the right side of a divide.

This chapter explores white, Anglo-Saxon Protestant domesticity in the twentieth century by looking at the marketing and description of familial health in domestic and mainline denominational family magazines. Concern for freedom from ill health and from any potential germ in the universe is a sign not only of the time covered here but also of the social sector that supplied both the expertise and the readership for these publications. Magazines like *Parents'*, *Ladies' Home Journal*, and *McCall's* functioned as the conduit for feminine and maternal proficiency from the turn of the century forward. Their readership was markedly Anglo-Saxon, mainline Protestant. By the postwar period, as marketing to nuclear families reached a new height and breadth, churches like the Methodist church brought out their own offerings

---

4. The seminal reading of this dynamic in the South is Lillian Smith's *Killers of the Dream* (1949).

for the domestic magazine-reading mother. For reasons both demographic and personal, I will pay close attention to the first years of *Together: The Midmonth Magazine for Methodist Families* (1956-73). Methodism — my own tradition — emerged as the largest mainline Protestant denomination during the twentieth century; the Methodist church is, in a rich, symbolic sense, America's church.[5]

A close reading of the early issues of *Together* illumines a split within modern, forward-thinking Protestantism in the United States during the twentieth century. This magazine put front and center the very arrangement of child and family highlighted in domestic magazines: the normative mode of holy family life involved a carefully coifed child in church, decked out in Easter hat with flowers in hand, gazing importunately upward (see fig. 1.2).

The children whose images graced the magazine's covers and photographic spreads were particular children. They had well-kept hair and even well-trained dogs (as epitomized on the inaugural cover, where a pair of perfectly matched twins flank what readers are told is a real descendant of Lassie). In "Publishing for Christendom (1945-1960)," a chapter from the two-volume history of the Methodist Publishing House by Walter Newton Vernon, Jr., *Together* is described as the "big bang" among Methodist publications of the era.[6] The magazine's "slick" presentation reflected the aim of its founding fathers, as summarized by Bishop Paul B. Kern of Nashville in his announcement of the undertaking at Methodism's General Conference in 1952: "We call for a bold venture for the creation of a Methodist periodical, combining the best of modern craftsmanship and aimed at a circulation, within twelve months, of not fewer than one million copies. It can be done and we are the people to do it."[7]

The link with the "modern craftsmanship" of domestic periodicals was not coincidental. Bishop Kern had been persuaded by publishing agent Lovick Pierce that the current form of Methodism could not compete with "a colorful abundance of eye-catching secular periodicals" to be found on "the coffee ta-

---

5. See, e.g., Peter Williams, *America's Religions: From Their Origins to the Twenty-First Century* (Urbana: University of Illinois Press, 2002): "Methodism had by the twentieth century acquired a reputation as the most typically American of the 'mainline' denominations. A Gallup poll taken in 1967-68 revealed that the Methodist church was the religious group 'most liked' by members of other denominations. It was also the largest single American religious group other than the Roman Catholic Church until its curve of declining membership intersected with the growth curve of the Southern Baptists in the late 1960s" (pp. 365-66).

6. Walter Newton Vernon, Jr., *The United Methodist Publishing House: A History,* vol. 2 (Nashville: Abingdon, 1989), pp. 431-35.

7. Cited in Vernon, *United Methodist Publishing House,* p. 432.

**Figure 1.2.** *Together,* cover photograph for April 1960

bles of the nation."[8] In changing times, during "the age of television," a new venture was called for. The critics cut through this "bold" strategy with insight. Dan Wakefield's review of *Together* for the *Nation* in January 1957 called it the culmination of the "current industrialization of Christianity," a periodical intent on showing that "religion can be fun," dedicated to a "forward-looking" people whose eyes were "fixed more often on the vision ahead than above."[9] *Christian Century* suggested that it simply reinhabited an old caricature of Methodists as "superficial, hail-fellow-well-met Christians."[10]

8. As later described by Herman B. Teeter, *The General Periodicals of Methodism* (Park Ridge, Ill.: United Methodist Publishing House, 1975), p. 48; cited in Vernon, *United Methodist Publishing House,* p. 434.

9. Dan Wakefield, "Slick-Paper Christianity," *Nation,* January 19, 1957, pp. 56-57.

10. Theodore A. Gill, "General Conference: Cont'd.," editorial, *Christian Century,* May 23, 1956, p. 639, discussing a special preview issue put out for the 1956 General Conference in Minneapolis.

By one reading, *Together* itself sealed the mortar between the blocks of mainstream postwar culture — "forward-looking" progress, the nuclear family, and "fun" Protestant faith came together *almost* seamlessly. The pattern of the family often played off the patterns of aspiring parenthood from decades prior, and that haloed glow almost overwhelms a differently flickering light within the magazine. A "slick" cover with a crystal-blue swimming pool, blonde mother and daughter giggling together in the water, reinforced an understanding of the family that renders almost unintelligible the life displayed in an essay named on the very same cover. The heroine of "Country Deaconess — a Pictorial," a woman who daily tended to the physical and spiritual needs of vulnerable people not her blood kin, seems quite the eccentric saint. Normative families were thus encouraged to practice a form of charity that could be properly dispensed from a safe distance. The charity pictured in the magazine too often reflected a sort of hazy, spiritual love given mercifully by those whose lives were safely on the other side of a divide between the normatively pressed and the pitiably disordered. At its worst, this design of charity became a justification for both vaguely sentimental pity and, as its flip side, what theologian Karl Barth called a sort of "Christian 'Marshall Plan,'" a plan to bring order and safety to the world through grand, providentially warranted strategies. Put differently, "the germ-free home" warranted both a safe, albeit prayerful, distance from *others* and bold plans to tidy the globe. This is one reading of *Together*.

But there is a counternarrative in *Together*. For "outsiders" like the *Nation's* Dan Wakefield, *Together* seemed such a travesty in no small part because Methodist history also included the courage to preach, not so much "good, comfortable fun," but "good works" born of risky faith.[11] Thus, the "country deaconess" is also a part of Methodism, even if her picture was not featured on *Together*'s slick cover. Her work is also a part of the heritage out of which *Together* grew.

The Methodist movement, started in Britain by an Oxford graduate who dared thwart the regularized, hierarchical Anglican status quo, also embraced the holy work of open-air stump preaching, coal-mine conversions, women preachers (who were likely disconcerting in any context), and worship that mixed shopkeepers, factory workers, and Oxford-trained dons in ways that seemed ill conceived to many in power. During a century when most in the Church of England were intent on maintaining clear boundaries of class hierarchies and proper bloodlines, John Wesley had read in the gospel a call to what amounted to ecclesial miscegenation.[12] Those who followed

11. Wakefield, "Slick-Paper Christianity," p. 57.
12. Regarding Wesley and the relation of the Methodist movement to class propriety, see

**Figure 1.3.** *Together,*
**cover photograph for**
**August 1958**

Wesley's legacy westward in America did so in saloons and brothels, and not always with the aim (and certainly not always the result) of bringing Bostonian respectability into the lives of frontier Christians.[13]

This Methodist legacy of holy unconventionality made its way even into a magazine striving for *Better Homes and Gardens* status. Stories of unlikely hospitality and blurred lines of kinship peek out from behind the polished

E. P. Thompson, *The Making of the English Working Class* (New York: Pantheon Books, 1964). Thompson narrates the influence of Methodism, through its ecclesiology of mixed bands and organized prayer groups, as the critical force behind the indefinite delay of a class revolution in England. John Wigger uses the term "religious miscegenation" to describe a charge against Methodists made by critics of the camp meeting movement in the late eighteenth–early nineteenth century. John H. Wigger, *Taking Heaven by Storm: Methodism and the Rise of Popular Christianity in America* (New York: Oxford University Press, 1998), p. 120.

13. On this point see Nathan Hatch, *The Democratization of American Christianity* (New Haven: Yale University Press, 1989), and Christine Heyrman, *The Southern Cross: The Beginnings of the Bible Belt* (New York: Knopf, 1997).

cover of nuclear normality. A delicate hope can thus be found in *Together,* as if growing resiliently between the cracks of the proper domesticity displayed. Each issue featured essays that pushed beyond the boundaries of normative family life, calling Methodist readers to consider their faith in ways that seem counternormative to postwar America. There is evidence here of a Methodism that sought to be of good witness, not so much through cover-perfect children and hygienic homes safely on the right side of a divide, but by risking whatever normative status it had achieved as America's church by calling for an altogether different set of alliances.

## The Gospel according to *Parents'*

### *"The Future of the Race"*

From its beginning in the mid-1920s until 1951, *Parents'* magazine closed its editorial page by quoting from one of the most beloved hymnists in American Protestantism, Phillips Brooks. Beneath a Peter Pan–esque drawing of lithe figures dancing across the page with hoops and bonnets, the magazine's credo ran thus: "The future of the race marches forward on the feet of little children."

**Figure 1.4. *Parents'* image: "The future of the race marches forward on the feet of little children."**

But during this same time period different words from this same man expressed hope for the future — words about a child who, for Christians, *is* our hope and our future. In Victorian English, Brooks narrated for generations of American Protestants the birth of one baby, the holy Child:

O little town of Bethlehem, how still we see thee lie;
    Above thy deep and dreamless sleep the silent stars go by.
Yet in thy dark streets shineth the everlasting light;
    The hopes and fears of all the years are met in thee tonight.

The contrast between these two perspectives on the future, summed up in two quotations from the same churchman, is significant.

In the first half of the twentieth century, magazines like *Parents'* promoted the Anglo-Protestant values seen then to be at the core of the nation. The first issue of *Parents'* ran an editorial by Franklin D. Roosevelt, governor of New York, on the "fundamentals of human relationships . . . based on certain age-old human and divine laws."[14] *Parents'* was in fact a kind of mainline denominational magazine, given its broad appeals to "the scripture-old Golden Rule" (again quoting Governor Roosevelt) and to the words of the much-beloved hymnist. The intertwined messages of the default civil religion and the growing field of household know-how reinforced the sense of importance conveyed in its pages.[15] The "future of the race" depended on the appropriate care and training of children, and the forward-thinking Protestant spirit lent an air of Providence itself to the daily tasks of domesticity. Alongside advertisements for potty-training devices, scientifically enhanced infant milk, and selective summer camps, readers of *Parents'* found not only the conceptual tools to form children who would participate in the march forward, but also a heightened sense of the holy purpose of parenthood.[16]

Connecting mainstream Protestantism with domestic propriety involved a kind of split between providentially blessed and ill-fated families. The racialized character of that split is implicit in most of the articles in domestic magazines, as it is in the reference to "the future of the race" in the *Parents'* motto. African American mothers and their children surface only rarely, and then in ways that make the race divide explicit. In her metaphorically salient essay "For Better or Worse — Servants Influence Children" (fig. 1.5), Ruth Sapin issues an important reminder that a mother who brings outsiders into her home needs to consider carefully the inevitable effect upon her children: "Women with servants frequently go about looking for unswept corners and chipped china and completely overlook the harm that can be done their human possessions."[17]

When someone from "outside" crosses the threshold of the family home, the influence can be "for better" or "for worse." The title of the essay is placed

---

14. Franklin D. Roosevelt, "Fundamentals: An Editorial Message," *Parents'*, August 1929, p. 12. For a similar analysis of the role of *Ladies' Home Journal* regarding mainline Protestant domesticity, see Jennifer Scanlon, *Inarticulate Longings: The Ladies' Home Journal, Gender, and the Promises of Consumer Culture* (New York: Routledge, 1995).

15. See Colleen McDannell, *The Christian Home in Victorian America, 1840-1900* (1986; reprint, Bloomington: Indiana University Press, 1994), esp. pp. 151-53.

16. Scanlon makes the same point about *Ladies' Home Journal* at the turn of the century; see Scanlon, *Inarticulate Longings*, p. 53.

17. Ruth Sapin, "For Better or Worse — Servants Influence Children," *Parents'*, January 1929, p. 21. References to this article have been placed in parentheses in the text.

on the page so that the word "Servants" reads as the bridge between "For Better or Worse" and "Influence Children," highlighting the import of the matter. An illustration by Louise Claster Rumely spreads over the first two pages of the piece, spanning the center page break, or, as magazine people call it, the gutter. On the left side of the gutter is an African American woman, sitting in a chair with a bowl in her lap and a spoon in one of her hands. On the right side are two young white children. The older of the two sits in a chair directly facing the African American woman; the younger child stands behind the chair, looking at the woman with a grinning side-glance. The woman is extending her empty hand, palm open, beckoning the children across the divide.

Viewed together, the carefully arranged title and the divided drawing prompt the reader visually to recognize the basic conundrum. The servant represents a potential threat to the reader's children. She enters one's home, bidden for her service, but she also calls one's children into a world not their own. She is invited into the house to stir the batter in a bowl, but at the very same moment she extends a hand in summons to the children. While she tends to the cooking, she also suggests to the children that they cross over. How may one supervise the various actors in this scene to bring about a "satisfactory" conclusion? The maternal task is traced here in a way that is implicit in much that we will cover throughout the book.

The mother of the two children does not appear in the illustration; she is the one with a God's-eye view, looking onto the scene. She is clearly the reader of the magazine, the human subject to whom this piece is addressed. Highlighted, italicized text describing the essay runs alongside the table at which the African American woman sits to mix the batter: "Whether you employ servants who live in your household, part-time workers or, perhaps, a mother's helper they affect and are affected by your children. This author brings up points often overlooked and yet of the utmost importance if a satisfactory relationship is to be achieved between your family and its helpers." Sapin assumes the reader is the household administrator called upon to manage the tension illustrated in the drawings and explicitly named in the title. Put simply, the mother of the two children is the "you" of the essay. The other woman is named consistently as a "servant," as one in the reader's "employ." She is a "worker" whose existence appears as a potential help but also as a potential hindrance to the aims of the "you" to whom the magazine is addressed.

> To harmonize the various elements of her household is, of course, the problem, the very great problem of the thoughtful modern woman. *The adjustments she must make between two important elements in that household, the child and the servant, require infinite patience and sacrifice of time*

# For Better or Worse—
# Servants
# Influence Children

By
RUTH SAPIN

*Illustration by
Louise Claster Rumely*

*Whether you employ servants who live in your household, part-time workers or, perhaps, a mother's helper they affect and are affected by your children. This author brings up points often overlooked and yet of the utmost importance if a satisfactory relationship is to be achieved between your family and its helpers*

*and energy.* With all her effort, the woman of today may never secure for her children an ideal companion like Stevenson's beloved Alice Cunningham, whose "most comfortable hand" led him "through the uneven land" of childhood and serious illness. But her thoughtful attention to the problem of the child and her helpers will go far to secure the fine functioning and consequent happiness of the family as a whole. (p. 42, emphasis added)

This is why the essay exists — to help the "you" of the domestic situation properly place the "mother's helper" so that she remains a source of blessing and not bane. The "servant" will inevitably "affect" one's children and also be "affected" by associating with them. The author's aim is to bring to the fore points that are "often overlooked" by the "you" of the essay, so that the reader may be adequately prepared for the "constant" supervisory work of "infinite patience and sacrifice of time and energy": "A constant supervision of the maid who is much with the children, a constant awareness of what is going on in her home is incumbent upon the woman who is seeking to han-

*The negro servant with her exuberance and strong dramatic sense, the fun-loving Irish girl, the peasant maid of any land can frequently broaden our children's horizons*

**Figure 1.5. "For Better or Worse — Servants Influence Children."** *Parents'*, January 29, 1929

dle the problem of the child and the servant" (p. 21). With planning, the "you" who is the director of the domestic scene, serving as both head of casting and stage manager, may ensure that her servant is truly of benefit to her children. With "constant supervision" and "constant awareness," a mother may thus ensure that difference maintains its distance.

Again, the visual impact of the drawing and set-apart text reinforces the importance of this point. On the right side of the essay, in bold text running alongside the kitchen cabinet and above the children's heads, is the author's key to resolving the problem: "The negro servant with her exuberance and strong dramatic sense, the fun-loving Irish girl, the peasant maid of any land can frequently broaden our children's horizons." The mother's task, in the midst of this domestic challenge, is to establish her children as the axis around which the servants revolve. The maternal task is to cultivate a perspective.

The wording of this resolution addresses head-on the starkest marker of difference in the United States. By carefully perceiving this African American woman as "the negro servant," a mother may accept such a woman as a source of "exuberance" for her children. Named as "negro," seen as bringing with her both "exuberance" and a "strong dramatic sense," the woman becomes manageably strange, even interesting. The article itself narrates blackness at the extreme of difference, at the far reaches of "courtesy": "One of the important factors in the excellent domestic service one finds abroad, particularly in England, is, I have always thought, the tradition of courtesy between employer and employee. Children can be imbued early with the idea that courtesy is due all who contribute to their well-being, from black Juliet, who comes in by the day to wash the clothes and do a bit of cleaning to Nana, the capable nurse who is summoned when mother is ill or goes off on a trip" (p. 21). Sapin thus places race at the far end of a continuum of difference, with "black Juliet," who is capable of a "bit of cleaning," set as the extreme and "Nana, the capable nurse," set as a temporary substitute for "mother" herself. (Nana's race is not named, presumably because she, like the reader, is set as the default mode of whiteness.)

In her resolution to the domestic problem, Sapin links particular configurations of domestic help, a concatenation of both labor and potential danger. After the "negro servant" is the "Irish girl," an immigrant apparently of benefit inasmuch as she may have brought over with her a love of "fun." Covering all other possible signifiers of danger, Sapin names the "peasant maid of any land," who may, with constant supervision, bring with her to the proper American household a taste of broadened horizons. The negro "servant," the Irish "girl," the peasant "maid" — each is described in such a way as to distinguish her from the default mother situating her children's household for the sake of the future of the race. The human beings collapsed within the headings of "negro," "Irish," and "peasant" represent those on the other side of a divide. Yet these very markers of other-sidedness may not be a problem so much as a help if one's own children are firmly established as the definition of normative "humanity."

But the continuum is delineated even further. As Sapin links in otherness the "negro" with the "Irish" with the "peasant maid of any land," she also links in familiarity those faraway humans on the normative side of the divide. Her narration builds a bridge across the Atlantic, to relate the task of normative, American motherhood with the task of mothers in England and Europe similarly blessed with the charge of ensuring courtesy, purity, and broadened horizons. Likewise, the reader's own children are kin with those mothers' "young charges": "In the reminiscences and autobiographies of many famous European writers, . . . it is interesting to note what a large part servants played in their childhood. Here were servants who filled the fascinated ears of their young charges with folk songs and folk tales, servants who, though uneducated, nevertheless by their industry and practical experience of life contributed a firm, strong thread to the tapestry of the artist's background" (p. 20).

In the end, the potential danger illustrated in the two drawings may be resolved by maintaining the centrality offered by *Parents'*. The children may cross over and yet not be contaminated. They may safely move to the other side at the behest of one's "negro servant," because a mother privy to the author's tips will have adequately established the children as center of the known world. "Children bridge the chasm of class much more effectively than do even the most democratic of employers. They are genuinely interested in the maid's experiences. By sympathizing with her, by seeking to make her lot happier and her position more tolerable, children often gain their earliest training in fair play and justice" (p. 42). In other words, if the children are defined as the default mode of knowing, different individuals may enter their perspective and add merely a broadened view, extending out from the center of established "fair play" and "justice." The well-attended children exposed to the "fun," "exuberance," and "peasant" stories of their servants need not be thrown off center. The properly situated home thus becomes the benignly governed, colonial world in microcosm. With proper planning, careful exposure, and safely governed sympathy, the children of mothers in need of "help" will be well trained for their futures.

### *"Four Policemen for Hire"*

Maltine ran a series of advertisements in *Parents'* that featured four uniformed men protecting one little child, around whom they were arrayed (fig. 1.6).[18] Given that a key ingredient in Maltine is cod liver oil, the uniformed men may be there to make sure the child actually submits to his dosage. But the overall impact of the series is clear. The men appear as "four watchmen to guard your child's health." They are labeled for the four essential vitamins: Officer A, Officer B, Officer C, and Officer D, all surrounding the child with their protective properties against "infection . . . rickets, scurvy . . . and nervous disorders," among other ailments named. The text of one version of the advertisement begins: "The four vitamins are like policemen. They help us resist skulking infection." The basic, medical message of the series is of course indisputable — children need these vitamins in their diet in order to grow and flourish. But the accompanying illustration and the imagery throughout the text play on an anxiety and presumption involved in the marketing of domestic science to mothers in the first half of the twentieth century.

18. In addition to figure 1.6, see *Parents'*, January 1929, p. 35, and *Parents'*, January 1930, p. 31.

Figure 1.6.
Maltine adver-
tisement in
*Parents'*, February
1930

*These four watchmen*
*guard your child's health*

# DAY AND NIGHT!

RAISING a child, as every mother knows, is no eight-hour job. Each complete day should bring him growth, health, a contented mind—a victory over disease.

Some of the most insidious diseases of childhood are those caused by vitamin-deficiency. General lowering of resistance—especially to the common cold—nervous disorders, rickets, soft teeth, scurvy... each is associated with lack of vitamins.

Think of the vitamins as policemen of our bodies. They guard against disease and promote normal growth. But when children are finicky with their foods, it is difficult to be certain that they are getting enough vitamins from their meals. Often the discovery comes too late.

Fortunately, medical science has developed a simple food combination which is known to carry all four vitamins. A leading biological chemist has proved that Maltine With Cod Liver Oil —added to orange juice in adequate dosage— *provides a sufficient quantity of all four vitamins (A, B, C, D) to promote health.*

Seventy per cent of this preparation is Maltine, a concentrated extract of malted barley, wheat and oats—rich in Vitamin B. The rest is pure vitamin-tested cod liver oil (a bountiful source of Vitamins A and D). Taken in orange juice

(Vitamin C), this preparation gives your child adequate protection against vitamin-deficiency. Keep a bottle nearby in the kitchen cabinet, and stir it in with your child's morning orange juice.

Send for a free copy of the booklet, "The Doctor Talks About Vitamins." In simple language it tells you the important facts about the four necessary vitamins. The Maltine Company, 20 Vesey Street, New York. Established 1875.

### The A B C's of Vitamins

**A** "OFFICER A" *is essential to normal growth and helps protect against certain infections, especially those that attack the respiratory system. Maltine With Cod Liver Oil is a recognized rich source of Vitamin A.*

**B** "OFFICER B" *is most essential. Lack of Vitamin B results in loss of appetite, a cessation of growth, and the appearance of certain nervous disorders. Vitamin B is found in abundance in Maltine With Cod Liver Oil.*

**C** "OFFICER C" *prevents scurvy. Orange juice is everywhere recognized as very rich in Vitamin C. That's why we recommend this policeman.*

**D** "OFFICER D" *is also necessary. A deficiency of Vitamin D causes rickets, that weakener of child bones. Sound teeth depend upon it. It is meager or lacking in all our ordinary foods. Maltine With Cod Liver Oil is rich in Vitamin D.*

# Maltine

## WITH COD LIVER OIL

*Accepted by the Council on Pharmacy and Chemistry of the American Medical Association*

"Your child" is at risk from various "skulking" menaces. He might suffer ill health of various sorts if a mother is unable to detect the symptoms or the source of menace. It would take experts like the "biological chemist of recognized standing" (whose "report" would be sent on request) to help mothers perceive and meet the needs of the "child." To repeat the closing line from the ASHA poster of "The Baby" (fig. 1.1), "*Real* motherhood develops by the addition of knowledge and understanding to the mother's instinctive love." While we are mammalian, and motherhood is therefore in some sense "instinctive," truly *human* motherhood makes use of the *gnosis* available only from those in the know — from those medically and/or scientifically trained. A sense of parental presumption is clear throughout these, often full-page, *Parents'* ads. The sector of the population for whom experts stood at the ready was targeted by such magazines. The child of the reader was the focal point of the various men in uniform who were researching, publishing, and producing the goods marketed in upscale women's magazines. Two other images from the series make this meaning unmistakable. The four policemen stand ready as watchmen "for hire," at the command of the mother and her child.

While the Maltine "fact-book on vitamins" was to "answer every mother's questions" on the "vital subject" of childhood nutrition, the child at the center of the effort was a specific child. During the first half of the century, advertising to mothers in the magazines of domestic hygiene and health played upon the aspiration of their audience to ascend above the struggles and joys of other women and other women's children.

This is at points implicit, as in the 1929 advertisement for "The University Plan of Character Building" (fig. 1.7). If one were to raise a child who would reach the end point of "Success" (here pictured as a castle in the clouds), one could never begin too early drawing on the "unique" information that would allow the child to get ahead. The image shows the still-crawling infant poised to ascend a staircase — from Obedience to Cheerfulness to Self-Control to Generosity to Orderliness to Courage to Self-Reliance to Respect for Others to Honesty to Initiative to Leadership and onward through the doorway marked Success. The plan is touted as "Unique — Practical — Necessary" and features "authentic information on every phase of the child problem" from "nationally known educators."

The advertisement has two words for the potentially intimidated reader, one encouraging and one foreboding. First, even the "busiest mother" will find her "task lightened" by the "simple and practical" plan for childhood Success. But second is a word of warning, for "experimenting means making mistakes," and surely "your child is too valuable for you to make mistakes in training." This message is characteristic — that maternal work in the home is

39

**Figure 1.7. "The University Plan of Character Building."** *Parents'*, **April 1929**

*Step by Step*

*Character*

*Leads to*

*Success*

(staircase labels, bottom to top:)
OBEDIENCE
CHEERFULNESS
SELF-CONTROL
GENEROSITY
ORDERLINESS
COURAGE
SELF-RELIANCE
RESPECT FOR OTHERS
HONESTY
INITIATIVE
LEADERSHIP

SUCCESS

## The University Plan of Character Building

### Unique — Practical — Necessary

Sterling character is not the result of chance; the rules by which it develops are found in The University Plan for Character Building.

It contains authentic information on every phase of the child problem.

It will help you prepare your little child mentally, physically, socially, and morally for the day when he enters school and will show you how to understand and how to co-operate with the aims of the school for the older child.

It places at your finger-tips the experience and knowledge of nationally known educators.

The University Plan for Character Building is so simple and practical that the busiest mother finds her task lightened.

Experimenting means making mistakes and then trying again; your child is too valuable for you to make mistakes in training.

**THE UNIVERSITY SOCIETY INC.**

**468 Fourth Avenue      New York, N. Y.**

*Frederick E. Bolton, Ph.D., Dean of College of Education, University of Washington:* It will be very valuable not only to teachers, but to parents who are earnestly seeking light on the rearing and training of their children.

*William A. McKeever, LL.D., School of Creative Psychology, Topeka, Kansas:* The most complete and comprehensive work of the kind I have ever seen.

*Olive M. Jones, ex-President of the National Education Association:* One of the most useful things brought out by any organization interested in the development of character.

*Elizabeth J. Woodward, The Woodward School, Boston:* Problems receive First Aid at the turn of a page.

*Henry Neumann, Ph.D., Leader Brooklyn Ethical Culture Society:* The advice to fathers and mothers is sound.

*S. Parkes Cadman, D.D., Central Congregational Church, Brooklyn, N. Y.:* I heartily commend The Home University Bookshelf to all who are interested in the welfare of children.

━━━━━━━━Mail this Coupon To-Day━━━━━━━━

THE UNIVERSITY SOCIETY, 468 Fourth Avenue, New York, N. Y.
    Gentlemen    Please send me, without obligation, further information about "The University Plan of Character Building."

*Name* ...................................................................................................

*Address* ...................................................................................................

58    *All advertisements conform to standards on page 79.*

40

fraught with occasions for error, occasions to lead one's children in the wrong direction, toward the "commonplace." Mothering construed in this way requires a scrupulous eye, a watchman vigilance for detecting the subtle differences that make up domestic success or failure.

The message that "some mothers make mistakes," to quote a Rubens Shirts advertisement from 1914 (fig. 1.8), plays upon two related fears, a fear of inadequacy and a fear of not being seen as adequately distinguished from the sorts of mothers who do not properly prepare their children to climb the stairway to Success. The sense that *choosy* mothers will choose according to the wisdom of the experts seems applicable to the marketing of almost any parenting item for sale. The suggestion that the readership of domestic magazines needed to purchase and prepare for their children goods beyond the "commonplace" pervades the advertising to mothers. Two examples from disparate goods may suffice. "Professor Anderson's way" of puffing wheat and rice for the Quaker Oats Company, for example, could help ensure that one's children had the benefit of "scientific foods."[19] The professor's expertise also guaranteed that "your" children were greeting the morning with a *superior* version of breakfast.

While at play in seemingly minor decisions about cereal or undershirts, this dynamic is even more pronounced in the marketing of items directly related to education. An advertisement for the Chautauqua Desk claims that "thousands of boys and girls have discovered and developed unsuspected latent talents and have thus begun a successful life career." In a manner similar to "The University Plan of Character Building" and the Maltine advertisement, the Chautauqua Desk advertisement subtly suggests that a child may fail to flourish without the proper tools for uncovering that which is otherwise hidden. The 1929 advertisement asks: "Is your home equipped in 'The Chautauqua Way'?"[20] The clear implication is that if the answer is no, then "your" child may be at risk of floundering, blocked from a "successful life career" with her talents unsuspected, undiscovered, and uncultivated. The nomenclature of "The Chautauqua Way" itself drew on the then decades-old, aspiring middle-class prestige of the Chautauqua Lake Sunday School Assembly of New York, a program for "vacation learning" founded in 1874 by two Methodists. The testimony that closes the advertisement, from Rev. Lewis F. Freyberg of Ohio, helps complete the circle of parental success: "The desk is something more than just a plaything to amuse and keep a child busy." The girl or boy meticulously trained for accomplishment "The Chautauqua Way" would develop the habits of proper education. The girl or boy not so trained would remain outside, below, elsewhere.

19. *Ladies' Home Journal,* February 1914, p. 48.
20. *Parents',* January 1929, p. 56.

Figure 1.8. Rubens Shirts advertisement. *Ladies' Home Journal,* February 1914

### *"Water Babies" and "Pigmy Games"*

Indeed, what of the child not privy to "The Chautauqua Way," the child who ate each morning a "commonplace breakfast," whose mother did "make mistakes"? Or, to put the question in its most stark, economic form, what of the child of the mother who cleaned up after and broadened the horizons of the child being groomed for Success?

To read the simple advertisements through this lens is to bring into focus a significant query about race, class, and the normative account of childhood in the twentieth century. The implied danger of one's "household help" in Sapin's essay was that they might bring one's children over to the other side — the wrong side of a divide that involved race and class, failure and success. A child whose mother wanted to raise him in "The Chautauqua Way" could, through lack of "constant" maternal vigilance, end up embodying the other side and thus not meet his potential. A well-educated, well-attended child would be able to perceive cultural difference from a hygienic place, safe from cultural contamination, as if there were neither a germ in the universe nor a "black Juliet" in the house. The normative mother reading *Parents'* would provide the constant watchfulness necessary to ensure a particularly classed version of white centrality. The well-brought-up child who would advance the future of the race would remain normatively white, even though the woman daily caring for that child was "negro" or "Irish" or "peasant." Thus, by one possible reading, the most-to-be-avoided specter haunting the warnings in many advertisements and essays in *Parents'* was the "negro" child, the child at the apex of difference and the nadir of presumed "civilization." This makes it important for us to consider how "negro" children appear in the pages of *Parents'*. From 1929 to the late 1950s, such a child was almost without exception referenced only implicitly as the child whose existence was to be avoided by mothers in the know. The exceptions reinforce this point.

In a regular feature of *Parents'*, readers were invited to Keep Posted! through "News of the Better Parenthood Movement, Child Welfare, Education, and Other Matters of Interest to Parents." The first Keep Posted! for 1930 asked the question, "Can the games played by pigmies of far-off Africa be adapted to the use of children in America?" Announcing that Mrs. Delia J. Akeley had been "sent out under the auspices of the Brooklyn Children's Museum . . . for the purpose of answering this very question," the editors explained that she had previously discovered "original ideas" and "unusual cleverness and skill" in the children's games of "the pigmy natives along the Congo River."[21] The short news item (with an accompanying caricature drawing) promised findings that might be "well adapted to the needs of American children."

Later that year the editors ran "Water Babies of the South Seas." Reading as a field report from Margaret Mead, the essay explained Mead's connection with the American Museum of Natural History.[22] The leading, highlighted text reads: "Courage, resourcefulness, the ability to hold their own are traits we would develop in our children. Perhaps we have something to learn from the training of primitive brown children whom this author lived among and studied." The text sums up the stance of the article, and its use in the *Parents'* milieu: "The proficiency of these little brown children is so startling that one well may inquire how it is brought about." Through this article as well as others, scientists could bring the world of the American Museum of Natural History into a reader's own parlor.[23]

21. "Pigmy Games," in Keep Posted! *Parents'*, January 1930, p. 27.

22. Margaret Mead, "Water Babies of the South Seas," *Parents'*, September 1930, pp. 20-21, 61.

23. It is worth noting here, in anticipation of chapter 3, that the American Museum of Natural History was at this point headed up by Henry Fairfield Osborn — president of the Sec-

The literary allusion on which the Mead article plays — "water babies" — may help contextualize this story of "brown-skinned" children in *Parents*. First published in 1863 for the English *MacMillan's Magazine*, *The Water-Babies* is to this day a beloved text in England. Written by Canon Charles Kingsley, adviser to Queen Victoria and keen social Darwinist, the book has run in the hundreds of printings in a myriad of excerpted and complete forms and can be found dog-eared and cheap (as well as gold-embossed and expensive) in used bookstores and church charity bins across the United Kingdom.

To make a very long and enchanting tale short, *Water-Babies* tells of a little chimney sweep who enters into a magically naturalistic, watery world wherein he is washed clean and also transformed into a sort of embryonic form, eventually developing into a true little boy of whom a good mother could be proud. Thus, a white child begins the story covered in soot, appearing in some illustrated versions of the book as though in blackface, and ends the story scrubbed white, having experienced the recapitulation of the human species.[24]

Whether it was Margaret Mead or the editors who chose the title "Water Babies of the South Seas," the reference is key. By the complicated logic of racism and evolution at the end of the nineteenth century and into the twentieth, African or "negro" people (as well as, in England, Irish people) could serve almost simultaneously as the epitome of the virile, natural human and as the example par excellence of atavism. Mothers wishing to bring up their own courageous, resourceful children might "have something to learn" from this anthropologist's study of the ways "primitive brown children" flourish. The knowledgeable study of presumed primitivism could lead to wisdom regarding modern motherhood.

The stress put here on the gymnastic strength of peoples considered "primitive" is consistent with a potent message throughout these issues of *Parents'* to foster what was presumed to be a latent vitality within children. "Setting-Up Exercises for the Baby," also appearing in 1930 and written by Zella Van Ornum Glimm, tells modern-minded mothers they have much to learn from scientific specialists who have studied the marks of instinct written onto the bodies of their young. "Here are muscle strengthening exercises for the baby based on movements children make instinctively from birth," she

---

ond Eugenics Congress in 1921 and host to the Third Eugenics Congress in 1932. Both meetings were held at the American Museum of Natural History.

24. In his 1868 *History of Creation* and his 1899 *Riddle of the Universe at the Close of the Nineteenth Century*, Ernst Haeckel sought to prove that the development of the human embryo involved a "recapitulation" of evolution.

explains. By watching one's infant with anthropological skill, a mother could encourage even her incipient instantiation of the race toward an ever more flourishing form. By keeping a "conscientious record of the new exercises the baby does each day," a mother would discover an "astounding variety in a few months' time."[25]

The importance of keeping a "conscientious record" is quite palpable (and bleak) in "I Am the Mother of a Behaviorist's Sons," by Rosalie Rayner Watson, wife of noted behaviorist John B. Watson. The headlined text promises what readers might gain by paying attention to the children of the Watson household.[26] "Dr. John B. Watson has two young sons who can swim, skate, box, hang from trapezes, stand on their hands and get along with people," the editors suggest. How might parents coax their children into similar feats? First, the mother must recognize that she is the one ultimately responsible: "for even the ultra modern mother or the business mother has not yet been able to deny the fact that it is with her that the responsibility and the care of the baby lie." Rayner Watson continues: "She may engage a trained nurse for the infant, but after all, she selects her and sets the pace for her." The pace to be set, it turns out, was a pace of determined independence, so that, like the Watson boys, one's children could fly outside the nest as soon as possible: "Now both of my boys accept the fact that I go when and where I please, and their lives are organized so independently that they don't care. They don't rely upon one human being for their happiness. From their earliest moments, we taught them to play with objects instead of people, and one of the greatest struggles I had with nurses (when I could keep one in our household over a month) was restraining them from entertaining the children." (One has to wonder whether her parenthetical statement was intended as irony.)

The editors also ran a "Certified Advertisement" for John Watson's books in the same issue, exclaiming: "Dr. Watson is helping 50,000 mothers to bring up happy children."[27] The text of the advertisement promises: "A Famous Psychologist Tells You What to Do When Your Child . . ." with a list from "sucks his thumb" to "is a 'mother's boy'" to "is a cry-baby." The reader learns that *Atlantic Monthly* has proclaimed Watson to be no less than "A godsend to parents!" and the *New York Herald Tribune* has suggested that Watson's first book is "perhaps the most important book ever written." Here,

25. Zella Van Ornum Glimm, "Setting-Up Exercises for the Baby," *Parents'*, October 1930, pp. 20-21.

26. Rosalie Rayner Watson, "I Am the Mother of a Behaviorist's Sons," *Parents'*, December 1930, pp. 16-18.

27. *Parents'*, December 1930, p. 67.

according to the publisher, is "the psychology of enlightened common sense." W. W. Norton and Company promises that the book will "give you knowledge instead of guesswork to apply to your biggest job," helping a mother "to avoid mistakes your own parents made." This sentence sums up the message quite well: "That is why these two books bring happiness to the families that own them." Through careful attention to a child's nature, with meticulous supervision of the domestic sphere, a mother could craft from the natural clay of childhood a model of success.

The fact that the advertisement and spousal testimony to Watson's methods appeared in December — alongside advertisements for Christmas trees and children's books — might seem counterintuitive today. Yet the strange juxtaposition of maternal sentiment and behavioral observation, of motherly sympathy and shrewd assessment, seems inherent in the message of expertise in dealing with the small bodies under a mother's charge. Proper mothering involved habituation to train toward progress. To repeat again the ASHA message with which this chapter started: *Real motherhood develops by the addition of knowledge and understanding to the mother's instinctive love.* Thus, it is apparently not incongruous to run Rayner Watson's testimony to behavioralism on the same page as Elspeth MacDuffie O'Halloran's poem "Holy-Day," the final sentence of which is "Someone very small and sweet / Wakes — smiles — and sleeps — / Mary, bless each mother who / Her first Christmas keeps!"[28] Nor is it surprising to hear Rayner Watson ask, with perhaps more than a hint of wistfulness: "I wonder how many parents eat their evening meal at a reasonable hour with the children, light the fire afterwards and have at least a social hour or half-hour together? In our family we do this on birthdays and holidays. The result is that the occasion so excites the children that the whole family becomes emotionally exhausted and very grateful when bedtime arrives."

"Water Babies of the South Seas" and instinctual exercises for children, behavioralism, and "Holy-Day" are linked to another December 1930 item from Viking Press. A parent could order in a boxed set both *Human Children* and *Animal Children.* The expertise of the author is described thus: "The author's keen, patient observation has caught the tender appeal of childhood. With sympathy and wisdom he describes the charm of babies and young children, their elemental impulses and the gradual awakening of consciousness."[29] "Observation," "elemental impulses," and "sympathy" were all part of

28. Elspeth MacDuffie O'Halloran, "Holy-Day," *Parents',* December 1930, p. 18.

29. *Human Children* and *Animal Children* are by Paul Eipper; *Parents',* December 1930, p. 92.

the work of mothering, for "human beings, too, are mammals" (again, to quote the ASHA poster on "The Baby"), and their movement forward toward the teleology of the race required a tricky combination of "instinctive love" and proper "knowledge." A mother reading *Parents'* during Advent could move from a feature entitled "Christmas Gifts for Children" on page 88 to an advertisement for "sterilized baby powder" on page 91 to the Viking advertisement for "tender" photographs from *Human Children* on page 92 to an advertisement for the Doo-Tee Infant Trainer on page 93. As the last advertisement explains, even the most basic of natural functions required this "scientific Infant Trainer" for proper results: "Psychologists say 'Health is a Habit!' and certainly the habit of health in babyhood, childhood and maturity depends on another habit — that of proper and regular elimination."[30]

The caricature of "pigmy" children and their anthropological observer in the Keep Posted! feature of *Parents'* (fig. 1.9) may be set within this matrix of hygiene, habit, and progress. If the future of the race marches forward on the feet of little children, the study of faraway "natives" might give a parent insight into the proper habits of childhood. The children of "far-off Africa" could function as both the intensely natural and the purely objectified, serving as "The Child" to be observed from a sterile, evaluative distance. The caricature names a tension and also offers a raced resolution. A mother wanting to shape her own child in the habits of progress might also find herself strangely torn between instinct and knowledge. As Rayner Watson's "behavioral" essay subtly suggests, sentiment and pediatric science might not always mix well in a mother's (or, in Rayner Watson's case, a servant's) mind, as she is tempted indiscriminately to coddle rather than properly habituate her charge. Indeed, in the "Pigmy Games" caricature, the woman dons a field hat and glasses over her persona as a modern mother, picking up pen and paper to observe and classify the childhood play of these "far-off" children. She is shown as a bespectacled woman with field hat, skirt, blouse, and heels. The exclamation points and sweat emanating from her head suggest both the importance of her discovery and, perhaps, the level of her surprise in finding here, among these distanced children, tools for raising the children of the *Parents'* readership. Her task is to link the anthropological study of these children with the lives of "children in America." Mrs. Delia J. Akeley (note the "Mrs.") is in some way every mother (which is to say, every mother reading *Parents'*)

30. In the same issue, Juvenile Wood Products, Inc., ran an advertisement for its Little Toidey infant training toilet seat, with the headline "Christmas Is Coming! Christmas Is Near!" Such a gift would "teach self-direction, reliance and skill / Bringing zest of achievement and joy and good will" (*Parents'*, December 1930, p. 96).

in her attempt to read together a primitive natural and the presence of "original ideas" and "unusual cleverness and skill."[31]

Her work may be more zoological than anthropological. While the drawing is not meant to be realistic, the anthropologist/mother is shown as significantly more human than the children. The "pigmy" children are drawn as if engaged in a physically impossible game. One child balances, on one toe, on the nose of another child, who is performing a back bend. The balancing child swings what appears to be a monkey above his head while also catching rings, tossed by a third child, on his extended leg. Each child is the same size. Each child is wearing the same grass skirt. Each child has the same spindly limbs, potbelly, white mouth, and large eyes. The "pigmy children" of "far-off Africa" are presented as nonpersons, as interchangeable specimens of the human mammal.

When considered in relation the same artist's sketch of white, American children on the same page, the problem with the drawing becomes clearer. These children, of different sizes and with different clothing, with varied gestures and with small, skillfully drawn faces, illustrate a different entry on the Keep Posted! page, regarding the addition of a cow to the Lincoln Park, Chicago, zoo. The juxtaposition suggests that the reader should see the pigmy children as specimens *to be viewed*. As the rural cow seems "as strange as the mountain lion and the rhinoceros" to the city children in Lincoln Park, so the pigmy children are to be considered as exotic and primitive, yet (perhaps *as primitive*) worthy of scientific consideration, at least inasmuch as their unexpectedly clever games may be adapted for use by American mothers.[32]

Preceding "Water Babies of the South Seas," another article by Margaret Mead, "South Sea Hints on Bringing Up Children," had run in September 1929. This extensive essay was introduced by a highlighted editorial endorsement: "Can the Samoans teach us anything about child training? You will ask yourself the question after reading this amazing article. The author is an anthropologist who was sent out by the American Museum of Natural History to make a study of adolescence in this primitive society."[33] In this piece, Mead pithily summarizes her *Coming of Age in Samoa*, leading in with three prodding paragraphs in which she seeks to throw the reader off center. But her anthropological description of the decentering, given the overall context of *Parents'*, neatly applies the observational method to *others* — extending a purportedly objective gaze to "this primitive society," as the editors word it.

31. "Pigmy Games," p. 27.

32. "What Is a Cow?" in Keep Posted! *Parents'*, January 1930, p. 27.

33. Margaret Mead, "South Sea Hints on Bringing Up Children," *Parents'*, September 1929, pp. 20-21. In this discussion, the parenthetical page references in the text are to Mead's article.

***Pigmy Games***

CAN the games played by pigmies of far-off Africa be adapted to the use of children in America? Mrs. Delia J. Akeley, sent out under the auspices of the Brooklyn Children's Museum, is going to live for a year in the villages of the pigmy natives along the Congo River for the purpose of answering this very question. On a former journey into the Belgian Congo, she found the children's games full of original ideas and demanding unusual cleverness and skill. She believes they might be well adapted to the needs of American children.

***What Is a Cow?***

CITY-BRED youngsters may now marvel over the strange looking animal known as the cow. A pure-bred Holstein cow and calf have been given quarters in the animal exhibit at Lincoln Park, Chicago, zoo for the benefit of children to whom they are as strange as the mountain lion and the rhinoceros. The newcomers were shipped from the stock farm of Mrs. Ruth Hanna McCormick, near Byron, Illinois. All city zoos take notice.

**Figure 1.9 and 1.10 Sketches from the Keep Posted! page. *Parents'*, January 1930**

By "limiting our observations to our own country, our own language group, insisting, blindly, that what is true of ourselves is necessarily true of the whole human race," as Mead puts it, *Parents'* readers have developed an inadequate way of seeing themselves and their children.

What Mead's article cannot decenter is the way in which her readers, at least here, are already acculturated to read the Samoans as "primitive." The reading of "our own country" and "our own language group" is not vaguely, generally blind but myopic in a particular way, through a raced ideology of human development. Mead's description of her comparison "control group" as "adolescents of a primitive community" and her narration of her choice of locale — "an island inhabited by a few hundred of brown South Sea Islanders" — suggest her own perspective (p. 22).

What Mead recommends as a method for "looking over the fence into other civilizations" is supposed to bring an appreciation of "this inadequately explored earth." However, her characterization of the other-people-to-be-explored is dubiously related to her characterization of the expert explorers. The anthropologist is the "student of mankind at all times and all places," able to be herself the center in order to bring to her own people the "queer things about human nature" to be learned from "other civilizations" (p. 21). Moving easily from the "East Coast African" to the "Eskimo," the anthropological voice stands as the observer of variation, able to posit the malleability of humanness sufficient to call into question the plight of "adolescence" in the United States. Indeed, in years hence, others would argue that Mead brought with her to Samoa a romanticized quest for a purer, uninhibited people — Adam, Eve, and their children prior to sexual shame. The anthropologist sought to find people who "consider sex as natural," and, behold, she discovered "graceful young Samoans in their shady, peaceful villages," children whose "young days" were "untroubled" and "unpoignant" (pp. 49, 52).

Mead's comparison between this Edenic existence and the "complicated" society of the *Parents'* readership is key to understanding the use to which her work was put in *Parents'*. "Our" children were growing up in a "very difficult and expensive world," a world "coming to recognize personality as a value and cherish choice and individuality of thought" (p. 52). If "the future of the race" was marching "forward on the feet of little children," parents of children in such a complicated, real world would need to learn all they could from observational experts like Mead. An "American" female on the verge of moving from girl to woman was facing a myriad of choices and new responsibilities, and would require guidance. The lessons of primitive children could, ostensibly, be used by a mother preparing her daughter as they together determined her route. Not incidentally, the editors ran "A Wardrobe for the College Girl" immediately following Mead's essay. Its elaborate illustration by Herbert Johnson depicts a lithe young woman with bobbed hair sorting through multiple silky dresses and four pairs of fashionable shoes with a decidedly choosy air. By recognizing the "best choice" of ensemble to wear to the campus football game, for example, a girl might be prepared to proceed through her complicated, individualized existence (see fig. 1.11).[34]

### "Being Washed Is No Easy and Casual Matter in the Slums"

There is a color of cleanliness, and as an introduction to two examples of race ideology, hygiene, and parenthood in *Parents'*, we note the existence of the Gold Dust Twins, "always quick and always sure," the personification of the washing powder made by the Fairbank Soap Company in Chicago. The company used the image from the early 1900s into the 1930s.[35]

One postcard advertisement (fig. 1.12) explicitly linked the middle-class woman's married plight with the work of the Gold Dust Twins. Admonishing that "A word to the WIFE is sufficient," the message played on the adage "a word to the wise," with "WIFE" underlined and bolded to accentuate the shift in status from woman to WIFE. To the left of the text is a drawing of a couple in full wedding regalia. To the right stand two black children, with red skirts on which is written "Gold Dust," one child with a washrag and the other with

34. Marian Park Baldwin, "A Wardrobe for the College Girl," *Parents'*, September 1929, pp. 23, 58.

35. From *Ladies' Home Journal*, March 1914, p. 56.

# ᴀ Wardrobe *for the* College Girl

*Illustrated by*
Herbert Johnson

By Marian Park Baldwin

¶ *Written by a college girl, this article gives inside information as to what's what on the campus. Actual prices and budgets adapted to thin, medium-sized and bulging purses are published at the end of the article*

Getting ready to go away to college is such a thrilling adventure! Out comes the dusty old trunk from the attic, or if the would-be college student is more lucky she hies herself to a luggage shop and looks at rows and rows of shiny new trunks, and finally comes home with one that has shelves and drawers and a rack that pulls out to exhibit many hang-

There is such a deliciously free feeling about slopping around in the rain and not having to

**Figure 1.11. "A Wardrobe for the College Girl."** *Parents'*, **September 1929**

a scrubbing mop. The text is salient for our purposes: "When you're married / Your trouble begins / Unless you adopt / The GOLD DUST TWINS." If a wife would only "adopt" the labor of these two black cherubs, she would have no trouble with her own work of cleaning up. Likewise, she would not be over-tired by her efforts: "Don't wear yourself out dishwashing," one advertisement reads, for Gold Dust "cleans everything."

The images of the Gold Dust Twins appeared on many Fairbank advertisements, as well as on the box of the powder itself, with the motto "Let the Gold Dust Twins do your work." Again, while the WIFE to whom the washing powder was being marketed could be read as a domestic cleaning tool of a sort, she was not merely so. The white WIFE is not a caricature; she is fully

51

**Figure 1.12. From a postcard. Courtesy of Duke Special Collections**

clothed in the one image, rather royally so, and her hands are full size in the other (fig. 1.13). By contrast, the children in two of the images are miniature, the size of a hand or a scrub brush, and in the other they are oversize, as if perhaps to suggest their strength for the task at hand. The caricatured imaging suggests that they are essentially serviceable, essentially to be of use. That two African American children could be more than merely *figuratively adopted* by the couple on the postcard is beyond the realm of possibility. The narrative humor posed regarding two African American children and their adoption into a white, middle-class home presumably adds to the appeal of the Gold Dust advertisements.

The work of cleaning "everything" to the point of proper, domestic hygiene is reflected racially in two illustrated articles in *Parents'* — "So Early Monday Morning," by Mary Ormsbee Whitton, and "Dey's All Got Debbils!" by Elizabeth McFadden.[36] The former situates race and childhood in such a way as to erase through nonaddress any possible concern about the children of women who are washing the clothing of other women's children. The latter configures the plight of children who are black (even blue-black) so as to transfer all culpability onto the washerwoman's shoulders. There may be problems, serious

36. Mary Ormsbee Whitton, "So Early Monday Morning," *Parents'*, November 1930, pp. 28-29, 75-77; Elizabeth McFadden, "Dey's All Got Debbils!" *Parents'*, October 1929, pp. 22-23, 65-66.

Figure 1.13. Advertisement for Fairbank Soap Company. *Ladies' Home Journal,* March 1914

problems, in the "slums," but McFadden's narrative brilliantly launders the issues at stake, leaving the *Parents'* readership whiter than Ivory Snow.

"So Early Monday Morning" promises to address "How best to deal with that white elephant — the family washing." Illustrated with stylized drawings, the essay reflects a spectrum of washing among the relatively upper class, from the mother who sends all her washing out, to the mother who considers the servant responsible for her washing, to the tennis-playing mother for whom "ten cents worth of electricity buys effective wash-day release." The two illustrations on the left side of the two-page spread contribute to the "we're all in this together" tone of the essay, as Mary Ormsbee Whitton compares various ways to save money and make use of the "new servant" in the home, the electric washer. The tennis mother and her bob-haired daughter wave good-bye to the washing machine, the former glad for the respite and the latter happy to have mother to herself.

The other illustration shows another option, in which a mother collects the family's dirty laundry and makes it someone else's problem (fig. 1.14). The text above the photograph — "This has been known to happen in the best-regulated families" — offers an insider's chuckle, as four children, in neat, descending order, follow mom to the laundryman's van, trailing their washables. Father, in black suit and evident distress, leans out the door to offer his dirty socks.

The article's third illustration appears across the page break, on the other side of the divide. In this picture (fig. 1.15), a brown-faced child is shown next to the *other* mother, the servant who is expected to do the family's washing. The caption's reference to "Old Dinah" indicates that the caricature is specific to the backward South: "Old Dinah never heard of washing machines, but her tony niece up North wouldn't skin her knuckles on a washboard!" While the commercial laundry employees who were actually washing, drying, ironing, and folding the clothing of the "best-regulated families" were behind the scenes, kept completely beyond the ken of the *Parents'* readership, Old Dinah could sturdily symbolize all forms of domestic help. The trinity of illustrations trades on a well-worn caricature of the African American woman, long since emancipated in the technical sense and yet here infinitely serviceable to signal both the privilege of those who employ her and the superiority of the Northern families who instead employ her "tony niece up North."

In front of Old Dinah is a child under her watch. The child sits on the floor with a basin of soapsuds, blowing bubbles. The child's hair, clothes, bare feet, and corncob bubble pipe signal the dehumanized happiness attending the pickaninny caricature. The readership of *Parents'* was disproportionately

**Figure 1.14. Illustration for Mary Ormsbee Whitton, "So Early Monday Morning."** *Parents'*, **November 1930**

**Figure 1.15. Illustration for Mary Ormsbee Whitton, "So Early Monday Morning," *Parents'*, November 1930**

Illustrated by
WALTER
VAN ARSDALE

Old Dinah never heard of washing machines, but her tony niece up North wouldn't skin her knuckles on a wash-board!

New England blue blood, and the editorial board overwhelmingly so, and the tried and true other-ing of Southern, racialized caricatures served well to reinforce the class dynamics of the essay. The aspiring class of the mother who could not deposit her dirty bundles with her own servant or a group of invisible laborers could nonetheless remain on the privileged side of the divide by way of the serviceable Old Dinah and her dehumanized charge. The tennis-playing mother could, by way of the caricature, remain a page break away from those sorts of women who do other people's laundry. As for the servant's own child — whose existence was significantly bound by the economics of domestic labor and whose childhood was marked by the work of her own mother for the mothers of other children — this child is depicted as happily playing with bubbles, blithe and hardly human.

The themes we have followed up to this point — of hygiene, race, safety, and the normativity of a particular version of whiteness — all intersect in an essay by Elizabeth McFadden, the illustration for which features another African American mother at her washboard, with two of her children nearby. Written as a first-person account of an attempt to find and reform a "congenital criminal," "Dey's All Got Debbils!" promises a helpful lesson in how not to parent: "You couldn't teach Mother Woolly anything about bringing up children. Hadn't she buried ten? But her mistakes are common to other parents and the solution will apply in many cases."[37] The essay uses a potent combination of racialized caricature, maternal dehumanization ("woolly" being no less than a well-worn racial epithet), and class presumption to resolve the quandaries, both explicit and implicit, posed by the essay. The explicit quandary may be stated thus: How is a woman reading *Parents'* to think about the problem of "slums," child labor, and juvenile delinquency? The implicit quandary may be stated a bit differently: How is a woman of decent conscience reading *Parents'* to think about the problem of "slums," child labor, and juvenile delinquency so as to absolve herself of any responsibility? McFadden's "solution" — a firm warning from a white woman with a police badge to a black woman from the slums — neatly answers both quandaries.

The essay starts with the question of congenital taint, and it ends with a skillful reinforcement of racial ideology and a clever cleansing of any residual class guilt. By the end of the essay a "prominent . . . successful" adherent of a form of eugenic ideology — "Some boys are just naturally born bad!" — may have been discredited, as well as the "happy pickaninny" caricature in "So Early Monday Morning." The juvenile thief is not a born criminal, and neither is he inherently a beast of burden. This does not, however, necessitate an overhaul of a privileged woman's perspective. The "ignominious" child laborer is narrated as in some way "the child" to be under protection by the four policemen metaphorically pictured in the Maltine advertisements. But the menace to *his* health is the kind of "other" mother who is prone to make "mistakes." That damned spot of privileged culpability for the plight of *other women's children* is handily removed.

The rhetorically rich illustration crafted by Robb Beebe (fig. 1.16) uses page layout to state and resolve the article's question. On one side of the two-page spread is a little boy carrying a heavy load of laundry. Unlike the pickaninny caricature, the child strains under the load, looking across the divide of the page with a plaintive fear. His face is not markedly caricatured as "negro," and his clothing and hat neatly fit him, even in his strain. The little boy's carefully drawn, detailed countenance is situated in immediate proximity to the author's name. His body is turned toward the far side of the left page, as if to carry him out of the essay altogether, but his face is turned back in evident fear of the divide and, beyond it, Mother Woolly.

She stands on the other side of the divide with three washtubs, a wash-

37. McFadden, "Dey's All Got Debbils!" p. 23. In this discussion, the parenthetical page references in the text are to McFadden's article.

board, a scrub brush, and, quite notably, a shadowed sketch of another child, rendered in a significantly different form. She stands with a scowl on her face, fisted hands on her hips, looking down and over at the child across the divide. The child on Mother Woolly's side of the divide is posed in recline, his hands resting on his stomach, his eyes closed. In large print, the highlighted text begins: "YOU couldn't teach Mother Woolly anything . . ." In smaller print, next to Mother Woolly's wash pail, the text reads: "After school George Washington has ter stay right beside me and wuk, he does. I doan believe in no foolishness fer kids."

On one side of the divide is a child worthy of and even summoning the author's attention. On the other side is the problem of his mother and the ill-drawn shadow child, a child who sleeps while his brother strains to depart the washroom altogether.

The highlighted text delivers the essay's rhetorical punch. The reader couldn't teach Mother Woolly — this "Zulu warrior," this "broad, black, fierce . . . prowling panther of a woman" (as she is called elsewhere in the piece) — anything about bringing up children. The next line is ripe with scorn, pitched across the divide with such sarcasm that it took my breath away when I first read it: "Hadn't she buried ten?" Given that the readership was largely made up of mothers intent on keeping their own babies safely guarded within a germ-free universe, the toss-away reference to the rate of childhood mortality among African Americans is powerfully dismissive. The author asks, in effect, "Hadn't Mother Woolly already discarded ten of her own children?" Her mistakes are characteristic of her class, the author argues, and the solution offered will be of use in slums everywhere. Determined to prove or disprove the notion of the "congenital criminal," the author had to work hard, eschewing "chocolate sundaes and golf" in search of "wild beasts" who would of course "shun the open." McFadden uses the language of a hunter: "I should have to track my bad boy to some hidden lair."

Having made her way "to the school in the second worst slum of our town," the author was introduced to George Washington Woolly. We are told that "George Washington may have been a misnomer but Woolly was right," for the child was "almost blue-black, round-eyed with ingenuous candor," with "the sort of a face that belongs with a luscious watermelon, but that is out of place behind a mask of lonely fright." McFadden's casual reference to the watermelon urchin, happy in his lot, serves well her purposes. This was a child who should have been happy but was instead hiding behind a "mask" of fear. And what was the cause of his "lonely fright"? Here enters Mother Woolly, the clearly marked villain of the essay. Dehumanized as merely animal by the narrative and vilified by the drawing, the mother of

# "Dey's All Got Debbils!"

## By Elizabeth McFadden

A PROMINENT man, a successful man, had started me off on my strange search. "Some boys are just naturally born bad!" he had said. Was he right? I was determined to know, so I set out on a hunt for a congenital criminal. But this business of finding a bad boy is not all chocolate sundaes and golf. Wild beasts shun the open. I should have to track my bad boy to some hidden lair. I went to the school in the second worst slum of our town where I had been made probation officer and invaded the office of its principal.

"If I'm to be probation officer in this school," I said, "I'd like some good hunting."

"All right," grinned the principal cheerfully. "How would you like a thief?"

"A real thief under twelve? Let's have him."

The principal went to the telephone.

"Please send me George Washington Woolly," he said.

"This boy," he explained to me, "was arrested the other day for stealing a dozen footballs."

I gasped. "Most of the college men I know are proud of capturing one."

"These were not blown up," explained the principal. "He slipped them under his coat."

"But what did he want so many for?" I asked.

"He doesn't seem to know himself. However, he has been selling them to the other boys in the yard. That is the way we came to learn of it."

The boy arrived. George Washington may have been a misnomer but Woolly was right. Small for his age, twelve, black, almost blue-black, round-eyed with ingenuous candor, he had the sort of a face that belongs with a luscious watermelon, but that is out of place behind a mask of lonely fright.

Here was a serious matter. George must learn he could not steal footballs. His parents were summoned. Mother Woolly arrived alone. She was enough. She made me think of a Zulu warrior, nearly six feet in height, broad, black, fierce, a prowling panther of a woman.

You couldn't teach *her* anything about bringing up children. Hadn't she buried ten? Yassam! Her vast experience had given her an invincible assurance in dealing with all the problems of childhood. Beatem! That was her panacea. Drive out de debbils. Dey's all got debbils! Yassam! Evidently she belonged to the same school as my judicial-minded friend.

My zeal for disciplining that nervous little woolly lamb, black sheep though he might be, began to evaporate. I saw that any punishment I could wreak upon the Son of the House of Woolly would be dew from heaven compared to his mother's ordinary hand-out. I must get

**Figure 1.16. "Dey's All Got Debbils!"** *Parents'*, October 1929

*YOU couldn't teach Mother Woolly anything about bringing up children. Hadn't she buried ten? But her mistakes are common to other parents and the solution will apply in many cases*

*Illustrated by*

ROBB BEEBE

*"After school George Washington has ter stay right beside me and wuk, he does. I doan believe in no foolishness fer kids."*

through to him and make my point on a heart and brain worn to iron by beatings.

"George, you want to have people like and respect you when you grow up, don't you? Don't you, dear?"

I took one little black paw and stroked it. That registers with a dog, why not with a beaten little boy?

Sudden tears glittered in the brilliant black eyes.

"Yassam, shore do."

"Then you must keep the laws, and never, *never* take things that belong to other people."

"Whut you mean, mam,—'long ter other people'?"

"Well, you have some things that are yours—toys,

haven't you?" I explained.

"No, mam."

"You haven't any toys? Not one?"

"No, *mam*."

I stared at his mother.

"No, mam, I don't believe in no sich foolishness fer kids," she pronounced.

"What does he do after school?" I asked.

"He stays right beside me and wuks, he does."

"No games? No play?"

"Whut he wanter play fer?" his Amazonian mother demanded. "One time he did git out, what'd he do? Went off an' stole an' got me an' his pap in bad. Ah'll fix him, youall leave 'im ter me."

A virtuous panther.

I turned to the trembling boy.

"George, you have your clothes. They are your own?"

No, *mam*. Desyer clothes, de wuz (*Turn to page* 65)

the child is situated as the problem to be solved. "Her vast experience had given her an invincible assurance in dealing with all the problems of childhood. Beatem! That was her panacea. Drive out de debbils. Dey's all got debbils! Yassam!"

The problem besetting the child trying to make his way courageously across the magazine's divide was, quite simply, his mother — a woman who beat her own offspring, thus joining forces with the eugenicist who had summarily dismissed her child as congenitally bad.[38]

The narrator thus realized that her aim had been misplaced. She was not called to discipline the Woolly child but instead to enfold him in her maternal care. Only then would the child move into the realm of the human. The text is worth quoting here at length: "My zeal for disciplining that nervous little woolly lamb, black sheep though he might be, began to evaporate. I saw that any punishment I could wreak upon the Son of the House of Woolly would be dew from heaven compared to his mother's ordinary hand-out. I must get through to him and make my point on a heart and brain worn to iron by beatings. . . . I took one little black paw and stroked it. That registers with a dog, why not with a beaten little boy?" (p. 23). When the author then tried to explain to the child that he should "*never* take things that belong to other people," she was shocked, *shocked,* to discover that even the clothes on the child's back were not, technically, his own, having belonged before to his brothers, named, not incidentally, Thomas Jefferson and John L. Sullivan.

The author's accusatory gaze thus turned in astonishment to the boy's mother. Why? Why was this child without a toy of his own? Mother Woolly responded: "I don't believe in no sich foolishness fer kids. . . . He stays right beside me and wuks, he does. . . . Whut he wanter play fer?" Using yet another racial epithet, this time "Amazonian," the author situates the boy's mother as the clear, sole source of his problem. She has forbidden her child to play. She has sided with those who believe in congenital badness by speaking of "debbils"; she has sided with the slaveholders by enslaving her child to her own washer work; she has made him old before his time. The necessary course of action is for a woman like McFadden quite literally to "turn on" a woman who makes such mistakes. What is called for is a law sufficient to bring her to heel. The culminating exchange warrants, again, full quotation:

---

38. As McFadden herself notes: "Evidently she belonged to the same school as my judicial-minded friend" (p. 22).

"Lor, Miss, youall don't know how to talk ter dat nigger. Now you jes' let me tell him erbout dis."

I yielded the floor.

"You, George Washington, you lost soul, you know whut? Disyer lady she's de wife ob a cop!"

"No, no, Mrs. Woolly."

"Yassam, dat's de truf, an'" (she turned back to the quaking George) "ef she hears ob you layin' yer little finger on anything again, she'll send her husband an' de patrol wagon an' have him trow you right in de ribber."

"Not in the river, Mrs. Woolly," I cried aghast.

"*Yassam! In de ribber!* An' de shark'll git 'im. An' de hants!"

The terror in George's eyes put steel into my soul.

I turned on Mother Woolly. I displayed my badge.

Mother Woolly knew a police badge when she saw it. The effect on her was electric.

"Are you listening, Mother Woolly?"

"Yes, mam!"

"Very well. There are two things that George must have from this day forth. If he does not get them, or if you take them away from him, I am going to summon *you* to ride in the patrol wagon and come to court. First, he is to have two hours every day to play out-of-doors with the other boys. Second, he is to have something he wants for his very own. It's to be *his own*. Nobody is to take it away from him. Do you understand?"

"Yassam." A cowed panther now.

I turned to George.

"George, what would you like to have to play with? What would you rather have than anything else in the world?"

The small brow knit. George was thinking more intensely than he had ever thought before. A sudden idea! (p. 65, emphasis in original)

In this way, through the strong, alternatively maternal correction of the law, "George got his hammer and the loveliest assortment of nails and became thereby a man of property and a responsible and happy citizen." Having been brought out from beneath the cruel arm of his mother by the loving arm of the law, the thief was transformed into a citizen. The narrative is thus concluded: "Bad? Perish the thought!" Through the hard work of McFadden in facing down the enemy, Mother Woolly's child became a "helpful, honest, friendly, industrious little soul" (p. 66).

The commentary brings the individualized, personal narrative to bear on the patterns of "truancy" in the "slums." Why were children not privy to the joys of education? Not due to the exploitative labor practices of the people employing their parents. Not due to the systematic, racialized ideology of capitalism in the United States. Who was responsible for the problems besetting children like George Washington Woolly? Why was he not able to align himself fully with the author, walking out of the narrative altogether? He and children like him were beset by the overzealous cleaning habits of their mothers.

> I discovered a whole ignominious army of children forced to forego the delights of learning in honor of the social institution known as the semiannual bath. *Being washed is no easy and casual matter in the slums.* The child would disappear from school as mysteriously as though he had been spirited to the Bastille under a *lettre de cachet* of Louis the Fifteenth. Many of the mothers were afraid of the truant officers and when quizzed by them, opposed a front of complete ignorance as to their child's whereabouts. . . . Gradually the rites of the Nights of the Bath were revealed to me.
>
> The candidate for the distinction had to be unsewed and taken carefully apart. Then the party of the first part, hereinafter called Johnny or Susie, was scrubbed pink in the family washtub and put to bed. There he remained while the party of the second part, hereinafter called "Yerclothes," was soaked and rubbed and dried and ironed and aired and reassembled. Then, and only then, did one return to school. (p. 66, emphasis added)

This accusation — that the problem facing a child not privy to the "delights of learning" was due to his mother's fixation on bathing — is, in the context, truly rich. Taking the reader's own fixation on hygiene, throwing it out, away from the reader, in order to exculpate her of any blame regarding the hardships besetting children in the poorest neighborhoods, was a masterful move on McFadden's part. Yet the accusation would boomerang on the reader. As aspiring women strove to justify and secure their own households as hygienic and sound, they would find their own lives and bodies being "unsewed and taken carefully apart."

But before we dig more deeply into what we term the Lysol habit, a few words about the domesticated version of faith foundational to the magazine. To understand the cleanliness that was considered akin to godliness, it is essential to understand the vaguely civil form of *Parents'* religiosity.

### *"The Meaning of Easter: An Editorial Message"*

A friend of mine was once much concerned because her seven-year-old son was more interested in the notion of God he received from their very religious Austrian maid than in the more abstract being of whom she tried to tell him.[39]

The version of Christianity at play in the pages of *Parents'* was so bland as to be virtually useless in addressing the divide reinforced by text and imagery. By a more suspicious interpretation, the form of religiosity underlying hygienic domesticity was itself racially encoded. Christianity was construed in such a way as to make the life and death of a Jewish servant crucified in a neglected part of the Roman Empire into a formless generalization about "humanity." What is more, the "humanity" characterized by the Christianity of *Parents'* was a particular humanity — a culturally normative humanity represented by the readership. *Parents'* civically palatable faith assumed the existence of an "abstract being" (to quote Sapin). The editors wrote into their pages a deity abstracted from any specific, biblical narrative. "God" became philosophical Silly Putty — able to take onto itself the words and images and colors of normative, elite whiteness.

The editors of the magazine wrote messages at Easter and Christmas of 1929 that may characterize the interplay of progressive Protestantism and the work of parents to ensure "the future of the race." "The Meaning of Easter," from April 1929, begins with a capital *E* illuminated by grapevines and lilies. So also the December 1929 editorial, "Old Christmases for New," begins with an illuminated letter. Both titles are in large print, with the text bordered in a scalloped pattern that ends with the boxed drawing accompanying the message from Phillips Brooks. The visual impact of the pages is considerable in the overall copy of the magazine. These matters were not peripheral to the purpose of *Parents'.*[40]

The editors begin "The Meaning of Easter" with a carefully crafted narration of Easter's history: "Every early association of the word Easter has to do with youth and its promise. The word is derived from an old pagan festival in honor of Eastre, the Saxon goddess of spring and dawn." Continuing the story, the editors tie together pagan spring and dawn with the "Jewish passover [*sic*]," described as a "paean of thanksgiving for the saving of the firstborn of each family in Israel." In the "Christian feast" of Easter, the pagan and

39. Sapin, "For Better or Worse — Servants Influence Children."

40. "The Meaning of Easter: An Editorial Message," *Parents',* April 1929, p. 15; Anne Pierce, "Old Christmases for New: An Editorial Message," *Parents',* December 1929, p. 11.

the Jewish are joined in the supposed common emphasis on "youth and its promise." The first paragraph closes with a quotation from no less an authoritative Christian than Bishop Ambrose (noted as "bishop of the Church of the 4th century"). According to the editors' characterization of the quotation, Ambrose notes the proper "symbolism" of Easter as "the real beginning of the year . . . the new revival of the seeds . . . , [for on Easter] God relights the sun and gives light to the moon."

Shorn of any explicit reference to Christ's death and resurrection, and tied to a serviceable construal of "Jewish passover," the "symbol" of Easter is freed to flow into the second paragraph. Moving from "youth and promise" toward parents themselves, Easter becomes "a period of renewal." For "busy fathers and tired mothers," Easter offers insight "through the mist of years" into "the procession of parents marching down the centuries." What Easter provides is the occasion to note that the procession is not descending but ascending, evolving, marching forward; the procession of parents is moving toward "the high goal."

Again, without defining the telos of parenthood with any explicit reference to the resurrection of Jesus Christ, the "high goal" of the march through the ages is sufficiently symbolic for the editors to link Easter with a "new covenant" made by parents with their children — to "make home the center" and "keep youth's point of view in their hearts." The covenant requires parents "above all to have faith in the integrity, the adventurous, level-eyed fearlessness of youth of today." Therefore, the editorial closes, readers may "Lift up your hearts and be glad!" With "trust" in the "great law which sets the constellations in the heavens, makes the trees clap their hands in gladness," and "stars the earth's bosom with flowers of every hue," parents may perceive that the same "renewal" alive in Easter is alive with "promise" for today's children and tomorrow's parents. The last paragraph is a brilliant combination of the magazine's emphases on youth, promise, progress, and parenthood, cast in the reconfigured language of Isaiah ("the leaves clap their hands"), Ecclesiastes ("the earth's bosom"), and even (perhaps inadvertently) an old English Christmas hymn echoed by Joseph Smith ("Lift up your hearts and be glad!"). The mix allows for a creative continuity between Bishop Ambrose and a magazine offering advances in cleaning fluids and vitamin A.

"The Meaning of Easter" concludes with a twofold charge: "Welcome the advance of intelligence in science and art and their contribution to the profession of parenthood. Have faith in your children and they will have faith in you. Thus the march along the way will be with stronger and firmer steps." With new intelligence in science and art, with the old covenant newly contextualized to be primarily a "new covenant" between parents and their children, the "faith" of Easter becomes a "faith" in the "future of the race" marching "forward on the feet of little children."

And what of the second high holy day of Christianity? Associate editor Anne Pierce begins "Old Christmases for New" by noting the readership of the magazine, one plausibly "immersed in the welter of ribbons and tissue paper, cards and gifts, tinsel, electric lights and special cookery." Pierce's contrast of the "old" Christmas with the "new" involves a reading of the incarnation by way of a sentimentalized "Silent Night" or "O Little Town of Bethlehem." The reason "the Child" could not be born in the inn was because it was "crowded," in contrast to the "hush of a dimly lighted stable." The wise men came "noiselessly," "bearing their few rare gifts," in contrast to the commerce and "welter of ribbons" today. These "few rare gifts" are disentangled from their marks as foretelling the criminal's death of Emmanuel. Rather, the gifts of the magi "symbolized love, praise and remembrance" — "the warm glow of wonder that diffuses itself" through the Christmas narrative. This warm glow is sufficiently diffuse to apply to the inn and to the magi and to the entire meaning of Christmas, construing the name Prince of Peace as indicative of "peace and refreshment" from the "fast-flowing, phosphorescent current of our electric commercial age." This Prince of Peace is the pause in the midst of the hustle and bustle of Pierce's readers. It has "its own sheer beauty" that exists "beyond and above all theologies and creeds."

The two editorials share one crucial pattern. The elements of the narrative are rendered in such a way as to be "symbolic" and "diffuse" and to float "beyond and above all theologies and creeds." This sort of serviceable distillation renders the real meaning of Easter and the real celebration of Christmas consonant not only with the messages of *Parents'*, but also with the vaguely mainline-Protestant Esperanto of the day. Defining beauty by this melody helps harmonize the parental aspirations of the readership and the story of a Prince of Peace, born without a place to sleep, who would go on to die — still bearing the wounds even after the resurrection. Pierce can thus move from the "hush" of the stable to the Prince of Peace to the wish that her readers might enjoy "above all else a peaceful Christmas with a fire on the hearth, a candle in the window, a community tree outside, a warm glow about the heart, and children bright-eyed and eager." This leads her to quote Plato on "wonder" and "inquiry" as the "root of all knowledge," the "same inquiring wonder" that led the magi "on their quest to find The Child." Yet finally, "The Child" becomes "the child," brought into focus so that we might "know what he really is" and "give him every opportunity to unfold," avoiding "all cynicism, hardness and world weariness." The eternal life through Christ conveyed indeed through Christian theology and creed becomes instead a "never-dying wonder concerning the deep undercurrents of life and an increasing tenderness for the births and crucifixions of all its strivings." The symbolization of the narrative is complete — the birth, life, and death of one Child becomes a prompt for remembering an older truth, a truth as old as Plato and the pagans who celebrated Eastre. This is the newfangled natural-theological creed above and beneath and beyond the *particular* creeds of any *particular* church. This is the serviceably inchoate message of the "Old Christmas" recommended to the readers of *Parents'* magazine.

One way to render two high holy Christian days into days of vague, universal significance is to address the *Parents'* readership as if they represented quite simply "the common life of human beings." The authors of the Easter editorial ostensibly addressed parents in general — parents en masse and across the ages — by suggesting that "Love and life, birth and death have been their constant companions, while ever at their side have moved the victories, the defeats and all the experiences that go to make up the common life of human beings." In this summary "human beings" become a universal concept described as holding in "common" their loves, lives, births, and deaths. The victories and the defeats are sufficiently held in "common" as to be told within an overarching story of human creation and a subsequent climb toward a "high goal." This is the narrative within which Easter and Christmas could become consonant with the goals of proper parenting in the United States. This was a problematic interpretation for the readership itself, inasmuch as the aspiring upper-middle-class home thus became the site for blessing, and the children within the vehicles of salvation.

But the message about "human beings" and their "common" struggles was problematic on another, related level. The supposed "common" constructed in the magazine was not general but specific. The magazine contained constant reminders that the "race" that epitomizes the "human race" is the particularly raced existence of a particular class with a particular creed.

### "Get the Lysol Habit"

Reflected in the shiny pans cleaned by the Gold Dust Twins is a home seemingly under attack by menacing germs. The refrain "does what soap and water can't" in the Fairbank advertisements seems also at play in many other ads that promoted cleaning in ways superior to those of one's grandmother. Simple soap would not suffice for the modern mother. Women without the proper products, the advertisements implied, are the kinds of mothers who "make mistakes." The safety of children depended on the advance of domestic

**Figure 1.17. Advertisement for the Cleanliness Institute.** *Parents'*, October 1930

hygiene through advanced products. The goal, as suggested in ads for products to clean everything from kitchen to bathroom to floor to clothing, was to eliminate germs. It was not enough simply to make things appear clean; one's home needed to be clean in ways that only a microscope could confirm and only a scientifically proven formula could achieve. The sense of hidden germs, skulking, lurking beneath the surface of one's domestic life, pervaded domestic magazines in the first half of the century, and arguably echoes still today. The road to germ-shielding grocery-cart covers from OneStepAhead was paved with many an advertisement for Lysol, which would protect one's children from the incalculable dangers invisible to the human eye.

The incalculability of the effort was perhaps key to the advertising. One could never be *sure* one had achieved a germ-free universe. The image of a mother reaching up to a sink beyond her grasp appeared courtesy of the "Cleanliness Institute: Established to promote public welfare by teaching the value of cleanliness" (fig. 1.17). The drawing was intended to prove through humor a serious point about children having access to a place to wash their hands. Children who were not provided a step stool could hardly be blamed for losing the war against germs. In numerous ways mothers reading the magazine were encouraged to make cleanliness the focal point of their children's existence.

The image works on another level as well, as the task of achieving the presumably godly form of cleanliness seemed almost by design beyond the grasp of a mother. Perfectly safe hygiene raced ahead, an always elusive goal of securing one's home against the menace of encroaching microorganisms. The imagery used was at times bizarrely militaristic. Children and their mothers were to "go on the war path against dirty hands," to quote one Lifebuoy advertisement, which featured "two little 'Injuns'" registering their "regular use" of Lifebuoy's "antiseptic lather" that would provide a *"real health safeguard"* for "Heap Big Bobby" and "Sister."[41] Lifebuoy even offered a free "Wash-Up Chart" to be posted on the wall for the sake of regular cleanliness.

It could be said that the war on germs threatened to split apart a mother's own body by turning her into a site of warrior-like vigilance. There seemed an insurmountable gap between a Zulu/Amazon/panther/servant woman and a vigilant/responsible/careful woman. Yet there was always also, at the same time, the danger that the latter would be mistaken for the former. The ever-elusive goal of perfectly safe hygiene could be seen as part and parcel of the divide between mothers who did not make mistakes and mothers who did. The gap was explicitly death dealing on one side and more subtly so on the other. Given that the readers of *Parents'* were merely human, given that their bodies were not foolproof and their homes not secured against all error and their children clearly not infallible, it was perhaps inevitable that the suspicion and other-ing of *other* women, so key to the *proper* mother's identity, would become internalized. Represented in the magazine is a sense that even a normative woman's body was not, in any helpful way, her own. The alienation between servant and mistress involved also an alienation from one's own embodiment as a dust-to-dust mortal.[42]

Lysol has regularly advertised in women's magazines from its beginning, with its crucial uses ramifying throughout the household, the school, and, as we shall see, even a modern mother's body. The war against germs was presented in these advertisements as no small thing but rather as the difference between a home that is "safe" and a home that is "deadly." One advertisement asks: "Are your door-knobs safe for little hands to touch?" The accompanying photograph (fig. 1.18) is of a little girl reaching up, her carefully brushed hair shining in the light. She is wearing a floral dress with a crisp white collar. Yet even such an attentively groomed girl is prone to put her hands where they don't belong, reaching, as the text below the image reads, "From door-knob, to fingers . . . to mouth!" What is a good mother to do?

Even amid the fear of "the common diseases which every mother dreads" there is a subtle reference to the inability of a mother to keep her home com-

41. *Parents'*, October 1930, p. 57, emphasis in original.
42. I am here indebted explicitly to Lillian Smith. Elizabeth Fox-Genovese introduced me to Smith's *Strange Fruit* (1944) in a seminar while I was an undergraduate at Emory. Later, reading and teaching Smith's *Killers of the Dream*, I realized how Smith's reading of white Southern womanhood could also so helpfully illumine what was at stake in the germ-free home.

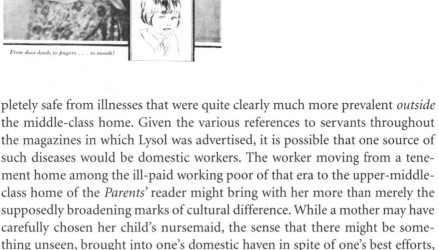

Figure 1.18. Lysol advertisement.
*Parents'*, April 1929

Aᵣe your door-knobs
safe for little
hands to touch?

Hᴬⱽᴱ you killed the germs on them with "Lysol" Disinfectant?

No matter how thoroughly you clean, with soap and water, the places little hands touch, germs remain to do their deadly work — to spread the common diseases which every mother dreads.

Kill them! Really protect your home against them! It is easy — as easy as cleaning in your regular way. Simply add a tablespoonful of "Lysol" Disinfectant to each quart of your cleaning water, *each time you clean,* and proceed as usual. That's all.

Send for our free booklet, "Preventing the Spread of Common Diseases." Keep it for constant reference as many thousands of mothers do. And in the meantime get the "Lysol" habit. Buy a bottle today. Full directions come with every bottle.

Sole distributors: Lehn & Fink, Inc., Bloomfield, N. J.

Lehn & Fink Radio Program—WJZ and 14 other stations associated with the National Broadcasting Co.—every Thursday at 8 p. m., eastern time; 7 p. m., central time.          © Lehn & Fink, Inc., 1929

*Lysol*
Disinfectant

*From door-knob, to fingers . . . to mouth!*

pletely safe from illnesses that were quite clearly much more prevalent *outside* the middle-class home. Given the various references to servants throughout the magazines in which Lysol was advertised, it is possible that one source of such diseases would be domestic workers. The worker moving from a tenement home among the ill-paid working poor of that era to the upper-middle-class home of the *Parents'* reader might bring with her more than merely the supposedly broadening marks of cultural difference. While a mother may have carefully chosen her child's nursemaid, the sense that there might be something unseen, brought into one's domestic haven in spite of one's best efforts, seems to pervade the advertisements for newfangled cleaning solutions.

This one reads: "No matter how thoroughly you clean, with soap and water, the places little hands touch, germs remain to do their deadly work — to spread the common diseases which every mother dreads." With Lysol, a mother could deal with germs summarily — "Kill them! Really protect your home against them!" Within copy advocating particular uses of Lysol, the company often offered free booklets by mail, such as the one promoted in this ad, *Preventing the Spread of Common Diseases*. The text here plays on a familiar theme: "Keep [the booklet] for constant reference as many thousands of mothers do." The proper form of motherhood involved time to turn (constantly) to a booklet about disinfecting. By buying a bottle today, a mother would show her allegiance with women like herself, vigilant for the sake of their own little ones and for "the future of the race."

Yet one could never be too safe. By sending one's children out into the world, to schoolrooms populated by other children, one was exposing them to a whole host of germs. The theme of securing one's child's health and happiness by crafting the properly wholesome environment was not always stated in terms of germs, even when the concern was a kind of cultural contamination.

"Choose your Children's Companions by Having School at Home" runs one advertisement for homeschooling materials. The language that opens the appeal is characteristic: "How happy the mother who can safeguard her children's future by guiding their selection of schoolday chums. Many mothers, instead of sending their youngsters off to school each morning, have found a better way."[43] The scene shows several children playing peacefully outdoors, floating their little boats in a stream. The sense that a mother with school-age children might be letting her most prized possessions walk around ready for the spoiling is written into the many references to the importance of clean living. "Should We Hand-pick Our Children's Friends?" one essay asks, posing what it calls a "big question." The "elementary" answer is to ensure that "unfit companions are eliminated, and that only the fit survive" — admittedly, a principle for which "the difficulties in the way of its practical application loom large." How could parents know "which among their children's friends are the sheep, which the goats."[44]

In one Lysol advertisement the potential menace lurking among one's schoolmates is a matter for pedagogical and maternal concern.[45] "Johnny is

43. *Parents*, August 1929, p. 5.
44. Helen L. Kaufmann, "Should We Hand-pick Our Children's Friends?" *Parents*, August 1929, pp. 16-17.
45. *Parents*, February 1930, p. 51.

home sick today." With these words the teacher begins to wonder: "How many of his schoolmates will catch the germs he spread?" Likewise, "the mothers of the other little boys and girls" in the classroom wonder whether Johnny has contaminated their children. What to do? Make sure your child's school is "thoroughly disinfected with 'Lysol' at the end of each day." And "teach your children not to get near youngsters who cough or sneeze or sniffle." You can never be too careful in friendships. The advertisement invokes the internalized, maternal fear of contamination from others and simultaneously, if more subtly, the fear that other mothers will suspect your household of menace.

The fear lending its pull to the advertisements for products ranging from Kleenex to Dr. Denton's Sleeping Garments to Cream of Wheat was that others might not associate your children with the right sorts of people.[46] Much worse, your children might be, through a sniffle or a cough, edged into association with the wrong sorts of people.

Playing off the partially lighthearted image of the mother reaching helplessly into an oversized washbasin, we ask how making hygienic vigilance a habit affected the aspiring mother? She was to perform her work perfectly, whether in supervising others or in doing the work herself, but not in a way that was unnaturally intrusive. Like a gently flowing stream, a mother was to be a source of calm and of watchfulness. "Listen to a woman work and you can judge her efficiency," begins the article "Noiseless Housekeeping." Nell Nichols thus warned that "Troublesome noise is born of destruction, faulty methods and carelessness." With effort, by cleaning silently, a mother's household could be conducive to "calmness and quiet," "stability and poise." An accompanying photograph shows a determined woman in heels and dust coat reaching with an extendable dust mop over the head of a child, who is peacefully observing a small terrarium. A home was to be, in a way, a sort of carefully tended terrarium, cautiously controlled but instinctive — scientifically informed but natural. By reaching even into the crevices of a ceiling, a mother was to achieve the "quiet, systematic daily cleaning" that "keeps the house fresh and neat without confusion, noise or fatigue."[47] Without fatigue? How

---

46. The advertisements running for Cream of Wheat in 1929-30 are worth a section to themselves, featuring brief stories, drawings, and professional photographs of up-and-coming girls from the best of families. See, for example, the feature on Elizabeth Stuyvesant Fish, "a member of Washington's 'youngest set,'" *Parents'*, October 1929, p. 31. Through the simple move of buying and preparing Cream of Wheat, a mother could associate her children with the best sorts of families.

47. Nell B. Nichols, Consultant in Home Economics, "Noiseless Housekeeping," *Parents'*, October 1929, p. 30.

was one to be the right sort of mother without adding to confusion or noise, without even the appearance of exertion as one carefully tends the hidden corners of one's household?

The manifold pressure is similarly evident in the ways the appearance of mothers made its way into the magazine. The "Look Your Best" series on maternal beauty begins with an encouraging word: "Good looks and health are priceless assets. Children respond to them."[48] Author of the series, and previously of the richly titled piece "The Etiquette of Beauty," Dorothy Cocks begins the first essay by telling of her calling: "Perhaps an impish god of the business world found delight in taking me, a daughter of Quakers, with a before-the-war education, and tossing me into the toilet goods business during several boom years. Whatever the prank may have done for the industry, it humanized me." By humanized, Cocks meant it prompted her to accept the natural need for cosmetics. "Now I don't think the use of toilet preparations is silly. I think it is gallant and splendid." They are no longer extraneous to the work of basic etiquette but truly basic to a proper woman's life: "I think they are necessities, staples, a part of the business of living." "Perhaps you think of toilet preparations only as make-up and therefore artificial and horrid. . . . If that is your attitude I'd like to take you by the hand and lead you around with me for a few days." Being led in this way, a woman might be able to come to the more "humanized" perspective.

Cocks was faithful to embodied etiquette, a form of physical habituation that became written on the very bodies of the women responsible for habituating hygiene for their children. The future of the race was written in small print onto the bodies of such women: "If you kept at it for a few nights, to establish a routine, and then repeated that routine a few more nights to form a habit, you would soon go through a little bedtime facial treatment as mechanically and as swiftly as you now clean your teeth — and as faithfully."[49] The scrupulous eye with which a mother was to appraise first her servant, then her neighbor, then her neighbor's children, then the corners of her own house, then her own children — this perspective reflects back across the magazine's divide, onto the narration of an aspiring mother's own body. The way Cocks describes the stakes in the December 1930 entry of "Look Your Best" suggests the subtle boomerang effect of the germ-free home: "Every mother seems beautiful to her small children, but critical appraisal will come sometime. Be ready for it." The first "Look Your Best" ran alongside a Lysol advertisement that announced: "The world today is using more than 7 mil-

48. Dorothy Cocks, "Look Your Best," *Parents*, October 1930, p. 44.
49. Dorothy Cocks, "Look Your Best," *Parents*, December 1930, p. 44.

lion *gallons* of 'Lysol' Disinfectant a year for general disinfection and for feminine hygiene."[50] The piece named two free booklets — *Protecting the Home against Disease* and *The Facts about Feminine Hygiene*.

We interrupt the historical narrative to examine a series of Lysol advertisements for feminine hygiene. Jodie Boyer, a graduate student sifting through early volumes of *Parents'* for images relevant to my research, came across a number of Lysol ads that I had, quite frankly, overlooked. I had written them off as more of the same — admonishments for women to keep a pristine home by rubbing Lysol on doorknobs, sink counters, and toilet seats. But Jodie had read the fine print. Later another graduate student, Sarah Sours, went with me through the volumes Jodie had marked for attention. We were both baffled. Surely these "frank booklets" on "the scientific side of health and youth" were not about what they seemed to be about. Surely they were simply suggesting that women wash their feminine hygiene products in Lysol. But no. They were suggesting that women use Lysol *itself* as a feminine hygiene product!

One 1929 advertisement features a woman sitting at her drawing room desk, preparing to write an appreciative letter to Lysol for sending her the booklet *The Scientific Side of Health and Youth*. The text of the ad confidently states that Lysol had been the "standard disinfectant — the safe and certain disinfectant — for feminine hygiene" for forty years, which means from before the turn of the twentieth century. Into the late 1950s the Lehn and Fink Products Company of New Jersey continued to suggest that its product be flushed into a woman's body for vaginal "hygiene." The advertisements suggest several crucial facets of the domestic hygiene movement during the development of "scientific motherhood." In the midst of "constant reference" to the rules of domestic vigilance, a woman was also encouraged to suspect her own body of hidden dangers and impurities. After probing further into the implied meaning of "health and youth," aided in particular by an article by Andrea Tone in the *Journal of Social History*, it became obvious to Jodie Boyer, Sarah Sours, and me that one of the hidden dangers of the female body as construed by the advertisements was the perceived danger of unplanned pregnancy.[51]

---

50. *Parents'*, October 1930, p. 44, emphasis in original.

51. See Andrea Tone, "Contraceptive Consumers: Gender and the Political Economy of Birth Control in the 1930s," *Journal of Social History* 29 (1996): 485-506. Tone notes the "legal euphemisms" made necessary by federal and state laws that severely restricted the distribution of contraceptive information and devices: "Publicly, manufacturers claimed that feminine hygiene products were sold solely to enhance vaginal cleanliness. Consumers . . . knew better. Obliquely encoded in feminine hygiene ads and product packaging were indicators of the product's *real* purpose; references to 'protection,' 'security,' or 'dependability' earmarked purported contraceptive properties" (p. 486, emphasis in original). Dorothy Dunbar Bromley, writing in 1934 in

Touted as a "frank and explicit" guide "written in simple language by an eminent woman physician," the Lysol booklet was to be a "constant reference" for bodily hygiene. Of course, "a fastidious woman" prefers not to discuss such "intimate questions" with others; thus the booklet would offer a guide for guarding one's health and "youth."

Another advertisement, titled "What *Every* Woman Wants," presents the universally sought quality of "that vivacity and youthfulness of spirit which arise from a healthful, well-cared-for body." Although Lysol appears to have focused its message on marital romance after World War II, this ad from 1929 depicts a woman in a sparkling Hollywood gown surrounded by, and the obvious focus of, no fewer than four men in tuxedos. The suggestion to the reader is clear. One may aspire to such admiration while young, but "beauty is only skin deep" and thus "fades with the years." There are "other precious qualities," however, that "have so much to do with her happiness — her health and her charm" that "can be protected by the wise practice of feminine hygiene."

There are at least two layers of subtext here. One layer suggests that the protection of a woman's internal "health and charm" involves her ability to remain internally youthful, so to speak. The hidden causes of what might be called unfeminine qualities (given the language game going on here) are best addressed by the use of Lysol. The other layer of meaning is related but somewhat different. Given that women were using Lysol to "disinfect" themselves of sperm as well as germs, the "vivacity and youthfulness" promoted in the advertisement also involved a woman's ability to remain without child.

In her article on the subtle marketing of feminine hygiene products for contraception in the 1930s, Andrea Tone suggests that the growth of such advertisements involved "Americans' desire to limit family size in an era of economic hardship."[52] The language repeated in advertisements during the Depression seems intensely admonitory, as in one *McCall's* ad from May 1933 entitled "The Incompatible Marriage: Is It a Case for Doctor or Lawyer?": "She was a lovely creature before she married. . . . But since her marriage she seems forever worried, nervous and irritable . . . always dreading what seems inevitable."[53] As Tone notes, the language of imminent peril is matched by the

---

*Harper's Monthly,* pointed to the opportunistic marketing of unsafe "chemical preparations" and other "products of dubious merit" in "thinly veiled terms in even the most respectable magazines." Manufacturers' pitches to women readers included such "seductive" captions as "Calendar Fear," "Can a Married Woman Ever Feel Safe?" and "Young Wives Are Often Secretly Terrified." Dorothy Dunbar Bromley, "Birth Control and the Depression," *Harper's Monthly Magazine,* October 1934, p. 572.

52. Tone, "Contraceptive Consumers," p. 485.

53. *McCall's,* May 1933, p. 107; cited in Tone, "Contraceptive Consumers," p. 495.

level of expertise posited as necessary for any proper counsel on the matter of prevention. Rather than consulting her mother or grandmother or friend, a woman was to turn to the "experts" who could understand the "scientific side" of the matter and thus recommend products like Lysol for "health and youth." Although economic pressures were unquestionably at play during the 1930s, the "scientific side" of beauty, feminine hygiene, and pregnancy prevention was also portrayed — particularly in the prior decade — as involving leisure and perceived marital pleasure. For the class targeted by publications such as *Parents'* and *McCall's,* the concerns addressed by the magazines' advertisements were quite simply different from the Depression-era fear of another mouth to feed from a limited larder.

An advertisement from *McCall's* in 1928, "Still 'the Girl He Married'" (fig. 1.19), makes this point palpably. The text is worth quoting at length:

> When they were first married, five years ago, they liked to dance together, go motoring together, play golf together. They still like to do those things together today.
>
> She is still the girl he married. During the years following her marriage, she has protected her zest for living, her health and youthfulness, and "stayed young with him" by the *correct* practice of feminine hygiene.

In the image a young couple are waving to their little boy as they depart in a convertible. The husband is wearing a summer suit with a cap rakishly angled. The wife is wearing a flapper cap and what appears to be a women's driving suit. Waving to his parents from the steps of a large house, the little boy holds the hand of a maid, who is herself wearing a black frock with white collar, white apron, and white ruffled cap. The maid looks down with a smile for the little boy.

The message seems quite clear: the use of Lysol for "feminine hygiene" has allowed the mother to remain "the girl he married." She has "protected her zest for living, her health and youthfulness," by pregnancy prevention. According to the proper domesticity presented in this advertisement, personal hygiene is necessary to avoid the contamination that would have been more children. The large house, the maid in strict uniform, the convertible, and the parents' attire all suggest strongly that this is not the use of Lysol for the sake of economic necessity. The sense is that a woman, after becoming a mother, must use Lysol to regain her status as a fully independent consort for her still dancing, motoring, golfing husband. She is to remain "the girl he married" by avoiding through disinfectant her shift into motherhood and his shift into fatherhood.

This threat, that a woman might lose her husband if she does not remain

**Figure 1.19. "Still 'the Girl He Married.'" Lysol advertisement.** *McCall's*, July 1928

Figure 1.19. "Still 'the Girl He Married.'" Lysol advertisement. *McCall's*, July 1928

a "girl," seems also at play more subtly in advertisements appearing two decades later. By taking a "Love-quiz . . . for Married Folks Only" (fig. 1.20),[54] a woman could learn more about her plight. The advertisement shows a woman with fresh-from-the-beauty-shop hair, wearing a pastel dress and pearls, clutching her hands in barely suppressed agony as her husband, wearing a tailored suit and carrying his topcoat, leaves by the front door. While making his exit he turns back with a look of apparent regret, perhaps also frustration. Why is this woman in agony? "Why does she spend the evenings alone?"

The answer from the "Love-quiz" brings together the themes of hidden peril and the vital importance of scientifically verified hygiene in the home. This woman's husband is leaving each evening for a tangled knot of reasons:

54. I am grateful for Harry Finley for the reference and the image.

## Love-quiz ... For Married Folks Only

### WHY DOES SHE SPEND THE EVENINGS ALONE?

**A.** Because she keeps her home immaculate, <u>looks</u> as pretty as she can and really loves her husband, BUT she neglects that one essential . . . <u>personal feminine hygiene.</u>

**Q.** Is this <u>really</u> important to married happiness?

**A.** Wives often lose the precious air of romance, doctors say, for lack of the intimate daintiness dependent on effective douching. For this, look to reliable "Lysol" brand disinfectant.

**Q.** Is "Lysol" safe and gentle as well as <u>extra</u> effective?

**A.** Yes, the <u>proved</u> germicidal efficiency of "Lysol" requires only a small quantity in a proper solution to destroy germs and odors, give a fresh, clean, wholesome feeling, restore every woman's confidence in her power to please.

**Q.** How about homemade douching solutions, such as salt and soda?

**A.** They have no comparison with the scientific formula of "Lysol" which has proved efficiency in contact with organic matter.

ALWAYS USE "LYSOL" in the douche, to help give the assurance that comes with perfect grooming . . . confidence in "romance appeal."

**Check these facts with your doctor**

Many doctors recommend "Lysol," in the proper solution, for Feminine Hygiene. Non-caustic, gentle,

"Lysol" is *non-injurious* to delicate membrane. Its clean, antiseptic odor quickly disappears. Highly concentrated, "Lysol" is *economical* in solution. Follow easy directions for correct douching solution.

**For Feminine Hygiene—always use**

**FREE BOOKLET!** Learn the truth about intimate hygiene and its important role in married happiness. Mail this coupon to Lehn & Fink, Dept. C.—483, 192 Bloomfield Avenue, Bloomfield, N. J., for frankly informing FREE booklet.

NAME_____

STREET_____

CITY_____STATE_____

*Product of Lehn & Fink*

**Figure 1.20. "Love-quiz . . . for Married Folks Only." Lysol advertisement. *Cosmopolitan*, March 1948**

"She keeps her home immaculate, looks as pretty as she can and really loves her husband, BUT she neglects that one essential . . . personal feminine hygiene." The text continues: "Wives often lose the precious air of romance, doctors say, for lack of the intimate daintiness dependent on effective douching." While the word used here is "daintiness" rather than "youth," it seems to mean something similar — she is no longer a lass. Her home, although "immaculate," is not secure against the concealed indelicacy of her own body. She herself is not immaculate. The "air of romance" is an ephemeral thing, warns the text, and a woman may lose it if she does not adequately rely on "effective douching."

The two layers of symbolic interpretation apply again here. Her body is problematic because she is aging, but her body is also implicitly tainted as a body that may become maternal and thus insufficiently romantic. The advertisement promises that "reliable 'Lysol' brand disinfectant" will grant a "fresh, clean, wholesome feeling" that will "restore every woman's confidence in her power to please." While by all outward appearances a woman might seem to be meeting the various norms of proper aesthetics and hygiene, Lysol wants her to be aware that "perfect grooming" within the home requires Lysol.

Lysol has added what is perhaps both the reassuring and the authoritatively intimidating countenance of the family doctor to the advertisement; he represents the authority with whom one should "check these facts" about Lysol's proven efficiency for granting the "power to please."

## To Save the World?

> But that is just what Methodism is out to do. Its great desire is not to preserve itself as an organization; it is not even wedded to the name; *its sole purpose is to save the world.* And for the accomplishment of this great end it desires to cooperate with every other agency that has the same aim and to follow as the Spirit leads into whatever form of organization the great Church of the future should take.[55]

By my reading of the Lysol habit, mothers were to habituate domestic privilege and providential promise by distinguishing themselves from women configured as servants. By the Lysol habit (1926 forward) and the University Plan of Character Building and the Chautauqua Way (1929), the future of the race would indeed march forward on the feet of *(our)* little children (1929-51). I derive this from a sample of available resources for mainline parenting during the first half of the twentieth century. But this sampling helps to situate problems posed by a close reading of *Together: The Midmonth Magazine for Methodist Families.*

One way to discern dominant conceptions of parenthood in the United States is to consider the confluence of hygienic domesticity with proper Protestant parenting. The quotation above from Gilbert T. Rowe, editor of the *Methodist Quarterly Review,* crystallizes much that was Methodism in America during the twentieth century.[56] During a "mighty modern time,"

55. Gilbert T. Rowe, *The Meaning of Methodism: A Study in Christian Religion,* Training Courses for Leadership (Nashville: Cokesbury, 1926), p. 233, emphasis added.

56. I am very grateful to Miriam and Justin Snider for pointing me to Rowe's book and to this section.

Methodism was able to work with various other agencies, to flow along on the "great ocean of human interest" and the "whole current of human aspiration."[57] The "idea of progress," so central to the development of modern America and to modern parenting in America, also helped to make this denomination the largest mainline Protestant body in the twentieth century. A church that aspired to a "Christian century" (the name of the mainline, ecumenical journal of the era) had as its aim no less than the salvation of the world.

A denomination so construed as the savior of the world had few rhetorical/theological resources available to name the rift between and within women's bodies or to heal the rift thus represented in the body of Christ. *Together* offered glimmerings of hope on this score, and signs of a thoroughly different neighborliness, one that acknowledged real differences while witnessing to one bread, body, and blood. But before we consider fully the work of such hope, we must note the ways that the "slick-paper Christianity" of the 1950s reinforced the dismembering form of domesticity of an earlier generation.

I must first risk what may seem to some readers to be an overly uncharitable, even grimly suspicious reading of *Together* to describe what I believe was at stake then and is at play now in mainline Protestant America. There were many reasons for postwar Protestants to adhere to the hopes and dreams of *Parents'* and *Ladies' Home Journal* and *McCall's* rather than of incarnate, boundary-crossing discipleship. Redolent in most conduits of domesticity was an undercurrent of threatened shame and an overcurrent of class ambition. Aspiring, middle-class Methodist women, taught by their mothers and grandmothers to fear the scrutiny of women who sat across from them in the pew (and above them in the pecking order), had few resources during the postwar period to risk association across the rifts of racialized class and classified race. Believing themselves to be living in a good-housekeeping panopticon, many Methodist women were sufficiently preoccupied with their own families' appearance to stave off a call by Jesus to live outside the suburban box. Or, to put this another way, there was insufficient incentive toward something like solidarity. By the time Methodism was flourishing as the postwar norm for religi-

57. Rowe, *The Meaning of Methodism*, p. 225. The full quotation reads thus: "The idea of progress is congenial to the Methodist mind. Methodism believes that Jesus Christ is in the stream of this mighty modern time, that he rides its flood and controls it for good. It does not feel that it must remain apart in utter isolation, but, like the gulf stream, it flows upon the bosom of the great ocean of human interest and mingles its warm waters with the whole current of human aspiration."

osity, there were too few resources to enable the groundbreaking, ecclesial mis-cegenation for which Methodists should have been infamous.

Methodism was in its heyday during the postwar period, a period during which the nuclear family exemplified properly sanctified life in America. Margaret Lamberts Bendroth is helpful again at this point: "Mainline Protestants are, in many ways, the neutral backing to the ethnic crazy quilt of American diversity, the mythical standard by which everyone else becomes an 'other.'"[58] By the time of the Ad Council's 1956 public service campaign to "Build a stronger, richer life" through family worship, Methodism was arguably the quintessential mainline denomination, spanning the country with largely homogenous congregations.[59] The stronger, richer life was epitomized by the foursome on the posters for the campaign. The white, Anglo-Saxon Protestant family came to symbolize Middle America, complete with Mom, Dad, Dick, and Jane, baseball, hot dogs, and General Electric. American Methodism played no small role in this powerful symbolism. My people had in the first decades of the twentieth century lent our passion for civic sanctification to the newly concerted social hygiene movements of the Progressive Era.

Several decades later, Methodism named the postwar emphasis on middle-class domesticity to be a holy vocation. By a certain reading of "Faith and the Atomic Age" (as phrased by one of the Ad Council posters; fig. 1.21), the nuclear family was the chief conduit through which civilization was to be *saved*. This is quite bluntly rendered by the title of the 1954 Methodist National Conference on Family Life: "The Christian Family — the Hope of the World." Bishop Hazen G. Werner, in the conference's opening address, put it thus: "This conference rests upon one irrefutable fact — that of the importance of the home. . . . The home is the fulfillment of our needs. It fulfills our desire to belong, to be wanted, to be secure. . . . The miracle of birth and the miracle of mother love and the miracle of family unity: preserve these, and you preserve not only the wonder of living, but you preserve the integrity that alone can help us perpetuate both our culture and our church."[60] Here we

58. Margaret Lamberts Bendroth, *Growing Up Protestant: Parents, Children, and Mainline Churches* (New Brunswick, N.J.: Rutgers University Press, 2002), p. 1.

59. An announcement for the campaign, part of the council's eighth annual Religion in American Life Program, ran in the second issue of *Together*, November 1956, p. 74. The non-profit Ad Council's public service campaigns have been "raising awareness, inspiring action and saving lives" since 1942. Accessed 2005: www.adcouncil.org.

60. Bishop Hazen G. Werner, "The National Conference on Family Life: Opening Address," in *Report: The Christian Home — the Hope of the World: Second National Conference on Family Life of the Methodist Church* (Nashville: National Conference on Family Life, 1954), p. 2.

may note the bishop's resonance with the ASHA poster at the beginning of this chapter, extolling the assumed, instinctual love of "mother" and the addition of proper understanding. Bishop Werner would later articulate the family's salvific role even more explicitly:

> At a time . . . when the general public and Social Agencies of the land are turning to the family as the one hope for the growth of sound persons to make a safe world; . . . at a time when the home *that is to be our salvation* is itself under threat of the disturbing influence of the new mass media, the mobility of the home, the growing employment of wives and mothers, the tension of a troubled world — The Methodist Church is pressing toward the restoration of the religious life of the home, *summoning the family to its divine vocation.*[61]

The church was to save the world by way of postwar domesticity. This is one potent way to narrate the rise of the white, Anglo-Saxon Protestant family as the "mythical standard" by which families of other configurations were judged to be "other."

### *"Faith and the Atomic Age"*

The normativity of Methodism coalesces in *Together*, the denominational magazine most similar to *Ladies' Home Journal, McCall's*, or *Parents'*. These ostensibly civic magazines had been running for many decades prior, but by the midfifties several middle-class, mainline Protestant denominations had initiated their own publications on crafting life at home.[62] Mainline Protestantism was asserting in a new way the integral role that religion was to play in safeguarding the future of a civilized nation. The Methodist *Christian Advocate*, launched in 1826, had within five years achieved the "largest circulation on earth, the London *Times* not excepted" (as the editors of *Together* proudly noted in its first issue).[63] The Methodist bishops called on the churches to help this new publication achieve an ambitious starting circulation of at least a million, with a goal of tripling that number within the year.[64]

---

61. Hazen G. Werner and Edward Staples, "Report of the National Family Life Committee: For the Quadrennium of 1952-56," *Journal of the 1956 General Conference of the Methodist Church*, 1956, p. 1855, emphasis added.

62. See, e.g., *Hearthstone: The Magazine for the Christian Home*, 1949-72 (Christian Church [Disciples of Christ] and American Baptist); and *Presbyterian Life*, 1948-72.

63. Lovick Pierce and J. Edgar Washabaugh, editorial, *Together*, October 1956, p. 8.

64. Pierce and Washabaugh, editorial, p. 9.

With this *Midmonth Magazine for Methodist Families,* the Methodist church was doing its part to help further a faith that could bolster a family during the Atomic Age.

As reflected in the Ad Council's poster (fig. 1.21), the two icons of the age needed complementary religious narration. Mom, Dad, and their two (please note the appropriately spaced and gender-balanced) children descend the steps of the "big-steeple" church encircled by the symbol of scientific progress and human aspiration. They are the newly *nuclear* family. How were they best to face the future? To paraphrase the text of the advertisement, a "small, still voice insist[ed] on being heard," asking, "Where do [they] fit into the Atomic Age?" (Note the quite malleable use to which the poster put Elijah's revelation from God.) The answer to the persistent, still, small voice involved the effort to "Build a stronger, richer life" by "worship[ing] together every week." This strength, wrought in the home through truly good, scientifically and religiously informed parenting, would forge a hopeful tomorrow.

**Figure 1.21. Ad Council, Religion in American Life Program, 1956**

This notion of strength through properly narrated progress is not new, just newly situated. The 1929 editorial from *Parents'*, "The Meaning of Easter," concluded with a presaging, twofold charge: "Welcome the advance of intelligence in science and art and their contribution to the profession of parenthood. Have faith in your children and they will have faith in you. Thus the march along the way will be with stronger and firmer steps."

But the newest advance of intelligence in science, in the Atomic Age, had also wrought the potential of hell on earth. How were Americans to consider their children and their children's children in the nation that had ushered in the Atomic Age? They were to take them to worship each week. More specifically, they were to attend "churches and synagogues" wherein they would be able to "draw the courage to make the Atomic Age an age of promise and fulfillment." In the place of worship of their choice, American parents could "start now to build your life and that of your family on a firm foundation of truth and Faith." Thus, the role of faith was to aid the nuclear household in producing children capable of responsibly handling the newest result of human aspiration.

### *"Spiritual Efficiency"*

*Together*'s purpose might also be pithily described by way of its monthly feature Little Lessons in Spiritual Efficiency. By methodically gathering up the flotsam and jetsam of domestic life, ordering the home with spiritual efficiency, a household might become the epicenter of Hope itself. The decade from 1950 to 1960 involved a characteristically American push to the fore, and the small details of family life held national import. The organized family schedule on the avocado-colored refrigerator; the discrete domestic prayer closet; the homemade, crèche-inspired holiday cards — these were the pieces of incarnate, embodied life through which a newly fragmented world was to be made whole. Anxiety about the future is certainly not unique to that decade and this nation. But the emergence of the nuclear familial ideal (what Stephanie Coontz has aptly termed "the way we never were") warrants close interpretation.[65]

As the decade progressed, unease over the role the United States had undeniably played in the creation of nuclear weaponry mingled with growing Cold War tensions over Communism. To quote one 1956 *Together* essay, the postwar period was feared to be a time of "hunger, disease, and ignorance," when "evil and terrible men" would "undertake to entrap us with all manner

---

65. See Stephanie Coontz, *The Way We Never Were: American Families and the Nostalgia Trap* (New York: Basic Books, 2000).

of mental, bodily, and spiritual poisons." It was through small efforts, "little by little," that those who believed in Jesus would "win the victory," enable the "Kingdom," and save the world.[66] The mainline Protestant model for parenting reflected and reinforced the way forward. The Methodist mothers, fathers, and grandparents to whom *Together* was addressed were vital for securing a hopeful future. With effort, "the Christian home" would become the crux of the age — the site at the intersection of scientific progress, national security, and blessed, divine providence. As Lysol was to grant a "fresh, clean, wholesome feeling," to "restore every woman's confidence in her power to please" (quoting the 1948 advertisement discussed above), so would a properly cleansed and situated family restore every person's confidence in America's power to provide. What was hidden in the Manhattan Project would be disinfected during the 1950s, allowing a hygienic, safer, happier future for our children, and for the children worldwide.

We opened the chapter with a quotation from the 1922 ASHA poster for young women: "The human mother can bring more than the simple animal instincts to the aid of her new-born child. *Real motherhood develops by the addition of knowledge and understanding to the mother's instinctive love.*" This affirmation of "mother's instinctive love" twinned with science's indispensable contribution runs through the intervening years between the poster series and the first decade of *Together*. Images of focused motherhood, putting family at the center of her efforts, run alongside the dispensing of proper "knowledge and understanding" throughout.[67] Even sources traditionally considered within the humanities were put to scientific use, to help cultivate with scientific precision the intelligence and creativity of a child to be molded.

One of the major advertisers in *Together* was a resource for parents called, notably, *Childcraft*.[68] To quote a *Childcraft* advertisement (fig. 1.22), by

66. Roy L. Smith, "Herods and Shepherds," in Little Lessons in Spiritual Efficiency, *Together*, December 1956, p. 20.

67. The uneasy combination of supposedly instinctual motherhood and domestic progress through science is salient in another article in *Together*, "How We'll Live in '77" (January 1957), to which we will turn in chapter 4. Natural/scientific motherhood is epitomized in the image from this essay, in which an adoring mother puts her precious baby at the center of her life (as the culmination of the montage, in the center of the essay) by pressing a button and viewing the child on a video screen. Author Leo Cherne's reassurance accentuates what is already quite clearly stated in the illustration: "Life 20 years from now will revolve, as it always has, around the home and the family. The instinct to build a home and rear a family will be unchanged" (pp. 22-23). The task of motherhood was to use all the proper tools available to train her "instinctive love" toward knowledge and understanding.

68. Thanks to Hadley Kifner and Maureen Knudsen Langdoc for bringing the importance of *Childcraft* to my attention.

Figure 1.22. *Childcraft* advertisement. *Together*, March 1958

introducing a child to "music, poems, pictures, and stories," a parent could help the child gain an "appreciation for fine things in life," which are linked visually in the photograph with a fashionable, well-pressed, and perfectly unsoiled life. What one might assume to be the perfected aesthetics for a staged, church-directory photograph is here depicted as the default aesthetic of the everyday Christian home. Playtime with mother appears here without a wayward thread, a broken smile, or a stray bit of clay.

The free promotional booklet was entitled *Their Future Is in Your Hands*. The stakes involved in such parental work were ostensibly eternal — a striking assertion within a Christian periodical. During a period of Cold War uncertainty, one ecclesial answer was to sing out with a bold affirmation of God's universal providence: "He's Got the Whole World in His Hands."[69] *Childcraft*

69. The old Southern spiritual became a favorite among Americans with the release of a chart-topping recording by Laurie London in 1958. "People who were looking for any kind of security to latch onto found the very simple message in the song's childlike lyrics a spiritual anchor. The single quickly emerged from obscurity to become a life preserver in the stormy cli-

had a different emphasis, one that bled over from the full-page advertisements into the pages of *Together* itself. With help from "the 150 authorities on child development," *Childcraft* would enable a mother (for it was almost always mothers to whom the advertisements appealed) to achieve "the power to shape a life, *to guide a destiny*."[70] The little girl in the photograph was molding a pretend person, forming a miniature out of clay. Yet her mother, looking on with careful, knowledgeable admiration, was molding a real person. With resources like *Childcraft*, a parent could "make her dreams come true." This is one construal of eschatology quite saliently at play in the pages of *Together*.

### *"People and Profits"*

*Childcraft* touted its product as "the most important work of its kind in the world." *Childcraft's* worldwide significance and the mother at the white kitchen table in her pressed cotton dress existed within a particular cultural matrix: the promised nation within which the child would become a responsible consumer/citizen.[71] In the advertised edition of *Childcraft*, the culminating section, in the last volume, features a report on the Midcentury White House Conference on Children and Youth called by Harry Truman in 1950.[72] The conference, according to *Childcraft*, addressed "with courage and audacity" the responsibility of the United States in forming children. Indeed, "the future of the world lies in a healthy personality for every child." One could discern in this material a sense that the state of the world depended on properly crafting children of the United States.

One way the habituation of holy home life was portrayed in *Together* involved a middle-class family's participation in consumer capitalism. General Electric ran regular two-page advertisements in the magazine, with its motto summing up its role in Methodist lives: "Progress Is Our Most Important Product" (fig. 1.23). The nuclear family of this promising era was the epicenter of a much larger story — a story of neighborhood, regional, and national progress. The suburban good life was part of achieving a better life for one's

---

mate of an unsure world." Ace Collins, *Stories behind the Hymns That Inspire America* (Grand Rapids: Zondervan, 2003), p. 86.

70. *Together*, March 1958, p. 5, emphasis added.

71. For the formation of the consumer/citizen as a focus of domestic effort, see Lizabeth Cohen, *A Consumers' Republic: The Politics of Mass Consumption in Postwar America* (New York: Vintage, 2004). We will return to this construction of "childcraft" in chapter 4.

72. Leonard W. Mayo, "A Healthy Personality for Every Child," in *Childcraft* (Chicago: Field Enterprises, 1954), 15:167-74.

neighbors, or so suggested ads like this one. With the growing, suburban family at the center, the reverberations of industrial retail moved out, involving "everyone" in the importance of a "better business climate." With a good, middle-class home came employment for the physician, the dry cleaner, the gas station attendant, the milkman, and the florist.

It was thus part of a responsible, ethical life to encourage a "business climate" conducive of human flourishing in this form. Such a good business climate would include, among other features, "Fair taxes for both business and individuals, without restrictive regulations or discriminatory financial burdens." It would require "conscientious law enforcement which protects the rights of all citizens, corporate and private," including, presumably, law enforcement sufficient to deal with those who did not follow "responsible union leadership" patterns necessary for a truly "healthy" business climate for all. As the text of the advertisement suggests, the notion that "one job" could lead to a "chain reaction of benefits" for everyone in the "community" brought about a sense that partaking in the development of technology was in itself wholesome, patriotic, and faithful.

This emphasis is characteristic of much advertising of the era, put succinctly in another two-page GE ad in a 1958 *Together* (fig. 1.24). With the headline "People and Profits: Both Are Needed to Make America's Capitalism Work," this advertisement also appears as a sort of pictorial essay on the providential progress for which General Electric was to be known. The "People's Capitalism" that was America's "distinctive brand of capitalism" required both understanding and encouragement "by all Americans." For "all people — not just a few — benefit when businesses earn profits." The most important benefit of profit is "research and development and the expansion and modernization which lead to new jobs, products, and services." The "schoolteacher," the "grocery boy," the "baby capitalist," the "whole nation" made up of individual people voluntarily working toward a better, brighter future — each is pictured in the photo essay as participating in this vital work of progress through capitalism. The essay's text concludes: "*Profit is the incentive to take the bold and imaginative risks needed for progress.* Businesses are in free, vigorous competition to anticipate and satisfy the needs, the wants — and even some of the unspoken aspirations — of the American people. Companies that fail to provide what people want will become profit-starved and a national liability. Those that succeed are the underlying resource of a vital civilian economy and a strong national defense."

The photographs next to the text are indicative of the core message of the piece. The young couple with their new baby are placed between the friendly young schoolteacher, who will teach the "baby capitalist" to count his pennies, and the clergyman, who will explain the providential connection between peo-

**Figure 1.23. General Electric advertisement.** *Together,* **December 1958**

ple and profits. The text is succinct in naming the stakes of proper home life and civic responsibility. "People's Capitalism" depended on a vigorous will, a steely resolve. Without it the country could become enervated. Mother's new stove, father's new lawnmower — such products were not merely the results of progress. They represented the engine of progress, able to anticipate the future for which Americans hoped, for after all, a fit business would "anticipate and satisfy" the "unspoken aspirations . . . of the American people." A truly fit business could achieve a kind of foreknowledge, a type of prophetic enactment, that could shape a tomorrow to meet the silent prayers of a citizenry. General Electric went even further to name the "civilian economy" as the bedrock of a livable tomorrow. It is worth noting that GE's pithy claim — "Progress Is Our Most Important Product" — transitioned quite smoothly into the soothing, bell-toned tune promising another generation of Americans a better existence through its products: "GE — We Bring Good Things to Life."

### *"Sound Christian Ethics to Good Use"*

In January 1958 *Together* ran a full-page notice on page 2. This was to be a "banner year for Methodist families." In a project "sponsored jointly by *Together* and the General Committee on Family Life," the magazine would hold a competition to find the Family of the Year.[73] As detailed in announcements in the February and March issues (fig. 1.25), the selection process would have an air of democracy about it. Individual readers were encouraged, enthusiastically, to be a part of the selection. Members of congregations were to "look about" as they participated "in church and community affairs" for a family in their congregation that would best represent the congregation in the district, conference, and national compe-

73. Notices ran in the January (p. 2), February (p. 8), and March (p. 2) issues. I am greatly indebted to Maureen Knudsen Langdoc for discovering the contest series. Maureen is responsible also for the insight, discussed below, that the depiction of colored faces on the first announcement is representative of a pattern in the magazine.

# PEOPLE AND PROFITS:

## Both are needed to make America's capitalism work

Figure 1.24. General Electric advertisement. *Together,* May 1958

**GENERAL ELECTRIC:** *These capitalists come from all walks of life*

**GROCERY BOY**

Larry Cichy is learning early how America's capitalism works—his parents gave him his first shares on his 11th birthday.

**REPORTER**

Amy Jane Bowles is one of a growing number of women share owners; over half of General Electric's owners are women.

**WELDER**

Leopold Arbour was one of 14,000 new General Electric owners in 1957. The number of G-E owners increased 50% since 1952.

**MULTIGRAPH OPERATOR**

Mrs. Longine Furman is typical of people who participate in "People's Capitalism" by investing part of their savings regularly.

**TRUCKING-COMPANY PRESIDENT**

Arthur Gallagher is also a G-E supplier. His firm is one of 45,000 which furnish the company with vital skills and services.

**GENERAL ELECTRIC EMPLOYEE**

Mrs. Ann Shem is one of more than 133,000 employees participating in General Electric's Savings and Stock Bonus Plan.

**COLLEGE PROFESSOR**

Joseph Doty, Professor of History, teaches about the past and invests in the future with shares of General Electric stock.

**PENSIONER**

Mary Hammond supplements her income from General Electric's Pension Plan with dividends from General Electric stock.

**GENERAL ELECTRIC DEALER**

Share owner Allen Merriam also owns one of the 100,000 independent firms which sell and service General Electric products.

**Figure 1.25.
Announcement of
the Methodist Family
of the Year contest.
*Together*, March 1958**

*Last Chance*

*for your church to help select*

# The Methodist Family of the Year

A TYPICAL Methodist family you see here, outfitting the lovely teen-age daughter for Easter. But there's more here than meets the eye—how this family in its home and church and community exemplifies the best in Christian living.

You know such families in your church. And this is your last opportunity to nominate one for the 1958 Methodist Family of the Year. Each Methodist church has been asked to propose one family from its congregation for this honor.

Every reader of TOGETHER—any individual or group of persons in the local church—may suggest a family. The official board of each church will decide the local nomination. (No nominations may be made directly to TOGETHER.) Candidates will be screened by official family-life judges at district, conference, and national levels.

The 1958 Methodist Family of the Year will be guests of TOGETHER at the Third National Conference on Family Life in Chicago, Illinois, October 17 to 19.

Here are the special qualifications for the Family of the Year

1 Parents age 50 or under.
2 Two or more children, at least one teen-ager, baptized and church members, or in Sunday school.
3 Family exemplifies inspiring Christian family living.
4 Family applies Christian ethics in everyday life.
5 Family active in church and community life.
6 Family members are known as warm, good neighbors.

Now think of the families in your church who fit these qualifications. Then get the ball rolling to see that their names come before your official board. Remember, April 18 is the deadline. Your pastor should have complete details and entry blanks. You'll be proud to have your church represented in this selection of the Methodist Family of the Year.

titions. By carefully considering the qualifications of each family, assessing one's neighbors in comparison with one another, a reader of *Together* could choose the one family that would most make the congregation "proud."[74]

The contest easily represents the worst sort of horizontal rivalry and vertical elbowing that might emanate from the polished promotion of faith, aesthetically normalized beauty, and worldly success. (Had he waited until 1958, Dan Wakefield would have had a field day reviewing this example of Methodist hubris for the *Nation*.) But beneath the competitive spirit of the "selection" ran a message that is, to my mind, even more troubling than the specter of women peering at their neighbors with an eye of appraisal. Running through the announcements is the suggestion that the family chosen would be the norm to which all Methodist families should aspire. One could call it the new and improved holy family.

"You can help by suggesting the one family you'd be proudest to have

74. The language of pride appears in both the February and the March announcements.

represent your church at the Third National Conference on Family Life in Chicago next October 17-19," the February announcement read. Each congregation's nominated family would be the face of that congregation — they would be the potential cover family for the *Midmonth Magazine for Methodist Families*. Each church member could nominate a family to the official board of his or her congregation, which then selected one family from that church. This process of assessment would continue up the tree of the Methodist church, with each nominated family "screened by official family-life judges at the district, conference, and finally the national level."[75] The family chosen as *the* Methodist Family of the Year would indeed become the Methodist cover family. Having made it through the successive screenings — from local congregation to conference to regional to national — they would not only attend the Third Family Life Conference in Chicago as "guests of *Together*," but would also appear on the front of the November 1958 issue of the magazine.

Because all readers were invited to participate in the initial screening process, the competition was, in a sense, egalitarian. Every Methodist privy to *Together* could turn her discerning, evaluative eye on her neighbors and judge their fitness for participation in the contest. Yet, in an odd way, the initial announcement of the contest illustrates the problem with this form of egalitarianism. The disembodied heads floating around the page are, ostensibly, different, particular people (fig. 1.26). But they are, well . . . just heads, bobbing around the text. And their differences are also strangely disembodied. The Methodist church in this period did indeed have African American congregations across the country. The church was linked formally and through its Wesleyan roots to mission-field churches outside the United States, in India, Korea, and South Africa, to name only three places. Yet the variegated colors of the human countenances chosen by the editors are make-believe. The disembodied heads have been shaded to appear in different tones of green, purple, and brown. Even the brown heads appear unnatural — the color seems other than the true color of the faces featured. The individual human beings depicted in the initial announcement have been dismembered, cloned, and painted. By a charitable reading, the editors may have wanted to encourage the congregant peering across the pew not to limit her appraisal to only her Anglo-Methodist neighbors. But arguably, the effect was quite the contrary.

The two subsequent announcements fill out the class-specific details, through a list of requirements for eligibility as well as drawings and a relevant

75. This language begins in the February notice.

*Announcing*

# THE FAMILY OF THE YEAR

*Selection*

THIS WILL BE a banner year for Methodist families in Together. Already announced is the Christian Family photo competition. Now comes a chance for your church to enter the FAMILY OF THE YEAR selection.

This event is sponsored jointly by Together and the General Committee on Family Life. Every Methodist church is invited to nominate a family of its choice. The family chosen will be featured in Together and will be the guest of the magazine and the Third Family Life Conference in Chicago next October 17-19.

The February issue of Together will carry full details and tell you how to nominate a family from your church.

Parents must be 50 or under, with two or more children baptized and members of church or Sunday school. Parents must not be employed by any national Methodist church organization or directly related to persons in such connections. Nominees must exemplify Christian family life. Parents must apply Christian ethics in business or professions. The family must take a creative role in church and community, and be good neighbors.

Watch the February Together for complete details. Meantime, your official board will want to discuss taking part in the FAMILY OF THE YEAR selection.

**Figure 1.26.** Announcement of the Methodist Family of the Year contest. *Together*, January 1958

photograph. When considering which family to nominate, a congregant was to keep in mind that the parents could not be over fifty. The representative family of Methodism had parents of an appropriately normal age. The model of family configuration assumed here is also clearly nuclear. A familial situation that included a grandparent, aunt, or uncle as an integral part of family life was beyond the realm of consideration. Parents of the proper age needed also to have "two or more children, at least one teen-ager, baptized and church members, or in Sunday school." A family with only one child, or with three young children, or with a teenager called to another denomination was not quite what the family life judges had in mind. A properly eligible family would show "inspiring Christian family living," apply "Christian ethics in business or profession," take "a creative role in church and community life," and be "known as warm, good neighbors."[76]

We may note the parameters drawn around the scope of "creative" discipleship. The neighborhood in which one would be properly neighborly had a particular hue. The drawings that accompany the February announcement depict a couple looking at a baby in a ruffled, bow-tied bassinet, he with shirt and tie, she with curled hair and earrings. Another drawing shows father, daughter, son, and dog enjoying a cookout on the lawn. Even the dog is smiling. The daughter has a crisp pinafore over a Peter Pan–collared dress. She is wearing a bow in her combed-back Pollyanna-style hair. Even in his own backyard, the son is wearing a dress shirt under a striped vest. The father has an ample chest and neatly combed hair. The church building pictured is a large steepled structure with an expansive entrance. It very much resembles the church out of which the Ad Council family emerges in the public service announcements encouraging stronger families through faith.

The photograph in the final announcement (fig. 1.25) renders the implicit features of eligibility more precisely. The full-page announcement ran as page 2 of the Easter issue. Here, proper Methodist family life is linked specifically to the ability to outfit one's family, more specifically one's daughter, appropriately. The Easter banquet to celebrate the resurrection of a wound-bearing Christ requires proper, party attire. The text reads: "A typical Methodist family you see here, outfitting the lovely teen-age daughter for Easter." The family is pictured in a clothing store. A daughter is modeling a pale pink taffeta dress, wearing jewels at wrist and ears and shiny black high heels. Her mother looks on with admiration, as does her father. (Her younger brother, I am delighted to note, appears less enthusiastic about this scene.) There is no apparent blemish on any of the faces. No one is more or less than the aesthetically normative weight of

76. *Together*, February 1958, p. 8.

the period. There is no sign of acrimony, save the little brother's (blessed) un-willingness to look blissfully at his sister for the photo shoot.

This appearance of the narrated normal was *necessary*, but not quite *sufficient*, to get the family through the screening process. A judging congregant was to take an even more perspicacious look at a neighboring family who appeared from all other indicators to be properly faithful. Lest there be something hidden, behind the carefully scripted scene, that would disqualify a family from representing the best that Methodism had to offer the world, the text gave this word of caution: "But there's more here than meets the eye — how this family in its home and church and community exemplifies the best in Christian living." If the Christian family was to be "the hope of the world" (again to quote the Methodist conference four years prior), it was important to make sure to choose *the right* family to symbolize that hope.

In November 1958 the James Detweilers of Burbank, California, were featured in "their sunny home" as the 1958 Methodist Family of the Year — "the kind of folk you'd enjoy having as neighbors."[77] The family of five is photographed against sunlight pouring from a window of their church home, with even the young son's crisp white handkerchief aligned to match those of his father and older brother (fig. 1.27). The editors explained their selection: "the Detweilers so well typify Methodist families the country over who put Christian ideas and ideals into their lives seven days each week." The photographs feature the Detweilers "starting the day" like "any one of a million" families, including even the family poodle, Minnie Poo, who "gets up early to bring in the paper each morning."

While the family is depicted as the apex of Methodism, their suburban life in Burbank is also portrayed as universally normal: "What family doesn't devote Saturdays to yard work, shopping, recreation! And what father doesn't like to don a chef's hat while pretending he's relieving his wife of kitchen chores?" This short, humorous caption accompanies James Detweiler's smiling face. Father laughs amiably at the situation, but the message is potent. The sentence rhetorically erases the existence of a Methodist family without a lawn to mow, without the expendable income or even work schedule to shop on Saturdays, without a mother who is to be relieved of her usual oversight of the kitchen or a father with a penchant for pretending he is helping out by striking up the grill. "What family doesn't . . . ?" There certainly were Methodist families who didn't — they became through this selective process the *other* internal to the Methodist body.

James Detweiler was a research engineer for Lockheed. Leaving their

77. *Together*, November 1958, pp. 14-17.

**Figure 1.27. Methodist Family of the Year.** *Together,* **November 1958**

native Ohio and Nebraska, he and wife Dorothy settled in Burbank and joined the First Methodist Church. The first two pages of the feature depict the family going about their daily work, with Dorothy cooking breakfast and Jim using "sound Christian ethics" to earn "his daily bread" at Lockheed. Another photograph shows daughter Jeanie inviting a friend by telephone to attend a church youth meeting. Still another shows how "Day's end sometimes finds friendly Dorothy Detweiler playing hostess to one of her church groups, Jim's co-workers, or simply a social gathering of neighbors." The next set of photographs shows "husky Doug Detweiler, a champion swimmer," putting his inherited "do-it-yourselfer" attitude to work by swimming laps in the pool. At the local dress shop the two females of the family seal their "close mother-daughter relationship" by looking for new clothes (fig. 1.28). Dorothy serves as superintendent of the church school, and Jim "usually assists his minister during the morning worship service." Their pastor suggests that "as a family, it is their desire to grow in their prayer and devotional life and, with humility of spirit, ever to serve the needs of Christ."

**Figure 1.28. Methodist Family of the Year.** *Together,* November 1958

The feature portrays the presumed normality of a wealthy suburban family in California, with a mother who doesn't need to work outside the home and children with time to pursue their sports and shopping. The contours of "creative" discipleship, as specified in the February contest announcement, adhere appropriately to the expectations created in the announcements themselves. The Detweilers are depicted as indeed good neighbors to the other members of First United Methodist, to the people connected to Lockheed, and to the neighbors who live nearby. As the editors of the piece conclude: "Withal, they're a happy, healthy, fun-loving five who enjoy doing for others."

During a seminar at Duke, Maureen Knudsen Langdoc presented images of the contest for our consideration. The class (myself included) found ourselves laughing, wincing, and becoming increasingly uncomfortable as the presentation progressed. Our chuckles at the cheesy pictures felt slightly mean-spirited. After all, here was a real family, cooking, swimming, shop-

**Figure 1.29. Methodist Family of the Year.** *Together,* **November 1958**

ping, hosting, variously going about their day under the all-seeing eye of the *Together* camera. I would suggest that we were uncomfortable due to the vulnerability of a real family so exposed to a critical, evaluative gaze.

The article is disconcerting because the contest itself is disconcerting. Methodists were invited to turn their evaluative eyes on one another, looking for splinters and stray hairs and prodigal children and lack of faith. As I suggest now that we consider the Detweilers as primarily a tool for reinforcing a form of domesticity that is racially encoded, as I suggest that we consider them the apex of normalized Methodism, sadly shorn of a radical call to boundary-crossing discipleship, it is *apt* for the reader to respond with protest. The Detweilers were merely a mortal family, merely a busy mother, an amused father donning an absurd chef's hat (fig. 1.29), a younger son doing his best to look grown-up, an elder son working to follow in his father's footsteps, a daughter willing to be photographed (for all the Methodist world to see) in her Saturday-morning hair clips, each striving to put "sound Christian ethics to good use."

The form of such reader response is an integral part of my point. The divide promoted by the germ-free home is a divide between families who can stand up to the evaluative scrutiny of the "official judges" and families who cannot, screened out by those who determine the qualifications for a truly good household. To read critically the use to which a real family was put in the pages of *Together* makes the scrutinizing gaze explicit, and aimed at a family who is so very close to what we consider *home*. It is this protective, charitable, neighborly impulse — after all, this family is merely mortal, merely fallible, and they are *our* people — that I believe was undermined systematically in the habituation of holy hygiene. The 360-degree circle of hygienically safe association for one's children and one's household was drawn in such a way as to exclude those who "make mistakes."

## Connect the Dots . . . and See a ———

At this point I will split my interpretation. I wish to consider two different ways to trace the church through *Together,* reading a counterimage that runs sometimes incongruously in its pages.[78] The split in interpretation is possible, and arguably necessary, if readers are also to trace hope through the following chapters on the formation of the thoroughly modern family.

A regular feature of *Together* was Together with the Small Fry, featuring stories, activities, prayers, and puzzles for children. In the November 1956 issue that I studied at the Duke University Library, someone, possibly a small fry related to a librarian, turned to page 55 and traced the dots numbered from 1 to 42 that make up the outline of a steepled church with double-door entrance and side exit. This Methodist child would thus have been able to fill in the incomplete sentence above the drawing with the word "church." She would have been able to "connect the dots . . . and see a *church.*" In the copy I studied, the child pressed hard on her pencil and traced an image of this church structure onto page 57, two pages beyond the puzzle. At the risk of being overly precious, I suggest that the symbolism of the tracing is significant. A black-and-white photograph of a father reading to his children ran immediately behind the connect-the-dots puzzle, and the trace of the pencil picked up the print of that photograph on the backside, leaving a faint imprint of the church structure on page 57.[79] The hand tracing the dots to draw a church left an imprint on the subsequent pages.

These trace marks of the church structure intersect three book reviews under the heading "Looking for Good Children's Books?" by Edith Patterson Meyer. The review piece itself is worth interpretation, and in this case, the tracing suggests one way to connect the dots. The reader today may interpret across the magazine and, with point 1 starting in America, move across to points 12 and 13, to broaden the horizons of the child reader. The review intersected by the trace marks of the church dot-to-dot here is *The Coming of the King,* by Norman Vincent Peale. The reviewer writes: "Reading and hearing anew another birthday story, far older and greater even than that of our country, is part of every Christian family's Christmas celebration." With this

---

78. Those wishing to pursue the possibilities of hospitality among mainline Protestants in the United States would do well to consider two other mainline Protestant periodicals — the *Christian Home* (1935-86), which overlapped with *Together,* mainly under the aegis of the Board of Education of the Methodist Church, and *Hearthstone* (1949-72), published under the Christian Board of Publication (Christian Church [Disciples of Christ]) and the American Baptist Publication Society/Board of Education and Publication.

79. The image was of "Looks at New Books," *Together,* November 1956, p. 56.

book, a family like the one pictured in the intervening page could enjoy the story in a "distinguished, reverent, and wholly satisfying" form.[80] Patterson Meyer thus situates the reader within "our country." She also situates the Christmas story as a larger circle concentric with the story of the United States.

The other two book reviews tell children in "our country" about life elsewhere. A Methodist child who received for Christmas a copy of Elizabeth Foreman Lewis's *To Beat a Tiger, One Needs a Brother's Help* could read about the "astounding acts of bravery and of devotion" among "a band of refugees in wartorn Shanghai." Patterson Meyer explains that the author of the book had been a Methodist missionary in China. In the third book, *Lantern in the Valley,* by Faye Campbell Griffis, the life of the Yoshida family becomes "very real" to a young reader. In it a child could hear about the "work and play, the problems, pleasures, environment, and ways of thinking of the Japanese people of both country and city." "Such books," the reviewer explains, will "push back the horizons of young Americans and give them a friendlier, more knowledgeable outlook on this rapidly shrinking world of ours." The two-page spread following the book reviews is another advertisement from General Electric, "People's Capitalism — What Makes It Work for You?"[81]

This is not the only way to trace the lines of the church in *Together*. It is not even the only image of the church presented in the magazine itself. There are articles even from the first year that depict "unusual Methodists" who do not fit on the cover. There are images of people who are not "husky" swimmers or shopping daughters or hostess suburbanites in Burbank. There are stories of Methodists who visit with people who are alone — "I Specialize in Lonely People"; stories of Native Americans — "America's Indians Get a Chance!"; and stories of immigrant families — "Help and Hope for Hungarian Refugees" — even one right after the other, as in the February 1957 issue.[82] But the wording of the reviewer above, who saw the need for Methodist parents to expose "our children" to books that will "push back" their "horizons," seems characteristic of one tint cast on the image of Methodist family life in *Together*.

By one reading, the child at the center of the magazine is a specific child. The child for whom the world is shrinking is the child whose family is the black-and-white image on page 56, a staged photographic image through

---

80. Edith Patterson Meyer, "Looking for Good Children's Books?" *Together,* November 1956, p. 57.

81. *Together,* November 1956, pp. 58-59.

82. *Together,* February 1957, pp. 29-30, 31-34, 35-38.

which a trace of the dot-to-dot church is passed for interpreting "this rapidly shrinking world of ours." The normative family is the carbon image of what came to be defined as *the* Christian family, and the church formed by connecting the dots was to serve as a resource for bringing up responsible children in a particular nation. This tone in *Together* may itself be interpreted through a thematic trace from a much earlier issue for mainline Protestant families. Recall the wording of the *Parents'* magazine article from three decades prior: "The negro servant with her exuberance and strong dramatic sense, the fun-loving Irish girl, the peasant maid of any land can frequently broaden our children's horizons." By one reading of *Together*, the image of the family was traceable to an earlier form of domestic normality, and is traceable into a form of domestic security today.

We should not eschew this reading of *Together*. I suspect that this perspective on the family, one's children, and the church was ultimately inhospitable even to the real lives of families who had a prayer of making the cut for the district, conference, and national Methodist Family of the Year. But I am increasingly certain that this perspective was inhospitable to the lives of families whose overt difference disqualified them altogether. To be part of the church might have been — and for many Methodists surely was — otherwise. To be part of the church might have been — and for many Methodists surely was — to be knocked off center, finding one's identity and the identity of one's family as but a small part of a story beyond one's control and crafting.

### "Unquestioned Safety and a Share in World-wide Missions"

A salient image recurs in the first issues of *Together*, advertising a Rand McNally book entitled *Boys and Girls Who Knew Jesus*.[83] The image shows Jesus with a group of children around him. All the children have smiling, even joyful faces, and all have light skin. The image of children who knew Jesus (as well as that of the light-skinned and blond-haired Adam and Eve in one long pictorial)[84] stands in contrast to many of the images depicting mission-field work in the pages of the magazine.

The tension between the depiction of *Boys and Girls Who Knew Jesus* (and the Adam and Eve who first knew God) and the depiction of families such as the Navajo family is ripe for theological and cultural engagement. As

---

83. See, e.g., *Together*, November 1956, pp. 62 and 68.
84. "The Story of Creation," watercolors by Floyd A. Johnson, *Together*, December 1956, p. 41.

Favorite Poem-of-the-month.

# America
# The Beautiful

By Katharine Lee Bates

*O beautiful for spacious skies, for amber waves of grain,*
*For purple mountain majesties above the fruited plain!*
*America! America! God shed his grace on thee*
*And crown thy good with brotherhood from sea to shining sea.*

*O beautiful for pilgrim feet, whose stern, impassioned stress*
*A thoroughfare for freedom beat across the wilderness!*
*America! America! God mend thine every flaw,*
*Confirm thy soul in self-control, thy liberty in law.*

*O beautiful for heroes proved in liberating strife,*
*Who more than self their country loved, and mercy more than life!*
*America! America! May God thy gold refine,*
*Till all success be nobleness, and every gain divine.*

*O beautiful for patriot dream that sees beyond the years*
*Thine alabaster cities gleam undimmed by human tears!*
*America! America! God shed his grace on thee*
*And crown thy good with brotherhood from sea to shining sea.*

WHAT'S YOUR favorite poem? Let us know. We plan to present "favorite poem" each month. *America The Beautiful* was suggested by Ruth D. Fuller of Chicago, Ill. The photograph of the Navajo family in Arizona is from Ralph H. Anderson.—EDS.

*"And crown thy good with brotherhood. ."*

**Figure 1.30. "Favorite Poem-of-the-Month."** *Together,* **November 1956**

also with too many of the images of children and adults from countries other than the United States, the Navajo family members are not named. The editors stretched the realm of the possible by featuring the family's image, but they arguably did so in the interest of broadening their readers' horizons. The "Navajo family from Arizona" is situated next to "Katharine Lee Bates," who penned the accompanying lines of poetry, and "Ralph H. Anderson," who took the picture (fig. 1.30). Many images of unnamed Anglo-American families appear throughout these first volumes of *Together,* such as the one depicting "home movie fans" making Christmas cards (fig. 1.31). They are assumed to be the sort of family that reads the magazine, and thus need no cultural designation, because they are the default mode of Methodist. They are the normal by which the Navajo family is different, and by which another woman in the same issue is designated simply "Blackfoot Indian Woman."[85]

85. From "Looks at New Books," *Together,* December 1956, p. 58.

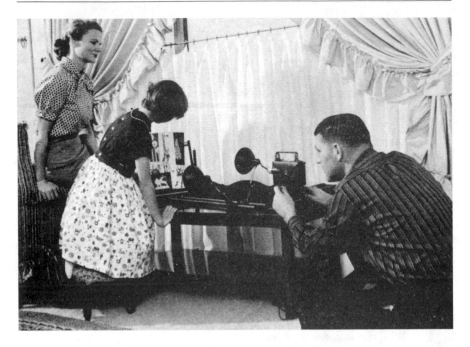

**Figure 1.31. Home movie fans making Christmas cards.** *Together,* **December 1956**

A small drawing of Native Americans around a fire accompanies the magazine's regular open-forum feature, but the official discussers in this "Midmonth Powwow" are almost exclusively Anglo-Methodist. African Americans appear infrequently — except for African American young men named to the "All-American Methodist University and College Elevens" football team each year.[86] This tension between default, domestic familiarity and perceived deviation from the norm runs through bits and pieces of the magazine, suggesting the need for an ecclesial resolution — suggesting the need for a different way to connect the dots and see a church.

The stress between a normalized, American Methodism and a church growing in regions considered to be "elsewhere" is apparent in many early articles. One short article makes this point. A news digest item from December 1956 shows "Bishop J. Waskom Pickett and a class of newly ordained Indian pastors" without designating the newly ordained by their names.[87] A choir and orchestra of "Indian Methodists" touring the United States to celebrate

86. See, e.g., *Together,* December 1956, pp. 32-33.

87. "One Hundred Years in India: Methodists Look to Future," *Together,* December 1956, p. 75. The news item ran on pp. 74-75.

Indian Methodism's centennial are described as "picturesque." Another photograph is captioned "A common scene in India: Villagers thresh grains as their ancestors did." India is called a "fiercely independent, young nation," and her century-old Methodist tradition is rendered from a distance. The short article labels many "Indian Methodists" without naming them, listing by name and association only the four missions representatives from the United States. The editors note with pride that "Methodists in India have helped bring about sweeping social and economic changes — the gradual disintegration of the caste system, improvements in the status of women, and better village living," but the article also highlights a pressure depicted in the images themselves.

After one hundred years of mission work by American Methodists in India, the church in India wanted its own identity. In answer to the question, "Do Indian Christians still want missionaries?" the church was answering, "'Yes' — with reservations." Visitors from the United States would be welcome inasmuch as they were "invited" and, importantly, came to "identify" with "the local church" — that is, inasmuch as they received hospitality and became decentered and newly named under a moniker from elsewhere, "Indian Methodists."[88] The call of the church in this small piece about a relatively new church from across an ocean and a continent is, by one reading, a call to cross the carefully constructed gutter of the magazine, to the other side, to the side of the "peasant," the "negro," and the variously situated "others" by whom several generations of aspiring mothers had gauged their progress. By one reading of this small piece in *Together*, "Indian Methodists" were inviting their brothers and sisters in the United States to reembody the church and, perhaps in the process, to be remembered as creatures dependent on another way.

According to the inaugural editorial in October 1956, *Together* was to continue "in the same evangelical spirit of reaching multitudes that marked efforts of our founder John Wesley as he preached to throngs on hillsides and in the pits of abandoned coal mines." For only as it was "exposed to many people" could *Together* "achieve a destiny of great service to The Methodist Church and to the larger purpose that called it into existence almost 200 years ago."[89] Yet by one reading of the magazine, mission work too often entailed paying someone to do the dirty work of coal mine conversions. In recurring advertisements for the Women's Division of Christian Service and for the Board of Missions of the Methodist Church, readers remain at arm's length to families outside normative Methodism. Such families are depicted as recipi-

---

88. "One Hundred Years," p. 75.
89. Pierce and Washabaugh, editorial, p. 9.

Figure 1.32. Notice for
Board of Missions Annuity
Plan. *Together,*
October 1956

ents of largesse that does not require proximity or the sort of decentering for which the "Indian Methodists" called.

It is striking that the older women to whom the advertisements were typically pitched were of a generation that did send many women off, across wide oceans, to live near the women and children they served. Here, in *Together,* this narration of the Wesleyan legacy is refracted through the postwar domesticity of the normal family. The ads for annuity and life insurance plans often play poignantly on the fact that many women in the generation aging in the 1950s did not want to be a "burden" to others, nor a "risk" to the next generation, bound as they were for a more promising future. Giving to others through a distanced form of charity would allow the nuclear family to avoid both risk abroad and the burden of its elders. The words of one satisfied annuitant are characteristic: "The future holds no financial worries for me. I have received peace of mind from a regular and assured income and I enjoy the inexpressible personal satisfaction of helping in the important work of building the Kingdom of God around the earth, thus contributing to the greater stability of the world." The ad copy continues: "Loss is impossible and blessing assured because you are in partnership with the Lord whose marching orders were, 'Go therefore and teach all nations and lo I am with you unto the end' — when you purchase a Life Income Gift Certificate [from the] Woman's Division of Christian Service."[90]

While often aimed at a generation no longer mobile enough to travel across town, much less across an ocean, the often large mission advertisements had arguably considerable impact. They spoke specifically about the absence of financial risk, but the rhetoric of protection from worry and interruption and of "security through Christian service" also carried with it an implicit distance from those with whom Christ identified himself. One could feed the poor, clothe the naked, and visit the prisoners virtually, by writing a check to one's congregation and to the Annuity Plan of the Board of Missions of the Methodist Church. The Methodist family could thus ensure, simultaneously, a "guaranteed high return, unquestioned safety and a share in worldwide missions" (fig. 1.32).

### "We Put Christ in Our Christmas Cards"

In her December 1930 *Parents'* essay on behavioralism, Rosalie Rayner Watson told of the tension in her own family around holidays. Naming Christmas as a time in particular when expectations were high but nerves raw, Rayner Watson wondered wistfully whether there were not a better way to celebrate — on a smaller scale, on a daily basis. The (perhaps intentional) irony woven throughout her essay on maternal know-how is that she seems to have come into contact with her sons only while supervising their live-in caregivers. Christmas was one of the few times when her two boys were all hers, their nannies having been given time off to share the season with their own families. (It is surely part of the mischief of Rayner Watson's narrative that her husband, the great child behavioralist himself, seems to have been thoroughly absent year-round.)

The maternal readership of *Together* faced a different set of complications for the holidays. While the early issues of *Parents'* ran frequent advice for the servant-employing mother, there is nary a trace to suggest that the readers of *Together* employed help. Even for the prize-winning Detweilers, the only extrafamilial "servant" seems to have been Minnie Poo, who reliably

---

90. *Together*, October 1956, p. 82.

trotted out to fetch the morning paper. The Methodist mothers reading the magazine were of a different social class living during a different time. Their responsibility for bringing Christmas to life in their domiciles involved a complicated combination of piety and the heightened domestic norms so characteristic of the postwar middle-class home. The *Parents'* editors had named as essential to the properly traditional Christmas in 1929 a vague "warm glow of wonder." The Christmas apparent in the pages of *Together* in the 1950s involved a juxtaposition of the one whose birth, life, and death was "the reason for the season" (to quote a contemporary phrase) and a properly staged family spectacle. A Methodist mother was responsible for displaying well within her own living room a properly staged family scene, worthy not just of receiving but also of *being* the hope of the world.

One of the most conspicuous contrasts in *Together*, between the message of the 1954 Methodist conference on the family and the 1954 hymn by Georgia Harkness, "Hope of the World," occurs in the midst of depicting Advent and Christmas. How was "The Christian Family — the Hope of the World" related to the "Hope of the world, thou Christ of great compassion"?[91] The tensions around celebrating Christ's coming are certainly as old as fights between orders vowing poverty and kings vowing cathedrals, but the postwar Methodist tension is worth noting. For one thing, preparing for the birth of the child on whom Christian hope ultimately depends brought into relief the similarity between the children to whom Methodists were to give from a safe distance and the family of Jesus himself. Jesus had no place to lay his head, and he suggested multiple times that those who were similarly homeless were the special recipients of his presence. When one was to give a party in his name, one was to invite the very people formerly prohibited from the table as unclean. Thus, some of the ways that postwar mothers reading *Together* were encouraged to bring Jesus into their middle-class homes seem quite strained. Some of the suggestions in *Together* for anticipating Christmas in one's family represent the strange maneuvering required if one was to bring Jesus into the home without challenging in some way the life of a "typical" Methodist family.

91. "Hope of the World," words by Georgia Harkness (1954, Hymn Society of America), *The United Methodist Hymnal* (1989), #178. Harkness wrote the hymn for the 1954 assembly of the World Council of Churches, whose theme was "Christ the Hope of the World." The theme speaker for the Methodist conference on the family saw fit to address the apparent incongruity between the two gatherings' titles, assuring his listeners: "There is no contradiction in these themes"; for the Christian family, embodying as it should the Father's "law of love," would carry that "unifying force" into "the community, the nation, and eventually the world." Bishop G. Bromley Oxnam, "The Christian Family, the Hope of the World," in *Report: The Christian Home — the Hope of the World*, pp. 3-6.

*We Put Christ in Our Christmas Cards*

WILL your family's Christmas cards reflect the true spirit of Christmas this year?

Ours will and yours can, too. As we did, you may find such a family project not only rewarding spiritually, but loads of fun!

For example, in our house at Christmas we always have a birthday cake for Jesus. One year we posed the children with it beneath a picture of the Madonna. Our Christmas card showed the scene, with our baby reaching for Christ's birthday cake (below).

Our favorite homemade, photograph-

*Three evenings of family fun yielded this Christmas card illustration.*

*A family scene with Christmas spirit.*

ic Christmas card illustrated the familiar hymn, *O Come, Let Us Adore Him* (above). Technically, this was the most difficult of any Christmas theme we've tried to photograph. We worked on this for three evenings. We set off a flash bulb inside the tiny stable, and to get the right expression on the children's faces we sang *Silent Night* and *Away in a Manger*, while we were taking the picture.

Before we had children, we were able to convey a religious message on our Christmas cards by illustrating vacation snapshots with appropriate verses from the Bible. It was easy to find texts that fitted perfectly our scenes of mountains, beaches, and peaceful valleys. And people seemed to appreciate this rather unusual touch in our family Christmas cards.

—DOROTHY L. YATES

35

**Figure 1.33. "We Put Christ in Our Christmas Cards."** *Together,* **October 1956**

Dorothy L. Yates begins "We Put Christ in Our Christmas Cards" (fig. 1.33) by asking readers, "Will your family's Christmas cards reflect the true spirit of Christmas this year?" In previous years Yates and her husband had sent Christmas cards showing the couple on vacation. "Before we had children, we were able to convey a religious message on our Christmas cards by illustrating vacation snapshots with appropriate verses from the Bible. It was easy to find texts that fitted perfectly our scenes of mountains, beaches, and peaceful valleys." The Yates family now sought to create a scene with their children that would fit perfectly with the theme of the season through various rituals involving card making. Dorothy encourages her readers: "As we did, you may find such a family project not only rewarding spiritually, but loads of fun!" The essay features two photographs of the three Yates children, one with the children "posed" under "a picture of the Madonna," with the baby "reaching for Christ's birthday cake."

But the photo most prominently featured in the article is the family favorite — one that "illustrated the familiar hymn, *O Come, Let Us Adore Him.*" Two of the Yates children stand by a crèche, looking in at the scene depicted with wooden figures. Taking the photo was no small feat. "Technically, this was the most difficult of any Christmas theme we've tried to photograph. We worked on this for three evenings. We set off a flash bulb inside the tiny stable, and to get the right expression on the children's faces we sang *Silent Night* and *Away in a Manger,* while we were taking the picture." Through such effort the family had been able to achieve the right expression, the right lighting, and the sense of hushed expectation of the proper Christmas. By one reading, Yates's essay "fitted perfectly" into a struggle going on in postwar, mainline Protestantism, particularly in the preparation for receiving Jesus.

The pages of *Together* also offer a different way to connect the dots of Christmas, suggesting a simpler way to "put Christ" into the Yates family's Christmas cards. We can think of this on both sides of the "gutter" dividing the two sides of *Parents'* magazine. First, by one connection of the dots, the Yates family might simply have recognized the face of Christ in each child in their home, regardless of whether the child had achieved the properly reverent facial expression. One way to "put Christ" into the postwar home might have been to see the reflection of Christ even in the face of a child who would not have been chosen to appear with Lassie's descendant on the cover of the magazine. Perhaps the Yates essay is characteristic of the era in no small part because they felt the pressure to expend three nights' work to achieve an image of the family good enough to appear on the cover of the family's own yearly missive. Representing the "typical" readership of the Methodist magazine, Mrs. Yates needed to put her family's best face forward.

But we may read another answer on the other side of the *Parents'* gutter. The families reading *Together* might also have put Christ into their holiday by inviting in those neighbors who were not welcome elsewhere. Interspersed throughout the pages of *Together* are images of families seeking hospitality from those already settled in America. The salience of these images is heightened in the Advent issues. For example, the Arab refugee families featured in one Advent essay from the first year of *Together* are visibly situated as akin to the holy family moving from Nazareth to Bethlehem (fig. 1.34). In juxtaposition with the women who are traveling like Mary to Bethlehem, the story of the American mother carefully situating her three children for an optimal photograph, to "put Christ" into Christmas, may be read as at least strained, and perhaps even strange.

The distance of such refugee families from the family comfortably serving their own similarly situated neighbors in suburban Burbank is consider-

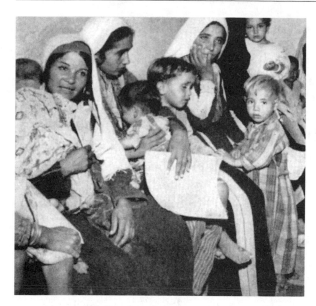

**Figure 1.34. Arab refugee families.** *Together,* December 1956. The caption reads: "Arab refugees await treatment in a camp clinic."

able. Yet perhaps the germ-free home had so taken hold by the postwar era that bringing into one's own carefully appointed home the very people one was to distinguish one's family from was almost unthinkable. To paraphrase a friend of mine, many a mother prepared for Advent in America in ways that involved trying to secure her home against the appraising gaze of her social superiors. One was to get one's house in order for the *right sort* of guest. Holidays were a time when domestic magazines in the United States heightened class aspirations through consumption and well-crafted, selective generosity. Inviting into one's familial celebrations those whom Christ suggested were indeed the form of his presence would have meant risking association with those who were to be kept at a distance. Those who followed this servant would have found it somewhat awkward, at the least, to celebrate his arrival on a simple ass when the hearth and home had been shaped by a habituation of aspiring, middle-class status.

The congregation preparing for the arrival of Mary on a donkey might have found itself strained in a way similar to the Yates children in their household. Moving one concentric circle out from the nuclear family, we may seek to connect the dots of the local congregation as it prepared for the celebration of Christmas. One extensive, full-color pictorial essay in January 1957 may help us name what was (and is) at stake in configuring the body of Christ in the local congregation during Advent. We can read it as an example of distanced charity in one church family, as a congregation in Minnesota staged a visual representation of Christ's presence.

"Art Gallery in a Church" featured the Hennepin Avenue Methodist Church in Minneapolis, a congregation that had inherited the Walker Gallery of Religious Art, a gift of Thomas B. Walker, "a Methodist layman who prospered from Minnesota's pineries."[92] The piece has limited text, most of its impact being visual, with full-color, mostly full-page photographs. It opens: "A 'PLACE TO SEE' in Minneapolis is the Hennepin Avenue Methodist Church — not only because of the beauty of its soaring gothic lines, but because it houses an art gallery that's more than an art gallery. In rooms and corridors lined with priceless canvases, children attend church school, choirs practice, women's societies meet, couples are married, and babies are christened." In addition to an opening picture of the spire, the text itself says the arrangement of the church building is consistent with classical, Western aesthetics. Internally and externally, the church building would be judged by the "typical" *Together* family as top-notch. Readers are further told that the current pastor, Rev. Chester A. Pennington, is the latest in a "long line of distinguished ministers," including one who had gone on to become a bishop and another who had become president of Garrett Biblical Institute. The people of Hennepin, along with its visitors, had access to "almost 300 oils and engravings from European and American masters." The photographs running through the essay show an all-Anglo, immaculately dressed congregation going about their worship, choir practice, Sunday school, and missionary meetings in rooms lined with "priceless canvases." The essay was not meant to intimidate, but to inspire, as Pastor Pennington explains: even "churches less favored by benefactions can partake" of "the great tradition of Christian art," by way of "reproductions of original work." Indeed, "church-school and parish-house rooms need not be drab."

The photographs opening the essay include one of a mother and her two small children beneath a newly budding tree and, towering above, the high-church spire. The three are tastefully coordinated with blue and gray coats. Across the opening page is also "Mrs. Forshee, wife of an associate pastor," who is showing her daughter a painting in the Walker collection. Both mother and daughter wear pastel, Sunday best, mother in a pink suit and daughter in a pink and blue smocked dress. The Furini painting they are studying depicts the Gospel of Luke's *Adoration of the Shepherds,* itself a seventeenth-century study of a story in which the equivalent of modern-day trash collectors are the first invited to pay homage to the infant king in a feeding trough. Mrs. Forshee is pointing to the haloed image of the baby Jesus.

92. "Art Gallery in a Church," *Together,* January 1957, pp. 35-42.

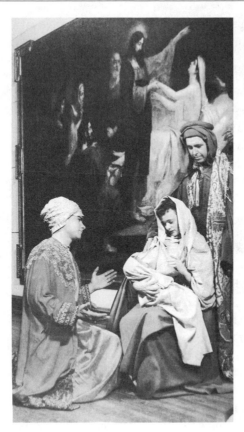

**Figure 1.35.** Members at Hennepin Avenue Methodist Church reenact Christmas story. *Together,* January 1957

*The Christmas story is re-enacted with a priceless painting as backdrop. It's "Christ Raising Jairus' Daughter," by Benjamin West, the American-born artist who became a court favorite of England's King George III. West painted it at the British monarch's own request.*

Continuing the Christmas theme of this January essay, the text explains that during Advent the congregation had "re-enacted" the Christmas story "with a priceless painting as backdrop" (fig. 1.35). A photograph shows a woman dressed in the traditional Marian blue, with a man, presumably depicting Joseph, behind her. They are portraying a different scene from the Christmas story, this one from Matthew, with one of the three magi kneeling before the bundle in Mary's arms (to all appearances, a plastic baby doll). A caption explains that the painting behind the human tableau is *Christ Raising Jairus' Daughter,* by artist Benjamin West, who "became a court favorite of England's King George III." The painting was evidently completed "at the British monarch's own request."

The editors chose for the December 1956 issue an image of a "modern Madonna" waiting with her child in the midst of "uncertainty" and in the blessing and vulnerability of a "borrowed" life (fig. 1.36). The accompanying poem appeared as an appeal from the Methodist Committee for Overseas Relief (MCOR), with the announcement that "Christmas offerings to MCOR help feed and clothe those in distress." With the photograph of woman and child, the poem stitches together a mother and child from the present with the mother and child in whom Christian hope resides. The poem begs for another reading at the intersection of the modern Madonna, the priceless painting depicting Christ raising a dead child to life, and the various efforts to "put Christ" into a family's and a congregation's Christmas celebrations. The text begs for a different way to connect the dots to find a church.

The mother in the photograph is not named. Neither is the poet. But the words name each child, each little one, as created miraculously — as created gratuitously by God. To put this same point differently, here the gift of a child is narrated as a *borrowed* gift, as one that is not fully a parent's own. Thus the recipients of the MCOR offerings, while in need, were not pitiable in their state of impermanence. The child's "borrowed clothes" were not a sign of shame to be rectified by the largesse of those who could afford firsthand clothes for their children. Here a reading of Mary, of the "hers" to whom the poem refers, is crucial. The Son of the One God was not Mary's possession but a gift to the world. The uncertainty of Mary's pondering — even in the fear of uncertainty — is a crucial part of the magi story, as they bring to Jesus signs of his royalty but also of his death. Again, it is possible to connect a different set of dots, pulling the lines together to find a sketch of a different church. The raising of Jairus's daughter may be read as signaling the borrowed life of each one — the gratuity of each child. Taking one more step back, one may also pull in the first painting depicted in the Walker collection. In her "study" with her daughter of the shepherds adoring the Christ child, Mrs. Forshee pointed to the One who received as his first followers an entourage of men who slept outside with sheep. By this reading, the tableau threesome from the Hennepin Avenue Methodist Church, reenacting the Christmas story, may be worshiping something other than a plastic baby doll.

A crucial postscript to the Hennepin Avenue Church story signals a possible mixing of stories and prayers across the gutter. In a 1957 essay in *Christian Century* entitled "Inclusive Church — Inclusive Theology," Martin E. Marty featured the Hennepin Avenue Methodist Church.[93] Marty begins the essay by suggesting that "Something's got to give." Noting the escalating tension between what was considered the "ivory-tower unreality" of theologians and "'American activism' with its emphasis on the externals of

93. Martin E. Marty, "Inclusive Church — Inclusive Theology: The Hennepin Avenue Methodist Church, Minneapolis, Minnesota," *Christian Century*, February 27, 1957, pp. 256-59.

*Song of a Modern Madonna*
*I hold my son—as she held hers.*
*My son, too, is a miracle of God's creation,*
*Making my mother's heart sing—even in the*
*fear*
*Of uncertainty. My son too wears borrowed*
*clothes;*
*He sits in the dust of a borrowed land;*
*He feeds from a borrowed bowl, filled with bor-*
*rowed milk.*
*He is my firstborn . . . and I hold him in love,*
*As she held hers, who mothered the Son of the*
*One God.*

Christmas offerings to MCOR help feed and clothe those in distress.

The Methodist Committee for Overseas Relief
150 Fifth Avenue, New York 11, N. Y.

**Figure 1.36. "Song of a Modern Madonna."** *Together,* December 1956

church life," Marty reads the test case for resolution in churches that are "found somewhere around midtown in almost every American metropolis." Such "'family' churches," as Marty names them, too often "seem to be existing on steam generated in the past," living in the midst of "suffocating self-contentment with size and success." Hennepin Methodist, with its four thousand members, four secretaries, five custodians, three ministers of music, four on-site clergymen, and housekeeper, engineer, business manager, director of religious drama, director of Christian education, and pastoral assistant, would seem the perfect test case. Headed by a senior pastor influenced by theologians Karl Barth and Emil Brunner, this church resembles a midsize Christian corporation — or an instance of the corporate Christ. If, as Barth wrote, Christianity has set ethics on a knife's edge, the programs in discipleship at Hennepin might be interpreted as an extensive attempt at smug Midwestern self-justification — or it might be, even simultaneously, a borrowed, gratuitous gift.

By Marty's reading, Hennepin could be the latter, in no small part because of the way the congregation held lightly its gift. The church school spent what Marty considered an uncommon amount of energy on education for children with disabilities, and the church had an active presence, both financial and embodied, in places of need across the city and the globe. Marty quotes Pastor Pennington: "The Christian gospel has a helping and healing word to speak to the whole range of human need. Nothing human is alien." But the sign of the incarnation Marty points to first is the one that also begs for a different reading of the congregation than the one prompted by the *Together* pictorial. The congregation had in 1954 issued a call to ecclesial miscegenation. A congregational resolution in 1954 had declared "A welcome to persons of all races." Yet, Marty says, the resolution might have sat dormant, as a sort of empty gesture, had it not been for a "test." In 1956 an urban redevelopment project had issued a plan to bulldoze a historically African American congregation. We are not able to discern from the account whether the Hennepin dignitaries had the power to redirect the city's plans and save the structure of Border Methodist Church. Although Marty does not even pause here, the possibility today should cause a full stop. As missions to places of need are empty without an investigation of the reasons for global poverty, so would a story about Hennepin fail unless readers today note that a congregation's home was bulldozed for the sake of city progress.

Yet, in the midst of lament for what might have been, it seems only apt to note what did occur. The same congregation *Together* highlights in 1957 for its "priceless canvases" had in 1956 voted to invite Border Methodist Church to join them in a merger. As Pennington describes the decision to Marty, the churches acknowledged that the reconfigured church would be "awkward at times." But Border Methodist accepted the invitation to marry the two congregations by a vote of 34 to 2, so that Christians might rightly "worship together regardless of race or cultural background." By one reading, they had refused the partition enforced by decades of habituated racial hygiene. To be sure, the photographs in the January 1957 *Together* show no sign of this merger, and were perhaps taken prior to it. The appearance of every choir member, of every Woman's Society of Christian Service member, is markedly middle-class Anglo.

But there may be another way to connect the dots and find a church. There is hope for a sketched tracing of the church in *Together* that marks a different future for such a faith. By one reading, during a time of marked, racialized violence, in a country that is still its most segregated during the worship hour on the Sabbath, Border Methodist and Hennepin Methodist had begun to embody a real Christmas tableau.

### "A Sort of Christian 'Marshall Plan'"?

In an issue of *Together* from 1963, Ferdinand Sigg, bishop of the Geneva Area of the Methodist church, narrates the discordant theology of Karl Barth.[94] He begins by telling of the First Assembly of the World Council of Churches in

---

94. Ferdinand Sigg, "Karl Barth: Theology for a World in Crisis," *Together*, August 1963, pp. 19-22.

1948. This vast gathering of Christians from around the world heard Karl Barth proclaim that the World Council had committed a theological category error. The theme of the assembly was "Man's Disorder and God's Design," but, Barth exclaimed, the theme should have read "God's Design and Man's Disorder." Barth's concern, as Sigg recounts fifteen years after the event, was that the World Council seemed to be embarking on "a sort of Christian 'Marshall Plan.'"

This may characterize a form of Methodism traced from carefully polished, "slick-paper" depictions of normative American domesticity, toward the dot-to-dot of General Electric's neighborhood, through an ethics put into practice at Lockheed, and traveling by way of certified check to missionaries practicing at a safe and organized distance "elsewhere." Such a Methodism may have had too little to say in the midst of a Cold War arms race or a domestic struggle for civil rights, and may today have too little to say about the effort to craft a perfect family. Family norms for domesticity, the promotion of science, and mainline Protestant faith became intertwined in a nation marching forward intent on forging a better future for itself through carefully calibrated procreation. The baby, the child, the well-timed and well-planned household became in the last century the site at which providence and progress coincided.

Margaret Sanger convinced most Methodists that there were simply "Too Many People!"[95] She suggested that people "from the Orient to South America, from Eastern Europe to the U.S.," would present "future problems potentially more dangerous than the H-bomb." "Have-not nations, with millions more mouths to feed each year, must spill over their borders in unending aggressions, searching for more and more food-producing areas."

Thus, by one reading of *Together*, the future of the world depended on responsible parenting, disinfecting, and planning ahead for the sake of "our" children in the world of tomorrow. By the reading to which we will turn in chapter 3, the tension implicit in the title of the 1960 *Together* article "They're Christians, They're Gypsies" required a sort of Christian Marshall Plan to control the populations of places like "teeming India," as it is named in Sanger's article.[96]

Yet, other readings, other ways to trace the church, are also possible. We could trace the church represented in *Together* by way of "Rosemary Goes to the Hospital," an essay that presents, not the cover-perfect twins

---

95. Margaret Sanger, "Too Many People!" *Together*, September 1957, pp. 16-18. We discuss this essay in our introduction.

96. "They're Christians, They're Gypsies," *Together*, September 1960, p. 76.

with Lassie, but instead a little girl whose parents go through the long and arduous medical procedures necessary for Rosemary to "triumph over cleft palate."[97] Another article in the inaugural issue, "How Donald Learned to Say 'Okay,'" is similarly potent. While the illustrator draws the child — also with cleft palate — with a hand over his face, unable or unwilling even to sketch the contours of a face still bearing the marks of imperfection, the article stands as a countertestimony to the polished average on the cover and in pages beyond. In the short narrative account, Donald struggles to master saying the word "Okay."[98] The understanding achieved by previously derisive fellow campers (and, by extension, the reader) is wrought through pity — Donald's father had left him in shame, unable even to "bear to look at him," and his mother had eventually "had a breakdown." But still, the story's attempt to resituate normality struggles awkwardly in a different direction than the attempt to "put Christ into Christmas" through three nights of perfectionist photography. This struggle is indeed also present in "Rosemary Goes to the Hospital." Rosemary's doctors stand near an impressive display of Rosemary's X-rays, peering at her skull as a project under construction. But the image of family life "with sister Noreen and brother Patrick" suggests that the receptivity of a child who is merely "near-normal" can be joyful, even while difficult. This is no small feat, as Methodists proceed through the decades toward prenatal testing and a 90 percent Down syndrome termination rate. A church capable of turning over its Marshall Plan identity by the prodding invitation of members in the two-thirds world may also be capable of reconfiguring the home to make way for the Christ child as she arrives, as the article puts it, "not . . . completely formed."[99] This tracing of the Methodist church is arguably not as thick and resilient as the one marching forward on the feet of well-planned and well-tested little children, but it is there nonetheless.

The fragile work of tracing a different church from point to point may take a cue also from another very early article in *Together,* one that also ran in anticipation of a Christmas different from that of the carefully crafted Christmas photo in home or congregation. In "Tenement Manger: A True Story," author William F. McDermott narrates a Christmas Eve "in the slums of Chicago."[100] Like the essays on cleft palate, the article teeters on the brink of ren-

---

97. "Rosemary Goes to the Hospital," *Together,* October 1956, pp. 19-21.

98. Charles Mussen, as told to Katherine J. Pitkin, "How Donald Learned to Say 'Okay,'" *Together,* October 1956, pp. 17-18.

99. "Rosemary Goes," p. 20.

100. William F. McDermott, "Tenement Manger: A True Story," *Together,* December 1956, pp. 11-12.

dering God's grace as itself a project to be performed by a strong, parental figure, here the American narrator. "Memories of festive days back in Bohemia and Poland and Italy kindled the minds of fathers and mothers as they sat in their shabby best and watched their children. The youngsters were thrilled. Their eager eyes were fixed on the curtained 'Stage Entrance.'"

Although the scene is hardly as majestic as the Advent scene at Hennepin Avenue Methodist Church, the story plays to a similar theatric impulse. "Costumes had all been adjusted, every detail was in readiness, and the first music of the Christmas program was about to be signaled." But the "little mission" wherein "great things had been planned" would receive unexpected, and unceremonial, joy by way of a hidden story occurring only in the background of the dominant narrative. One of the angels in the choir was missing, a child named Molly, who plays the role in this *Together* story of the Irish peasant: "A proud little thing she was, with the tilt of the head, the lilt of the voice, and the laughter in the eyes that bespoke the Irish blood within her." Later, after the Christmas Eve play was over and the congregation had sung (of course, it had to be) Phillips Brooks's "O Little Town of Bethlehem," the narrator and a makeshift Santa Claus moved through the neighborhood to distribute the "white gifts to the king" the congregants had reverently offered — "groceries, fruits, and meats for those even poorer and hungrier than their donors."[101]

Winding their way among the tenements, they came across Molly, who, as it turns out, had missed the play in order to help a neighbor give birth to a baby. The mother had two "youngsters" who were "huddled in bedraggled quilts spread on the floor" and a third, older child who had greeted the narrator at the door. The family had only half a loaf of bread and was, in sum, a vision of squalor. Yet McDermott narrates the event thus: "Then we realized we were in the presence of the greatest miracle of all — the miracle and mystery of creation. . . . A thought flashed through my mind — and I saw again a stable and a manger and a Child new-born. But this was not in Bethlehem of Judea on a starlit night, but in a midnight blizzard in an American tenement."

By one reading, by one possible connection of the dots, Molly is merely a bit actor, an Irish peasant girl (with "reddish-gold ringlets," no less) brought in from central casting to play a saint in the midst of the poverty at-

---

101. The author here refers to the "white gift" tradition, said to be the idea of an Episcopal minister's spouse in 1904, who adapted a legend from Cathay. In the adaptation, children bring gifts wrapped in simple white paper in order to designate the equally immeasurable, inherent worth of a child's gift, regardless of the contents inside the plain paper.

tending Catholic immigration in the slums of Chicago. But by another, she appears in this unhygienic scene as a witness, a girl who was willing to miss her time on stage in order to make time for a baby deemed by the dominant narratives of her time and place to have been, quite clearly, a mother's *mistake*. By this reading, McDermott's Molly is an invitation to exist in faith and risk right at the boundary between a mistress and her maid, right at the boundary of a miracle that upset everything. Through McDermott's narration, we learn that Molly grew up to greet him one spring, "a long time later," with an unexpected "Merry Christmas!" Her words to him, and thus to his readers, suggest a recalibration of Protestantism and a reformation of the germ-free home:

> "I'm an infant welfare nurse," she smiled. . . . "I didn't get a chance that night at the mission to speak my lines about 'the least of these,' but now I'm *doing* it instead!"[102]

### "The Idea of Progress"

> From the beginning [Methodism] has appealed to experience, and consequently it was not more at home in the eighteenth century than it is in the twentieth. By making experience the criterion of truth, instead of tradition, it has been able to keep pace with progress and to appropriate the best thought of the age without violation of its established principles. It does not look with disapproving or suspicious eye upon the effort of the historian to uncover the past or of the scientist to reveal the secrets of the natural world. The idea of progress is congenial to the Methodist mind.[103]

In *Taking Heaven by Storm: Methodism and the Rise of Popular Christianity in America,* John H. Wigger suggests that Methodism had early in its American manifestation begun "identifying with middling people on the make."[104] This allowed early Methodism to adapt to geographic and cultural context as needed to speak the gospel to disparate people. With a sense that each and every person was created with equally immeasurable worth and equally desperate need, early American Methodism was sufficiently nimble to reach across

---

102. McDermott, "Tenement Manger," p. 12, emphasis in original.

103. Rowe, *The Meaning of Methodism*, p. 225.

104. John H. Wigger, *Taking Heaven by Storm: Methodism and the Rise of Popular Christianity in America* (New York: Oxford University Press, 1998), p. 5.

geographic, racial, and class boundaries. Yet this capacity to morph to fit the varying American landscape also meant that Methodism had within it a tendency to adapt uncritically. By one reading, much of the established Protestant church "kept pace" with progress, to quote Rowe, even when that progress ran contrary to its core affirmation of created and baptized kinship. When "middling people on the make" came under cultural pressure to prove that they kept pace with progress, one means to do so was by leveraging their way upward, gaining traction off someone else's downfall. In the midst of this, many culturally adapted Protestants may have had few theological resources from their rather elastic theological tradition with which to push back. As the "idea of progress" in the United States became intertwined with carefully marketed science, using a didactic of class aspiration and shame, Methodists, like other mainline Protestants "on the make," may have found themselves eager to register their approval of and trust in the ability of science to make a better world.

One way to read the shift from chapter 1 to chapter 2, from "Holy Hygiene" to "The Corporate Breast," is as a shift from the domestic life lived on Sunday to the domestic life lived on Monday through Saturday. The "experience" that was to be "the criterion of truth" for many mainline Protestant women in the last century was experience as held up for examination according to the domestic magazines on which *Together* was modeled. In a 1957 *Together* article entitled "The Luxury of Being 50," Phyllis W. Heald suggests that there was in much of mainline Protestant "experience" a sense of class competition and neighborly scrutiny — the "haunting need of keeping up with the Joneses."[105] Heald homes in on family life with children as particularly fraught; the child-rearing years were considered the "'I must worry' stage." Yet by this postwar period, the worry was not primarily about child health. It was about appearances. The possibility that "the boss's wife" would call when "her house wasn't in order" was no small matter for an aspiring woman who was, in John Wigger's words, "on the make." Striking in Heald's piece is her sense that turning fifty brought her a freedom from "customs or restrictions" that had once bound her. Only the departure of children from her home allowed her to proclaim, "Now we are free!" A "happy feeling of complete, continued freedom" and a sense that "God is close and real" come after her work of scrutinized mothering is done.

By the first decades of the twentieth century, it was clear in consumer culture that the means for securing one's family against criticism were through products. "Better living" was to come "through chemistry," and the

---

105. Phyllis W. Heald, "The Luxury of Being 50," *Together*, July 1957, pp. 31-32.

sorts of Christians who were congenial to progress were the sorts of Christians modeled in the magazines that advertised DuPont. In chapter 2 we will consider the narration of scientific progress and maternal responsibility as it came to bear on a basic task of motherhood — deciding how to feed one's child. As those who were to raise the little ones on whom the future of the race rested, mainline Protestant mothers were to turn over their children to the scientists intent on forging a "century of progress."

## 2 The Corporate Breast

### "Scientific Motherhood"
### during the Century of Progress

*Be thou my Vision, O Lord of my heart;*
*Naught be all else to me, save that thou art;*
*Thou my best thought, by day or by night,*
*Waking or sleeping, thy presence my light.*

*Be thou my Wisdom, and thou my true Word;*
*I ever with thee and thou with me, Lord;*
*Thou my great Father, and I thy true son,*
*Thou in me dwelling, and I with thee one.*

*Riches I heed not, nor man's empty praise;*
*Thou mine inheritance, now and always;*
*Thou and thou only, first in my heart,*
*High King of heaven, my treasure thou art.*

*High King of heaven, my victory won,*
*May I reach heaven's joys, O bright heaven's Sun!*
*Heart of my own heart, whatever befall,*
*Still be my Vision, O Ruler of all. Amen.*

Translated by Mary Byrne, 1905; versified by Eleanor Hull, 1912

**Figure 2.1.** *Journal of the American Medical Association (JAMA)* **advertisement, 1933**

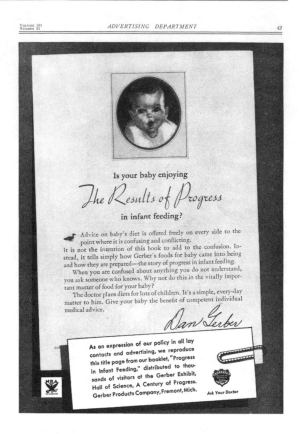

*The reproduction of the species — their nurture in the womb, and their support and culture during infancy and childhood — is the grand prerogative of woman. It is a noble and a holy office, to which she is appointed of God; and the duty is both pure and sacred.*[1]

This quotation is from Dr. Cook's handbook for women in the second half of the nineteenth century. The brochure in figure 2.1 features Dan Gerber's advice to mothers in 1933. The growing circle of expert authority, from a physician in 1866 to someone such as Mr. Gerber in 1933, is worth noting. In less than a century the authority of the physician, newly established,

---

1. William H. Cook, *Woman's Handbook of Health: A Guide for the Wife, Mother, and Nurse,* 5th ed. (Cincinnati: W. H. Cook, 1866).

had spread to those purveyors of progress who might invoke his advice. The good mother was to pay attention. To borrow a phrase from Dr. Cook's handbook, the "reproduction of the species" at the beginning of the twentieth century was a tricky business, even for women whose mothers were the relatively privileged, Protestant, native-born mothers to whom Dr. Cook wrote his lofty words about maternal nobility and holiness in 1866.[2] The foundation of "pure" and "sacred" reproduction was shifting from local, familial wisdom to the realm of *Hygeia* (1923-1949), the consumer magazine published by the American Medical Association and named after the Greek goddess of good health.

The title page of the brochure addressed to modern-minded mothers of 1933 featured a letter, signed by Dan Gerber, that asked, "Is your baby enjoying The Results of Progress in infant feeding?" Making the most of the changing ground of parental authority, Mr. Gerber began his letter with well-worded sympathy: "Advice on baby's diet is offered freely on every side to the point where it is confusing and conflicting." The letter continued: "When you are confused about anything you do not understand, you ask someone who knows. Why not do this in the vitally important matter of food for your baby?" And who better to clarify the "confusing and conflicting" information than the pediatrician? "The doctor plans diets for lots of children. It's a simple, every-day matter to him. Give your baby the benefit of competent individual medical advice." In a way characteristic of the age, Dan Gerber mapped the road out of maternal confusion into the doctor's office, for that was the location of "someone who knows."

The shared "advice" between physician and corporation flowed both ways and out into the reading, traveling public, through print advertising as well as spectacles such as state and national fairs. Not incidentally, the "someone who knows" was increasingly privy to the particular version of maternal knowledge advanced by Gerber, Mellin's, and Nestlé's, by way of articles and advertisements aimed at medical professionals. The message was reinforced to mothers through advertisements in *Hygeia,* a periodical touted by experts in women's and parenting magazines as a way to "keep your child well": "Every statement in the articles is passed upon by high medical authority. You can depend implicitly on *Hygeia.*"[3] Medical authority and expertise were also promulgated heavily at statewide and even national events to promote prog-

2. Cook, *Woman's Handbook of Health,* p. 229, referenced in Rima D. Apple, *Mothers and Medicine: A Social History of Infant Feeding, 1890-1950* (Madison: University of Wisconsin Press, 1987), p. 191.

3. American Medical Association, 1929, in *Parents',* January 1929.

ress. According to the note added to the reproduction of the Gerber letter in *JAMA*, the brochure *Progress in Infant Feeding* was handed out to "thousands of visitors" at Gerber's exhibit in the Hall of Science at the 1933 Century of Progress Exposition in Chicago. The exposition itself was a momentous effort to transform what many progressive Northeasterners thought was a provincial, bucolic Midwest into the epitome of industrial and scientific progress. The much-heralded (and variously worded) theme was "Science Finds — Genius Invents — Industry Applies — Man Conforms [or Adapts]."

Seven decades and several generations later, in 2003, a mother Googling "ADHD" would have found at the top of the list an advertisement inviting her to visit www.welcometoordinary.com. At the site she would have seen a green road sign with large white lettering: "*Welcome to* ORDINARY." This sign popped up throughout Lilly Pharmaceutical's first run of advertisements for Strattera, indicating the route toward (quoting a 2003 brochure) "An uneventful trip in the car. A relaxing family dinner. A project started and completed." Through Strattera, a mother might discover "an ordinary day." The accompanying photograph features an elfish, blue-eyed boy smiling over his spaghetti (fig. 2.2). Little sister, dressed in baby-doll pink, sips pink soda pop through a straw. Father's gaze is clearly focused on the children, his arm resting comfortably on the seat back behind the boy. No traces of spaghetti or soda pop stain faces or clothing. According to the text below the picture, the family was at the table for an entire hour. This pristine domestic "ordinary" is, according to the brochure, "A place that most people take for granted."

One way to consider critically the norms of parenting during the century of progress is through particular, mainstream practices and products, and looking at the supposed "ordinary" anew, as if we were strangers from a far-off land. Mention the connection between infant formula and medical ethics, and most people immediately think of the results of marketing formula to mothers in the two-thirds world, precipitating a worldwide boycott of products from Nestlé. Such a pattern of patently immoral corporate behavior warrants ongoing engagement, but the implications of scientifically produced infant nourishment are domestic as well as international, subtle as well as overt. In this chapter we will remain within the domestic scene, considering more critically the American marketing of childhood progress through corporately produced infant food by studying that marketing in its broader, cultural context. We will move out from the central hub of infant formula to consider various spokes of the wheel, from potty training to the Century of Progress Exposition to Playtex girdles and Seven-Up.

At the close of the chapter, I will attempt to make this particularly complicated wheel hit the ground, so to speak, by considering the mainstream market-

**Figure 2.2. "Welcome to Ordinary." Image from Eli Lilly, 2003**

ing of medications for behavioral disorder in the United States. I did not pick attention–deficit/hyperactivity disorder (ADHD) and its treatment at random, but rather because of my suspicions about the medicalization of childhood and my fear of new, scientifically potent designations of childhood "deviance."

But the conclusion could have gone elsewhere — to the marketing of Baby Einstein products and their kin to promote infant genius, or to the likelihood that formula companies will eventually market explicitly "value added" formula that is, once again, hailed as superior to mother's milk for producing a maximally healthy and intelligent baby. On the other side of the road, I could have addressed in the conclusion some of the problematic ways that La Leche League (the international mother-led effort to support breast feeding) has drawn on the rhetoric of *discriminating* motherhood — playing subtly on fears of being associated with "bad mothers" by producing a subpar infant. While I have found La Leche League to be invaluable in my life as a mother who breast-fed both of my daughters (one adopted and one by birth) into toddlerhood, I wince to remember one League leader advising a group of new mothers: "Babies who drink formula just *smell* different. They are just not as *sweet* as breast-fed babies." These words soured in my mind when I gratefully used formula to supplement feeding my adopted daughter.

I would thus invite the reader to take the wheel of the chapter, and to take it on different roads, to continue the metaphor, but I will in the chapter's conclusion ask in particular: How did the pharmaceutical summons "Welcome to Ordinary" make its way into American culture? How did many American mothers come to the point of trusting Lilly, Shire, and others to provide a "much-needed relaxing family dinner"? Put a bit differently, how did Mr. Lilly become the modern-day Mr. Gerber? What sorts of cultural changes and pressures have coincided with the diagnosis of hyperactivity as a disorder and the assumed recourse to pharmaceuticals as a cure?

This is not to say there are not children who visibly benefit from ADHD medications, whose behavior, on medication, is more predictable, regular, and ordered. Conversation after conversation with parents of children designated as ADHD has convinced me that the medicine does, in a tangible way, help some parents see the possibility of getting through each day. But even conceding the efficacy of pediatric pharmaceuticals, it seems appropriate to back up and ask about the context in which so many parents find recourse, often reluctant and hard-pressed recourse, in a solution wrought from highly potent and little-understood drugs brought to them by a multibillion-dollar industry. Gratitude for the apparent efficacy of a product need not silence criticism. The emergence of ADHD as a highly lucrative pediatric disorder can be questioned in many ways. I will offer only one, I believe plausible, narration by way of another development in parental progress — the marketing of scientifically approved infant feeding and care during the century of progress.

## "Scientific Motherhood"

### "Ask — Your Doctor — Your Grocer — Your Husband"

The shift to medical science as the conduit of reliable parental advice was complete by 1936. A mother needed to "ask" the appropriate experts before deciding what to feed her baby. Similar to the condescending tone of the Gerber advertisement, a Heinz strained foods ad, which ran in the *New York Herald Tribune* in 1936, assumed a mother's befuddlement (fig. 2.3). The photographs depict her travel from doctor's office to grocery store to living room

Figure 2.3. Heinz strained foods advertisement. *New York Herald Tribune*, 1936

to "make a poll of all the authorities [she] know[s]." The images do not show her calling on her mother, her aunt, her matronly neighbor, or even a local nurse. Instead, she puts on her fashionable hat and suit to consult three smiling, suited men — her doctor, her grocer, and her husband. Only then will she be able to determine "the best kind of strained food for baby."

The advertisement brings together responsible maternity with medical authority and consumerism, featuring not only doctor and white-coated grocer but also "the Seal of Acceptance of the American Medical Association" and an invitation to learn more about Heinz products through the "Heinz Magazine of the Air" — a regularly scheduled radio show that dispensed advice for the home and indeed "everything of interest to women." Her doctor, she is assured, will verify that the foods are "safe," and her grocer's "long personal experience" qualifies him to weigh in on the matter. Thus, what might have been the authenticating claim of grandmother two generations prior — "long personal experience" — has transferred to the local grocer. The cherubic, blond infant in his high chair looms over the proceedings, his happiness apparently the goal of the process.[4]

In *Mothers and Medicine: A Social History of Infant Feeding, 1890-1950*, Rima Apple explains that from 1890 to 1940 many American mothers moved from the default mode of breast feeding to bottle feeding under the supervision of a medical doctor.

> Discoveries in bacteriology, physiology, and nutrition effected a new understanding of infants' diets. Coupled with analyses of high infant death rates that often demonstrated the inadequacy of mother's milk, these scientific advances suggested how to protect children's lives through new "scientific" modes of infant feeding. These, in turn, were used to establish and maintain successful business enterprises — both manufacturing concerns and medical practices. Employment of these new methods also enhanced the prestige of their users by denoting such medical practitioners as "scientific" and such mothers as "modern."[5]

The enhanced prestige attending medical science and those who could afford its goods remained a palpable part of the formula industry, but the movement toward a perfected, artificial infant food had its roots in a suspicion of default motherhood. Apple traces several factors at play as the turn to infant food began, one being a heightened sense of maternal responsibility, infant fragility, and domestic risk. With the late-nineteenth-century elevation of maternity came the fear that most mothers were not up to the task. With the discovery of bacteria came the possibility that other forms of menace could be lurking, hidden, as well. Mothers represented the apex of social hope — and thus also the locus of social peril. They were simultaneously potent and incompetent, the font of wisdom and uninformed. They needed a team of experts to equip them for their assigned work of shaping the social body by way of shaping each tiny, individual body. And fundamental to that shaping was the matter of infant feeding. For reasons symbolic as well as scientific, "medical writers and research-oriented physicians attracted to pediatric studies focused much of their attention on the problem of infant feeding and infant foods."[6]

Periodicals such as *Good Housekeeping* and *Ladies' Home Journal* had been advocates for what Apple calls "scientific motherhood" through newly defined expert advice since the turn of the century. But by 1920, women's magazines had changed their perspective on infant feeding, moving from ar-

---

4. I use the male pronoun for the infant because the advertisement itself does.
5. Apple, *Mothers and Medicine*, p. 16.
6. Apple, *Mothers and Medicine*, p. 6.

ticles about milk supply to articles about medically regulated formula.[7] Advertising targets shifted from physician to mother in the 1940s and 1950s, as formula companies increasingly sought to engender among mothers themselves a trust in scientific technology for the sustenance of their children. The methods by which advertisements encouraged such reliance on formula became more complicated during these decades, as maternal appearance came quite obviously into play. In *Ladies' Home Journal* during the early 1950s, formula advertisements appeared alongside those for girdles and bras that would enable a mother to return to her prematernal, "girlish" figure. In both subtle and overt ways, the advertisements from 1950 on also encouraged women to see formula as a means for enjoying a more active life outside the home. By the 1960s and 1970s, the message had shifted explicitly toward the working mom, encouraging women to pursue careers apart from the toils of nursing; the formula advertisements appeared alongside those touting preschool toys that required little if any parental guidance or contact.

The historical developments in formula feeding present a helpful focal point for interpreting the multiple changes that have led to the prevalence of pediatric psychopharmaceuticals. I suspect that marketed, scientifically regulated infant foods emerged as a crucial part of a larger cultural turn toward medical-technological answers to parental questions and that the particular questions posed by parents were influenced by the marketing of those answers. The suggestion that a mother needed to "ask" the (most often male) experts about the care and feeding of her baby made way for the allure of corporately scientific products: *scientific* sense emerged as the *choicest* common sense on which to draw when dealing with whatever parental problem arose, from infant growth to maternal convenience to, eventually, perceived economic necessity, as middle-class mothers began to stay in the workplace even during the nursing years. Our examination of this particular application of nutritional science may open us to questions of both parental reliance on technology and the methodical effort to create a culture wherein the pervasive use of products such as infant formula makes sense.

### *"The Dangerous Business of Being a Baby"*

By the end of the nineteenth century the maternal breast had come to signify not only the security of the hearth but also the threat of an unregulated, irregu-

---

7. For the shift to scientific motherhood, see in particular Apple, *Mothers and Medicine*, chapter 6, "The Noblest Profession," pp. 97-113; for the shift to bottle feeding in particular, see chapter 7, "The Doctor Should Decide," pp. 114-32.

**Figure 2.4. Nestlé's Food advertisement.** *Ladies' Home Journal*, **March 1914**

lar home. The Nestlé's Food advertisement in figure 2.4 ran in *Ladies' Home Journal* in 1914, reminding readers of "the dangerous business of being a baby." Repeating the ominous statistic that one out of every six babies born in the previous year had succumbed, Nestlé's implicitly offered its product as a preventative to infant mortality. The infant mortality rate did plummet from 1915 to 1997, and one of the reasons was the regulated homogenization of cows' milk.[8]

But the causes of infant mortality were complex. The women to whom *Ladies' Home Journal* appealed, and at whom Nestlé's aimed its message, were already in a different health sector than women tending families in poverty-stricken urban areas. The dangers of being a baby were significant when viewed against the infant mortality rate today, but as is the case even today, the dangers were quite unequally distributed.

Still, the fear of losing a child in the first year, and the fear of not doing everything possible to better that child's chances, was very real even for the unquestionably advantaged readers privy to the ad. This would prove a selling point for Nestlé's and many other companies in the infant-feeding business. The appeal ostensibly focused on "dirty dairies" and "sick cows," but the im-

### The Dangerous Business of Being a Baby

DANGEROUS indeed when we see the tiny little bodies menaced by dirty dairies, by sick cows, by ignorance, by disease; and dangerous indeed when we know that one baby out of six—last year—died.

But the danger grows less—Doctors and Scientists have learned much about how to keep our babies; and now the mothers of the nation have joined in the movement for "Better Babies."

"Better Babies" means, first, healthier mothers; second, mothers who know.

It means mothers who know that their Babies' food is of most importance. Who know of the dangers for little babies in cow's milk. Who know that the Government Inspectors found only eight Clean Dairies in every hundred, and that in one State alone—under strict laws—there are 200,000 infected cows. Who know that even when cow's milk is pure it is too heavy in curd for little babies. All milk contains curds. But nature provided a light, fleecy curd for babies, and never intended the heavy, tough curd of cow's milk for such delicate little stomachs.

# Nestlé's Food

is nearer to mother's milk than any other diet you can give your baby. In NESTLÉ'S the curd of the milk is rendered soft and fleecy as in mother's milk. The best cow's milk is the basis of NESTLÉ'S FOOD—the milk from clean, healthy cows, in Sanitary Dairies, that are carefully inspected. Then to it are added other food elements your baby needs, and that cow's milk does not contain.

Send the Coupon for a free trial package of twelve feedings and our 72 page Book for Mothers.

NESTLÉ FOOD COMPANY,
77 Chambers Street, New York
    Please send me, FREE, your book and trial package.

*Name*

*Address*

---

8. The city of Chicago had been the first to pass a compulsory pasteurization law, in 1908. Centers for Disease Control and Prevention, "Achievements in Public Health, 1900-1999: Healthier Mothers and Babies," *Morbidity and Mortality Weekly*, October 1, 1999, pp. 849-58. Accessed 2004: www.cdc.gov.

plication carried also into the warning of maternal "ignorance." The advertisement warned that the "tiny little bodies" were "menaced," and that mothers were rightly joining "the movement for 'Better Babies.'" Part of this movement involved being among the "mothers who know," and Nestlé's wanted its readers to know that its food came only from "clean, healthy cows, in Sanitary Dairies." The ad also offered a free trial package of twelve feedings. Within ten years, most mothers from the class that had the leisure and interest to subscribe to women's magazines were turning to the scientifically monitored corporate breast.

As Apple narrates the story, the key figure in the movement toward the scientific approach was Thomas Morgan Rotch (1849-1914), a faculty member at Harvard Medical Center and the first American pediatrician to be named to a full professorship in that discipline.[9] Rotch's concern about infant feeding was twofold. (1) He was suspicious of entrepreneurs in the infant-feeding business; "non-medical capitalists" were hardly qualified to offer their "proprietary foods" for the care of infants.[10] (2) Yet neither were mothers themselves a truly reliable source of sustenance.

As Rotch and others measured the composition of mother's milk, they discovered that lactation varied widely over time and among individuals. There seemed to be so much that could go wrong in such an unregulated environment. Apple summarizes the concern: "A mother's milk could be totally unfit for her infant if, for example, the woman did not nurse at regular intervals, or if her temperament was 'undisciplined,' or if she was not 'willing to regulate her diet, her exercise, and her sleep according to the rule which [would] best fit her for her task.' Medical intervention in infant feeding meant, first of all, the responsibility to explain to a mother how to *fulfill her nursing duty by regulating her life.*"[11] What had been thought to come naturally for the vast majority of new mothers now came under scrutiny. Medical scientists, newly equipped to diagnose myriad inadequacies with one's breast feeding, were the new source of expertise in solving them.

In a previous generation the first recourse of mothers with financial means who could not (or did not wish to) breast-feed had been to enlist the aid of a wet nurse. Yet if the moral and physical consistency of mothers in

9. Apple, *Mothers and Medicine*, p. 24; Harry Bloch, "Thomas Morgan Rotch (1849-1914), America's First Full Professor of Pediatrics: His Contribution to the Emergence of Pediatrics as a Specialty," *Pediatrics* 50 (July 1972): 112-17.

10. Apple, *Mothers and Medicine*, p. 24.

11. Apple, *Mothers and Medicine*, p. 25, emphasis added. Apple here is quoting Rotch, "The General Principles Underlying All Good Methods of Infant Feeding," *Boston Medical and Surgical Journal* 129 (1893): 505.

general was now suspect, this suspicion was magnified tenfold for the class of women usually employed as wet nurses. As Janet Golden explains in *A Social History of Wet Nursing in America,* while physicians serving the upper classes, and the women themselves, assumed the need for infant nurses and (often) wet nurses, the overall sense by the turn of the century was that women from the immigrant classes were unsuitable to suckle the infants of superior, native-born stock.[12] "Beyond the understandable concerns about diet, drink, and drugs that troubled doctors lay murky questions regarding the influence of passion, heredity, and character on milk."[13] The product of the medical laboratory, created under careful scientific observation, was undoubtedly preferable, even "sublime" (to quote one doctor), when compared with the product of the wet nurse.[14] It was perhaps merely a matter of time before physicians and the mothers they most often served decided that the bodies of even upper-class women were sufficiently irregular and unreliable as to warrant displacement by the corporate breast. After all, to quote again another medical advocate of the bottle, "it is easier to control cows than women."[15]

### "Physicians' Babies Are Better Babies"

Predictably, the same moral passion for quantification and regularity came to bear on the babies themselves. Eavesdrop someday on mothers of infants and toddlers at the children's museum in an American city and you will likely hear percentages: "He's in the top fifth percentile." "She's in the lowest tenth percentile." "She has always been right around the fiftieth percentile for her age." Someone not accustomed to this ritual might think parents were bragging about or confessing their child's proficiency or deficiency, but these mothers are explaining their children's size in comparison to their peers — a

12. Janet Golden, *A Social History of Wet Nursing in America* (Cambridge: Cambridge University Press, 1996). Golden quotes Dr. I. N. Love, influential physician and vice president of the American Medical Association, who wrote in the *Archives of Pediatrics* that it was "better by far for [an infant] to have been wafted to the angels than for our first-born to have breathed the same air for a day with the moral monster in the shape of a wet nurse" (Love, "The Problem of Infant Feeding — Intestinal Diseases of Children and Cholera Infantum," *Archives of Pediatrics* 6 [1889]: 585, quoted in Golden, p. 154).

13. Golden, *Social History,* p. 151.

14. C. Cleveland, "The Wet-Nurse vs. the Bottle," *Archives of Pediatrics* 1 (1884): 346, quoted in Apple, *Mothers and Medicine,* p. 7.

15. Edward F. Brush, "How to Produce Milk for Infant Feeding," *JAMA* 43 (1904): 1385, quoted in Apple, *Mothers and Medicine,* p. 56.

percentile established through decades of data points garnered from requests of "sit him on the scale, please" and "let's just measure her little head now." This practice of plotting weight and height and cranial circumference against an average — against a norm established as ordinary — began as routine medical care during the same years that saw the meteoric rise in the use of infant formula.

Only one generation after Dr. Rotch vowed to stem the tide of "nonmedical capitalists" entering the world of infant feeding, local pediatricians, medical scientists, and formula entrepreneurs were cooperating to sell mothers products that ostensibly required such monitoring — and, not incidentally, promised a considerable profit for industry and medicine. While women were encouraged to invest in devices like the Detecto-Lette baby scales to "watch" their babies' weight,[16] it was to pediatricians that they were to look for expert charting and calculation of baby's feeding. Indeed, the symbiotic circle of medicine and industry was effectively closed by companies like Mellin's and Mead Johnson, which provided written instructions for mixing and administering their products only to doctors. This practice kept the mother out of the loop, but it also heightened her sense that she was procuring for her little one the best possible food for his progress. A 1930 Mead Johnson advertisement ran with a large-print heading in all caps, "Physicians' Babies Are Better Babies." Two mothers, wearing fashionable hats and floral dresses, smile as chubby toddlers sit amiably on scales. The text put the matter succinctly: "Regular visits to the doctor's office where the baby is carefully examined, measured, weighed and recorded, and the individual formula specially prescribed, are far more satisfactory than the mother's attempting to feed her baby without professional advice. Mead Johnson and Company have preached and supported for many years the fundamental principle that 'Physicians' Babies are Better Babies.'"[17]

The "better" could be registered on a scale — and baby became a quantifiable gauge of maternal and medical success. A 1930 Dextri-Maltose advertisement put this point in visual terms (fig. 2.5). Rats with diets rich in the Dextri-Maltose supplement vitamin B grew impressively, moving the little arrow on the scale in clockwise jumps, while rats with diets deficient in the supplement slowly registered their devolution counterclockwise. The text reinforces the idea that the product is an advance — the result of scientific ingenuity applied to the age-old problem of human nourishment: "NEW to the profession generally" yet "OLD in laboratory background"; proved

16. *Parents'*, March 1929, p. 61.
17. The ad ran in *JAMA*, September 1930.

**Figure 2.5. Dextri-Maltose advertisement. *JAMA*, 1930**

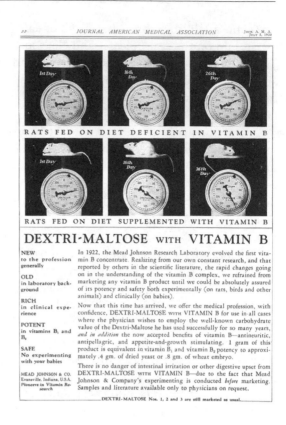

"RICH in clinical experience" and "POTENT in vitamins B1 and B2." It is also "SAFE — No experimenting with your babies." These sorts of advertisements sent a message contrary to the tacit "breast milk is best under the best of all possible circumstances" message. The climate was such that a mother "in the know" knew to turn to those who truly knew — to the medical scientists who could produce a fatter rat, and a fatter baby.

This Mellin's Food Company advertisement (fig. 2.6) allowed a picture to speak volumes over the text: "We do not claim that Mellin's Food and milk is better than mother's milk, but we do claim, emphatically, that, if an artificial food must be used, Mellin's Food is the best artificial food in the world for babies." The Ashley twins, Dorothy and Donald, sit together on the bed — Donald, "raised on Mellin's Food," seeming on a different scale altogether than Dorothy, "nursed at the breast." Indeed, Donald seems on a scale much more like the rat fed with Dextri-Maltose's vitamin B.

The production of "better babies" was not merely a matter of personal

Figure 2.6. Mellin's Food Company advertisement. *Good Housekeeping*, 1907

pride; it was a matter of responsibility, for a good mother was the conduit for good citizenry. The "grand prerogative of woman" (again to quote Dr. Cook's 1860s summons to maternity) involved her ability to produce a child who would not just subsist but would also thrive and discernibly contribute to the good of future society. A later run of the Mead Johnson "better babies" advertisement in the straight-to-the-consumer magazine *Hygeia* (1938) reminded mothers themselves: "The mother who takes full advantage of her physician's command of these resources improves her child's immediate as well as future health and at the same time contributes her share toward the improvement of the race."[18]

The message of improving the race through good motherhood was in-

18. Mead Johnson, 1938, in *Hygeia* 16 (1938): 1057, reproduced in Apple, *Mothers and Medicine*, p. 129.

termingled, even in these early years, with messages of maternal convenience. During the 1920s, images encouraged mothers to "take baby and go!" (fig. 2.7). Canned Pet Milk would allow the modern mother to don the fashionable attire of her age and take baby (and attending nurse) on her adventures. "Whether you go by trail or train, the bottles packed in the bags will be ready for every feeding of the day." Pulling her infant up by the "scruff" of its little jacket, the mother in the advertisement could be assured that the milk was "*more* than pasteurized," being also "*sterilized* — scientifically clean." She need not sacrifice mobility, convenience, or scientifically verified purity in the care of her baby. The class cues of the advertisement are overt, with the promise of traveling itself a relatively elite (or at least aspiring) appeal, and the presence of the uniformed nursemaid solidifying the interpretation. A fashionable woman, on the go, would find Pet Milk the natural choice.

This quite transparent message of convenience and privilege would not return full force until the 1960s, and the tension between the 1920s message of "take baby and go!" and the duty of selflessly focused motherhood is apparent in a Mead Johnson "Types of Mothers" advertisement from 1930. Taken together, the advertisements reflect a shift nationally, even among the flapper class, from mobile whimsy to financial difficulty by 1929. "Types of Mothers and Their Infant-Feeding Problems" was again focused on physicians themselves, running in *JAMA*. With the physician centered on the page, stethoscope in hand, his silhouette resituates the supposed criteria for judging infant food — medical expertise. Still the expert, he also serves as a key witness in Mead Johnson's defense to the readers of *JAMA*. The writers seem intent on reassuring doctors that the typical "business-going mother" (apparently "No. 1" among mothers with "infant-feeding problems") is not using their product frivolously but is instead turning to formula only after "the economic shoe is pinching pretty tight." The physician takes her case study and proclaims her appeal "more excusable" for its necessity.

The message of the advertisements is mixed, reflecting the convoluted messages middle-to-upper-class women (i.e., those who could afford ladies' magazines and a pediatrician) were receiving at the time. The "business-going mother" is dressed in flapper cap and ruffles, with heels. Her clothing does not signal a mother on the verge of economic necessity, nor is she obviously matronly by the standards of the decade. Yet the text reassures physicians that their trusted colleague at the center of the scene has judged her case "excusable." "Of course, you know, Mrs. Rush, that breast milk is best for your baby. In every way, it is far ahead of the best formula. It is free from bacteria and dirt, it never sours, it is always correct in temperature, and quicker as well as cheaper than bottles. I haven't much respect for the mother who won't

Figure 2.7. Pet Milk advertisement. *Saturday Evening Post*, May 24, 1924

nurse her baby." This enumeration of the benefits of breast milk is clear, and the writers have touched all the high points of concern for what Apple calls "scientific motherhood." Breast milk is, according to the 1930 text, clean, reliable, cheap, and eminently respectable.

Yet in 1931, a *JAMA* editorial weighed the various considerations and ruled in conciliatory favor of artificial feeding. The editorial noted that "breast feeding has become irksome if not actually difficult for many mothers of the present generation," concluding with "cheer" that "artificial feeding can be made far more safe and satisfactory than seemed to be the case in former times."[19]

With the mother's fashionable dress and the centrality of the validating physician, the Mead Johnson advertisement subtly undermined its almost ex-

19. See "Breast-Fed and Bottle-Fed Babies," *JAMA* 96 (April 11, 1931): 1231.

haustive list of the benefits of breast feeding. Running underneath the company logo was text that overtly reinforced the endorsement of formula — in an age eager to be back on the road toward progress, readers were reminded that Mead Johnson and Company were "pioneers in vitamin research," and they were further encouraged to note that "Dextri-Maltose with Vitamin B is now also available for appetite-and-growth-stimulating properties." While the ostensible message of the advertisement was about working mothers, even the mother whose household shoes were not pinching too tightly might be encouraged to consider the benefits of Dextri-Maltose.

An advertisement from 1935 (fig. 2.8) assured the doctor that "Gerber advertises . . . so that mothers will cooperate with you," but the authority of the physician (again, front and center) simultaneously reinforced the impression that medical expertise and corporately produced infant foods went ineluctably hand in hand. As Gerber maintained that "our advertising has always emphasized the importance of regular medical supervision of a baby's feeding schedule," they also recommended their direct-to-consumer booklets *Mealtime Psychology* and *Baby's Book* for the doctor's approval. If he approved, Gerber would send "as many copies as you require for free distribution." For women who were privy to the myriad of messages regarding their likely inadequacy as milk producers, the appeal was strong to partake of products that had been tried by scientists, recommended by physicians, and proven true by modern mothers.

Mothers were introduced to the products of infant feeding in the physician's office, through conversation with other mothers, and through advertising in women's magazines, which continued even while formula companies reassured physicians that they advertised only for maternal compliance. To better understand the cultural context of the turn to safety and regularity through infant formula we consider the framework within which infant-feeding advertisements appeared. From the beginning of publication, *Parents'* promised readers that every product advertised in the magazine had been scrutinized by "our experts"; using "the same high standards as in selecting our editorial material," the editors reportedly drew on the expertise of leaders "in the field of health, education, child welfare, nutrition, clothing, play equipment, the arts, etc." With this vow featured in a full-page announcement, mothers reading the magazine in 1929 were faced with a multitude of products to bring up baby, the importance of which were magnified by the articles themselves. Not only did the covers and articles carry the messages of technologically and scientifically enhanced parenting, but even the smaller advertisements and the fine print in the back of the magazine suggested to mothers the importance of domestic progress.

GERBER ADVERTISES.. *so that mothers will cooperate with you*

Figure 2.8. Gerber advertisement. *American Journal of Nursing*, 1935

When you tell a mother that it's time to start her baby on Gerber's Strained Vegetables, she's very apt to say: "Oh, yes, I know them."

Back of this ready acceptance lie years of groundwork carried on by Gerber. We haven't left to you the burden of explaining the nutritional value of strained vegetables in a baby's diet. Through consistent advertising we have been educating women on the special values of Gerber's Strained Foods and their advantages to her and her infant.

More than this, our advertising has always emphasized the importance of regular medical supervision of a baby's feeding schedule. Never has Gerber given feeding instructions or formulas.

We believe this policy of active cooperation with physicians has been helpful to them. In addition, we have planned our special literature to mothers to save the doctor's time, by covering routine details that would otherwise call for explanation. The cordial reception given by the medical profession to our booklet on "Mealtime Psychology" has prompted us this year to introduce a new booklet for mothers—"Baby's Book."

If you have not seen this book, we will be glad to send you a copy. In Gerber advertising it is offered mothers at 10c. If you find the booklet helpful, we will be glad to supply you with as many copies as you require for free distribution

•   •   •

*Strained* Vegetable Soup . . . Tomatoes . . . Carrots . . . Green Beans . . . Beets . . . Prunes . . . Spinach . . . Peas . . . 4½ oz. cans. Cereal . . . 4½ oz. and 10¼ oz. cans.

NOW AVAILABLE EVERYWHERE AT NOT TO EXCEED 10¢.

**Gerber's**
9 *Shaker - Cooked Strained Foods*

GERBER PRODUCTS COMPANY, Fremont, Michigan JN-9 (In Canada: *Grown and Packed by* Fine Foods of Canada, Ltd., Tecumseh, Ont.)
Please send sample copy of the new Gerber booklet, "Baby's Book."

Name
Street
City                                State

Page 67 of the February 1929 issue of *Parents'* is indicative. On the top left, Clapp's Approved Baby Soup and Strained Vegetables displays "The Badge of Health" for its foods "To Supplement the Milk Diet." The badge features a fair-haired, chubby-cheeked baby chewing on two fingers as if teething. Clapp's products are "Prescribed by over 5,000 Doctors — *Because* they are scientifically prepared under surgical standards of cleanliness and supply the elements needed for sound growth." Although Clapp's also mentioned cost and convenience, front and center was the promise that these foods were prepared under "surgical standards of cleanliness." Few mothers would confidently say that the average household kitchen could come close. The evidence of physician endorsement implied that physicians themselves did not expect most mothers to be capable of meeting the standards of superior hygiene.

On the upper right of the page is an advertisement for Pyrex Nursing

Bottles, with a drawing of a mother's hand holding the bottle over boiling water and then under a running tap. The text opens with the announcement: "DOCTORS URGE the use of Pyrex Nursing Bottles because of their absolute safety in boiling and in quick changes from hot to cold water. They say that regularity in feeding is so important that this boil-proof bottle is a real step toward higher infant health standards. Follow the advice doctors are giving all over the country. Do not run the risk of upsetting your baby's schedule by having his bottle break just as his feeding is ready." Anyone who has scrambled in the predawn light for a clean bottle will appreciate the *convenience* of unbreakable containers, but the message here is ratcheted up several notches above mere convenience. The emphasis on regularity is tied to an emphasis on "higher infant health standards." Pyrex nursing bottles contribute not only to maternal convenience but also to the good health of children "all over the country," through the "advice of doctors." The baby's schedule is so important that the "risk" of upset warrants the purchase. Mothers were reminded in subtle ways throughout the magazine that they were involved in a large, cooperative effort toward better regularity and health, for the sake of the nation. And regularity in input was linked to regularity in outflow.

Below the Clapp's Baby Soup advertisement is one that announces: "Mothers! If you have a child between the age of 6 months and 5 years get the youngster an Ah Mah Tiny Toilet Seat." Available in blue, green, orchid, and white, this "necessary" and "sanitary" tool could be procured "complete" for $1.50. The Cotton Buckle and Tag Company from Memphis, Tennessee, had entered the market related to infant bowel regularity — a market that warrants a narrative detour.

### The "Doo-Tee" of Regularity

At the same time that women were turning to infant formula to ensure regular weight gain, hygiene, and health, the medical wisdom of the time became obsessed with the responsibility to "fix a regular time for bowel action," to quote one American Social Hygiene Association poster for young women (1921). One interpretation of this focus involves the need for the home to become as efficient and controlled as were the newly routinized places of American industry.

In the middle of the *Parents'* magazine page we have just considered, sandwiched between the Clapp's "Badge of Health" soup, the Ah Mah Tiny Toilet Seat, and the Pyrex "boil-proof bottle," is the continuation of an article entitled "Mother: General Manager of the Plant." The author writes: "The business manager knows the economic resources of his plant, the fiscal reserves, the income and the outgo. So should the homemaker."[20] This idea that children were, in the words of a *Hygeia* advertisement, "little human machines under your care" implied also that they required a certain kind of managerial proficiency.[21] The sense that a mother's work required not just counting out cups of flour for the morning's biscuits but also measuring with accuracy an infant's milk was one of the selling points for formula. A woman could not be sure about the amount of milk going from breast to mouth, but she could measure the amount gone from a bottle and count the number of bites consumed from a bowl of cereal or a jar of strained spinach. Indeed, in many "mothers' registries" and baby books, mothers were encouraged to record these numbers on paper, day by day, week by week, to ensure that everything was moving along as planned. This focus on the minute, quantitative statistics of homemaking encompassed elimination as well.

One of the first articles in the January 1929 issue of *Parents'* — by "Norma Selbert, R.N., Department of Public Health, College of Medicine, Ohio State University" — was "Train Your Baby to Regularity."[22] Next to a photograph of a cheerful, naked baby, the italicized opening text reads, "Begin early and be systematic," for "That's the secret of success in helping your baby to establish good habits." The article elaborates in meticulous detail a system for training the bowels, which should be implemented "as soon as the umbilicus (the navel) has healed." Selbert opened the essay by emphasizing the long-term as well as immediate benefit of such regularity: "The care of the healthy baby should be systematized as early as possible. A system will make automatic and habitual useful actions which help to maintain health. A system will also guard against growing into irregularity, and ways which are undesirable. Moreover, it minimizes the work of the mother and assures time when she and the baby are free to enjoy rest or recreation."

It is worth noting some of the details. Selbert advised that "elimination will occur regularly if the infant is healthy, is fed regularly, and receives sufficient water between feedings." A mother was to note precisely when during the day her "regularly" fed baby was, well, *regular,* and then regularly hold the baby over a "pan or vessel" at that time, "day after day, to establish the habit of regularity." If the baby did not do his business in a timely manner, mothers were to "hasten evacuation" by inserting "a cone-shaped piece of softened castile soap" or "glycerine suppositories." Selbert warned: "Never permit an

20. Chase Going Woodhouse, "Mother: General Manager of the Plant," *Parents',* February 1929, p. 67.

21. *Parents',* January 1929, p. 39.

22. Norma Selbert, "Train Your Baby to Regularity," *Parents',* January 1929, pp. 17, 36.

exception to occur until the habit has been established. One break in the continuity will undo the effects of the routine." Moving on to urination, Selbert instructed mothers to wake their children "several times during the night" to establish the proper "self-control" and "discipline" so that they might join the ranks of the "many children of two years [who] go through the night without wetting the bed." The last line of the essay encouraged mothers not to give up: "Praise and rewards given when the child has practiced self-control strengthen his desire to establish right habits."

"Baby's Second Summer" was the title of another *Parents'* article, by Edwin F. Patton, "physician and surgeon to children," in 1929.[23] The featured photograph is also of a naked baby, and the headline reads, "The 'Fearful Second Summer' is a thing of the past but the second year is the time to establish right habits of eating, sleeping and elimination." The author notes that the "chief enemy is conquered," namely, the dangers of "bacterial contamination of milk" in a baby's summer after weaning, but there new issues must be addressed in the "development of the toddler." While babies were no longer afflicted with "diarrheal diseases" resulting from bacteria, their proper training in "elimination" was crucial for future patterns of behavior.

From 1929 on, advertisements about such training appeared in various forms throughout the magazine. The Little Toidey seat, from Juvenile Wood Products, Inc., in Fort Wayne, Indiana, drew the testimony of a mother whose "little lady [had] become rather careless" and who thus wanted to use the "Toidey Steps, which I think will *restore* her *pride* and *perfect behavior* again" (fig. 2.9). The advertisement features a drawing of an infant secured on the potty, as well as a toddler using the steps to wash her hands, climb into bed, and reach the potty. The highlighted text of the advertisement, when considered against the backdrop of the emphasis on order, hygiene, and maternal duty, reflects the pressurized sense of maternal accomplishment and failure: "the little lady grew careless" and *"Will restore her pride and perfect behavior again . . . !"* Reflected in "the little lady" is the sense of apparent urgency, for mother and for daughter, in training for "perfect behavior."

The apparent importance of the process is accentuated in the advertisement for a duck-headed potty seat. The Doo-Tee Infant Trainer would ensure "bathroom cleanliness" and "keep babies from handling themselves" (fig. 2.10). The vow that the contraption is "recommended by leading specialists" might seem a bit overblown if not for the many articles testifying to the importance of precision in such matters. In the Battle Creek Sanitarium Health Foods advertisement, parents are warned that "When food is too dainty *then*

23. Edwin F. Patton, "Baby's Second Summer," *Parents'*, July 1929, pp. 20, 54.

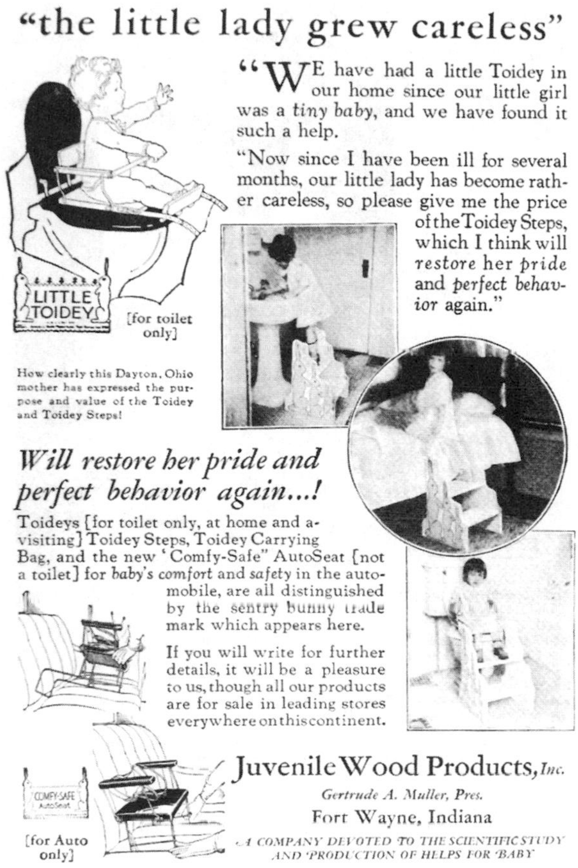

Figure 2.9. Juvenile Wood Products advertisement. *Parents'*, January 1929

*Nature rebels.*" The first paragraph reminds readers that "Growing children need bulk or roughage as much as their parents," and homes in on the problem: "Many childhood ailments may be traced to delayed elimination." But parents could rest assured, for "Nutrition experts at Battle Creek have worked for 50 years on this one problem." Repeating the offending characteristic, the ad explains that "Dainty, concentrated foods are responsible for more constipation than any other one thing."

On the other side of the spectrum, "223 Hospitals warn: 'Harsh toilet paper may cause serious trouble.'" While foods may have been overly dainty, one needed tissue paper for the toilet that was "Soft as old Linen" (the ScotTissue motto). Another Scott Paper Company advertisement in the same series warned of "15 painful troubles either directly caused or aggravated by inferior toilet paper." The photograph features a fashionable woman and her

**Figure 2.10. Doo-Tee Infant Trainer advertisement.** *Parents',* January 1929

## DOO-TEE INFANT TRAINER

*Lightens Work—Improves Results
Recommended by Leading
Specialists*

BATHROOM CLEANLINESS. Doo-Tee keeps the toilet seat and bathroom floor clean by directing all of the water into the bowl.

KEEPS BABIES FROM HANDLING THEM-SELVES. They sit close up to the duck's back and the duck's head occupies the attention of the child's hands—a point baby specialists especially approve.

PREVENTS FEAR. The head of the duck and the high back with the strap across the front holds children securely and prevents fear of falling.

BODY CLEANLINESS. Doo-Tee automatically separates children's legs uniformly apart, insuring body cleanliness.

If your department store or plumber cannot supply the Doo-Tee Infant Trainer, **$4.95** mail the coupon to the factory with

**DOO-TEE CORPORATION**
615 23rd Avenue        Oakland. Calif.

DOO-TEE CORP., 615 23rd Ave., Oakland, Cal.
Enclosed find $4.95 for which send one blue pink Doo-Tee Infant Trainer.

Name .................................................

Address ........ ..............................90

bob-haired child with a bespectacled, grandfatherly doctor who smiles with paternalistic understanding. "Your own family doctor will tell you that harsh, inferior toilet paper may produce inflammation or even serious infection," the advertisement counsels, and poses to mothers a question that appeared time and again, in advertisement after advertisement — for bottles, for tissue, for formula, for strained peas, for toilet seats: "Why take chances" when the product advertised met the "strictest medical requirements"?

### *"Is Your Child above Normal . . . ?"*

In her *Eugenic Design: Streamlining America in the 1930s,* Christina Cogdell traces the imagery of control, regularity, flow, and efficiency in the work of notable figures from the streamline school of design. In her research on advertisements for everything from kitchen appliances to women's dress gloves, Cogdell discerns a pattern: "I became convinced that in the decades surrounding the turn of the twentieth century, evolutionary thought in its numerous guises served as a common ideological foundation upon which modernists in almost every field constructed their work, arguments, and perceptions of the world and themselves, either consciously or unconsciously."[24] One way to read the role of "progress in infant feeding" and the "Doo-Tee" of infant regularity is by way of Cogdell's thesis, which provides a way to perceive what was at stake for mothers who read *Parents'* and other such magazines.

While scientists and social theorists disagreed on fundamental and finer points of evolutionary theories, middle-class parents received messages that were at times quite blunt. Many versions of the theory that hit the ground reflected an idea expressed openly in the full title of Charles Darwin's *On the Origin of Species by Means of Natural Selection; or, The Preservation of Favoured Races in the Struggle for Life.* The thinking that life was inherently a struggle, with resources adequate for only a select few, and that those who survived were within the "favoured races" of a species, put a particular spin on the task of parenting children. One very obvious growth from this vein of thought in the United States was the overtly, unapologetically eugenic movement, to which we will turn in the next chapter. But even the turn to pediatric science during this time bears the marks of a concern with progress, development, and establishing oneself and one's children as climbing up, rather than slipping down, the evolutionary track. The cultural diffusion of Darwinian thought was sufficient to reach into the basic assumptions of parenting among the aspiring classes.[25]

One key interpreter of Darwin in Germany, the United Kingdom, and the United States was Ernst Haeckel.[26] After reading Darwin's *Origin of Species,* Haeckel left his medical practice for full-time scientific research and teaching. In his 1868 *History of Creation* and his 1899 *Riddle of the Universe at the Close of the Nineteenth Century,* Haeckel sought to prove that the development of the human embryo involved a "recapitulation" of evolution. While

24. Christina Cogdell, *Eugenic Design: Streamlining America in the 1930s* (Philadelphia: University of Pennsylvania Press, 2004), p. 5.

25. Thanks to Sarah Johnson for the term "cultural diffusion."

26. A summation of Haeckel's serviceability for Nazi Germany appears at the University of California, Berkeley, Museum of Paleontology Web site. Accessed 2004: www.ucmp.berkeley.edu/history/haeckel. The referenced quotation reads: "The Nazi party, rather unfortunately, used not only Haeckel's quotes, but also Haeckel's justifications for racism, nationalism and social darwinism."

Haeckel's theory itself was considerably more complicated, the ways that it filtered through the popular German, British, and American imagination were predictable. (I will not dwell on whether these filtered popularizations were true to Haeckel's own thought.)

Recapitulation theory involved the basic idea that the individuals within superior races of people would move through the various stages of animal life, on toward the form of life characterized by intellectual, physical, and aesthetic excellence. Those within inferior races would remain at a stunted stage, a stage technically proper to their race. Individuals within superior races who remained at a prior, less developed stage were thought to be atavistic — temporal and racial anomalies that evinced the abiding presence within even superior peoples of their less developed past. This is the theory that influenced Dr. John Langdon Down in naming some of the individuals under his care as "mongoloid," supposing their features to be similar to the people of Mongolia — in his view, a stunted race. The continued use of the term "simian crease" for a hand trait, often associated with Down syndrome, thought to represent a prior, apelike stage of human evolution reflects the enduring influence of Haeckel in scientific parlance.

A particularly important pattern of thought Cogdell traces in her research of aesthetic design during the late 1920s and the 1930s is the idea that some discernible types of individuals or groups could be a "drag" on the efficient flow of a society. The explicitly eugenic tracts and displays of the time were clearly shaped by this concept, with Henry Fairfield Osborn, head of the American Museum of Natural History in New York from 1908 to 1933, calling for the social control of certain types of "parasitic" peoples: "In the United States alone it is widely recognized that there are millions of people who are acting as dragnets or sheet anchors on the progress of the ship of State."[27] Drawing on this statement as characteristic of the time, Cogdell suggests the common social and aesthetic sense of the era affirmed a particular understanding of the social body, one that saw control and regularity as essential for the social body to progress: "Smooth flow could be restored to the nation's evolutionary stream and political economy only by shifting the balance of the national birthrate from the dysgenic to the eugenic in the interest of national efficiency."[28] Looking for analogous bodies in the natural world, artists and engineers together found the greyhound particularly apropos, drawing on

27. Henry Fairfield Osborn, address to Third International Congress of Eugenics, New York, August 22, 1932, quoted in "Birth Control Peril to Race, Says Osborn," *New York Times*, August 23, 1932.

28. Cogdell, *Eugenic Design*, p. 131.

the aerodynamic "thoroughbred" as a perfect type.[29] The "America" float at the New York World's Fair in 1939-40 featured a giant white greyhound in forward flight, and the "Fitter Families for Future Firesides" of the American Eugenics Society attracted participants in the "Fitter Family" competitions by asking, "Are you a human thoroughbred?"

It is not a stretch to assume that the fundamental concepts of competition, scarcity, "favoured races," and the threat of being judged as not in the march of humankind made their way into the science of domesticity, adding a new kind of pressure to maternal feeding and toilet training. Even for the types of mothers in the relatively privileged, physician-going class, the heat was turned up considerably in October 1929 as the sense of scarcity became reality. Children who were weak and irregular were problems not merely for their own middle-class households. A mother needed to be able to say with some assurance, and without what was increasingly judged to be blinkered sanguinity, that her child would contribute to the overall advance of the nation.

Cogdell's research grants a conceptual backdrop against which to consider a book (fig. 2.11) offered by the editors of *Parents'*. *The Modern Baby Book and Child Development Record* was marketed as a way to "keep a scientific record of your child." The advertisement for the book, which was offered in blue or pink in standard and deluxe editions, maintained that purchase of the book was not merely a matter of preference, for "Doctors, educators, and physicians urge you" to keep such a record. The repetition of "doctors" and "physicians" and "scientific" strengthens the impression that this book is a matter of basic, parental responsibility. This "modern" book is different from previous such albums:

> For generations the conventional Baby Book has been a sentimental household document, used as a photograph album and a record of trivialities. Now two child specialists have made a real scientific record and guide to parents on their child's development from birth to the sixteenth year. . . . This book contains scientific records of the greatest value to parents, doctors and teachers. . . . A section on family history is followed by the birth record, and a section on general health containing blanks for recording height, weight, teeth, operations, diseases and accidents.

29. Cogdell, *Eugenic Design*, p. 148. Cogdell quotes one eugenic sermon that humans needed to breed toward the "ideal type," whether drawing on the ideal type of rose, orange, cow, athlete, or scholar (p. 153, quoting A. Wakefield Slaten, sermon 25, American Eugenics Society Papers, American Philosophical Society, Philadelphia).

**Figure 2.11. Advertisement for**
***The Modern Baby Book and Child***
***Development Record. Parents',***
**December 1929**

The contrast between, on the one hand, "conventional," "sentimental," and "household" and, on the other hand, "modern," "specialists," and "scientific" was also a contrast between past and future, between those families whose routines and practices were merely "sentimental," full of "trivialities," and those parents who had opened themselves for apt scientific scrutiny, judgment, and counsel. This same logic of comparison is evident in the form of the book. The opening set of questions played on the concerns of parents eager to be judged as "modern" and "intelligent": "Is your child above normal, normal, or perhaps a little under normal physically, mentally, or in social adjustment? How is his character developing? Are there traits which need correcting? What abilities in him are most outstanding? How can they be further developed? The importance of recognizing difficulties early enough for quick and easy correction. An amazing new development record unlike anything of its kind ever published. A scientific guide in the intelligent handling of your boy or girl."

The first question in the series is reiterated throughout the book, as further described in the advertisement. *"Normal standards of development"* were *"presented for comparison with the individual record"* so that a parent could answer accurately, with scientific precision. The question was, in effect, Just where is your child on a continuum of physical, mental, and social abilities? How could parents be sure their estimation was not born of "sentiment," mere "conventional" wisdom, or triviality? The book offered parents a set of "significant facts to be observed" in their child at "three, six, nine, twelve and eighteen months," and for "every year thereafter," so that they might be involved in "guided observation" in their estimation and, not incidentally, make a more precise "comparison with other children."

The image on the cover of *The Modern Baby Book* most obviously depicts the growth of one's children from birth to young adulthood. But the imagery of the graph, when read alongside the emphases of discernible gain at play during the period, may take on another significance. The child was not to be judged day by day for growth on his own chart but to be compared with the patterns of discernible normality as quantified by the "scientific method" of the experts who wrote the book. The text left little for interpretation here. The child was to be compared with other children, to map whether he was above or below them in the various forms of ostensibly measurable abilities recorded in the modern version of childhood development. Without comparison to other children, parents would not know how their own child measured up.

## The Century of Progress

The Gerber Products Company sponsored an exhibit in the Hall of Science, in the Fountain Rotunda, at Chicago's Century of Progress Exposition in 1933-34. An ad inviting physicians to view the exhibit assured them that the "Gerber policy of active cooperation with the medical fraternity maintained in all Gerber advertising will be followed rigidly in lay contacts at the Century of Progress" (fig. 2.12). The nurse employed for the purpose, "Miss Harriet E. Davis," was "particularly well qualified, thru her professional work and training, to impress on lay visitors the importance of relying only on a physician's advice on all questions connected with Infant Feeding." The official Century of Progress photograph of the Gerber exhibit gives some idea of the slight discord between appealing to mothers and appealing to physicians in the display itself.[30] The Gerber baby drawing, appearing in the center, on the

30. See *The Official Pictures of A Century of Progress Exposition, Chicago, 1933-34* (New York: Encyclopaedia Britannica, 1933), p. 136.

**Figure 2.12. Gerber's strained food advertisement.** *Journal of the American Medical Association*, **1933**

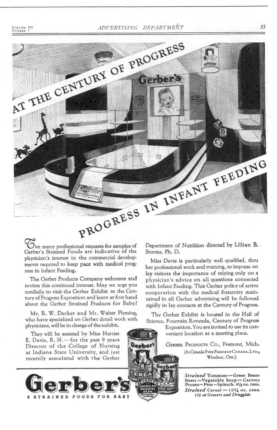

lampshades, and in the display window of foods, along with the tumbling ABC blocks, seems intended to appeal to one sensibility, while the polished silver and jet-black color scheme seem intended for another aesthetic. Perhaps the vaguely vehicular shape of the display case was meant to indicate the forward movement of progress. The display contained no rocking chairs, no plush toys, no signs of childhood per se, but rather a symbol of the ideal baby amidst the architecture of sophisticated modernity.

Despite its apparent aesthetic variance, the design of the Gerber exhibit fit well into the overall blueprint of the Century of Progress. Regarding the architecture of the exposition, the official photographic record, published by the Encyclopaedia Britannica in 1933, explained: "It is in no way a reminiscent architecture; refusing to avail itself of the sentimental force which is inherent in imitation, it breaks away sharply and confidently from all traditions. But it is a strong architecture. It might be called, figuratively, athletic. One of the traditions from which it breaks away is the tradition of waste, . . . because it is so fined down for efficiency, because it is in such beautiful condition (to continue with the athletic figure)."[31] In this commentary James Weber Linn (nephew and biographer of Jane Addams) pulled together key themes of the age. To be modern and progressive was to refuse sentimentality, to name all traditions as mere reminiscence and instead move confidently into the future, shedding the "tradition of waste" by being "fined down for efficiency."

In his description of the Century of Progress, Linn reflected the sensibility of the *Modern Baby Book,* refusing as it did to recapitulate the sentimentality and triviality of an earlier era. He drew on a cultured admiration of the thoroughbred, whether canine or equestrian, with the imagery of streamlined, regularized, athletic, and efficient bodies. And Linn struck the (evidently important) note of elimination, nodding to the architecture's purging of "waste."

### *"Forward! Ever Forward!"*

The Century of Progress was meant to epitomize progress itself, catapulting the heartland from a local, agricultural, and tradition-bound region to an industrial, scientific runway of progress. As summarized in the introduction to *Fair America: World's Fairs in the United States* (2000), the "veritable web" of world's fairs beginning in the mid–nineteenth century lent "form and substance to the modern world." "To say that world's fairs have exerted a formative influence on the way Americans have thought about themselves and the world in which they live probably understates the importance of those expositions."[32] The millions of visitors to the various fairs across the United States were exposed to the very intentional, minutely planned messages of the fairs' organizers and contributors. Even those who did not attend learned of a fair's aims in reports and in advertising in regional and national publications. This was serious business. The corporate and civic leaders organizing the various events did not perceive them primarily as a means for entertaining the public but rather as a means for shaping the civic imagination around a particular, chosen theme.

The aim of the Century of Progress Exposition in Chicago was, from the outset, to expose the public to the promise of scientific progress. Linn described Chicago's past and present with strong contrast, drawing a distinct line between, on the one hand, "recollection" and "sentiment" and, on the other, the working of true "imagination":

31. James Weber Linn, introduction to *Official Pictures,* p. 6.

32. Robert W. Rydell, John E. Findling, and Kimberly D. Pelle, *Fair America: World's Fairs in the United States* (Washington, D.C.: Smithsonian Institution Press, 2000), p. 1.

A Century of Progress was planned, by architecture and arrangement as well as by exhibits, to throw the minds and the imaginations of men forward, into the future. It was not to look back, but onward. It was to be a projection, not a recollection. This book asserts and demonstrates the success of that daring intention as a whole, by giving innumerable examples of its success in detail. The "World's Fair" of 1893 appealed directly to sentiment, A Century of Progress appeals to the imagination. It is the difference between a story and a prophecy.[33]

One of the first images in the official pictorial record is a color drawing of the Travel and Transport Building, and the caption below echoes Linn's emphasis on movement away from the traditions of the past into an unfettered tomorrow: "Larger than the dome of St. Peter's or that of the Capitol in Washington, this sky-hung rotunda of the Travel and Transport Building strikes a new note in architecture — first application of the principle of the suspension bridge — the largest unobstructed area enclosed anywhere under a roof."[34] The language of "new," "first," and "largest" ran throughout the fair's exhibits and literature. Although planning for the exposition was well under way when the stock market crashed in 1929, the insistent tone of "Forward! Ever Forward!" (again to quote Linn's official commentary) seems magnified by the contrasting economic downturn occurring in the nation at the time. The way out of the morass was "Forward! Ever Forward!"; those sounding notes of concern or doubt needed not apply. "To forget the achievements of the past is impossible, to deny the inevitability of change absurd, to turn away from the immediate and from the promise of the future cowardly," the exposition warned. There would be space in the future only for the "determined and unquenchable curiosity" and the "spirit of scientific inquiry" that had "changed the world and set it on its new path of progress."[35]

The metaphor of yesterday's faith outdone by the science of today is apparent. The Travel and Transport Building had surpassed St. Peter's in scope and freedom. Electricity was newly christened as "The Servant That Has Transformed the World."[36] Paeans to the "miraculous" events of human ingenuity ran throughout the official guidebook to the fair and the exhibits themselves. "The Miracle of Light" enabled the fair to continue past sundown, past the usual constraints of nature, and the designers made much of the technology to illumine the many towers. A reproduction of Antwerp's St. Nicholas

33. Linn, introduction, p. 5.
34. *Official Pictures*, p. 11.
35. Linn, introduction, p. 5.
36. *Official Guide Book of the Fair* (1933) (Chicago: Cuneo, 1933), p. 53.

church stood in the midst of the Belgian Village, where one could enter the "sixteenth century" as if a time traveler–tourist, enjoy "craftsmen in the costumes of hundreds of years ago," and enjoy the "ancient folk dances" and "merry milk-maids" that added to the "picturesqueness of the village."[37] If St. Nicholas — referred to merely as "an old church" in the guidebook — was charming yesteryear, the Hall of Religion represented the modern faith of today and tomorrow. The guidebook's opening description of the hall displays the American, mainline Protestant spirit of the fair:

> Near the Twenty-third Street entrance, and north of the Midway, or street of carnival, stands a unique building. It strives to express the spirit of modernism, that is the voice of the Fair, and the more mellow, more traditional spirit of holy things.
>
> Its tower-carillon chimes religious melodies, and within is a chamber of quiet, a chapel of meditation and prayer. It is the Hall of Religion. Here, the followers of many faiths tell the story of man's rise through religion. Jew and Gentile, Baptist and Methodist, Presbyterian and Lutheran, Christian Scientist and Episcopalian, join in a solemn manifestation of the supremacy of God.[38]

The superiority of Anglo-Protestantism as the culmination of moral, "social-evolutionary development" — as William R. Hutchison writes of the Parliament of Religions at Chicago's 1893 Columbian Exposition — was apparent as well in the spiritual universalism described in the 1933 Hall of Religion.[39] While "all religions" were represented at the 1933 fair, the "world's best known religions" were melted, mellowed, and molded into a calf that looked remarkably like the "spirit of modernism." The pride of place among the "holy things" of tradition was given to the Chalice of Antioch, "one of the rarest relics of Christianity." Representing "the golden age of Hellenic art," the chalice appeared as a museum piece among the murals attesting to an evolved sense of spirituality — "man's universal aspiration for God." Off the main lobby were exhibits by the American Bible Society, the Christian Century Press, and the Protestant Episcopal Church of America.[40]

---

37. *Official Guide Book* (1933), p. 124. The church is identified in Samantha Gleisten, *Chicago's 1933-34 World's Fair: A Century of Progress in Vintage Postcards* (Chicago: Arcadia, 2002), p. 108.

38. *Official Guide Book* (1933), p. 82.

39. William R. Hutchison, *Religious Pluralism in America* (New Haven: Yale University Press, 2003), p. 175.

40. *Official Guide Book* (1933), pp. 82-83.

The practical focus of the fair was on advancement. Many of the exhibits featured contrasts between the world of yesterday and the world of tomorrow; from bathing to canning to baking, displays of the ways of the future included also, in a mural or a corner show, displays of the clearly inferior ways of the past. There were advances in transportation, "from wagons to wings," to quote the guidebook, signaled by the sleek Greyhound "auto-liner" buses (with the sleek Greyhound icon) that whisked people around the fair, as well as the airplanes that flew in formation overhead. The fair was replete with advances in foods and agriculture, such as the Wonder Bakery's "truly perfect" (i.e., fully automated) assembly line, which baked breads "scientifically" — "never touched by human hands."[41] General Electric presented a House of Magic, including a sparkling white Electric Kitchen in which home cooking could be almost as sanitary and advanced as the Wonder Bakery.

The Dairy Industry had its own building, with the cow featured in a drama depicting bovine progress, from "the bringing of the first cows to the Plymouth colony" to "today's organized dairy industry."[42] Above the entrance to the exhibit was written "A Vital Story of Human Progress." The caption beneath the photograph in the photographic record reflects the going assumption regarding the use of cows' milk for infant feeding — in the imagery, both mother and Mother Nature had been methodically supplanted: "The Dairy Building, where is portrayed the story of the foster mother of mankind, the cow."[43]

Bread baked exclusively by machines and industrialized cows as foster mothers signal a theme carried forward in another popular exhibit — the Baby-Incubators that featured "living babies" (figs. 2.13 and 2.14). To better interpret this seemingly bizarre extension of scientific progress, we return to the beginning of the industrial formula movement, to Thomas Rotch in particular.

Rotch, a pediatrician at Harvard, was the first in his field effectively to champion artificial infant formula, bringing infant feeding under the watchful eye of the burgeoning discipline of infant and child medicine. As Jeff Baker notes in *The Machine in the Nursery: Incubator Technology and the Origins of Newborn Intensive Care,* Rotch's development of the incubator, or "brooder," and his commitment to scientific infant feeding reflect his sense of nature as technically malleable, and open to improvement: "In each case, he took a product from agriculture (the incubator and cow's milk) and modified

41. Gleisten, *Chicago's 1933-34 World's Fair,* p. 70.
42. *Official Guide Book* (1933), p. 77.
43. *Official Pictures,* p. 78.

Figures 2.13 and 2.14. The Baby Incubators. From *The Official Pictures of A Century of Progress Exposition, Chicago, 1933-34.*

it along the lines suggested by the study of human physiology."[44] Rotch's sense for marketing his perspective was also astute, in that he played in both cases on the "traditional divisions of class," calling on his audience's "middle-class sympathy for scientific motherhood as contrasted with the traditions of the lower-born nurse, whose experience he dismissed as consisting of 'ignorance rather than of intelligence.'" The appeal for the discipline was also strong — "The idea that science could enable physicians to create a perfect living environment for a prematurely born infant held great excitement for the young pediatric profession" — but the cost and impracticality of the device were prohibitive, and the movement for incubator technology foundered.[45]

Baker narrates a complicated interplay of obstetrics in France and pediatrics in the United States, with a web of medical contacts spanning decades. But the technology eventually found its way to Coney Island through a man named Martin Couney, a "self-designated missionary for the incubator crusade."[46] It was Couney's adaptation of a French method for promoting and financing the premature infant incubator that led to the display at the Century of Progress Exposition.

### "Mistakes and Mishaps" of Retrogressive Culture

The baby incubator with live babies offers a conceptual link between the exposition's "Forward! Ever Forward!" exhibits of science and industry and the Midway, at the center of the fair, with such attractions as Ripley's Believe It or Not Odditorium, a sampling of "freak shows," Darkest Africa, and the Old Plantation Show. Positioning the "odd," "freakish," "mysterious," and "quaint" right in the midst of the overall message of the Century of Progress may seem at first counterintuitive. But at second, deeper glance, the arrangement makes sense. As "mankind" progressed upward, forward, and away from merely mortal limits, it seemed necessary to those crafting the exposition to place at the center a midway — a titillating reminder of the "uncontrollable" and "accidental" in nature and culture. The scientifically perfected wombs with "live babies" offered fairgoers a chance to view human life in a palpably vulnerable and nascent form — struggling at the point of viability — as a sort of scientifi-

44. Jeffrey P. Baker, *The Machine in the Nursery: Incubator Technology and the Origins of Newborn Intensive Care* (Baltimore: Johns Hopkins University Press, 1996), p. 131. For the discussion of the Rotch-Putnam brooder, see pp. 82-83.
45. Baker, *Machine in the Nursery*, pp. 132, 134.
46. Baker, *Machine in the Nursery*, p. 86.

**Figure 2.15. Scene from the Midway. From *The Official Pictures of A Century of Progress Exposition, Chicago, 1933-34***

cally macabre cross between the fully mechanical Wonder Bakery and the Midway's Midget Village. Would these babies make it, or would they not? Were they destined to die, as freaks of an older Mother Nature, or were they creatures on the cusp of progress? The barely live babies presented the question of the Century of Progress Exposition in symbolic form.

The lives exhibited at the Midway were clearly on the other side of a divide. The live babies in the incubators posed a question, but the "Real Two-Headed Baby" gave a clear answer (fig. 2.15). The theme of the fair was "Science Finds — Genius Invents — Industry Applies — Man Conforms [or Adapts]," and here was humanity left behind. The Midway represented humanity beyond the reach of scientific findings, inventive ingenuity, and the applied industry of progress. From the Temple of Mystery to the Thrill House of Crime to the Old Plantation Show, this section of the fair displayed nonconforming and ill-adapted man. The Thrill House of Crime allowed viewers to step inside a safely contained world of menace populated by clearly distinct types, including the "white slaver," the "suicide," the "coke addict," the "kidnaper," the "fire bug," the "drug slave," the "bomber," and the "maniac." The apparent discord between the "odd" and "criminal" and the theme of progress makes sense when viewed from a particular perspective. The various

159

"other" peoples on display were live examples of "incredible truths, wonders and paradoxes" (to quote the Ripley's brochure for the fair) amidst the exposition's overall "prophecy" of improvement. Science and methodically engineered industry were to eliminate "waste" along the "path of progress" (again quoting Linn on the fair).

One postcard from Ripley's Odditorium is of particular interest to my inquiry (fig. 2.16). The pressure of optimally responsible parenting posed by the *Modern Baby Book* was arguably unhelpful for the mothers at whom the authors aimed their pointed messages. But the exhortation to throw off "sentimentality" and "triviality" for the sake of a scientific comparison of childhood attributes takes on a menacing tone when one considers the implications for children who did not fit within the narrative of progress. The spectacles of "nature's mistakes" at play during the Century of Progress served a rhetorical function — as the placeholders for that-which-must-be-avoided. They were the ones from whom the modern mother should distinguish her own children. Betty Williams, a "Baby with 4 Legs and 3 Arms," and Freda Pushnik, "The Little Half Girl Born without Arms or Legs" (both part of the Odditorium), served simultaneously two related purposes. These children were reverse icons, the opposite of Gerber's iconic baby. They provided both a visual paradigm of the accidental, mistaken Natural that scientific progress could leave behind and an extreme border beyond which fairgoers could be certain to progress. They provided viewers with the consummate form of "other" children in comparison with whom their own children could be judged "modern."[47]

Linn suggests that the exposition served, through its display of "miraculously developed mechanical ingenuity," a "valuable work of demonstrating to the nation that it is a unified nation, a high-hearted nation, a nation undiscouraged and unafraid . . . [a nation] in oneness of hope and spirit."[48] There were some fairly obvious, and rhetorically serviceable, fissures in this technological "oneness," however. In its Midget Village (fig. 2.17), the exposition offered a glimpse at a down-scaled city where "sixty Lilliputians" lived in their "tiny houses" and conducted their "diminutive activities." Viewed within the cultural assumptions of Haeckel's Darwinian recapitulation theory, the Midget Villagers represented a kind of backward, not-yet-fully-formed culture. They were the past of human evolution, away from which science was progressing.

47. Ripley's "attractions" at the fair can be seen at http://hometown.aol.com/chicfair/ripley.html.
48. Linn, introduction, p. 10.

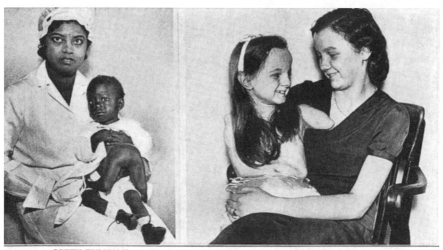

BETTY WILLIAMS
15 Months Old Baby with 4 Legs and 3 Arms

FREDA PUSHNIK
The Little Half Girl Born without Arms or Legs

**Figure 2.16. Image from Ripley's postcards from the Century of Progress, © 2007 Ripley Entertainment Inc.**

What the Midget Village portrayed overtly, various other villages suggested more subtly, by designed, exploitable differentiation. Among the foreigners participating, the contrast between British and western European cultures and everyone else was clear. There were cultures to visit as tourists of the dark, old, and exotic, and there were cultures capable of contributing more directly to the ingenuity of progress. While the Swedish Pavilion and the Moroccan Village were both featured in the fair, the former modeled "the simplicity and dignity . . . typical of the trend in modern Swedish architecture," while the latter was described thus: "The streets are paraded by typical Moors in costume, who sell their barbaric wares in this wonderful reproduction of Northern Africa."[49]

Many of the villages at the exposition were set up to accentuate the distance between the "World of Tomorrow" and the peoples of yesterday. After visiting the Ford Symphony and Park, fairgoers could, in quick succession, take in the sights of the Midget Village, the Old Plantation Show (with "60 Hand-Picked Colored Entertainers"), and the Living Wonders exhibit (presenting "human mistakes and mishaps" — the "largest collection of strange and curious people ever assembled").[50] The *Official Guide Book of the Fair* ex-

49. *Official Guide Book* (1933), p. 96.
50. *Official Guide Book* (1933), p. 166.

**Figure 2.17. Midget Villagers.** From *The Official Pictures of A Century of Progress Exposition, Chicago, 1933-34*

plicitly linked the sites of the Midway, assuming associations that ran from the "breath-taking roller coaster" to the "tricks of magic" to the "beauties of the Orient [who] dance to strange tunes" to "glimpses of Cairo, Damascus, Tunis, Tripoli, and Algiers" to "the Siamese Twins, giant people, and other 'freaks' gathered from the four corners of the earth."[51] Many of the cultures represented in the various villages stood in for the "mistakes and mishaps" of retrogressive culture, with the Oriental Village positioned in a way that made it seem as symbolically backward as Darkest Africa (fig. 2.18). The guidebook issued for the fair's 1934 continuation promised Hawaiian Village entertainment featuring the climactic "sacrifice of an Hawaiian girl" in the "flaming

51. *Official Guide Book* (1933), p. 123.

**Figure 2.18. A fire walker. From *The Official Pictures of A Century of Progress Exposition, Chicago, 1933-34***

crater" of a volcano.[52] What the "mishaps" and midgets offered in individual form, the inhabitants of such villages displayed in cultural form — serving as oddly reassuring reminders of the retrograde beyond which a Century of Progress could move.

Arguably the most egregious of such symbolic uses of entire peoples were the ways Native Americans and African Americans functioned in the rhetoric of progress and blunder. The differences portrayed in "Forward! Ever Forward!" were predictably the most blatant as they hit home in the United States. The Century of Progress poster (fig. 2.19) is representative of many displays: the old America of 1833 was that of the Indian; the future, that of the

52. *1934 Official Guide Book to the Fair*, cited in Gleisten, *Chicago's 1933-34 World's Fair*, p. 92.

Figure 2.19. Official poster for Chicago World's Fair by George B. Petty, 1933, Chicago History Museum (Chi-06172)

embodied initiative of Anglo-Saxon America. The Century of Progress between the incorporation of Chicago as a city (in 1833) and the 1933 celebration involved the movement away from the world of Native America and toward the world of General Motors, General Electric, and Frigidaire. The Hall of Science, which claimed pride of place for the entire exposition, featured not only "The Transparent Man" (a slim, Nordic figure with his plastic arms raised to the stars, brought over from Dresden, Germany) but also an exhibit that contrasted "primitive" and scientific medicine. According to the guidebook, the fairgoer could view "the antics of an Indian medicine man, practicing his primitive medicine," as well as "the progress medicine has made."[53]

The menace of the primitive was clear in the "Tragic History" revisited at the Drama of Old Fort Dearborn. Here visitors could recall the shift from "friendly" to murderous Indians. The pioneers of 1812 had faced "the circling redmen" with courage, but the Indians, that day, had prevailed.[54] The Indian Village feature at the 1933 fair was housed in the U.S. Army Camp. The images of the village appear as caricatures, in no small part because of the juxtaposition of the Indian encampment with the extensive Home Planning Hall section of the fair. One of the "official pictures," published in a volume by Encyclopaedia Britannica, shows a small boy carrying a watermelon almost as large as he is. The caption reads "Small Injun (Navajo) — Heap Big Watermelon!"[55] The cultural reference from watermelon to "Injun" subtly links former inhabitants of "Darkest Africa" with the survivors of an older America. Although supposedly the Native American tribes were to be on display as distinct peoples, another caption below an image from the guidebook is telling: a mother and child are labeled merely as "Types in the Indian Village."

The depiction of southern African Americans in the Old Plantation Show merely scratches the surface of the underlying racism involved at the Century of Progress. There were those workers who would be involved in harvesting the rubber for the high-speed race of progress and those who would reap the benefits, as signified in the Firestone brochure (fig. 2.20). This was powerfully symbolized by the names assigned to the two towers holding up the famed Sky-Ride of the Century of Progress, which moved fairgoers from one side of the exposition to the other. They were dubbed "Amos" and "Andy," after the characters from the radio minstrel show, which had originated in Chicago in 1928.[56] Almost unbelievably, one feature of the

53. *Official Guide Book* (1933), p. 40.
54. *Official Guide Book* (1933), pp. 128-32.
55. Image from *Official Pictures*, p. 35.
56. For more on the background of the radio beginnings of Amos and Andy, see Melvin

**Figure 2.20.** *How Firestone High Speed Tires Are Made.* Pamphlet printed for the World's Fair, Chicago, 1934

fair was "African Dips," which gave visitors an opportunity to drop an African American into a tank of water by hitting a bull's-eye with a ball.[57] The depiction of "African" culture (as if it were a monolith) painted with bold strokes what was more subtly implied at the other villages. The exhibit was called Darkest Africa and featured shows of "Firewalkers" and "The Funny Native," in which a "native" and a white actor with academic demeanor por-

Patrick Ely, *The Adventures of Amos 'n Andy: A Social History of an American Phenomenon* (New York: Free Press, 1991).

57. Rydell, Findling, and Pelle, *Fair America*, p. 84.

trayed a series of supposedly humorous miscommunications.[58] Although the fair also featured exhibits from the National Urban League and a few African American colleges, the situation of race at the Century of Progress was deeply divisive.

The differential benefits of the fair were not merely symbolic. Some people would be moving forward, while others would not. Chicago had been one of the primary destinations during what historians call the Great Black Migration. From 1910 to 1920, the African American population in Chicago had more than doubled, to 109,000, and by 1930 it had grown to 234,000.[59] As the authors of *Fair America* reveal: "Virtually absent from the Century of Progress were African Americans. . . . Although the fair created many jobs, few went to African Americans during either the construction or the run of the fair. The only African American in the fair's management hierarchy headed the toilet concession, and most African Americans who did work at the fair cleaned toilets; a few others worked as maids, police, and demonstrators in a few exhibits."[60] The language of unity notwithstanding, the world of the Century of Progress was limited. Those who were excluded served a purpose.

### *"Is Your Baby Enjoying The Results of Progress?"*

"Is your baby enjoying The Results of Progress?" the Gerber brochure inquired. The definition of progress may be read as subtly dependent upon a distinction between families that represented the past and those that represented the future. These themes came together in the Lullaby Furniture Corporation mural "Progress of Furniture for Children" (fig. 2.21). The mural features a mother from 1833 B.C. who drapes her child on a tree and a mother from A.D. 1833 who holds her baby over a small rocking cradle. A horse-drawn wagon, a spinning wheel, and a Native American offering a fur pelt provide the background. The mother in the center, the mother of 1933, is on a different scale than the other two, her figure elongated into an unnaturally streamlined style. She is wearing a Romanesque dress of simple elegance.

The interwar years were loaded in various ways for mothers with the fi-

---

58. This is my best bet as to what was going on, by the picture in the Encyclopaedia Britannica version of the fair.

59. Nicholas Lemann, *The Promised Land: The Great Black Migration and How It Changed America* (New York: Knopf, 1991), p. 16.

60. Rydell, Findling, and Pelle, *Fair America*, pp. 83-84.

Figure 2.21. "Progress of Furniture for Children." Lullaby Furniture Corporation. From *The Official Pictures of A Century of Progress Exposition, Chicago,* 1933-34

nancial and cultural wherewithal to conform to the norms set out in fairs like Chicago's Century of Progress Exposition. To quote one author, the "homemaker" was, "collectively," "the greatest single purchasing force in the market."[61] The pull on a certain class of mothers to use their purchasing power to build up the vigor of the social body was considerable. Drawing on an analysis of Depression-era fairs, held in San Diego, Dallas, Cleveland, San Francisco, and New York in addition to Chicago, the authors of *Fair America* summarize the cumulative message as twofold:

> In all of America's depression era fairs, the dominant theme continued to be America's national progress toward a future utopia, but that theme contained a shift in emphasis. Progress, in addition to its other definitions, now meant increased consumer spending as world's fair sponsors

61. Woodhouse, "Mother," p. 67.

tried to persuade Americans that they had to set aside older values such as thrift and restraint and become consumers of America's factory and farm products. . . . America's depression era fairs contained another message. Those expositions also encouraged Americans to place their faith in the ability of scientists and engineers to design the world of tomorrow.[62]

According to the official photograph of the "Progress of Furniture" mural, Lullaby also offered at the exposition three small wooden cradles much like the one beneath the woman of 1833, but they were flanked in the display by two large cribs similar to the one featured front and center in the mural. For a mother of means, the choice might be clear. For those unable to afford either the space or the cost of the 1933 model, the sense of being on the wrong side of a divide was part of the message of advertising during the period. In the midst of a precarious time nationally, it was important for the aspiring homemaker to pinch pennies or even go into debt to stay well within the Century of Progress and away from the human mistakes of the Midway.

Allow me to depart from the historical narrative and cultural analysis here to answer a question likely pressing on at least some readers. Weren't the good new days of pasteurized milk and refrigeration and automobiles indeed quite a bit better, on any scale, than the bad old days of summer milk poisoning and horse-drawn carriages? To quote one amused great-grandmother after one of my lectures on the norms of holy housekeeping (at St. Olaf in Minnesota), "Your presentation was terrific, love, but so were electric refrigerators and laundry machines." There were indeed many women who also found infant formula to be a great gain in their daily life with baby. Writing from a perspective very different from that of Rima Apple, Ann Hulbert, in *Raising America: Experts, Parents, and a Century of Advice about Children,* notes that many women preferred the convenience and reliability of artificial feeding and thus resisted the supposedly authoritative advice of leading physicians who encouraged breast feeding as the best bet for baby.[63]

The perceived gains in domestic organization, aesthetics, and health at the Century of Progress were unquestionably considerable for many women in the United States. But the appeal for scientific motherhood was intertwined with at least two dubious messages, at times implied and at times quite explicit. I suspect that these messages were deleterious for the women reading *Ladies' Home Journal,* and I am certain they were deleterious for the women from whom those readers were to distinguish themselves. From "the

---

62. Rydell, Findling, and Pelle, *Fair America,* pp. 11-12.

63. Ann Hulbert, *Raising America: Experts, Parents, and a Century of Advice about Children* (New York: Knopf, 2003). See especially pp. 64-69.

dangerous business of being a baby" to "progress in infant feeding," there was an underlying assumption that women's bodies were potentially unreliable and possibly even dangerously disordered, and that the process of childbirth and infant feeding needed the discipline, order, and expertise of (almost exclusively male) science. This suspicion of one's embodied, incarnate self — this sense that one's own womb and one's own breasts and one's "sentimental" repetition of one's grandmother's household were problems to be solved and even supplanted by scientific precision — may have driven the expansion of an industry that brought gains to women, but those gains came at a cost. And the costs, like the benefits of progress, were paid differentially.

This leads me to the second dubious message at play in the advertising of infant formula (as well as baby cribs and potty contrivances and such). There was during this time (as, I will argue, in our own time) an appeal not only to a basically misogynist suspicion of embodied maternity but also to a newly *scientific* distrust of certain types of people within the social body. The advertising to women in the mainstream of the United States appealed to their gender fears and their class aspirations. To bring forward a family fit for the "future of the race" (to recall the motto of *Parents'*), a woman was to distinguish the fruit of her womb from the potential waste of another's.

## The Corporate Resolution

### *"Well, What Do YOU Know about Babies?"*

Several key components of "scientific motherhood" during the first half of the twentieth century converge in the Johnson & Johnson advertisement from midcentury shown in figure 2.22.[64] Appearing in *Ladies' Home Journal* in February of 1950, the pitch for baby oil and baby powder has the knowledgeable physician and the fragile baby morph into the figure of an infant/doctor with a medical bag and stethoscope. The "dangerous business of being a baby" (to quote a 1914 *Ladies' Home Journal* ad discussed above) required expert advice, and what did the average, *Ladies' Home Journal*–reading mother really *know* about babies? The images and text encompass the time's prevailing themes of maternal insecurity, comparison of one's baby with the baby of another, fear that human infants were from another land altogether, and tension between medical and grandmotherly influence. The first picture shows a mother standing with hands on

64. Thanks to Bryan Langlands, who found this particularly apropos image for me in *Ladies' Home Journal*.

Figure 2.22. Johnson's Baby Powder advertisement. *Ladies' Home Journal,* February 1950

hips, amused/bemused by her bald-headed baby; the mother next to her is holding a baby with a full head of hair. Should she worry? No, the voice of the baby/expert tells her, "don't fret!" Does the baby have a "language" to which she may not be privy? Yes and no, the voice of the baby/expert replies. If she is able to "listen carefully," she will "learn to recognize the hunger cry, boredom cry, pain cry!"

The third question reflects both the tension and the clearly corporate resolution of the turn from sentimental to scientific motherhood. "Should grandmothers have a say in bringing up baby?" The inquiry itself reveals the extent to which the perceived naïveté of maternally transmitted knowledge had been supplanted by scientifically verified truth, but the answer is also telling. Maternal and scientifically verifiable wisdom met in the "trusted" product lines advertised in magazines like *Ladies' Home Journal*. "Should grandmothers have a say in bringing up baby?" Well, the baby/expert replies, "your doctor is your best bet." However, "grandmas *are* gold mines of work-and-worry-saving tips!" The grandmother, wearing a fashionable black dress and pearls, will likely "approve Johnson's Baby Products for baby's nursery tray just as your doctor does." After generations of advertising to mothers, scientific advice, maternal aspirations, and corporate marketing had come together — maternal good sense could predictably unite with scientific good sense precisely in the brand names of baby care represented by Johnson & Johnson. A *good* mother and a *good* grandmother could agree on medically tried-and-true names like Gerber, Kellogg's, Ivory, and Johnson & Johnson.

For two decades Gerber had promised physicians that "Gerber Advertises . . . so that mothers will cooperate with you," and the effort had paid off, at least for Gerber. By targeting mothers as well as health professionals, the producer could create demand from two sides. Elitism combined with suspicion of maternal know-how led to a different version of maternal know-how — a maternal preference for food that was both "select" and "scientific." One Gerber advertisement (fig. 2.23) reminded physicians that "Anybody can put vegetables through a sieve . . . but there's more than that to Gerber's!" Through "selected seed in selected soil" and through "scientific control" "established by the Gerber research laboratory," Gerber offered a product superior to that created by any old mom in any old kitchen. Citing "feeding experiments at Michigan State College and Columbia University," Gerber suggested that it was "distinctly worth [physicians'] while to specify Gerber's." By doing so, they could "remove one factor of uncertainty in infant feeding." The photograph shows the pristine innards of the corporate body, with women in white uniforms and nursing caps reporting to their nursing-capped supervisor for the twice-daily "hand, nail, and general appearance inspection" and white-coated scientists working hard around laboratory tables.

Within two decades the marketing industry could reliably appeal to a mother's trust in the disembodied doctor, often represented by key advertising words such as "modern" and "endorse" and "patented." While still advertising to physicians, corporations could in some sense circumvent the family doctor by playing on the well-cultivated desires of the magazine-reading mother with an even moderately expendable income.

Arguably no less ludicrous/serious than the Doo-Tee toilet training aid of 1929 were ads during the 1950s for products such as the "Marvelous New Spill-Proof Heinz Baby Tumbler!" which, according to a 1952 ad, would "scientifically" control the flow of liquid so as to guard against "gagging and chok-

VOLUME 102
NUMBER 4    ADVERTISING DEPARTMENT    13

Figure 2.23. Advertisement for Gerber. *Journal of the American Medical Association*, 1935

ing." Promising that "leading doctors everywhere" were endorsing the Heinz Baby Tumbler, the advertisement declared it to be "revolutionary."[65] The sense that a mother needed to procure, through seemingly insignificant little purchases such as a sippy cup, the importantly selected, controlled, and medically enhanced knowledge of domesticity has been quite extensively documented by the generations of more skeptical women who followed.[66] But it is still worthwhile to note here, again, the ways women were encouraged, from many sides, to purchase the "doctor-approved" tools requisite for truly *knowledgeable* motherhood. The expert/baby returned again and again to ask questions like the one that framed a 1958 advertisement for *The Book of Knowledge*.

65. See *Woman's Day*, December 1952.
66. Note Betty Friedan's *The Feminine Mystique* (1963) and Barbara Ehrenreich's book on "expert" advice to women, *For Her Own Good* (1978).

Above the many images of a blond little boy going about his daily routine is the question, in bold print, "How Many Can You Answer?" As he asks things like "Where does the day begin?" "Where does dust come from?" "What makes Johnny's dimple?" "What makes me hungry?" "Do dogs dream?" "Why does soap make me clean?" his mother, vacuuming in dress and shiny high heels, is to answer. After all, the text intones, "Nothing is so vital to your child's future as the right answers . . . right now."[67]

The stakes involved in the quest for proper knowledge were brought home repeatedly in advertisements for infant feeding. Clapp's Baby Food asked, "Will your baby's future tell this story?" implying that a choice against Clapp's might result in a less salubrious ending for one's baby. Naming the child pictured, as if a condensation of the *Modern Baby Book,* the advertisement explained that "Hugh Starke started life with two wonderful gifts. *The first* — a wise Mommie who followed her doctor's advice. *And second* — a wise doctor who took care to prescribe the best for Hugh." The ad's photographs show Hugh at six months, eighteen months, and twelve years — clearly, *"a youngster who had a good start!"*

The specter of a child who did not receive a good start is the focus of the Ovaltine ad in figure 2.24.[68] "Sissy . . . they called him," the bold print reads. "But he was just too frail to keep up!" The ad copy suggests that a mother beset by such a problem could "try this for the nervous underweight child," and the smaller print warns that "a lifelong complex can easily develop in a child who lags behind the others." The recommended "health insurance program" of "2 to 3 glasses of Ovaltine" per day would allow a mother to "be sure [she had] done just about everything . . . to insure proper nutrition."

### A New "Natural"

The sentimental and the scientific coexist in awkward symbiosis in many other advertisements from the 1950s. The images of the period presented both a sense of precarious childhood — your child might become a "sissy" — and a sense that a good mother would choose carefully the proper bits of consumer culture to form a secure, calm, and unsoiled nest for her little one. The task was to protect and beautify — and medical studies were on hand to warn about the stakes and recommend the solutions.

ScotTissue brought home the message that baby's tender skin needs

---

67. *Parents',* February 1958, p. 7.
68. Sarah Sours found this image in her research.

Figure 2.24. Ovaltine advertisement. *Ladies' Home Journal*, March 1950

**Figure 2.25. Advertisement for ScotTissue.** *Ladies' Home Journal,* March 1950

mother's "constant/devoted/wise care" with a series of advertisements featuring aesthetically normative women dressed in white and gazing lovingly at baby, always against a willowy white background (fig. 2.25). "As Soft as old Linen," ScotTissue would enable mother to meet the needs of her fragile baby, who was, not incidentally, always described with the male pronoun. "You are his only safeguard against discomfort, you know, and your baby's skin really is thinner than yours." While women were simultaneously offered a growing cornucopia of products to protect their own skin, the tissue advertisements reminded them that their first priority needed to be the protection of the skin on their baby boy's buttocks, for "skin studies show that it would chafe more quickly, be 'injured' more easily." The pristine white backgrounds gave visual credence to the superior cleansing power of the gentle tissue. There was certainly no sign, however oblique or symbolic, of the substance that ScotTissue was presumably to clean up. But the text made that point as well: ScotTissue offered "high absorbency for clean, *clean* cleansing."

Against this diaphanous, immaculate backdrop, mother was also to choose breast feeding. The voice of the expert now accentuated the need for mother's breast. At the turn of the century the maternal breast had symbolized the potentially chaotic influence of natural variation, but by midcentury mother was again to breast-feed. Scientists were back in the fray, persuading even the privileged and savvy mother to offer her baby the breast. It was deemed the most "natural" method of feeding baby — and now "natural" was, somehow, inherently good. Yet the messages of domestic advertising, relying as they did on the expertise of male-dominated medicine, simultaneously reinforced a message that mothers needed the constant aid of medically monitored expertise. The home was potentially perilous, but it could be rendered "clean, *clean*" through a mother's reliance on the trusted products of corporate science. While the infant/expert called upon her dependence on corporately marketed, scientific motherhood, he also commanded her to trust that her body would provide the best possible food for baby. It is little surprise that the renewed turn to breast feeding would take decades, and even then it would be manifest largely as an act of rebellion against the whole ball of (laboratory tested) wax that had become the male, corporate breast.

The tense coexistence of the supposedly "natural," beautifully default bond of mother with infant and the assumed crucial role of science in the practice of responsible motherhood is apparent in a poignant photographic essay from a 1950 issue of *Ladies' Home Journal* (fig. 2.26). Entitled "Baby's First Year," it chronicles a year in the life of a typical family in pictures taken by staff photographer Wayne Miller, beginning with the birth of his third child, a daughter. It begins with a two-page spread of photographs taken in the hospital, as Dana Miller was born to parents Wayne and Joan. In the first photograph two masked, white-coated medical professionals, a male and a female, stand over Joan's head. The male holds a towel over Joan's eyes as both professionals clearly watch the lower half of her body. If Joan watched the birth of her third baby, the photographs do not show it. The reader views her. The medical professionals view her. But she is shown blindfolded. The opening text is similarly loaded: "One March evening in Chicago's Frank Cuneo Hospital, a nurse picked up a delivery-room chart and entered the birth of a 'small female, weighing four pounds six ounces, generally in good condition and well formed.' Thus unemotionally recorded, Dana Miller, third child of photographer Wayne Miller and his twenty-six-year-old wife, Joan, began life."

The way Dana Miller began her life was characteristic of the shift to hospital birthing, which was almost complete by midcentury. According to one caption, 85 percent of American babies were born in hospitals by 1950. Dana "began life" officially through the "unemotionally recorded" statistics of her weight, condition, and formation. She was measured and assessed by a

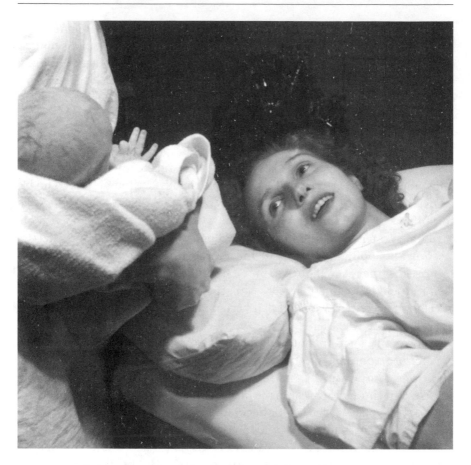

**Figure 2.26. "Baby's First Year."** *Ladies' Home Journal,* **March 1950**

doctor, charted by a nurse, and, after three days' incubation ("because of her slightness"), sent to be with her mother in the hospital room. The text describing baby Dana's care offers the expert witness of another medical professional to the need for such bonding between mother and child: Arnold Gesell, director of Yale University's Clinic of Child Development and an advocate of "rooming in." Summarizing the Gesell school of child rearing, the article suggests, along with "many doctors" who agree with Gesell, that the baby will thrive best on a "self-demand" schedule: "He need not live by the clock on the wall, but may be fed when he cries, allowed to sleep till he's done sleeping, and, best of all, enjoy *a more natural intimacy* with the first lady in his life" (emphasis added).

The call for mothers to establish "a more natural intimacy" in the midst of the hospital is rich with symbolism. The "natural intimacy" they were to pursue was introduced while they were fully surrounded by the expertise and equipment of medical science, was established secondary to the official "unemotionally recorded" evaluation of the newborn, and was recommended by no less than the director of Yale University's Clinic of Child Development. The article further suggests that "most homes can flex to self-demand," but one wonders whether life so configured will be able to "flex" sufficiently to accommodate both medicalized, unemotional motherhood and the "natural intimacy" of breast feeding. The birth of the baby is described as "a harsh experience" wherein "a human being [must] face so suddenly so many facts of a world he never made." The same thing might be said of mothers reading *Ladies' Home Journal*.

Postwar motherhood, as it entered the atomic era, saw the application of science for the sake of national security, but it also reflected the sense that there was much at stake in home economics. No detail of domesticity was too small for the researchers eager to help ease and anchor the life of the middle-class family. Medical science had taken great steps in infant care, as exemplified in Johnson's Baby Lotion's ability to "prevent impetigo, prevent raw buttocks, prevent diaper rash, prevent heat rash" (fig. 2.27). In the ad a doctor in lab coat and medical mask peers intently into a baby's nether regions; another physician shows on a chart the drop in infant skin problems owing to the use of Johnson's Baby Lotion; two nurses fixedly study a chart while an "Impetigo epidemic rages"; and, eventually, a mother cares for a baby at home, preventing "excoriated buttocks" and the suffering of "miliaria (heat rash)."[69] By 1955 *Ladies' Home Journal*, "The Magazine Women Believe In," combined warnings of impetigo and the "miracle" of protected buttocks with the "timesaving" nylon from DuPont (fig. 2.28) that would grant mother the minutes necessary to coif hair, arrange pearls, and practice a tune on the piano.

As discussed in the previous chapter, the norms of apposite domesticity were intensified by the professionally arranged color photographs appearing in the now mass-marketed magazines of proper homemaking. The advertised summons to trust in one's maternal, scientifically verified natural instinct appeared within a context of a beautifully perfect world of clean babies and happy mothers in clean kitchens.

There was also the matter of the husband. The "time-saving" products of corporate science were important in no small part because of the presence (or presumed presence) of another person in mother's life who counted her as his "first lady." The standards of motherhood for middle-class mothers

69. *Ladies' Home Journal*, April 1950, p. 241.

**Figure 2.27. Advertisement for Johnson's Baby Lotion.** *Ladies' Home Journal,* **February 1950**

**Figure 2.28. DuPont Nylon advertisement.** *Ladies' Home Journal,* **March 1955**

Timesaving *Du Pont Nylon* in party clothes means more play for children, less work for mother. Nylon stays neat lots longer, launders easily, needs a minimum of ironing! Nylon is one of Du Pont's modern-living fibers.

(and for those who hoped to be judged as normal by such) involved nothing short of what Betty Friedan famously named (in 1963) the "feminine mystique." The period during which doctors hoped for a renaissance in breast feeding saw also a new emphasis on the romantic dyad of husband and wife — the sense that a middle-class woman could be maternal, youthful, and sexually accessible through the magic of Max Factor and Maybelline. The symbolism is perhaps most overt in the marketing of women's girdles — enabling an elasticity of identity. The "figure of the fifties" would militate against the official advice to breast-feed.

### *"The Feeling of Freedom"*

It may be time to step aside once again and address a question likely on the minds of some readers. Was DuPont polyester not indeed a time-saver? Should we not praise DuPont Nylon as indeed a freedom fabric? Only a mother who has never ironed 100 percent cotton frocks would think that the creation of polyester was not a gain! Perhaps. Goodness knows that I myself wear, wash, and dry plenty of polyester each week.

But the time-saving devices of 1950s motherhood reinforced through advertising an impossibly configured version of the domestic "normal." The time-savers emerged as a new necessity during an era when mothers received unprecedented pressure to conform to an image of perfection. The "normal" at play for mothers during the postwar period involved a woman's responsibility (a) to keep her son's derriere both *clean* clean and unchafed, (b) to protect him from playground taunts, (c) to ensure that he was informed about the origin of dust and the dreams of dogs, and (d) to dress him and his sisters in impeccably matched clothing. This was all while also protecting her hips, breasts, and hands from any signs of her labor. So, before I concede touché to my imagined interlocutor, let us concentrate on the Trushay advertisement.

Trushay's run of ads for their "beforehand" lotion featured an appeal to "every woman who leads a double life" (fig. 2.29). The split between "Efficient You!" and "Enchanting You!" was literal, as the advertisements depicted one half of a woman able to "whiz through the dishes, suds up [the] clothes," and "whisk away dust 'n' dirt" and the other half of the woman able to look her "loveliest for BIG evenings!" Her hands would be "in and out — in and out — of hot, soapy water," but she would still seem, from outward appearances, to be hardly lifting a finger. A woman was to be "efficient" in her cleaning but still retain a side of herself that was "enchanting" to her husband, and to others. This required a kind of illusion of leisure — hands that carried out the

*For every woman who leads a double life…*

**HOME-LOVING YOU!** Cooking up your specialties, washing the dishes, polishing up the house! Your hands are in and out—in and out—of hot, soapy water. But you'd hate to have rough, red hands when evening comes, for then it's . . .

**PARTY-LOVING YOU!** *Giving* a party—*or going* to one—you want your hands soft and *smooth.* That's why Trushay—the "beforehand" lotion—is *very specially yours!* Read below how this unusual lotion guards your hands while you work!

**TRUSHAY** . . . *the "beforehand" lotion . . . guards your hands even in hot, soapy water!*

YES IT'S YOURS INDEED—velvety Trushay. Yours—and every woman's whose hands—th from one soapand-water task to another.

Fragrant Trushay—a new and different idea in hand care!

A lotion so oil-rich, you smooth it on BEFORE doing dishes or rubbing clothes—and it protects your hands right in the hot, soapy water! Actually helps prevent de-drying, chapping damage. Softens your hands—preserving their smooth loveliness—while you work!

Don't let daily washing tasks spoil your hands. Adopt Trushay's "beforehand" care. And remember, Trushay leads a double life, too! It's marvelous "beforehand"—and it's a wonderful lotion to use any time. So keep a bottle on your dressing table, as well as in your kitchen.

Use Trushay as a skin softener, a body rub, a powder base. And always smooth it on before you go out in cold weather. Creamy Trushay makes your skin much softer—and guards against painful, ugly chapping. So begin today to use Trushay.

**TRUSHAY**
THE
"BEFOREHAND"
LOTION

A PRODUCT OF BRISTOL-MYERS

**Figure 2.29. Advertisement for Trushay lotion.** *Ladies' Home Journal,* **March 1950**

"quick, capable" tasks of hygienic motherhood without bearing the marks of the effort required. Trushay would help prevent the "rough, red hands" that would be the telltale signs of work.

The Trushay advertisements visibly represented the split between the role of mother and the role of wife at issue in the Atomic Age. Another powerful image of the tension in living according to the plan of aesthetically normative motherhood is from the advertisements for Playtex girdles. The series for the new "Invisible Playtex Pink-Ice" was particularly provocative, with images of a woman moving "freely" while quite obviously frozen in a large block of pink ice (fig. 2.30). She was in motion, freed for movement, but only as a series of stills set in transparent latex. The contrast between, on the one hand, the movement of the model playing tennis (in ice) or leaping over a block of wood with a single bound (fig. 2.31) and, on the other, the "Hollywood" model posing for her close-up is indicative of the strange message conveyed in the series. A woman was, in movement, free — but only inasmuch as she remained enveloped in latex. The devices were "made of tree-grown liquid latex," and were therefore, presumably, conducive to a natural liquidity of form. From the "slim silvery tubes" to the models elongated on the page, the message was about streamlining the female body. But it was also clearly about moving from the postmaternal to the prematernal, even adolescent, body — to the body whose hips had not been spread by childbirth. Not a one of the models featured in the advertisements wears clothing that looks even remotely motherly. Instead, the reader was to take her cue from Hollywood: "Nowhere in the world is a woman's figure so noticed as in Hollywood. Nowhere is the *look of youth* so important."

Although feminist historians have been quick to note the postwar era's concentrated attention on domesticity and traditional female roles, the Playtex girdles represent visually the optimal version of the 1950s mother. She was to be simultaneously a wonderful cook and a lady of leisure, open to her children and their needs, but not in a way that would hold her back or visibly distinguish her from the Hollywood goddesses.

The area of the feminine body on which the girdle concentrated was "from waist to hips to thighs," and one could, through this purchase, meet the aesthetic norms of "supple, young lines." The repeated appeal throughout the advertising of Playtex girdles during this period was to the "Figure of the 1950s," a figure that was "slim, young, supple," with "fluid lines" and a "young, vital silhouette." This was the "feeling of freedom" encased in roseate ice. "To be sure that you have that new figure," one "so perfectly slim," a woman would need to "wear Playtex." This was the aesthetic context in which the women reading *Ladies' Home Journal,* and several key magazines

**Figure 2.30. Playtex girdle advertisement.** *Ladies' Home Journal,* **May 1950**

**Figure 2.31. Playtex girdle advertisement.** *Ladies' Home Journal,* **March 1950**

like it, were to decide whether to breast-feed or to turn to the sleek, supple lines of Evenflo, a line of products for feeding that "makes happy babies."

The baby fed with an Evenflo nurser would be able to truly "enjoy" his milk, controlling the flow for quick or, if he preferred, quite leisurely feedings (fig. 2.32). Evenflo nursers would enable baby to have "precision" in his meal, even before he was able to speak; he could "relax, feed at the speed he wants." This would lead to "healthy gains in weight." The sense that a bottle-fed baby was a healthier, more contented, more *in control* baby was new in the 1950s. The appeal to physician expertise is less present in these advertisements, perhaps in part because the American Medical Association was by then concentrating its efforts on convincing women to breast-feed.

Appearing also for the first time since the Roaring Twenties was the appeal to a particular version of infant convenience and maternal ease. A woman's transition from mother to "cover girl," as depicted in the Silhouette Figure Form International advertisement (fig. 2.33), would be simpler if she drastically reduced her caloric intake and donned a latex girdle and form-fitting brassiere. These practices and patterns were of course practically ill-suited for nursing an infant. But beyond the technical difficulty of breast feeding while determined to achieve a sleek and youthful figure, the sleek and youthful figure that was the norm signaled the need to move beyond motherhood. The Houston-based Silhouette Figure Form International made this clear in their text, wherein they offered "Special courses for new mothers . . . designed and regulated to restore firm body tissues — [to] help regain a youthful figure. Silhouette's ingenious equipment . . . prescribed, personalized courses under the supervision of experienced instructors guarantee that you will have the lovely figure nature intended for you." The "figure nature intended" for mothers was not one with postpartum hips and breasts full of milk but instead one that was "youthful." The "ingenious equipment" of the era would redefine the natural, supposedly "freeing" women for movement.

The physician/baby who asked, in the Johnson & Johnson advertisement, what a mother *really* knows about babies had now grown into a boy who not only needed to know everything in the *Book of Knowledge* but also hoped to have a "cover girl" for a mother. From medical advice to "experienced instructors" — from obeying one's doctor to obeying the purveyors of the beautiful in Hollywood — a mother reading magazines like *Parents'* or *Ladies' Home Journal* would need to turn to the products of tomorrow to achieve her "youthful" status of yesterday. With a Perma-Lift Brassiere and a "poof" of Stopette, she could present herself as both youthful and unencumbered by the stresses of motherhood (fig. 2.34). With warnings like the one in

Figure 2.32. Evenflo advertisement. *Parents'*, January 1958

### America's Most Popular Nurser

Mrs. William Millar of Darien, Conn. feeding baby daughter, Anne.

## Feeding is easy with
# evenflo

It is easy to feed baby with Evenflo Nursers. Evenflo's precision feeding lets your baby relax, feed at the speed he wants. Moreover, Evenflo's patented, self-regulating Twin Air-Valve Nipple makes formula flow *evenly*, whether it is thick or thin. Baby finishes his Evenflo bottle easily, makes healthy gains in weight.

Widemouth Evenflo bottles are easier to fill and clean, and the sanitary sealing of nipple inside bottle is convenient for refrigeration and carrying.

*Since it is easier to nurse, handier to use, more mothers use Evenflo than all other nursers combined.*

25¢ Complete Unit
10¢ Nipples

## evenflo®

*Everything to feed your baby*

### EVENFLO, RAVENNA, OHIO

Mothers <u>can</u> be **COVER GIRLS!**

A surprising number of America's top fashion models actually are mothers . . . some of three or four children. It isn't that these envied women don't have figure problems . . . it's simply that they know how to take care of their lovely figures. And how . . . ?

**MANY OF AMERICA'S GLAMOROUS MODELS ARE MEMBERS OF SILHOUETTE!**

Special courses for new mothers are designed and regulated to restore firm body tissues — help regain a youthful figure.

Silhouette's ingenious equipment . . . prescribed, personalized courses under the supervision of experienced instructors guarantee that you will have the lovely figure nature intended for you.

*The Internationally Famous Silhouette Guarantee . . .*
**3 MONTHS FREE**
If we fail to get the following results in 60 days:
OVERWEIGHT        UNDERWEIGHT or AVERAGE
Lose 15 Pounds.          Add 2 Inches to Bustline
3 Inches Off Hips and Waist. Improve Posture and Re-Proportion
Take One Inch Off Ankle.      tion Body Measurements

JANUARY SPECIAL!
Enroll at any Silhouette
Figure-Form Studio For Only $8.00 per month

On a Membership Basis, Treatments Average Only 35c

You'll marvel at the ease and speed of this new concept in figure perfection. You'll be delighted with the lovelier figure that Silhouette promises . . . the dramatic results achieved without Spartan dieting!

There are no classes to attend, no appointments to make. You arrange visits to suit *your* convenience as often as you like. FREE, private figure analysis and trial treatment. No obligation . . . ever!

### Silhouette
**FIGURE-FORM INTERNATIONAL**
•United States • Canada • Mexico • England

The Silhouette Salon Nearest You is Part of the World's Largest and Finest Chain of Health Studios, with Over 200 Studios Located Throughout the United States, Canada, Mexico and England. Your Membership is Good at All Silhouette Figure-Form Salons.

For FREE literature, write Peg Maxwell, Dept. PS, Silhouette Figure-Form International, 3517 Montrose Blvd., Houston, Texas or call "Information" for the phone number of the salon in your city.

Figure 2.33. Silhouette International advertisement. *Parents'*, January 1958

**Figure 2.34. Advertisements from**
*Ladies' Home Journal*, **March 1950**

**Figure 2.35. Listerine Antiseptic advertisement.** *Ladies' Home Journal*,
**May 1950**

the advertisement for Listerine Antiseptic, mothers were advised that their choices were loaded (fig. 2.35). If mere bad breath could cost you your man, what kind of toll would breast feeding take on your marriage? The taxonomy of the maternal body was complicated at this time: Was the breast to be lifted to the mouth of one's infant or lifted by a powerful brassiere to be admired by one's husband?

Arguably, by the close of the 1950s advertising to women in mainstream America was potent enough to allow a woman to think she was choosing, quite freely, to take control of her own figure and her own marriage through her choice of infant formula. In the Johnson & Johnson advertisement featuring the baby/doctor, the executives could trust that the affirmation of grandmother's knowledge would not undermine the appeal of their product. Scientific expertise mattered, but industrial science had long since learned to magnify, not mitigate, the prevailing norms of aesthetic desire and gender. On the cusp of the 1960s, the *Parents'* seal of approval stood not so much as a seal of professional expertise as a seal of parental approval — a sign that women like the reader herself, not incidentally married to men like the reader's husband, approved of the product bearing the seal. This "feeling of freedom" — feminine autonomy as aesthetically streamlined — would gain momentum as the next generation declared itself to be liberated from the tasks of traditional domesticity.

### The Rise of the Medicated "Ordinary"

The bizarre version of what nature intended may be best characterized in two Seven-Up advertisements (figs. 2.36 and 2.37).[70] The corporate breast had become, by this point, virtually unrecognizable, as a mother's hand reached out to offer her eleven-month-old son not her bosom but a green-tinted bottle of fizzy liquid. This might look like mere whimsy to the twenty-first-century reader, but the message was delivered in straight-on sobriety. The drink was "for any family occasion." Not only were "Freddie and Kay" to enjoy their soda pop, but their little brother in the push pram could also enjoy the drink of choice, the "cheerful, clean-tasting" Seven-Up. The language echoed the appeals to scientifically approved infant feeding in decades prior: "Seven-Up is *so pure — so good — so completely wholesome* that even the very youngest can 'fresh up' just as often as they want . . . and with as much as they want, too." The language of "wholesome" and "purity" had become quite service-

70. Thanks to Bryan Langlands for finding the image in figure 2.36.

**Figure 2.36. Seven-Up advertisement.** *Ladies' Home Journal,* **August 1950**

**Figure 2.37.** Seven-Up advertisement. *Ladies' Home Journal*, September 1955

able. The 1955 advertisement focused precisely on the youngest member of the family:

> This young man is 11 months old — and he isn't our youngest customer by any means.
>
> For 7-Up is so pure, so wholesome, you can even give it to babies and feel good about it. . . . By the way, Mom, when it comes to toddlers — if they like to be coaxed to drink their milk, try this: Add 7-Up to the milk in equal parts. . . . It's a wholesome combination — and it works!

A pastel-pink-and-blue baby ball and a plush lamb with a pink bow add the touches. The designations "so pure" and "so completely wholesome" were given validation by two seals immediately to the left of the text in the 1950 version. One seal signified that the product had been "Commended by the consumer service bureau of *Parents' Magazine*," and the other seal presumably denoted medical approval, with "Advertised — American Medical Association Publications." Hygeia, the goddess of health, had come a long way, baby.

Although I generally refrain in this book from making my own appeals to a *more natural* natural, this advertisement almost begs for such an argument. As the initial turn to mass-marketed infant formula in the early twentieth century reflected not only a medicalized culture but also a growing market of scientifically verified domesticity, the shift to one part soda/one part milk reflected not only a fast-food culture but also a growing market of family entertainment. We can take up the question of "the natural" by asking this: When a human process that had seemed for centuries to be natural (breastfeeding an infant) is transmuted into something hardly recognizable as such (the "wholesome combination" of milk and soda pop), who gains from the transmutation?

This advertisement makes the answer fairly transparent. Seven-Up is suitable "for any family occasion" and thus should be purchased in bulk: "Order a case where you see those bright 7-Up signs." But the small print offers another clue to the answer of the transmuted natural. To the right of the baby's arm is a gentle reminder that the new and improved "Family Occasion" in the family room of the 1950s involved a little box: "Watch 'Soldiers of Fortune.' For exciting adventure, see this 7-Up show every week." Television would serve (up to the present) as a newly natural conduit for the milk of corporate advertising. The toy ball and the plush lamb would be as handily supplanted as had been the mother's breast.

### *"So Much Going On . . ."*

Television made a hit debut at the 1939-40 New York World's Fair, with exhibits from General Electric, Westinghouse, the Crosley Radio Corporation, and RCA. To sum up the claim made to the fairgoing public, the new technology would "revolutionize public communication and private life."[71] Sixteen years after the fair, *Life* ran an image that visually depicts the revolution in private life brought to Americans through television. The first page of the two-page ad pictures a sealed television box with the text "Open *before* Christmas! here's why." The second page shows the family crowded around the half-exposed, glowing set (Junior's nose nearly touching the screen), apparently too mesmerized by the show to finish the unpacking (fig. 2.38).

The promise that there was "so much going on in NBC Big Color TV . . . every night!" captured a population that had previously gotten their news primarily through magazines, newspapers, and radio. As Lynn Spigel notes in *Make Room for TV: Television and the Family Ideal in Postwar America,* postwar domestic magazines featured not only advertisements for televisions themselves but also advice for rearranging the living room around this new focal point of domestic life.[72] As the 1960s began, television was a normal part of American family life. What was so overt in the advertisement was the alluring promise of becoming a part of what was "going on" through television news and entertainment. The television era offered families the opportunity to bring the real news and the real world into their own living rooms — *virtually* — transforming the home into a place where Mom, Dad, Junior, and Sis could access, together, the newly defined *public.*

The shift to a new sense of domestic knowledge and entertainment had already occurred to some extent with radio, decades prior, but the appeal of being able to travel toward an exciting elsewhere, together, while remaining at home in one's living room was given new power as sound met sight. DuMont ran a series of advertisements in 1946 and 1947 with the mottoes "Get the Most out of Life . . . with TELEVISION" (fig. 2.39, 1946) and "Get More out of Life with Television" (1947).[73] The series showed families sitting together viewing sports and circuses and grandly staged musicals. The "Life" that mat-

71. "The 1939 World's Fair: Television in the World of Tomorrow," MZTV, the Museum of Television History. Accessed 2004: www.mztv.com.

72. See Lynn Spigel, *Make Room for TV: Television and the Family Ideal in Postwar America* (Chicago: University of Chicago Press, 1992). See in particular chapter 4, "The Home Theater," pp. 99-135.

73. The advertisements appeared, for example, in the *New York Herald Tribune, New York Times, New Yorker,* and *New York Times Magazine.* Thanks to Dan Rhodes for this reference.

there's so much
going on in
NBC BIG COLOR TV
...every night!

**Figure 2.38. NBC Color Television advertisement.** *Life*, 1956

No matter what day of the week your new Color TV set arrives, tune it in and start enjoying NBC Big Color. There's lots of it . . . *every night!*

Night after night on NBC, you can see great shows like Alcoa-Goodyear Playhouse, the new Walter Winchell Show, Robert Montgomery Presents, Dinah Shore's once-a-month Chevy Show, Kraft Television Theater, The Perry Como Show, Noah's Ark, Bob Hope's Chevy Show, and Lux Video Theater . . . all in Color! And most weekday afternoons, NBC Matinee Theater brings you a live, full-hour, Big Color play.

*More* Big Color news! This Saturday night, the Esther Williams Aqua Spectacular, October 5. Dinah Shore's first full-hour Chevy Show.

October 15, William Wyler's production of Somerset Maugham's gripping drama, "The Letter," on Producers' Showcase. And, on October 28, Mary Martin stars in "Born Yesterday" on the Hallmark Hall of Fame.

That's just October. Between now and Christmas, there'll be a dazzling succession of Big Color shows on NBC. You can see them all in black-and-white, of course. But why wait till Christmas for Color? You could be enjoying so many NBC programs so much more . . . *right now.*

*Exciting things are happening every night on* **NBC** COLOR **TELEVISION** *a service of*

tered, by way of the messages in such advertising, was the life that was viewed through the box.

The turn from the actual to the transmitted virtual in living rooms across the country may be read as a part of a long trajectory toward the carefully arranged pretend, a trajectory on which world expositions like the one in Chicago had a distinct place. Visitors to the Century of Progress were able to move from a pretend, futuristic living room, in which no one was actually living, to a pretend, atavistic village, in which people pretended to live. Moving from constructed image to constructed image, from stage to stage, is an opportunity as old as the carnival. But the carnival within the home, and the flipping from channel to channel, or the awaited change from show to show, may have transformed the home itself — as family meals, conversations, leisure time, and even furnishings were rearranged according to the

**Figure 2.39. DuMont advertisement.** *New York Times,* **1946**

possibilities of getting more out of life, with television. The sense not only of viewing but also of being viewed may have thoroughly transformed the sense of ordinary. Two decades into the age of television, some parents already worried that the inventing "genius" at the Century of Progress had gotten out of control — the carnival had hit home, and man was being required to conform and adapt.

We can interpret the rise of the medicated ordinary by way of the cultural history of marketing infant nutrition and progress. ADHD medications warrant critical consideration in and of themselves, given the controversy surrounding both the drugs and the diagnosis. The diagnosis of ADHD came about through a long process, beginning roughly at the beginning of the twentieth century when British doctor G. F. Still named a pattern among some children as a "defect of moral control."[74] By the 1950s, stimu-

74. G. F. Still, The Goulstonian Lectures on "Some Abnormal Psychical Conditions in

lants were being employed to treat what was by 1980 deemed by the American Psychiatric Association to be a "disorder," labeled attention deficit disorder. The name would change in 1987 to attention–deficit/hyperactivity disorder (ADHD). The stimulants often prescribed for pediatric ADHD are the most addictive drugs still legally available in the United States, yet two to three times as many children and adolescents were taking some type of psychiatric drug in 1996 as in 1987, with Ritalin (a stimulant) among the most frequently prescribed.[75]

This pattern alone begs for attention, apart from the larger questions of marketing biotechnology to parents. But the pattern is significant precisely for the larger questions of marketing domestic normalcy in the United States. The turn from the breast to the bottle reflects features of a turn to medically verifiable data and, ultimately, to carefully marketed, corporately produced tools for the raising of America's children. A plausible way to interpret the meteoric rise in pediatric psychopharmaceuticals is through the provocation voiced by cultural critic Wendell Berry, who suggested that technology will solve the problems that technology creates and will create the problems that technology solves.[76] One need not accept in every detail Berry's distinction between "the natural" and "the technological" to worry about the way biotechnological answers are given as the new default "natural" answers to perceived problems in childhood behavior.

There are some rather compelling cultural accounts of the perceived rise in hyperactivity among children in the twenty-first century. We will name these up front. Simultaneous with the new diagnoses of pediatric behavioral disorders has been a decrease in quantity time between parents and children in postindustrial America. For a relatively brief period, middle-class Americans took advantage of labor laws, advances in agriculture, and labor-

---

Children," *Lancet* 159, no. 4104 (April 26, 1902): 1163-68; cited in Ian N. Ford, "Socio-educational and Biomedical Models in the Treatment of Attention Deficit/Hyperactivity Disorder and Related Neurobehavioural Disorders in Childhood and Adolescence, and Their Implications for Adult Mental Health," *Child and Adolescent Psychiatry Online*, 1996. Accessed 2005: www.priory.com.

75. Kate Zernike and Melody Petersen, "Schools' Backing of Behavior Drugs Comes under Fire," *New York Times*, August 19, 2001; Erica Goode, "Pills and Children (University of Maryland Report on Increase in Psychiatric Drug Usage)," *New York Times*, January 19, 2003. Goode reports that the use of "anti-psychotics, so-called mood stabilizers, and other potent drugs also jumped sharply."

76. See Wendell Berry, *Life Is a Miracle; An Essay against Modern Superstition* (Washington, D.C.: Counterpoint, 2000), p. 21. The actual quotation reads: "Many of the calamities from which science is expected to save the world were caused in the first place by science — which meanwhile is busy propagating further calamities, hailed now as wonders, from which later it will undertake to save the world."

saving devices in the home to spend time in some form of leisure in the evenings. But according to the National Research Council's Board on Children, Youth, and Families, by the late 1980s children were spending on average eleven fewer hours per week with their parents than they had spent in 1960.[77]

Another change involves that box that brings us "every night" our entrée into what is "going on." This is what researcher Marie Winn has termed "the Plug-In Drug."[78] I will argue below that the strong pull of ADHD as a medically defined and treatable diagnosis has no small part to do with the fear among middle-to-upper-class parents that their children may be out of control. Yet, although the American Academy of Pediatrics reports that nearly one thousand studies have indicated links between aggressive behavior in children and media violence, and the National Television Violence Study concluded that 60 percent of all television programs had violent content (and this, before 9/11), the average American child still watches four hours of television every day.[79] One study found that children committed seven times as many acts of aggression in play after viewing one episode of *Mighty Morphin Power Rangers* (a show that in retrospect appears almost wholesome) than children who had not viewed the show.[80]

This is not even to dig into the many documented links between large class size and reported hyperactivity among public school children, the link between artificial additives in children's food and reported hyperactivity, or other hypothesized and variously linked environmental factors in the emergence of what has been seen as a national epidemic of middle-class childhood deficit and disorder.

Yet, as compelling as these possible environmental answers are, they seem not to be taking hold of the parental imagination, and even less so the public-decision-making imagination. In my many conversations after lectures at churches, civic groups, and universities, I have met only a handful of (often exhausted and financially stressed) mothers who have managed to throw out the family television and cut back on out-of-home work hours in order to address nonmedically their children's designation as ADHD. The lat-

77. See S. Small, G. Eastman, and S. Cornelius, "Adolescent Autonomy and Parental Stress," *Journal of Youth and Adolescence* 17 (1988): 377-91.

78. Marie Winn, *The Plug-In Drug: Television, Children, and the Family,* rev. ed. (New York: Penguin Books, 1985).

79. American Academy of Pediatrics Committee on Communications, "Media Violence," *Pediatrics* 95 (June 1995): 949-51; American Academy of Pediatrics, "Television and the Family," http://www.aap.org/family/tv1.htm.

80. Chris J. Boyatzis and Gina M. Matillo, "Effects of 'The Mighty Morphin Power Rangers' on Children's Aggression with Peers," *Child Study Journal* 25 (1995): 45-56.

ter decision is often simply financially unavailable to lower-working-class mothers and single mothers.

To better understand the rise of the medicated ordinary, we can extend the discussion of infant feeding and childhood regularity — two ways of ensuring domestic regularity and decorum during a century of progress — to contemporary culture. This brings us to another set of contentious puzzles facing mothers in the United States today. The American Academy of Pediatrics recommends that mothers breast-feed for at least the first twelve months, and the World Health Organization goes so far as to recommend breast feeding exclusively (excluding formula and even water) for at least six months, further suggesting that mothers continue breast feeding for at least two years.[81] Yet according to U.S. statistics, only 22 percent of American mothers are still breast-feeding at six months.

The reasons for this disparity between advice and actual practice are complicated. The maternity leave policies in the United States render most working mothers financially incapable of breast feeding their babies past six weeks — that is, if they are even able to take advantage of the federally mandated minimum of six weeks unpaid leave. (Part-time and casual employees are not guaranteed any leave at all.) But even this development in the story of infant feeding in the United States may be read alongside the evolving norms of childhood and parental regularity.

At the beginning of the last century, aspiring mothers were encouraged, even admonished, to bring the scientist and modern pediatrician into the nursery. Although women's magazines and medical journals still traded on the idea that parenting was "the grand prerogative of woman," a "noble and a holy office, to which she is appointed by God" (to quote again Dr. Cook's 1866 manual on infant care), as the century progressed, mothers were increasingly urged to turn away from homespun, commonly sensed sense and toward the new, scientifically vetted wisdom of medicine and industry. "The reproduction of the species" (again, Dr. Cook) required the new tools of corporate production. The primary movement of the human race, by all middle-class gauges, was not going on in the nursing chair or the bathing vessel or the training potty but in the world of science, genius, and industry. Educated mothers were to be the foot soldiers in the march forward. Within a few generations of the turn of the century, women quite predictably and understandably aspired to play a more active role in the direction of troops. Through so-

---

81. World Health Organization, *Global Strategy for Infant and Young Child Feeding*, World Health Assembly 2002 (Geneva: World Health Organization, 2003), paragraph 10. Accessed 2004: www.who.org.

cial work, nursing, teaching, and other professions, women sought to use their feminine expertise to reproduce the social body.

This rise in the number of women working outside their homes occurred simultaneously with a heightened pressure to conform to a particular aesthetic ideal. The newly pliant latex available in the late 1940s and early 1950s went not only into better nipples for bottle feeding but also into products like the Pink Ice girdle — so that even postmaternity women could achieve a "girlish" figure. Through the growing circulation of women's magazines, mothers were increasingly exposed to ever-higher standards of beauty and domesticity. As women began to leave the home to work elsewhere, the ideal of clean and conspicuously arranged domestic life was not adjusted. Mothers entered the workforce, but the workforce did little to accommodate them. Even many privileged women with relative power found that in the halls of business, medicine, and the academy they had to conform to an ever-expanding workweek and what the Duke Women's Initiative in 2004 called a culture of "effortless perfection." The Women's Initiative summed up the class and gender issues for working mothers thus:

> The arrangements that individual families make to deal with such issues in our society are often complex, tenuous and expensive. Here, as in other ways, economic class reinforces gender differences, since it is easier for highly compensated employees to pay for the kinds of arrangements that make parents feel comparatively comfortable working long hours outside the home. As one medical faculty member put it: "It really does take a village. And I've hired a village." For lower-paid employees, making ends meet and providing opportunities for their children often means that one or both parents work two jobs, and child care arrangements depend on the help of family and neighbors as well as affordable child care providers.[82]

If this has grown to be the case for female physicians, how much more is it the case for female orderlies? And this does not even begin to ask about the children of the low-paid workers who are hired as "the village."

The need for Enfamil, Midol, Prozac, Xanax, hyper-caffeinated coffee, and Ritalin may be read in part as a need for the tools with which a family may manage the barrage of financial expectations and on-the-job demands. Scientific motherhood has become a working assumption of what some social commentators call a "tunnel economy," in which only streamlined and

---

82. *Report of the Steering Committee for the Women's Initiative at Duke University* (2003), p. 8. Accessed 2003: www.duke.edu.

unencumbered lives make it through to the light of economic security. Scientific motherhood may have begun as an appeal to aspiration among rising middle-to-upper-class mainstream Protestant mothers, but it eventually made its way through the more broadly defined middle class. By the time Lilly marketed Strattera in middle-end women's domestic magazines in 2003, the sense that "most people" were able to "take for granted" the unspoiled "ordinary" displayed in the ads cut to the heart of a middle-class mother's duty — to deliver an aesthetically normal version of domesticity (one consistent with *good* housekeeping), even while working outside the home to generate the income necessary to procure it.

### *"Spend More Time . . . "*

The tensions between maternal time and infant demands were quite unconcealed by the 1970s, when formula companies advertised directly to expectant and new mothers.[83] The physician/baby became, in a 1974 Enfamil advertisement from *Good Housekeeping,* the "man of the house," expecting to be fed on time (fig. 2.40). The text reflects the underlying conflicts between physician advice, which had not changed since the 1950s, and perceived maternal responsibilities. Addressing the *Good Housekeeping* mother at her most vulnerable point, Enfamil reassures her: "No matter how good a mother you are, there are always times when your baby is ready for his formula. But his formula isn't ready for him." Even a *good* housekeeping mother could meet her infant's demands on schedule with "Ready-To-Use" formula, whose motto for 1974 ran: "Isn't it nice that the formula that's so convenient for you is also so good for him?" The more succinct version of the motto, "Good for You. Better for Your Baby," was given another valence in a second 1974 ad.

In one ad (fig. 2.41) the corporate breast supplants entirely the maternal breast, as three generations of men attest to the sufficiency of formula. The grandfather, dad, and baby all apparently thrived on the nourishment that was available quite apart from mother. The text again confirms: "How reassuring to know that the formula that's convenient for you is also good for the

---

83. The code of the World Health Organization (WHO) regarding formula advertising, accessed 2004: www.who.int/nut/documents/code_english.PDF. The various forms of infant formula marketing in the United States are in basic conflict with the International Code of Marketing of Breastmilk Substitutes (1981), adopted by both the WHO and United Nations International Children's Education Fund (UNICEF). The United States did not sign on to this agreement.

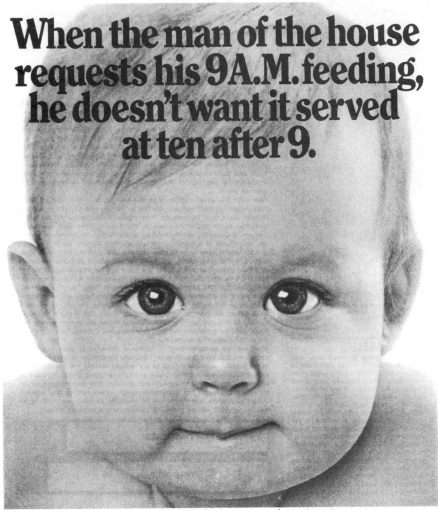

# When the man of the house requests his 9 A.M. feeding, he doesn't want it served at ten after 9.

No matter how good a mother you are, there are always times when your baby is ready for his formula.

But his formula isn't ready for him.

That's one of the many nice things about Enfamil Ready-To-Use. It's always ready when your baby wants it. No mixing. No mess. Just pour and you're feeding him as nutritious a formula as you can buy. Just ask your doctor and he'll tell you.

There's a full day's supply in each 32 fl. oz. can and because it's pre-mixed, you're always confident that it's mixed exactly right. And since you're spending less time making formula you can spend more time enjoying your baby.

Isn't it nice that the formula that's so convenient for you is also so good for him?

**Enfamil®
Ready-To-Use**

Good for you.
Better for your baby.

**Figure 2.40. Enfamil advertisement.** *Good Housekeeping*, June 1974

**Figure 2.41. Enfamil advertisement.** *Good Housekeeping,* September 1974

newest generation," and the notion that formula has been for at least sixty years the solution of mothers lends a sense of tradition to the message.

In the "man of the house" version of the ad, there is an appeal to both concerned mother and busy mother. The claim again circumvents the possibility of breast feeding, contrasting the difficulty of powdered formula with the ease of already-mixed feedings — "And since you're spending less time making formula you can spend more time enjoying your baby." No mention is made of the already-mixed convenience of breast feeding.

What might this sort of advertising mean for time spent between children and parents in middle-class America? Miriam Weinstein, author of *The Surprising Power of Family Meals,* uses cultural and historical analysis to suggest that the pattern of eating changed during the last decades of the twentieth century. She sums up her research in this way:

> We got the news about wanting to eat food that tastes good. But somewhere, as my daughter would say, we missed the memo about the pleasures of making it and eating it and sharing it with people we care about. We've perfected the segmentation of the family. Nobody has to eat the same food, watch the same show, listen to the same song, let alone sing it. We love to imagine the French with their lush tables, or the Italians with their big families, but we prefer to gobble our take-out, our home delivery, our single-serve microwave, on the run, in front of the TV, in the food court, or in the car, while we dream of quality time, of family vacations, of someplace far away.[84]

We can see the early manifestations of the on-the-run meal in the turn to "Ready-to-Use" Enfamil and its kin, as mothers were told that it would be easier to feed baby by bottle so that they might, ostensibly, have more time with baby. The world of domestic advertising in the 1970s gave the lie to this point, however, through ads like one from Fisher-Price that made rather apparent the shift from an idealized form of motherhood (requiring constant maternal attention to the dangerous possibility of excoriated buttocks) to one that made maternal attention almost obsolete. The ad's photographs were of infants with their toys, and there was not even a mother's hand in the mix. The text began by way of a newer, savvier sense of what baby needs: "Parents used to think that a bottle, a bath and some cuddling was enough to keep a baby happy. But now we know that babies learn as much about the world and themselves that first year, as in any year to come." The toys were each "a new

84. Miriam Weinstein, *The Surprising Power of Family Meals: How Eating Together Makes Us Smarter, Stronger, Healthier, and Happier* (Hanover, N.H.: Steerforth, 2005), p. 6.

and delightful way to widen their world." The large headline across the top of the advertisement put more candidly one of the questions at stake by the 1970s, as women with small children were working outside the home in greater numbers: "Fisher-Price knows that when you live in a crib you need lots of exciting things to do."[85]

The "exciting things to do" have increasingly involved an array of electronic devices to keep baby, and then toddler, and then child, occupied. Yet in the midst of this, acute pressure is also applied to the children and parents of relative privilege, the children of the upper and professional classes, to perform by the quantifiable standards of testing and the more nebulous standards of a "well-rounded" child. As the time parents spend with children is decreasing in the United States, the taut, even brittle, sense of adolescence is growing.

In her attempt to figure out why parents with even the most ample financial means to carve out not merely quality but also quantity time with their children are not doing so, Miriam Weinstein lands on the term "cultural capital," a term at play in the private school set, the first parents to turn to ADHD medications in large numbers. As she describes this phenomenon: "It's about parents investing in their children so the children can be worth more."[86] Weinstein quotes sociologist Teresa Arendell: "*Good* childhoods are intended not only to secure children's immediate psychological well-being and growth. They also aim to prepare children for their future roles as adults. . . . Steady involvement in organized enrichment activities enhances and secures children's individual *cultural capital,* readying them for participation in select strata of adult life."[87] Weinstein suggests that this push to produce a child who is able to "play soccer, study oboe, and work at the soup kitchen, preferably all on the same day" has much to do with the forces pulling such families apart.[88] The move to produce better children, children who are worth more, may be leading to the need for the sorts of psychopharmaceutical correctives that allow children bound for these "select strata of adult life" to perform in ways that will validate their parents' efforts.

Living as I do in a region termed the "new" South, supposedly a region

85. *Ladies' Home Journal,* July 1974, p. 23.
86. Weinstein, *The Surprising Power,* p. 84.
87. Weinstein, *The Surprising Power,* pp. 82-83, quoting Teresa Arendell, "The New Care Work of Middle Class Mothers," in *Minding the Time in Family Experience: Emerging Perspectives and Issues,* ed. Kerry J. Daly (Oxford: Elsevier Science, 2001), pp. 171-72, emphasis in original.
88. Weinstein, *The Surprising Power,* p. 83.

"too busy to hate," I have heard many testimonies that these pressures of privilege don't just trickle but gush down on working-class women and their children. As working-class, service-worker families try to navigate underfunded public school systems — in smaller cities that presume vehicles, expendable income, and facility with English — they wonder at the complaints of professional-class women who presumably have all the goods necessary to navigate the system well.

### "Welcome to ORDINARY"

In 2001 a physician named Laurence L. Greenhill of the New York State Psychiatric Institute ran a series of newspaper ads to elicit research subjects for a study of the safety and efficacy of generic Ritalin in preschool children. The study was called the Preschool ADHD Treatment Study, or PATS, and was initiated on the heels of an article in the *Journal of the American Medical Association* that had tracked "a twofold-to-threefold increase in the use of stimulant drugs, particularly methylphenidate [Ritalin], among 2- to 4-year-olds."[89] The study was intended to remove the drug from the category of "therapeutic orphans" — drugs approved for adults that, through "disclaimer labeling," may be legally prescribed for children without pediatric evaluation. The advertisement in the *New York Daily News* asked, "Is your preschooler just too active?" and offered "a comprehensive evaluation by our study team, as well as up to 14 months of treatment — all at no cost."[90]

A 2002 article on the study in the *New York Times* showcased the predicament of a couple with an extremely active only child — "politely speaking . . . a handful" — whom they had adopted after multiple attempts at fertility treatments. Readers were told that "Sam" had been born to a teenage mother, whom the parents only later discovered had herself (along with other birth relatives) been diagnosed with attention–deficit/hyperactivity disorder. The story narrates the shift that occurred as Sam's adoptive mother, a "believer in holistic medicine," and father, who previously believed his son was "just being a boy," came to accept their child as "a boy with a problem" — a problem in need of medication. At the end of the article, Sam's parents have just decided not to take him out of the study; he had developed a common, but discon-

89. Sheryl Gay Stolberg, "Preschool Meds," *New York Times*, November 17, 2002, p. 59; Julie Magno Zito, "Trends in the Prescribing of Psychotropic Medications to Preschoolers," *JAMA* 283 (February 23, 2000): 1025-30.

90. Stolberg, "Preschool Meds," p. 59.

certing, side effect while on the medication. The decision was indeed a dilemma, for Sam's behavior on the medication was significantly more manageable. Even Sam saw the difference. Asked about the "tiny pills," he replied, "They're for to help me." Help him with what? "'To help me with helping,' he replied, as if this were the most obvious thing in the world."

The pressure on parents and the rhetorical play upon parental anxiety that their child is not quite normal and their family not quite "ordinary" are hardly new. In a 1957 advertisement for *Childcraft* that ran in *Together*, a little boy rides on his rocking horse, waving his hat in the air, cowboy boots and even spurs completing the picture. The bold print reads: "School is closer than you think," with the underlying query in all capital letters, "Is he riding toward success or failure?" With *Childcraft*, "America's Famous Child Development Plan," a mother could be assured that her child would be ready for school. "In today's competitive world," the text reads, "no child should be denied this opportunity."[91] "Let *Childcraft* help remove your doubts," mothers were told. The stakes in such a "competitive world" were nothing short of staggering: "School can be a frightening new world or an exciting adventure for your child. One leads down the road to continuing failure; the other toward shining success. Which shall it be? The answer rests with you. Fortunately, today's parents can have the help of *Childcraft* in preparing their youngsters not only for school, but for life."

Another advertisement shows a school-age child, again a little boy, "just on the edge of all the fun." The bold-print question, "Does your child feel like an outsider?" runs above a drawing of five children playing joyfully on swing set and teeter-totter. Even the dog seems set for sheer "fun." Yet the one little boy is almost a mere outline, the barest hint of his particularity can be seen in the dark shadows beneath a tree. The ad's text again cuts to the heart of parental responsibility and proprietary shame: "Would you care to picture *your* child in the shadows? Behavior problems like this often have far-reaching effects in later years" (emphasis in original), and this is why *Childcraft*, privy to "150 leading child guidance and educational experts," was an essential purchase. "*Childcraft* can mean a better, happier way of life for you and yours."

The patterns that led up to the turn to mass-marketed psychopharmaceuticals are complicated, but the line from reliance on pharmaceuticals to the financial beneficiaries is a straight one. ADHD medications are among the top profit-making drugs for the major pharmaceutical companies that produce them. Strangely enough, Trushay "beforehand lo-

91. The *Childcraft* advertisements appeared in *Together*, March 1957, p. 75; October 1956, p. 83.

tion" was distributed in the 1950s by Bristol-Myers, the precursor to Bristol-Myers Squibb, today a major pharmaceutical company "whose mission is to extend and enhance human life."[92] In 2003, as the company sought to extend the application of its antianxiety medication BuSpar to children diagnosed with ADHD, it settled antitrust litigation concerning its attempts to block a generic version of the drug.[93] In 2001, three major drug companies broke a United Nations treaty from 1971 that was widely interpreted to prohibit the straight-to-consumer marketing of psychotropic substances.[94] What was perceived as an opening of the floodgates led to the mass-marketing of ADHD medications to women's magazines and women's television channels by pharmaceutical companies in the United States. The mothers and fathers who label and dose for deficit and disorder are not simply choosing freely from a marketplace of options. Parents in the United States are exposed to daily images beckoning toward a smoother life with their children. Set within the likes of *Ladies' Home Journal*, ADHD advertising is merely a part of the cornucopia of the familial "ordinary."

Consider one example of ADHD in context. A Shire Pharmaceuticals' Adderall advertisement in the May 2004 issue of *Family Circle* shows a little boy sitting on the steps with baseball glove and hat (fig. 2.42). The headline reads "Already Done with My Homework Dad!" This photograph of a successful boy, waiting patiently for dad to come home from work, appears alongside an advertisement for slipcovers. The "made over" furniture is graced by an impeccably dressed blonde mother and daughter sitting on either side of a ruggedly handsome power-dad with salt-and-pepper hair. The family dog lies at their feet. There are no plastic toys on the floor; there is no dog hair on the couch, no sticky jam on the child's dress. The articles running before and after this pair of advertisements tell readers how to "Succeed at Motherhood without Really Trying" (a humor piece) and discover the "7 Secrets of Supremely Happy Women." Such depictions of married life with children may seem, on the ground, evidence that our own messy lives and children are hopelessly disordered. Standing in the grocery line, I am compelled to wonder whether "ordinary" is a place that *other* people are able to "take for

92. Bristol-Myers Squibb. Accessed 2004: www.bms.com.

93. Rachel Zimmerman, "Drug Makers Find a Windfall Testing Adult Drugs on Kids," *Wall Street Journal*, February 5, 2001; Federal Trade Commission, "FTC Charges Bristol-Myers Squibb with Pattern of Abusing Government Processes to Stifle Generic Drug Competition," news release, March 7, 2003. Accessed 2004: www.ftc.gov.

94. Jim Rosack, "Controversy Erupts over Ads for ADHD Drugs," *Psychiatric News*, November 2, 2001, p. 20, available online at http://pn.psychiatryonline.org/cgi/content/full/36/21/20.

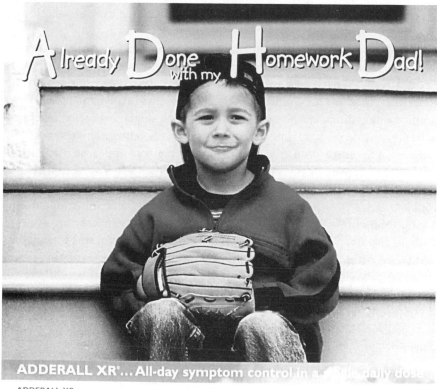

ADDERALL XR:

- Works fast for the start of the school day—with or without food
- Offers all-day ADHD symptom control
- Helps improve academic performance
- Shares a 60-year legacy of safety and clinical experience

ADDERALL XR was generally well tolerated in clinical studies. The most common side effects are decreased appetite, stomachache, difficulty falling asleep, and emotional lability.

Talk to your doctor if you have a history of high blood pressure or any heart conditions, glaucoma, thyroid problems, emotional instability, mental illness, or a known allergy to this type of medication. ADDERALL XR may not be right for you. If you are currently or have recently taken a type of antidepressant called a MAO inhibitor, you should not take ADDERALL XR. There is a potential for worsening of motion or verbal tics and Tourette's syndrome.

Abuse of amphetamines may lead to dependence. Report any new psychological symptoms to your physician.

*Please see brief summary of prescribing information on adjacent page. For more information, consult your physician*

**Shire US Inc.**
your ADHD support company
1-800-828-2088                    ©2003 Shire US Inc., Newport, Kentucky 41071

Talk to your doctor today to see if the all-day symptom control of ADDERALL XR can add new meaning to your child's life.

Visit us at **ADHDSupportCompany.com** or **ADDERALLXR.com**, or call 1-888-774-3000 for more information.

ONE DOSE DAILY

**ADDERALL XR** Ⓒ

5 mg, 10 mg, 15 mg, 20 mg, 25 mg, 30 mg CAPSULES
(Mixed Salts of a Single-Entity Amphetamine Product:
Dextroamphetamine Sulfate, Dextroamphetamine Saccharate,
Amphetamine Aspartate Monohydrate, Amphetamine Sulfate)

Patient-friendly ADHD treatment

April 2003          AXJA331          **Shire**

**Figure 2.42. Advertisement for Adderall.** *Family Circle*, May 2004

207

granted." And what, then, is wrong with *my* child, smearing spaghetti and spilling pink soda pop?

Pediatric ADHD advertisements do not appear in *Sports Illustrated* and other magazines aimed at a predominately male audience. Yet *the dad* appears frequently in ADHD ads. At least half of the advertisements promoting ADHD medications for children in the last five years involve the presence, or implied impending presence, of the child's father — playing softball, helping with homework, participating in family time over Scrabble. This seems a crucial part of the story. While the advertisements may not appear in men's magazines, men appear in the advertisements. A father helps with homework, smiling down at his son. Another father plays a game of checkers on the couch with his two children. Another sits down for a "relaxing family meal," taking time out — according to the advertisement, a whole hour — to be with his two small children. The scenes trade on a longing for this sort of normality — a normality where mom is not left to negotiate parenting a son alone. The "Welcome to Ordinary" image of the family meal is subtly retro, harking back to the diner of *Happy Days* and the family dinner that the mothers to whom the ads are supposed to appeal perhaps sense is lost.[95] The superimposed road sign itself, "*Welcome to* ORDINARY," appears against a rural, placid backdrop and signals through its plain text a simpler time.

This suggests a bleak underside to ADHD marketing. While the workweek balloons out of control and the amount of time that middle-class and professional parents spend with their children plummets, parents find themselves "choosing" pharmaceutical solutions. The message implies that this daily pill will quell the centrifugal forces pulling apart children and marriages. The "Welcome to Ordinary" series brings together many of the themes of pressurized but newly neglected childhood.

In the advertisement that opened the chapter (fig. 2.2), the photograph of "ordinary" focuses in on one little boy, the text indicating that the family meal and "relaxing" family time together are "much-needed." The clear implication is that this little boy is the center of the domestic problem to be solved. He is the reason family dinner is often interrupted. Another Strattera advertising pamphlet depicts a little boy building a model airplane with his father, and on the second page another child appears under the green sign of ORDINARY, with a clearly completed model. The timeline reads, "4:30 PM Tuesday — He started something you never thought he'd finish. 5:20 PM Thursday — He proved you wrong." The route to ORDINARY, a route that

---

95. Thanks to Dan Rhodes for pinpointing the retro-allure of the image from the Strattera advertisement.

involves a child actually starting a project and, within two days, completing it, is brought to the mother, to whom the advertising appeals, not so much by a recalibration of time as by the ADHD medication of Lilly laboratories. The boy is the problem, not the expectation of performance. The boy is the problem, not the overscheduled childhood. The boy is the problem, not the father's absence. Strattera goes straight to the heart of the problem, therefore, addressing the child who cannot keep up with parental expectations and the increasing sense among a segment of society that childhood involves, primarily, the training for efficient progress. This is perhaps most poignant in the Adderall advertisement. The implication of the ad is that the missing baseball game with dad has to do with the little boy's previous inability to complete his homework in time. He is the cause of the oft-postponed baseball toss with dad after work.

### "The Monsters Next Door"

Immediately following the Columbine disaster, the cover of *Time* featured the faces of the two boys who had murdered so many smiling out of the center of the page, with photographs of the children and teacher who had died arranged along the border.[96] Below the pictures of the two boys ran the words "The Monsters Next Door," with the word "Monsters" in red. *Time*'s multi-article special report opened with a reminder that Eric Harris and Dylan Klebold had recently posed for their official class picture, had only a month earlier attended their school prom, and were otherwise, all things considered, relatively *normal*. The ensuing articles and sidebars bore titles like "What Can the Schools Do?" "A Curse of Cliques," "Coming to Clarity about Guns," "Bang, You're Dead" (an essay on revenge in movies and television), and "Digital Dungeons."

The search for answers about the disaster involved soul-searching on the part of an entire nation, and few offered one-theory answers. But one way to interpret the visceral fear evoked by the story is that the monsters were indeed *next door*. The children who committed the ultimate acts of chaos on their fellow classmates and teacher were children of the suburbs, Littleton, Colorado, a relatively wealthy Denver suburb, and thus children who should have known better. They were, after all, "Little Leaguers," as the bold print, again in red, broadcast below their childhood photos. Beneath the pictures of

96. "The Monsters Next Door: A Special Report on the Colorado School Massacre," *Time*, May 3, 1999.

"The Dead," in a two-page spread, were indications, again, that these were children who were, as the text put it, "headed" somewhere. These were children whose lives were "cut short" by the boys next door.

The significant rise in ADHD diagnoses and prescriptions in the United States since the Columbine massacre can in part be seen as a response to the fear that violence is not merely a product of poverty, isolated in the parts of the United States abandoned by parents and children seeking the American promise. If it is not so isolated, then what of the children in communities like Littleton who are possibly at risk of perpetrating such acts of chaos and disorder?

The *Newsweek* special report, issued the same day as the *Time* report, pitched the story in a way that was subtly different. Rather than asking a series of questions in the form of essays on various factors promoting violence in the United States, the headline on the cover read "Why? Portraits of the Killers. The Science of Teen Violence."[97] The lead article in the special report was titled "Anatomy of a Massacre." In the second piece, "Why the Young Kill," the summary head asked, "Are certain young brains predisposed to violence?" Although the text itself went on to detail the various environmental factors that might "push them over the brink," the impetus of the piece was the "biological roots of violence," with the second two-page spread showing four digital images of a "normal" versus a "violent" brain.

After reading the two cover articles, and reports in mainstream media, one may have asked whether, perhaps, the "monsters next door" might have been detected, and treated, by reliable forms of medicine. The macabre of the Midway had broken violently into the homes of the future, and one solution was to figure out the precise anatomy of the invasion, in a way that would allow for adequate diagnosis and reliable medication.

One of the first mainstream media references to Ritalin was in the 1973 movie *The Exorcist*. In a scene ultimately cut from the film, Regan MacNeil's single, highly ambitious working mother received word from her daughter's physician that the little girl's condition might be hyperactivity disorder. In the scene, the doctor prescribed Ritalin. By one reading of the turn to scientific parenting during the Century of Progress, the children next door and in the relatively elite homes of middle-class parents in the United States became canaries in the mine shaft of a new economy. Their parents were under pressure within the tunnel economy to make their families leaner, more capable of moving quickly through toward human progress. With the Columbine murders, the Midway's House of Crime moved next door. Those whose physiog-

97. "Special Report: Massacre in Colorado," *Newsweek*, May 3, 1999.

nomies were to mark them as people capable of grave deeds seemed to don masks and move into our gated communities. Safely housed elsewhere, the danger of disorder may be vaguely titillating, but what are we to do when the chaos encroaches?

The combination of quantified, controlled parenthood, the march of progress in home entertainment, and the demands of a workday that has moved from nine to five to eight to six, or even seven, is arguably a witch's brew of family life — and the pharmaceutical companies know how to use all three ingredients to appeal to parents and a society eager to make things right. I fear that this is not only a mess for "our own" children, for the children depicted in the Strattera advertisements. I fear that it leaves largely to their own devices the children who are, after all, *not* next door but many neighborhoods away, whose physiognomies still vaguely connote to many middle-class suburbanites the menace of crime. Diagnosing their problem as medical, as inherited, as part of the structure of the "violent" brain, is a temptation with a pattern in the United States, a pattern that involves isolating and controlling the monstrous by way of genetic science. It is to that movement that we turn next.

# 3 To Form a More Perfect Union

## Mainline Protestants and the American Eugenics Movement

*My hope is built on nothing less*
*Than Jesus' blood and righteousness.*
*I dare not trust the sweetest frame,*
*But wholly trust in Jesus' Name.*

> *Refrain*
> *On Christ the solid Rock I stand,*
> *All other ground is sinking sand;*
> *All other ground is sinking sand.*

*When darkness seems to hide His face,*
*I rest on His unchanging grace.*
*In every high and stormy gale,*
*My anchor holds within the veil.*

> *Refrain*

*His oath, His covenant, His blood,*
*Support me in the whelming flood.*
*When all around my soul gives way,*
*He then is all my Hope and Stay.*

> *Refrain*

*When He shall come with trumpet sound,*
*Oh may I then in Him be found.*
*Dressed in His righteousness alone,*
*Faultless to stand before the throne.*

> *Refrain*

Edward Mote, 1834

**Figure 3.1. "The Christian asks: how many; how healthy?"** *Intercollegian,* January 1948

*The first urgency is to know the axioms of eugenics. We are not even well educated nor modern if we have no bowing acquaintance with its larger truths.*[1]

The image of two little boys (fig. 3.1)[2] is from 1948, and it accompanies an essay in the *Intercollegian* for young Christian men and women in America on the importance of family planning during the postwar period. The

1. The Reverend Phillips E. Osgood, 1926.
2. This image, with the caption "The Christian asks: how many; how healthy?" appeared in January 1948 in the YMCA/YWCA magazine, the *Intercollegian*, alongside two related articles: Paul Popenoe, "Surveying the Chances," and Helen F. Southard, "Planning Parenthood on Campus," pp. 9-10, 10-11, respectively. Popenoe was an active member of the American Eugenics Society and coauthor of the widely used textbook *Applied Eugenics*. Southard was an advocate for family planning. I am grateful to Rachel Maxson for finding these articles in the midst of her own research and for sharing the reference with me.

quotation above, from a sermon by Reverend Osgood, is from 1926, one generation prior. The grandparents of the children who were to be well planned during the postwar period would have been privy to sermons like his during their own youth, sermons offering a potent mixture of religiosity and the new science of inheritance. The notion that has run subtly through chapters 1 and 2 — that there is such a thing as good and bad blood, fit and unfit children, pure and impure races — emerges full force in this chapter.

Phillips Endecott Osgood's sermon "The Refiner's Fire" won top honors in the first of a series of well-received sermon contests sponsored by the American Eugenics Society (AES). Using Malachi 3:3 as his text, Osgood admonished the "temporary guardians of a miraculous gift" to respect their "partnership with God to keep it pure!" "The dross must be purged out" — and eugenics was the means for purging. The editors of the ecumenical journal the *Homiletic Review,* reprinting the sermon in 1929, registered their unequivocal assent: "A contest is worth while which evokes so excellent a sermon. Eugenics is an approved thing. It is no longer on trial."[3]

Twenty years later, an avid Protestant eugenicist named Paul Popenoe put the matter more subtly: the young Presbyterian, Methodist, and Episcopal men and women reading a YMCA/YWCA–sponsored magazine needed to take on the civic responsibility of "surveying the chances." Citing his own study of children in the Sonoma State Home, he warned that "feebleminded" families were reproducing at a higher rate than those able to provide "the best start." Reminding his mobile, collegiate readers that "cities always live as parasites on the rural areas," Popenoe emphasized their duty to consider patterns in "the nation's birth rate" when choosing their mates and planning their families.[4] It was incumbent upon the young people of the right sort to marry their own kind and to reproduce in ways that would lead to further success. Popenoe's article was linked in the magazine with one by Helen Southard, "Planning Parenthood on Campus." By the mid–twentieth century, the matter was largely settled among mainline Protestants: "The Christian asks: how many; how healthy?"

The history of the eugenics movement in the United States is seldom brought to the public eye. When popular historians do present the story, they safely place eugenicists on the other side of a wide intellectual and cultural gap. The eugenicists' science was faulty. Their ideas were blatantly racist. To

---

3. Phillips E. Osgood, "The Refiner's Fire," *Homiletic Review* 97 (May 1929): 405-9. Christine Rosen gives an account of Osgood's eugenic efforts in her *Preaching Eugenics: Religious Leaders and the American Eugenics Movement* (Oxford: Oxford University Press, 2004); see in particular pp. 3-4, 124-26.

4. Popenoe, "Surveying the Chances," p. 10.

quote one PBS narration, the "horrors of institutionalized eugenics revealed in Nazi Germany . . . doused [American eugenics] entirely as a movement" after World War II.[5]

Arguably, one of the trickiest tasks of narration is the one facing the writing staff at Cold Spring Harbor Laboratory in the United States. The lab celebrated "100 Years of Genetics" in 2004, reflecting a history that extends from Charles Davenport, lab director and mastermind of the Eugenics Record Office (ERO), to current chancellor James Watson, codiscoverer of the double-helix structure and advocate for "making better human beings" through genetic engineering.[6] In May 2002 David Micklos, director of the lab's Dolan DNA Learning Center, marked the seventy-fifth anniversary of the landmark eugenic sterilization case, *Buck v. Bell*, with a special online article, "None without Hope: Buck *vs.* Bell at 75."[7]

The way Micklos tells the story to the mainstream, Internet audience in the United States warrants close attention. *Buck v. Bell* was the original test of Virginia's sterilization laws. The case went to the U.S. Supreme Court in 1927, where Oliver Wendell Holmes, writing for the court, rendered the following verdict: "It is better for all the world, if instead of waiting to execute degenerate offspring for crime, or to let them starve for their imbecility, society can prevent those who are manifestly unfit from continuing their kind. The principle that sustains compulsory vaccination is broad enough to cover cutting the Fallopian tubes. Three generations of imbeciles are enough."[8] With characteristic clarity, Justice Holmes thus linked several key eugenic concepts. To prevent individual suffering, the state may compel the prevention of certain "kinds" of individuals. As an effective inoculation against degeneration, crime, and imbecility, the social body may "vaccinate" itself against the deleterious or parasitic "unfit."

Using subtle rhetorical cues, Micklos embeds this story of corporate vaccination within the longer history of genetics at Cold Spring Harbor, dis-

---

5. Public Broadcasting System, "Eugenics Movement Reaches Its Height" (1923). Accessed 2003: www.pbs.org.

6. Watson has gone on record in support of genetic engineering to eliminate physical suffering. He has also grown increasingly blunt in his support of inheritable genetic engineering to avoid people who "really are stupid" and to make "all girls pretty." The relevant sentences, as reported by the London *Times:* "People say it would be terrible if we made all girls pretty. I think it would be great," and "If you really are stupid, I would call that a disease" (Mark Henderson, "Let's Cure Stupidity, Says DNA Pioneer," *Times* [London], February 28, 2003, Home News section).

7. David Micklos, "None without Hope: Buck *vs.* Bell at 75," Dolan DNA Learning Center. Accessed 2002: www.dnalc.org.

8. *Buck v. Bell*, 274 U.S. 200, 207 (1927).

tinguishing between the lab's dubious past and its promising present. Although Cold Spring Harbor's home team, led by Davenport, paved the way for the sterilization of Carrie Buck after the birth of her daughter, Vivian, their science was, according to the *current* Cold Spring Harbor narration, sullied by the "biblical concept that 'like breeds like.'" Impure, their scientific methods were eventually discredited by a more *accurate* strand of genetics; coercive, their political methods were untenable after the Nazi atrocities. As evidence of the state's mistake, the site features a link to Vivian Buck's first-grade report card, telling readers that this supposed third-generation imbecile eventually made the elementary school honor roll. Micklos here brings the reader back to the point of the title of the online piece, "None without Hope." As it turns out, no lineage is "without hope," because the new science of genetics is revealing a complicated combination of factors — factors that might "predispose a person to autism" or "predispose to genius" — so that "one can never predict where genius will arise." Micklos situates the eugenics of the past on the other side of a chasm, distant from now-chastened politics and a science whose backward, biblical myopia has been duly corrected in our modern society. The piece concludes that the Buck girls would likely wish us to take this lesson of "hope" with us into our "Brave New World."[9]

    This chapter is in part my attempt to tell a different story than the safe one told by Micklos. One sign from the American Eugenics Society's Fitter Family fairs from the first half of the last century names a core assessment that still holds purchase today in American politics and, I found, in many mainline congregations: "Some people are born to be a burden on the rest." This gauge applied then to many kinds of difference; those who would judge scanned the horizon for those who variously did not "fit." Depending on the region, the signs of unfitness included poverty, disability, race, and religion.

    I believe it is important to complicate the standard narration of eugenics past and present. This core assessment of burden and birth led to an arsenal of biotechnological tools to plan, evaluate, and enhance children and to measure the worth of a given family — tools that today have become standard parental and political equipment. I suggest there are links between current hopes for genius and past attempts to vaccinate the social body against the menace of poverty, disability, and deviance. As individual parents navigate the strand of genetics that supplanted the science of Davenport and his ilk, they are choosing in rising numbers to terminate pregnancies that show

9. Micklos, "None without Hope."

**Figure 3.2. Sign from the American Eugenics Society's Fitter Family fairs, 1926. Courtesy of American Philosophical Society**

signs of genetic difference — choosing, in the majority of cases, to terminate for conditions ranging from physical disease to mental disability to gender ambiguity. At the same time, U.S. citizens view with increasing skepticism public spending on the supposedly indiscriminately bred children of poor African American mothers as well as on the "huge" families of recent Latino Catholic immigrants.[10] The cultural context in which individuals make what are increasingly seen as purely "personal" decisions and in which a society makes what are often deemed purely pragmatic decisions is shaped by the powerful rhetoric of eugenics.

The pregnant body, the social body, and the burden of certain "types" of babies are all culturally loaded in ways that reflect the vast movement in the past century in the United States to popularize eugenics. The quest to craft a more perfect union through "fewer and better babies" is alive and

10. The language is from the cover story of the March 15, 2004, issue of *Business Week,* featuring a photograph of two parents with their five sons. The article, by Brian Grow, is entitled "Hispanic Nation," and the cover warns: "Hispanics are an immigrant group like no other. Their huge numbers are changing old ideas about assimilation. Is America ready?" A graphic that accompanies the story charts "America's *Bebé* Boom."

well.[11] *Pace* Micklos, *pace* PBS, *pace* the tale often told, many eugenic ideas have jumped the gap from yesterday to today, bridging the chasm between overtly coercive eugenics and purportedly voluntary parental and social responsibility in the land of the free and among people supposedly freed for discipleship.[12]

The era on which we will concentrate, often called the Progressive Era, saw the professionalization of marriage, domesticity, hygiene, and charity. As with the rising interest in infant feeding and child nutrition, there were unquestionable gains in the care of children and family made by those newly charged and ready to organize "the race" for the future. Schools were built, children were clothed, and hungry mouths were fed. But along with the efforts came a newly potent, death-dealing distinction between those whose lives were *worth care* and those whose lives were not. Many of the participants in the progressive class of Protestants drew a line between lineages of hope and lineages of risk, peril, and civic menace. The distinction between auspicious and inauspicious lives was an integral part of the engine of mainline Protestant eugenics.

My suspicion is that the mainline Protestant men and women who accepted and promoted eugenics leveraged the lives of others. Mothers and fathers and their daughters and sons won Fitter Family medals by reinforcing a continuum of worth whereby some pregnancies, some children, and some families lost. To use the language I employed in chapter 1, mainline Protestants placed themselves on the right side of the gutter. Or, in the language of progress, they boarded the vehicle of science, moving closer to the ever-elusive promised land — where no one we truly cared about would suffer indignity or pain. My hypothesis is that eugenics gained popular support in large part through the endorsement of mainstream and progressive Protestant spokespersons. Mainline Protestantism continued to accept the thoroughgoing relevance of eugenic ideas long after Henry Ward Beecher, self-declared "cordial Christian evolutionist," endorsed with his pen and from his pulpit the social use of Charles Darwin and the social Darwinism of Herbert Spencer.[13] From

---

11. The phrase is from the title of a book by William J. Robinson, M.D., *Fewer and Better Babies*, published in multiple editions from 1915 to 1938.

12. Non-Southerners to whom I present this material are shocked to hear that the ERO was based on Long Island, New York, and that the AES had its headquarters in New Haven, Connecticut. The South has functioned in some ways to provide a second rhetorical divide, allowing people from elsewhere to dump most American ills in the supposed backwater of Southern culture.

13. See Richard Hofstadter, *Social Darwinism in American Thought* (New York: Braziller, 1959), pp. 29-30, 48.

Paul Popenoe's *Intercollegian* article encouraging white middle-class men and women to replenish the race to the current United Methodist endorsement of "responsible" parenthood in the UMC Social Principles, mainstream Protestantism has lent legitimacy to a trajectory of discriminating reproduction. Leading eugenicists in the United States used their own white, middle-class, literate, wholesome, productive, patriotic, native-born Protestant families as the standard against which to judge and measure other families. The eugenics movement was germinated in a relatively elite, academic version of scientific racism from the previous century, but it took root in the heartland of America arguably as a result of two primary forces: clergy eager to remain relevant in an era when other professionals, and scientists in particular, were gaining ascendancy; and middle-class laity eager to establish themselves as good, wholesome parents and productive, responsible, clean citizens. As an ordained Methodist minister, and as a "bright" child deemed by many to be one of the "promise," it seems only apt that I struggle through these texts. For I have found that these poisonous messages echo still, today, in my parishes and in my own living room.

The "born to be a burden" sign from the AES Fitter Family fairs warned with two intermittently flashing lights that of all persons born in the United States — that is, one "every 16 seconds" — a mere 4 percent, or one "every 7 1/2 minutes," was "high grade," able to "do creative work and be fit for leadership." A third flashing light underscored the associated economic toll: "Every 15 seconds $100 of your money goes for the care of persons with bad heredity. . . ." That this display carried such rhetorical weight — that across the Northeast and the heartland farmers and shopkeepers and homemakers and ministers' wives had their own and their children's heads and limbs measured and their extended family trees mapped for taint or purity in order to be identified among the "high grade" 4 percent — is a sign that the AES knew their constituency well. That this display evoked among mainline Protestants hopeful aspirations rather than holy offense is an important part of the story of American eugenics.

I will tell the story in this chapter without relief. While in the previous two chapters I picked out strands of hope in the images and text — finding threads of hopeful resistance — I will not pick out such strands here. Readers wishing to find a tapestry of resistance may turn back periodically to the beloved Methodist hymn that introduces the chapter. Or they might consider the title of the Cold Spring Harbor feature on the Virginia sterilization case, "None without Hope." On *whose* blood is our hope built?

## George Henry Napheys and the Advent of Eugenics

### *"Difficult, Delicate, and Dangerous"*

Drawing on Charles Darwin and Francis Galton — as well as William Shakespeare, the New Testament, and Aristotle (to name a few) — George H. Napheys wrote at the end of the nineteenth century on the "difficult, delicate, and dangerous" matters related to "the transmission of life."[14] His book reveals one prominent Protestant conduit through which the notions of two British scientists filtered down through Protestant America and into the minds of a generation of young laity and clergy — a generation that would then decide whether to heed Davenport's call to propagate eugenics in America. *The Transmission of Life* remained in print for more than twenty-five years, circulating among Congregationalists, Lutherans, Methodist Episcopalians, and Baptists.[15] In it Napheys wove together the latest in eugenics (the term would soon be coined by Galton — Darwin's cousin — in 1883), sociology, animal breeding, Christian faith, and good old "common sense."

The publisher's announcement for the book explains that "an untold amount of misery and crime springs from an ignorance of the nature and proper hygienic care of the sexual function." In an attempt to correct this ignorance and thus avoid both crime and misery, Napheys detailed everything from "the number of fallen women in the different cities and the classes into which they are divided," to "the avoidance and the limitation of offspring," to "how to have male or female children at will." The publisher notes that the

---

14. George Henry Napheys, *The Transmission of Life: Counsels on the Nature and Hygiene of the Masculine Function* (Philadelphia: J. G. Fergus, 1871). The descriptive phrase is from an endorsement by the *Lutheran Observer,* May 5, 1871, included in the book's front matter: "The subject of this book is at once difficult, delicate, and dangerous; and Dr. Napheys has been singularly successful in treating it in a way to subserve the public health and public morals. It is both scientific and practical. Its style is clear and plain, but does not offend the most refined taste" (p. xxv).

15. All references will be to the sixth edition of 1871. The book's first edition was widely recommended to laity by "the leading professional medical journals," as noted by the *New Englander and Yale Review* 39 (March 1880): 303-4, whose editors commended the 1879 edition as well. Napheys also wrote *The Physical Life of Woman: Advice to the Maiden, Wife, and Mother* (Toronto: MacLear, 1871), which differs in content and tone but also includes the sections "Inheritance" and "How to Have Beautiful Children." In the preface to this book for "woman," Napheys explains: "Had every person a sound understanding of the relations of the sexes, one of the most fertile sources of crime would be removed" (p. 18). A year earlier, Napheys cooperated with D. G. Brinton on *Personal Beauty: The Laws of Health in Relation to the Human Form* (1870), in which they discussed "offensive breath," "want of symmetry," "correct proportions," "the shape of the head," and "proper form and color of the eye."

latter guidelines are "strictly scientific," "also applicable to domestic animals," and "will therefore doubly interest most people."[16]

This endorsement, amusing as it sounds today, reflects one of Napheys's key rhetorical strategies — one that would later serve the AES. Napheys drew consistently on images and experts from animal husbandry. Depending on at least some lingering knowledge of domestic breeding among readers in newly industrialized areas, he interspersed newfangled sociology with old-fashioned farming common sense. He encouraged the idea among readers that the informed tasks of previous generations of farmers and others who worked in farming communities could now lend certainty to a set of male tasks that had recently become less certain. Speaking to young men living far from extended networks of kin who might otherwise provide guidance for marriage and the propagation of children, Napheys gave practical standards for choosing a wife who would issue forth "handsome, healthy, and intelligent" children rather than those who were "diseased, deformed, and weak-minded."[17]

The end of the nineteenth century saw not only the spread of syphilis and other communicable diseases but also the spread of the *knowledge* of the spread of disease. The city, whether it be Chicago, New York, or even Kansas City, seemed to many a place where all bets were off and all interactions a risky form of speculation. The growing sense that young men in these settings needed a printed resource for practical guidance and basic knowledge of human hygiene may have led to the *Lutheran Observer*'s pronouncement of Napheys's effort as "singularly successful."

Lengthy testimonials and endorsements precede the text. Napheys dedicated the book to the Reverend John Todd, an influential Congregational clergyman, author, and one of the founders of Mount Holyoke Seminary; the testimonials came from a similar set. The publishers took obvious "pleasure in presenting the following testimonials to the practical value, and the moral tone of this work." Listed are fifteen prominent clergymen, including two bishops of the Methodist Episcopal Church; the president of the New York Baptist Convention; the Reverend Horace Bushnell; the presidents of seven colleges, including Amherst and Trinity; and the president of Cornell University. While the list also includes a handful of physicians, the "experts" to whom the publishers overwhelmingly looked for support were clergy.[18]

16. Napheys, *The Transmission of Life*, pp. i, ii, iii.

17. Napheys, *The Transmission of Life*, p. iv.

18. Napheys, *The Transmission of Life*, pp. v-xxi. The list includes Rev. John Todd; Bishop Levi Scott, Methodist Episcopal Church; Rev. H. Clay Trumbull, missionary secretary for New

The coming turn of the century would mark a shift in the balance of moral knowledge, from clergy to scientist, but this book was published at the edge of the shift. Napheys gained credence by being "both scientific and practical," avoiding offense to the "most refined taste" by speaking of sex with "clear and plain" language for the benefit of "public health and public morals." The *Lutheran Observer* (Philadelphia), the *Christian Secretary* (Hartford), and the *Christian Radical* (Pittsburgh and New York) each registered the hope that, by heeding Napheys's advice, "every man of ordinary intelligence" might participate in the restoration of the "moral nature of the race."[19]

It is precisely the "moral nature of the race" that is at stake in "the married life," Napheys explains. The "union extends its influence throughout the whole fabric of social and political life." Given that marriage is a "union *for the purpose of offspring*" (emphasis in original), it is predictable that the trajectory of the book will lead to the telos of proper begetting.[20] Because "the whole fabric of social and political life" is at stake, a man must not "overlook health, nor undervalue beauty in the woman he seeks." Napheys here suggests that "a sickly, nervous, peevish, inefficient wife — qualities which are naturally associated" — will lead to an unfortunate alliance. "Although the boy Cupid is notoriously blind," the "prudent" boy will avoid "social vice" by keeping "his eyes open" when choosing the woman with whom he will "join irretrievably." Napheys concludes this section by answering affirmatively "the young man who asks us deprecatingly, 'Would you have me marry for beauty?'"[21]

The "father's care over the health of his child" thus begins "before its birth, nay, before its conception." Here Napheys refers directly to an expert horse breeder who has proven through both study and practice that "like will

---

England of the American S.S. Union; Rt. Rev. Thomas March Clark, Protestant Episcopal bishop of Rhode Island; Bishop T. A. Morris, Methodist Episcopal Church; Rev. Horace Bushnell, Hartford, Connecticut; Rev. Leonard Bacon, New Haven, Connecticut; Rev. Henry A. Nelson, professor of systematic and pastoral theology, Lane Seminary, Cincinnati; Rev. C. P. Sheldon, president of the New York Baptist Convention, pastor of the Fifth Baptist Church, Troy, New York; Rev. Abner Jackson, president of Trinity College, Hartford, Connecticut; Rev. George W. Samson, president of Columbian College, Washington, D.C.; Rev. Wm. A. Stearns, president of Amherst College, Amherst, Massachusetts; Rev. Samson Talbot, president of Denison University, Granville, Ohio; Rev. W. T. Stott, acting president of Franklin College, Franklin, Indiana; Rev. Cyrus Nutt, president of Indiana State University; Andrew D. White, president of Cornell University.

19. Napheys, *The Transmission of Life*, p. xxv, quoting the *Lutheran Observer*, May 5, 1871, and p. 132, quoting the *Christian Radical*, May 13, 1871.

20. Napheys, *The Transmission of Life*, p. 132.

21. Napheys, *The Transmission of Life*, p. 137.

produce like" — "hence the necessity of some knowledge of the parentage both of the sire and dam." A prudent man, wishing to "avert taints of the system," will not follow the caprice of stupid Cupid but will warily investigate the parentage of a young woman. For "he may marry a woman who will bear him healthy children, whereas his children by another woman may be doomed." Napheys concludes ominously: "The responsibility and the risk are his own."[22] To continue on a path of success, the young man should choose a young woman at least five years his junior and ensure a hygienic bedroom, well ventilated and set to wholesome specifications.[23] Napheys's counsel reflected the growing sense in his time that for the future of the relatively young country, young men and women needed to forge families capable of productive lives. These themes would continue in advice issued by the YMCA, the American Social Hygiene Association (ASHA), and others intent on contributing to a more flourishing union.

Choosing a mate carefully for the sake of producing stronger, keener, and more efficient offspring had been business as usual for slaveholders in the South. Marriages among the elite across the United States may have been founded on the acquisition of more intangible forms of power, but slaveholders sought wherever possible to force intimacy between slaves who would produce better workers. Napheys's advice, characteristic of his time, can be interpreted as an effort to encourage those who were, in a palpable sense, the building blocks of a post–Civil War economy to internalize the kind of discriminating criteria that would make for a better crop of future workers in an industrialized era. What Matthew Frye Jacobson notes regarding the rhetoric of immigrant workers — that those few who brokered the meaning of American citizenship did so in part as a function of waxing and waning needs for cheap labor — arguably applies also to those who brokered the meaning of procreation for the native-born to whom Napheys wrote.[24] Romantic whimsy is a costly indulgence for families dependent on reliably hearty children; it is perhaps similarly a luxury for a country striving to keep the wheels of industry turning.

The question of new European immigration is at play in Napheys's ad-

---

22. Napheys, *The Transmission of Life,* pp. 205, 206.

23. Napheys, *The Transmission of Life,* pp. 138, 171.

24. Matthew Frye Jacobson, *Whiteness of a Different Color: European Immigrants and the Alchemy of Race* (Cambridge: Harvard University Press, 1998), p. 20. Referring to Sinclair Lewis's satirical depiction of a "Nordic Citizen," Jacobson writes: "The Nordic's crass statement of the conflict between the ideal 'control of this great nation' on the one hand and the ever-pressing need for 'cheap labor' on the other fairly sums up a tension between the imperatives of democracy and the imperatives of capitalism that is integral to American political culture."

vice. He worries that "the native American population is actually dying out," suggesting that native-born couples have a "duty" to eschew the apparent trend toward "leading round a solitary, lonely child, or possibly two" rather than doing their part to rectify the growing disproportion in the United States between native-born and recent immigrants. This call to "duty" is tempered, however, by his assurance that they may meet it with willed precision. Rather than accepting the random distribution of fate, couples may now plan families according to both responsibility *and* desire, since the discovery of "the law which governs the production of the sexes." Albeit with "certain elements of uncertainty," "persons can have either a daughter or a son as they prefer," and it is apparently common sense that "the ideal family is composed of some of each sex." Here Napheys is at his animal-husbandry finest, referring to the work of "stock-raisers, bird fanciers, bee merchants, and all engaged in the breeding of the various kinds of domestic animals."[25] But of much more serious import than the work of producing boy or girl are the methods by which a well-chosen marriage may "avoid having diseased and deformed children," to cite the title of the longest section in his chapter entitled "Inheritance."

This crucial chapter makes explicit the stakes involved in choosing a mate. While conceding (as many who follow him will not) that "legislation upon this subject is, of course, impracticable," Napheys argues that the issue of inheritance "demands . . . the closest attention from the philanthropist and the moralist." For "the moral and social responsibility incurred, by marrying into a family of which one or more members have suffered from constitutional disease, is great, and should not be lightly assumed." The quest for "judicious marriages" is one to which every young person should commit, for good judgment alone can "eradicate all heredity affections."

Napheys gives the reader a guide to the "risk incurred under various circumstances," based on the work of a Dr. J. M. Winn from England.[26] He has in mind here not only extreme, fatal diseases but also mental and emotional conditions of various sorts, including theft, criminality, alcoholism, "cowardice, jealousy, anger, envy, and libertinage," to name only a handful.[27] Taking these patterns into account, couples need to avoid marriage if there is "a constitutional taint in either father or mother, on both sides of the contracting parties." If "constitutional disease is only on one side" but the "contracting parties" are both free of obvious taint, "healthy offspring may be the issue of

25. Napheys, *The Transmission of Life*, pp. 193, 189, 196.
26. Napheys, *The Transmission of Life*, pp. 210, 211.
27. Napheys, *The Transmission of Life*, p. 223.

the marriage." But, he warns, "if there have been no signs of constitutional disease for a whole generation, we can scarcely consider the risk materially lessened." It is only when "two whole generations have escaped any symptoms of heredity disease" that his readers may "fairly hope that the danger has passed."[28]

One generation later, another well-connected Protestant, Henry Fairfield Osborn, served as president of the American Museum of Natural History, from 1908 to 1933. As part of his mission to educate "a very large class of inquisitive but wholly uninformed people," he displayed accounts and photographs of "cacogenic" families, giving names and faces to the specter of inheritable "taint."[29] Napheys made effective use of this method as well, pointing to such cautionary examples as "the giant Chang," who was, "until recently, on exhibition in London"; "the Porcupine man," who had been "presented at the Royal Society"; and a set of "juvenile delinquents, at Parkhurst."[30] The latter menace, of the "distinctive criminal class in all our cities," runs through Napheys's section that answers, in the affirmative, "Is Our Moral Nature Inheritable?" He goes on: "This dangerous class is marked by certain physical and mental peculiarities" that allow the reader to "distinguish them . . . in any promiscuous assembly." His wording here is characteristic. Those who pose a menace may "be readily pointed out" for pedagogical purposes; those observable, displayed *others* should serve as warnings.[31] "Injudicious marriages are constantly being formed," Napheys explains, and the reader who would fully respect his own "Masculine Function" should heed the advice of people like Francis Galton, who has "given much attention to this subject."[32] Quoting Shakespeare's *Macbeth,* Napheys again links the

28. Napheys, *The Transmission of Life,* p. 211.

29. Osborn played a key role in international eugenics; both the second (1921) and the third (1932) international eugenics congresses were held at the museum. Thanks to Michon Scott at the Web site Strange Science for the Osborn quotation, from Henry F. Osborn, "Models of Extinct Vertebrates," *Science* 7 (June 24, 1898): 841-45, with two plates. The relevant quotation reads in full: "There are certain obligations resting upon the curators of metropolitan museums from which curators of university museums should enjoy a grateful immunity. These mainly involve the difficult undertaking of arousing interest and spreading accurate information among a very large class of inquisitive but wholly uninformed people. If these obligations are unfulfilled the metropolitan museum fails in its purpose and deserves the withdrawal of public support."

30. Napheys, *The Transmission of Life,* pp. 203, 204, 224.

31. Napheys, *The Transmission of Life,* p. 222.

32. Napheys, *The Transmission of Life,* pp. 212, 217. Napheys even quotes a Dr. Steinase, who observed in a child of "only three years" signs of an inherited tendency toward theft, by virtue of his "clandestinely" taking "more food than he could eat" (p. 223).

older classifications of animal husbandry with the new, genetically determined taxonomy of mankind:

> As hounds, and grayhounds, mongrels, spaniels, curs,
> Shoughs, water-rugs, and demi-wolves, are classed
> All by the name of dogs; the valued file
> Distinguishes the swift, the slow, the subtle.[33]

In distinguishing the swift, the slow, and the subtle, it is important to keep in mind "considerations of race." In this way Napheys closes this section of *The Transmission of Life*, narrating the full import of a new era in "physical science." Rather than writing his own prose here, Napheys "cannot forbear to quote the thoughts of an eminent theologian, Canon Charles Kingsley." Kingsley was the author of the classic English children's tale *Water Babies* (on which Margaret Mead played in her essay for *Parents'* magazine on "primitive brown children") and the official religious adviser to Queen Victoria during the development of her empire. Many theologians remember him as the churchman to whom John Henry Newman gave his answer in *Apologia pro vita sua*. Napheys gives Canon Kingsley the last word on the relation between science and faith.

> Physical science is proving more and more the immense importance of race. . . . She is proving more and more . . . how the more favored race (she cannot avoid using the epithet) exterminates the less favored, or at least expels it, and forces it, under penalty of death, to adapt to new circumstances; and, in a word, that competition between every race and every individual of that race, and reward according to deserts, is (as far as we can see) an universal law of living things. And she says — for the facts of history prove it — that as it is among the races of plants and animals, so it has been unto this day among the races of men.

Rather than arguing for the supremacy of science over revelation, Kingsley argues that, when read through proper spectacles, the "painful facts" of science are evident at the heart of Scripture itself. In so doing, Kingsley paves the way for eugenics, using the potent rhetoric of Christian supersessionism.

> The natural theology of the future must take count of these tremendous and even painful facts. . . . Scripture has taken count of them already. . . .

---

33. Napheys, *The Transmission of Life*, p. 222.

Its sense of the reality and importance of descent is so intense, that it speaks of a whole tribe or whole family by the name of its common ancestor, and the whole nation of the Jews is Israel to the end. And if I be told this is true of the Old Testament, but not of the New, I must answer, What? Does not St. Paul hold the identity of the whole Jewish race with Israel their forefather, as strongly as any prophet of the Old Testament? And what is the central historic fact, save one, of the New Testament, but the conquest of Jerusalem — the dispersion, all but destruction of a race, not by miracle, but by invasion, because found wanting when weighed in the stern balances of natural and social law? Gentlemen, think of this . . . by the light which our Lord's parables, His analogies between the physical and social constitution of the world afford — and consider whether those awful words, fulfilled then and fulfilled so often since — "The kingdom of God shall be taken from you, and given to a nation bringing forth the fruits hereof" — may not be the supreme instance, the most complex development, of a law which runs through all created things, down to the moss which struggles for existence on the rock?

Having interpreted Scripture according to this "law which runs through all created things," from humanity down to mere moss, Kingsley seemingly pulls back to take in the scope of creation by way of grace.

Do I say that this is all? . . . God forbid. I believe not only in nature, but in grace. . . . I believe that if he will

Strive upward, working out the beast,
And let the ape and tiger die;

if he will be even as wise as the social animals . . . then he will rise to a higher sphere; towards that kingdom of God of which it is written, "He that dwelleth in love, dwelleth in God, and God in him."[34]

Note, however, Kingsley's account of grace. Employing Alfred Lord Tennyson, this formulation of grace links us with even the moss that "struggles for existence" yet at the same time connects the human struggle with a characteristic elevation "to a higher sphere." By climbing above, occupying the newly distributed "kingdom of God," those within "the more favored race"

34. Napheys, *The Transmission of Life*, pp. 226ff., quoting Charles Kingsley, "The Natural Theology of the Future" (paper read at Sion College, January 10, 1871), published in *Macmillan's Magazine* 23 (1871): 369-78. The text appears also in *Design after Darwin, 1860-1900*, vol. 2, *Remaking the Watchmaker: Orthodox and Unorthodox Design Arguments*, ed. Richard England (Bristol, U.K.: Thoemmes Continuum, 2003).

may distinguish themselves not only from moss, ape, and tiger but also from those peoples who will *not* inherit the kingdom.

Kingsley was a thorough interpreter of Darwin, incorporating evolutionary thought into Christian theology for children as well as adults. Napheys was but one American conduit for Kingsley's thought, but by setting his words within a popular text for the "common man," Napheys effectively distributed a newly configured natural theology beyond the key Protestant clergy who endorsed his book. He placed practical eugenic theology into the hands of at least two generations of Protestant laity. What had been considered folk wisdom, or common sense — seeking somcone compatible for marriage — became, by the turn of the century, a scientific pursuit of significant import. The search for a comely, hygienic, moral mate with whom to have auspicious children became, in the natural theology of Kingsley, nothing less than a step toward a more faithful, dutiful, socially responsible existence. Many Protestant clergy considerably less prominent than Kingsley, Napheys, and the university presidents who endorsed *The Transmission of Life* took up this adjusted gospel with verve.

### "The Natural Theology of the Future"

In his *Social Darwinism in American Thought,* Richard Hofstadter suggests that no scientific theory has had a "greater impact on ways of thinking and believing" than evolution: Darwin did no less than "revolutionize the fundamental patterns of thought" in education, economics, and theology.[35] Napheys's characteristic handbook for new husbandry reworked morality using an astute combination of the old patterns and the new science of evolution — using both to prescribe individual and corporate responsibility for the upward climb. Hofstadter writes about social Darwinism (particularly as represented by British philosopher Herbert Spencer and Yale sociologist William Graham Sumner) as a movement that interwove "a kind of naturalistic Calvinism" with the new science of evolution. In this way, the "idea of competitive struggle" was given "the force of a natural law."[36] Napheys's use of Kingsley as the rousing culmination of his treatment of masculinity and life combined practical advice with a stirring call to shoulder responsibility for one's race. Kingsley's "higher sphere" of morality, "towards that kingdom of God," is arguably a theological gloss on the closing lines of Darwin's *The De-*

35. Hofstadter, *Social Darwinism,* p. 3.
36. Hofstadter, *Social Darwinism,* pp. 10, 6.

*scent of Man,* in which the *ascent* that represents the proper *descent* involves the virtues of "that heroic little monkey" that exhibits courage "in order to save the life of his keeper," or of the brave "old baboon" that rescues "his young comrade from a crowd of astonished dogs." This is what distinguishes the real man from the "savage" who "knows no decency, and is haunted by the grossest superstitions."[37]

Moral supremacy, race improvement, hard work, practical prudence, and good, honest competition — these made for a forceful ideology of progressivism for a new century. Napheys's book marked a transmission of sorts, from the authority of local, ecclesial, agrarian, and familial leaders to the emerging authority of a learned, professionalized elite. What Jane Ursel has called a shift from "familial to social patriarchy" was fostered by Protestants eager to participate in the ordering of a rapidly expanding country.[38]

The brokers of civic thought recalibrated to take on the new tasks attending a relatively complicated and diverse populace. Leading the charge, a new form of Protestantism called the Social Gospel movement deciphered the new science through the grammar of the old faith to meet a new set of political challenges. The movement's spokesman, Walter Rauschenbusch, wrote: "Translate the evolutionary theories into religious faith, and you have the doctrine of the Kingdom of God. This combination with scientific evolutionary thought has freed the Kingdom ideal of its catastrophic setting and its background of demonism, and so adapted it to the climate of the modern world."[39]

As Social Gospel and other Protestant leaders in the United States set up associations and organizations to monitor, measure, order, and aid the country, Protestant faith became newly intertwined with organized, civic aspirations. Those aspirations indeed involved the alleviation of suffering and the amelioration of horrific conditions facing the working poor in urban areas. But the "kingdom ideal," shorn of its "demonism," would also be privy to a set of demons let loose in the modern, rational world itself. Benjamin Franklin's faith in human ingenuity put on new flesh and strode methodically forward.

37. Charles Darwin, *The Descent of Man and Selection in Relation to Sex* (London: J. Murray, 1871), pp. 404-5.

38. Jane Ursel, *Private Lives, Public Policy: One Hundred Years of State Intervention in the Family* (Toronto: Women's Press, 1992), p. 3.

39. Walter Rauschenbusch, *Christianizing the Social Order* (New York: Macmillan, 1912), p. 90.

## ASHA and the Campaign for Social Hygiene

### *"What Kind of Children?"*

The question of marital hygiene — and of what kind of children would issue from a particular match — continued to press the growing Protestant middle class in the decades after the last printing of Napheys's book. Clergy, social workers, and other newly professionalized educators formed "purity alliances" to take on the scourge of prostitution and the spread of venereal disease. As Kristen Luker notes, the movement's leaders sought increasingly to attack the problem at its source, to produce at the grass roots a climate inhospitable to what was called the "Social Evil." At the same time, public-health physicians organized to promote "sanitary and moral prophylaxis." The purity movement and physicians movement eventually united to form the American Social Hygiene Association (ASHA).[40]

Through pamphlets and public displays, ASHA sought to bring the science of social and individual hygiene to young adults (fig 3 3). Two series of posters developed in concert with the U.S. Public Health Service and the YMCA encouraged young men to keep fit and young women to embrace the beauty and duty of youth and life.[41] ASHA archivist David Klaassen notes: "The posters offered a positive program [that] emphasized accurate information — sexual intercourse is not necessary to preserve manly health and vigor; seminal emissions and menstrual periods are natural occurrences — and recommended the need for plenty of vigorous activity and proper diet — get in the game; beauty comes from within, paint your cheeks from the inside out."[42]

"Keeping Fit" and "Youth and Life," the names of the series, cover a wide range of hygienic subjects. In "Youth and Life," "every girl" was reminded to brush her hair "clean and glossy," to "eat slowly" and "fix a regular time for bowel action," and to "devote herself to the welfare of humanity." The overall message of personal hygiene was that "most girls could be prettier than they

---

40. Kristen Luker, "Sex, Social Hygiene, and the State: The Double-Edged Sword of Social Reform," *Theory and Society* 27 (1998): 609-10.

41. "Keeping Fit" was produced in 1919 by the U.S. Public Health Service and the YMCA; "Youth and Life" was adapted from that series in 1922 by ASHA. Both series, available in the Social Welfare History Archives at the University of Minnesota, may be viewed online at http://special.lib.umn.edu/swha/exhibits/hygiene/index.htm.

42. David Klaassen, "Social Hygiene Poster Campaigns in the 1920s," Social Hygiene Poster Series, Social Welfare History Archives, University of Minnesota, http://special.lib.umn.edu/swha/exhibits/hygiene/essay.htm. Klaassen reports that by the early 1920s these images had been displayed in 13,000 settings and viewed by more than 750,000 people.

# What Kind of Children?

By courtesy of Edison Lamp Works

Children get their basic qualities by inheritance. If they are to be strong, keen, efficient, and great, there must be good blood back of them

If you want your children to be well-born, choose your husband because of fine qualities in his family as well as in himself. Then add the best training

These make a square deal for the children

Youth and Life Exhibit. Part No. 23. (Forty-eight Parts.) Copyright 1922, by The American Social Hygiene Association

**Figure 3.3. Youth and Life Exhibit. ASHA, 1922**

are because most girls could be healthier." In "Keeping Fit," alongside images encouraging "energy, endurance, and fitness," boys faced Teddy's intense gaze and were reminded that although he was "sickly and frail when a boy, Roosevelt by faithful training achieved the vigor of manhood." With cleanliness came not only godliness but also patriotism.

The ASHA leadership reads like a who's who of early Protestant progressivism — Harvard president Charles W. Eliot, a leading Unitarian who served as one of the organizers for the First International Congress of Eugenics of 1912; Presbyterian Jane Addams, founder of Hull House, Chicago; Grace Hoadley Dodge, first president of the YWCA; and progressive Baptist John D. Rockefeller, Jr., whose millions also supported various explicitly eugenic causes. Cooperating with the U.S. Public Health Service, the YMCA, and the YWCA, ASHA presented young Americans across the country with a program and a vision for healthy and conscientious reproduction.

Exercising, eating fruit and green vegetables, and spending time in sunlight were in service to a particular goal — to keep oneself productive, pure, and pleasing for a mate with whom to plan the clearly *good* life. Warnings about casual alliances and dissolute living contrasted with images of hearty young men and rosy-cheeked women tapping Vermont syrup or picking apples. The underlying message to avoid disease, irregularity, and dirt is less obvious than the message to seek out the proper kind of wholesome young man or woman. The best alliance would produce health from health, perpetuating promise.

The young men and women to whom the "Keeping Fit" and "Youth and Life" campaigns were directed join hands in the powerfully evocative Norman Rockwell illustration of a haloed young couple. The husband and wife sit comfortably in a chair decorated with flowers in bloom, she leaning back in spotless apron and stylishly crimped hair, with one shiny black high heel exposed, he leaning forward, clean shaven, white collared, pointing with index finger at architectural plans, presumably for their future home. Their golden-haired little one, in royal purple and white lace collar, looks up at the two while building a castle with wooden blocks. Although Norman Rockwell was capable of domestic realism, he beautifully conjured up for the "Keeping Fit" campaign an image of the idealized young family building their own and the nation's future. As with other posters, the message of the text bridged the newly indisputable *science* of mammalian reproduction to the well-informed aspirations of human reproduction. "Although man and many other animals reproduce their kind in much the same way, man differs from other animals in the way he treats his offspring," the poster explains. "The human father and mother form a union called the family," in which the "finest feelings of the race — comradeship, courage, loyalty, unselfishness, love — are developed."

The "Youth and Life" poster with the same image is even more candid: "Partners, fit and congenial . . . transmit their fitness for a finer race."

The threat of an ill-chosen mate is only in the background of Rockwell's illustration. The text from another poster is more explicit (fig. 3.3). With the ambiguity of the accompanying picture, the poster presents an admonition. "Children get their basic qualities by inheritance," it warns. "If they are to be strong, keen, efficient, and great, there must be good blood back of them"; thus, a young woman considering a prospective husband will be wise to look for "fine qualities in his family as well as in himself." The drawing shows a father at the threshold of his family home. The mother stands in the doorway with arms by her side, watching soberly as her husband embraces their golden-haired daughter. The portrait is faintly ambiguous. Is the father a man of "good blood"? Perhaps. Perhaps not.

Read together, the posters present the challenge of a prudent, well-informed choice. The "comradeship" and "unselfishness" to be developed as the "finest feelings of the race" are linked to "good blood," and perceptions may be deceiving.

The text that accompanies the smiling children advised viewers: "Every child has the right to be well born" (fig. 3.5). A "fair start in life" requires that one's parents think carefully long before engaging in the intimacy that will result in their child's birth. This caution is plainly portrayed in two other posters — one, from "Keeping Fit," with a syphilitic boy (fig. 3.4) and one, from "Youth and Life," with a girl whose eyes were infected by her mother's gonorrhea (fig. 3.6). If not careful, a mother hoping for a "keen" and "well-born" daughter may end up instead with a child like this one, "blinded by gonorrhea." The blinded youngster is alone, a groping, pitiful figure, pitching forward. The disfigured boy, also alone, gazes forlornly at the camera under the caption (in large red print) "Inherited Syphilis." The two images signal abandonment. In contrast to the bright color images of the ideal family, the potentially normative family, and the blond moppets riding their tricycles, the solitary, afflicted children appear in black and white.

Venereal disease was not the only risk facing the young men and women to whom the posters were addressed. The particularly stark menace of blinding or disfiguring disease resulting from illicit sex is generalized more subtly in the series taken as a whole. The import of "sex" is as social as it is individual, as political as personal. A poster entitled "What Sex Brings to the Race" features a drawing attributed to Procter and Gamble, with a turn-of-the-century mother in a flowing gown and a child in a nightshirt, waiting for her morning bath. Sunlight flows through tapestried windows. The text broadens the themes to inspire in those who would be "manly" and "womanly" the

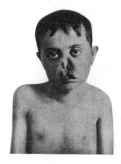

No. 27

## Inherited Syphilis

A man may transmit syphilis to his children

His children's children may pay the penalty of his mistake

B

No. 45

Every child has the right to be well born

Will you give your children healthy bodies and a fair start in life?

B

No. 39

Blinded by gonorrhea

If the mother has gonorrhea, her child may be blinded at birth

Simple medical treatment at time of birth will prevent such blindness

Men who think themselves cured sometimes infect their wives with gonorrhea. Chronic ill-health and inability to have children are often caused by gonorrhea. Many serious operations on married women are due to this disease

Youth and Life Exhibit. Part No. 39. (Forty-eight Parts.) Copyright 1922 by The American Social Hygiene Association

**Figure 3.4. "Inherited Syphilis." ASHA**

**Figure 3.5. "The Happiness of Children." ASHA, 1922**

**Figure 3.6. "Blinded by Gonorrhea." ASHA, 1922**

sense that "the attractions . . . between boys and girls" fuel no less than "the arts, the sciences, and the culture of civilization."

Cumulatively, the message of the two series is compelling. If one is to have the "kind of children" who will be "strong, keen, efficient, and great," capable of contributing to "the culture of civilization," one must ask probing questions about the family tree one's future child will inherit. Although the American Social Hygiene Association was founded as part of a focused effort at the turn of the century to squelch the "Social Evil" and its attendant, debilitating diseases, the two poster series sought more broadly to cultivate an ardent desire for a thoroughly wholesome future — free not only of gonorrhea and syphilis but also of other "unwholesome," socially burdensome conditions increasingly thought to be the product of a tainted heritage. One must take a more accurate and thorough measure, it admonished, of a person's intellectual, emotional, and aesthetic attributes.

If indeed "the future of the race marches forward on the feet of little children," many of those eager to "form" the nation saw their role as not only putting shoes on the unshod but also eliminating those who could not march. The message of their efforts promoted discriminating fecundity and, arguably, underwrote eugenics. First, they encouraged prospective parents, as well as the parents of the prospective parents, to approach mating with a discriminating caution. YMCA and YWCA participants were to put on their most discerning spectacles, stand back, and *appraise*. Was this young man or woman truly *worthy* of *the race?* Even the armchair historian knows the insidious pattern of miscegenation laws in the South. But the subtle message was formally similar, borrowing from an implied distinction between a "strong, keen, efficient" race, capable of "civilization," and persons to be written off as weak, stupid, and inefficient. Second, what of those children judged to have been bred in error? They function at the boundary of danger. At best they are objects of pity. At worst, like Carrie Buck's daughter, they signal the need for social vaccination through sterilization.

How was one to judge those worth marriage, those worth care, and those worth extinction? The leaders of the eugenics movement were intent on putting the tools for such measurements in the hands of the populace.

### "Worth-While Lives"

One of the posters from the "Youth and Life" series aims to inspire by naming women with "Worth-While Lives." The poster features a photograph of the Reverend Dr. Anna Howard Shaw, ordained minister in the Methodist

Protestant church, distinguished graduate of both medical school and theological studies, and president of the National American Woman's Suffrage Association (1904-15). Although the photo was taken late in life, she appears full of verve, even exuberance, with academic robes flowing and a city bustling behind her. Below her is a list that includes, among others, Jane Addams, Florence Nightingale, Madam Curie, Ethel Barrymore, and Elizabeth Barrett Browning. The message and image offer a slightly different take on the task of youth and the purpose of life. A "Worth-While" life might involve primarily domestic stability, but it might also involve, perhaps later in life, a vocation in medicine, film, or literature.

One pragmatic reason for a woman to pursue a healthier life and a promising mate would be to secure her prospects as a physician, an actress, or a poet. Young women in less promising circumstances could draw inspiration from the poster entitled "What One Girl Did": "Four years ago she saw only her physical handicap, her lameness. Today she is . . . a doctor's assistant." Bolstered by "a bit of encouragement, training, and education," she has attained not only health but also "a useful place in the world." The next poster in the series, the only one that depicts a clearly working-class woman, declares that even in apparent "drudgery," with the proper effort and will, "The Healthy Girl Can Enjoy Her Work."

For many Protestant women, leadership in movements like ASHA and the YWCA represented a chance to make conditions better for women from the canning factory to the tenement bedroom to the farm. Margaret Sanger, who eventually founded Planned Parenthood, certainly saw her participation in the American Eugenics Society (AES) in this light. The AES, the Eugenics Record Office, ASHA, and other such organizations were staffed and, at times, led by women hoping to make life more livable and even more "wholesome" for other women. The working definitions of domesticity were problematic, however, and arguably in ways that continued well after the Progressive Era. Under the leadership of Raymond Fosdick, younger brother of the Reverend Harry Emerson Fosdick, the Rockefeller Foundation had set out to foster a eugenic science of "economic productivity" and "social stability"; these efforts went hand in hand with a new science of domestic hygiene, which would "combat vice, raise moral standards, and improve human conduct."[43]

Matthew Frye Jacobson suggests that racism in the United States is "a theory of who is who, of who belongs and who does not, of who deserves

---

43. Lily E. Kay, *The Molecular Vision of Life: Caltech, the Rockefeller Foundation, and the Rise of the New Biology* (New York: Oxford University Press, 1993), p. 26.

what and who is capable of what." As was the case in what Jacobson calls "the contest over whiteness — its definitions, its internal hierarchies, its proper boundaries, and its rightful claimants," the contest over responsible parenthood and "good housekeeping" required losers as well as winners.[44] The homogenized definition of cleanliness and godliness that allowed various Protestant women to join forces for "productivity" and "stability" required also their sense of a common enemy — and actual families were labeled "unproductive," hopelessly soiled, "tainted," or "impure" in the process. There were women involved in the hygiene movement, most notably Jane Addams, founder of Hull House, who opened their doors and minds to the various configurations of immigrant families and migrating African American families arriving in Chicago. There were also undoubtedly social workers with ASHA who sought to stretch the boundaries of the American family and the beautiful child even while disseminating information about the deadly diseases often attending prostitution. But there were many wealthy and well-connected women who, like YWCA founder Grace Hoadley Dodge, seemed unable or unwilling to extend their service to "working girls" beyond the circle of white, native-born farm girls immigrating to the cities of the Midwest and Northeast. Protestant women like Dodge, who eventually founded the New York College for the Training of Teachers, were arguably in a position to challenge the eugenics movement. (Dodge herself was related by marriage to the Osborn men who led the AES.) Many, instead, took up the rhetoric and tools of conflict, chaos, and necessary ordering, arguing for extending social services to some while stigmatizing others as "potential threats to the advancement of civilization."[45]

## The ERO and Fitter Families

### "The Investigators"

A 1904 medical school graduate of Iowa State University, Florence Brown Sherbon had for several years been supervising Better Baby contests in Iowa with her colleague in domestic science Mary T. Watts when the director of the Eugenics Record Office (ERO), Charles Davenport, suggested that they join

44. Jacobson, *Whiteness*, pp. 6, 5.
45. Wendy Kline, *Building a Better Race: Gender, Sexuality, and Eugenics from the Turn of the Century to the Baby Boom* (Berkeley: University of California Press, 2001), p. 22. Kline is elaborating on the work of Douglas Baynton, *Forbidden Signs: American Culture and the Campaign against Sign Language* (Chicago: University of Chicago Press, 1996).

**Figure 3.7. Eugenics Training Class, 1914**

forces. The hope was to organize across the country a series of exhibits and contests in "Human Stock" sections of county and state fairs. The resulting movement — Fitter Families for Future Firesides — included lectures on the importance of heredity and elaborate contests in which couples or families were measured and judged by eugenic health professionals for gifts or taints. Displays informed the fairgoing public about the importance of *responsible human breeding*. Using family trait forms written by Davenport, Harry Laughlin, and others, questioners advised couples of their pedigree, and families of their genetic promise or peril. Field-workers, trained at the ERO, traveled also to potentially "dysgenic" or "cacogenic" regions to do measuring, judging, and questioning.

Apart from offering leadership for the social hygiene movement, the daughters of relatively privileged Protestant women also served as foot soldiers for organizations like the ERO, offering "their [supposedly] innate female understandings of women and children with their new, professional, and 'scientific' understanding of the human condition to solve the emerging problems of the new social order."[46] Trained in education, sociology, and medical science at the newly founded institutions of higher education for

46. Luker, "Sex," p. 614. Luker is speaking of domestic hygiene efforts more broadly and does not discuss the ERO or Protestant workers in particular.

women, many found employment through organized efforts to bring progress to rural and urban families.

The most dubious of these efforts involved the young women working for the ERO, the American Breeders Association (by 1914 the American Genetic Association), and other eugenics organizations (fig. 3.7). These were the citizens who volunteered to observe, measure, and judge prospective couples, infants, children, and families in order to further the movement to form a more perfect union. Such "service," however, was not without personal gain. Those who judged acquired prestige by *making use of* those they were judging.[47] As someone (perhaps one of the women) wrote playfully below a photo (fig. 3.8), they were "The Investigators," women who packed up their linen dresses and purchased crisp notebooks in order to follow men like eugenicist Ivan E. McDougle to places like Amherst County, Virginia. The three young professional women smiling at the camera likely helped McDougle compile the data that went into *Mongrel Virginians,* his text on cacogenic Virginians, published in 1924 to encourage the institutionalization, incarceration, and sterilization of an entire region in rural Virginia.

### "Indiscriminate Fecundity"

The fear of "indiscriminate fecundity" — the words of Margaret Sanger, pioneer of the American birth control movement — was fueled by apparent reproductive chaos in cities and in rural areas.[48] Some of the leading voices in favor of eugenic control embraced the movement after trying to bring solace to a desperately poor and growing immigrant population in major industrialized areas. Sanger and Walter Rauschenbusch both worked among the poorest of New York City during an era of unparalleled poverty and exploitation there, and both believed eugenics necessary for industrialized America to truly progress. People outside the boundaries of the city shuddered at the photographs of Jacob Riis, America's first photojournalist; they imagined the hell of living and working cramped in a tenement, hearing the "feeble wails of

47. Nicole Hahn Rafter, in her introduction to *White Trash: The Eugenic Family Studies, 1877-1919* (Boston: Northeastern University Press, 1988), notes that for ERO field-workers, the family studies "did more than extend professional horizons. They also *validated* that extension, giving it rationale, scientific authority, an aura of expertise and objectivity. . . . Furthermore, to authors (and readers as well . . .) the family studies gave the reassurance that they, in particular, ranked high in genetic worth" (p. 16, emphasis in original).

48. Margaret Sanger, *The Pivot of Civilization* (1922; reprint, Amherst, N.Y.: Prometheus Books, Humanity Books, 2003), p. 133.

I.E. McDougle
Gwendolyn Watson
Martha Lobingier
Eleanor Harned.
"The Investigators."

**Figure 3.8. "The Investigators," Ivan E. McDougle, Gwendolyn Watson, Martha Lobingier, and Eleanor Harned, in Amherst County, Virginia, 1924, Arthur Estabrook Papers**

those little ones," as Riis described an Italian neighborhood during a lecture in 1894.[49] Those who lived within the better-heeled parts of the city could readily sympathize with the author of *Fewer and Better Babies*:

> I thank my fates that it is but very seldom that I have to ride in the subway, but when I do, particularly if in the rush hours, the spectacle fills me with inexpressible sadness.
>
> Just look at the faces — not a happy, contented face in the ten cars of the express train. Just analyze them. Tense, gloomy, dissatisfied, grouchy,

49. The quotation is from text that accompanies the Riis photograph "Italian Mother and Her Baby in Jersey Street," circa 1890, Jacob A. Riis Collection, 90.13.4.160, Museum of the City of New York. Riis was asked to take part in a conversation on eugenics at the Episcopal General Convention of 1913; see "Pastors for Eugenics," *New York Times*, June 6, 1913, p. 10.

distinctly unhappy, cruel, stupid or vapid, such are the expressions of practically all the faces you see there. And what are they all doing there? For what reason are they jostling or being jostled . . . ? . . . Merely to make eight or ten or twenty dollars a week, just to support the body sufficiently to be able to work again.[50]

While some Protestant leaders also supported the growing labor movement of the Progressive Era, many found in eugenic ideas a more immediate answer to the apparent meaninglessness of a life born into poverty. The disturbing spectacle of the tenement poor was sufficient to convince quite a few Protestant millionaires to support the eugenics movement but apparently insufficient to force them to rethink significantly the patently exploitative labor methods by which they both made their wealth and ostentatiously displayed it. The urge to order and, when necessary, to eliminate those whose lives seemed interminably disorderly was more powerful than the call to organize.

In her introduction to a collection of rural family studies by the ERO evocatively entitled *White Trash: The Eugenic Family Studies, 1877-1919*, Nicole Hahn Rafter suggests that female professionals, newly trained in "psychology, social work, and sociology," were sent out to document the "degeneracy of country life."[51] The collection of studies complicates the common hypothesis that the eugenics movement grew primarily in response to urban immigrant suffering. While some may have signed on for the sake of starving children in tenement homes, Rafter surmises that the "scientific mythology" of eugenics involved also the methodical search for deviance, particularly among the rural poor. From their luxurious home in New York City, John D. and Mrs. Rockefeller felt compelled not only to establish the Museum of Modern Art but also to bring modern sensibilities and professional order to the rural, backward netherworld.

Those sent out to bring the gospel of proper living to regions suspected of degeneracy found, not surprisingly, a recalcitrant clientele. Rafter writes: "*These* poor were self-reliant, often indifferent to the charity and outright hostile to the values which some of the new professionals made a career of dispensing."[52] In turn, or possibly from the outset, women and men trained by the ERO to be the "Investigators" formulated what Rafter calls a "hieroglyphic world," producing a "language and myth" in order to craft an "ideo-

---

50. William J. Robinson, *Fewer and Better Babies: Birth Control; or, The Limitation of Offspring by the Prevention of Conception*, 35th ed. (1915; reprint, New York: Eugenics Publishing, 1929), pp. 103-4.

51. Rafter, *White Trash*, p. 7.

52. Rafter, *White Trash*, p. 17, emphasis in original.

logically charged mythology." By using "bumpkin pseudonyms" and "sending covert signals to readers," the investigators gave their benefactors a carefully constructed and distanced disdain for those already suspected of "defective delinquency."[53] Working variously for a connected configuration of eugenic efforts, including the official record office, a Rockefeller-funded project on degeneracy, the *American Journal of Sociology,* and the New York state legislature, the detectives used "animal and insect imagery" not only to "suggest danger" but also to "imply that the cacogenic would hardly notice if they were treated as less than human."[54] With titles such as "Hereditary Pauperism," "The Tribe of Ishmael," "The Smoky Pilgrims," *The Hill Folk,* "The 'Pineys,'" *The Feeble-Minded in a Rural County of Ohio, Dwellers in the Vale of Siddem,* and *Mongrel Virginians,* the studies presented real human beings and families as mythological symbols, serving narratively to underwrite plans to isolate, institutionalize, sterilize, and eliminate.

The images of families (figs. 3.9 and 3.10) were taken around 1915, as a part of A. H. Estabrook's follow-up study of "the Jukes" of Ulster County, New York. Estabrook, an official with the ERO, concluded of the family: "One half of the Jukes were and are feeble-minded, mentally incapable of responding normally to the expectations of society, brought up under faulty environmental conditions which they consider normal, satisfied with the fulfillment of natural passions and desires, and with no ambition or ideals in life."[55] In this summary, Estabrook makes a move common in the cacogenic studies. Not only does he judge their homes, their children, and their ways of life "faulty," but he also suggests that they are, on a fundamental level, subnormal. "Satisfied with the fulfillment of natural passions and desires," they are beneath human and thus prime candidates for the expert city-husbandman to categorize, select, and eliminate. The photograph "Four Generations in One Almshouse at One Time" charts the cacogenic pedigree of three women, judging them incapable of living within "organized society."[56]

One of the grandfathers of cacogenic studies was the Reverend Oscar McCulloch from the Indianapolis Plymouth Church, author of "The Tribe of Ishmael: A Study in Social Degradation" (1888). Having served soup to these

53. Rafter, *White Trash,* pp. 26, 1.

54. Rafter, *White Trash,* pp. 2, 26.

55. Arthur H. Estabrook, *The Jukes in 1915* (Washington, D.C.: Carnegie Institution of Washington, 1916), p. 85.

56. "Four Generations in One Almshouse at One Time, at Yaphank, Suffolk Co., N.Y.," 1917, Eugenics Record Office Records, courtesy of American Philosophical Society. Small print reads: "A border-line family, in which illegitimacy runs high, not quite able to care for itself in organized society."

**Figure 3.9. 1915**

**Figure 3.10. 1915**

people in his parish halls, he sought also to study them as specimens, thereby better to order their futures. He summed up his study:

> In this sketch, three things will be evident: First, the wandering blood from the half-breed mother, in the second generation the poison and the passion that probably came with her. Second, the licentiousness which characterizes all the men and women, and the diseased and physically weakened condition. From this result mental weakness, general incapacity, and unfitness for hard work. And, third, this condition is met by the benevolent public with almost unlimited public and private aid, thus encouraging them in this idle, wandering life, and in the propagation of similarly disposed children.[57]

In his "evident" three points, McCulloch reveals a pattern that runs throughout the series of studies. The sense that a family could be "poisoned" in a way that manifested itself through "licentiousness" or "mental weakness" or an incapacity for what was deemed *real* labor is one that became codified in the ERO field-record family trait forms. His conclusion that a "benevolent public" was merely "encouraging" the "propagation" of children who would live poisoned and parasitic lives also carried through the movement. Likening the "tribe" to the "Sacculina," a small parasite that attaches itself to hermit crabs, McCulloch urged his readers to "close up official outdoor relief," "check . . . indiscriminate benevolence," and "get hold of the children."[58]

The technique of renaming their specimens allowed investigators to retain superior distance — a kind of modern, demonic recapitulation of Adam's stewardship of the nonhuman animals in the Genesis story. Frank Blackmar, author of "The Smoky Pilgrims" (1897), named the people under his gaze after their "smoky and begrimed appearance," marking them as "shiftless, helpless, and beyond hope of reform."[59] Gertrude Davenport, wife of Charles, summarizing the Swiss report "The Zero Family" (1905), described a people of "such depths of degradation" as to be worthy of literally *no name*. Here are "criminals who are bred as race horses are bred, namely, by the process of assertive mating." "Such," she explained, "are outside the pale of beneficent environ-

---

57. Oscar C. McCulloch, "The Tribe of Ishmael: A Study in Social Degradation," in Rafter, *White Trash*, p. 51. Originally published in *Proceedings of the National Conference of Charities and Correction* 15 (1888): 154-59.

58. McCulloch, "The Tribe of Ishmael," pp. 49, 54.

59. Frank Blackmar, "The Smoky Pilgrims," in Rafter, *White Trash*, p. 60. Originally published in *American Journal of Sociology* 2 (January 1897): 485-500.

ment."[60] Florence H. Danielson wrote with Charles Davenport another report, *The Hill Folk* (1912), whose extensive diagrams chart numerically and descriptively the "matings," "percent of defectives," "cost of crime," and "cost of maintenance of state wards" in various branches of the family groups they studied. This study, like others, contrasts the few "energetic," "ambitious," "neat," "industrious," and "normal" strains with those who are "lewd," "shiftless," or "careless."[61] In "The 'Pineys'" (1913), another young professional woman, traveling from her post at the Vineland Training School in New Jersey, insisted that "the Piney and all the rest of his type have become barnacles upon our civilization." Elizabeth Kite entreated those concerned with the "high standards of our commonwealth" to take in hand those families whose members showed a habitual failure to pass the Binet intelligence test she had been trained to administer at the Vineland Training School.[62]

### "A Goodly Heritage"

The term Rafter uses for the collection of studies — *White Trash* — is indicative. The suspicion that there is "trash" even among the supposedly promising "native-born" stock is part of what seems to have driven not only the methodically dehumanizing studies of "cacogenic" families but also the Fitter Family contests. Images of the "tainted" and "impure" subtly underwrote the prestige gained by the model families who won silver trophies and "Goodly Heritage" medals by submitting to the various tests planned by grandmotherly women like Mary T. Watts and Florence Brown Sherbon and administered by corps of their young recruits. Each family member was tested with an Individual Analysis Card, "intended to accompany the Pedigree Chart," to determine whether his or her attributes were normal; everything from "speech," "walking gait," and "athletic ability" to "ability to profit from experience," "industry," "common sense," and "moral courage" appears for analysis.[63]

60. Gertrude Davenport, "Hereditary Crime," in Rafter, *White Trash*, p. 68. Originally published in *American Journal of Sociology* 13 (November 1907): 402-9.

61. Florence H. Danielson and Charles Davenport, *The Hill Folk: Report on a Rural Community of Hereditary Defectives*, in Rafter, *White Trash*, pp. 81-163. Originally published in the ERO Memoir series, no. 1 (Cold Spring Harbor, N.Y.: Press of the New Era, 1912).

62. Elizabeth Kite, "The 'Pineys,'" in Rafter, *White Trash*, pp. 164-84. The quotations are on p. 170. Originally published in *Survey: A Journal of Constructive Philanthropy* 21 (October 4, 1913): 7-13, 38-40.

63. See Individual Analysis Card, example 1, Individual Analysis Cards, ms. coll. 77, series VI, box 4, Eugenics Record Office Records, American Philosophical Society.

The perception of children who did not measure up in this context was formally similar to the perception of those cacogenic families identified as "trash." As the rural poor of the eugenic family studies were seen by a whole class of professionals as unredeemably unproductive, so infants, children, and adults with marked disability were seen by those with the power to judge as dangerously burdensome. At the Vineland Training School, where Elizabeth Kite learned to administer the Binet IQ test to "the 'Pineys,'" the school's leader, Henry H. Goddard, perfected the Binet-Simon measuring scale for determining whether a child had been born an "idiot," an "imbecile," or merely a "moron."[64]

Goddard, a Quaker whose mother had been a leader in the Quaker evangelism movement, saw himself as an advocate for children with mental disabilities. The author of perhaps the most notorious of the cacogenic family studies, *The Kallikak Family* (1912), Goddard taught several generations of well-meaning social workers and educators to determine whether a child was hopeless or held some remainder of promise. If the child was born of a seemingly promising and compliant family, the parents would receive recommendations as to their future reproduction. Parents less likely to comply with such advice would be registered for future studies of cacogenic inheritance. Births involving disability were thus markers, warnings of genetic territory in need of caution and control.

In their introduction to a collection of essays on the history of mental retardation in the United States, Steven Noll and James W. Trent suggest that during this era mental retardation was seen as a "condition to be observed, delineated, and classified." Those considered "other" were "utilized to examine 'normality,' and the mentally retarded were used as stock literary devices to hold a mirror to American society."[65] In a climate where normality increasingly meant industrial and aesthetic worth, those who were neither obviously productive nor comely were merely burdensome. Yet the poor, the shiftless,

64. See Leila Zenderland, *Measuring Minds: Henry Herbert Goddard and the Origins of American Intelligence Testing* (Cambridge: Cambridge University Press, 1998), pp. 102-3. According to Zenderland, Goddard's "New Classification (Tentative) of the Feeble-Minded" defined the groups as *idiot* ("one testing below a mental age of three on the Binet scale"), *imbecile* ("one testing between mental ages three and seven"), and — coining a new term for the highest group, since "feebleminded" had come to be used as a generic term — *moron* ("a person of arrested mental development, with an intelligence comparable to that of the normal child between 8 and 12 years inclusive"). Zenderland notes: "For the rest of his life, Goddard would regard this opportunity to add a word to the English language as one of his greatest accomplishments" (Zenderland, pp. 102-3).

65. Steven Noll and James W. Trent, eds., introduction to *Mental Retardation in America: A Historical Reader* (New York: New York University Press, 2004), p. 10.

**Figure 3.11. Photo is from an Individual Analysis Card**

the apparently useless, and the deformed arguably played a central rhetorical role in the "mythology" of eugenics (to recall Rafter's useful term). Photographs of the *other* kind of family and the *dreaded* type of child run throughout the eugenic publications. The image of a Quaker and Oberlin graduate who, in July 1922, posed for the picture in figure 3.11, to be included as part of her official ERO "pedigree," may be read in conjunction with Noll and Trent's suggestion. Her "goodly" heritage may be distinguished not least because of the implied presence, in the background, of those *from whom* she may be distinguished.

This mirroring of identity, whereby the superior traits of an individual or family line become clear in contrast to the inferiority of others, is conspicuous in the Fitter Family movement. The "-er" in "Fitter" is parasitic on the less than fit. The Fitter Family competitions involved photography to capture the faces, bodies, and familial configurations of the families who would contribute to, rather than burden, a relatively young country on the verge of success (fig. 3.13). These portraits of the "above average" family are distinguishable largely as a function of their contrast to those "other" families who fell below the average. Behind the scenes, as a necessary, negative backdrop to the prize-winning images, were recent immigrant families, African American families, and other families who failed to win a grade of B-plus or higher. Those with "a goodly heritage" (as affirmed by the phrase embossed on their medals — "Yea, I Have a Goodly Heritage," fig. 3.12) were so judged by a grading curve *that could not have existed* without families who received a B or lower.

248

**Figure 3.12. From the Fitter Families Collection, American Eugenics Society Records**

**Figure 3.13. From the Fitter Families Collection, American Eugenics Society Records**

I fear that the symbolic significance of this curve continues today, as Methodist, Presbyterian, Congregationalist, and Episcopal parents eager to forge a promising future for their families do so by way of technologies, neighborhoods, and schools of distinction, leaving behind those who do not measure up and cannot keep up in a competitive, streamlined market culture. The eugenicists of yesterday played on the fears of relatively privileged middle-class parents, encouraging them to identify upward and to eschew solidarity with those who were falling behind. The challenge before mainline Protestants today is to see the children in their homes, neighborhoods, and churches as unqualified gifts rather than projects, to identify "downward" rather than to climb, and to allow their strategically protected and planned lives to become entangled in the needs of families and children judged to be at risk and behind the curve. To face this challenge, Protestants will need to confront their role in the past.

## Holy Husbandmen — "Interpreting the Historic Faith in a Modern World"

### "Citizen" Clergy

One symbol of the eugenics movement in the 1920s and 1930s was a "EU-GENICS" tree, with roots branching out to tap the "many sources" from which the eugenics movement drew in order to become a "harmonious entity" (fig. 3.14). Through the "self direction of human evolution," eugenicists hoped to cultivate a tree that would flourish, bearing only good fruit for the future. Note that "religion" was relegated to a root well off to the far right, one of the farthest roots from the main trunk of the tree. Biology, psychology, statistics, mental testing, history, geology, law, and politics all had roles to play, with religion seemingly squeezed in almost as an afterthought — after sociology, to be precise. Yet the imagery of human advancement, hope, and flourishing fruit was rhetorically potent owing in part to the echoes of the same biblical faith preached by Davenport's Congregationalist father, and the movement needed clergy to keep those echoes resonant.[66]

Through the formation of the AES, eugenics leaders signaled that it would not be sufficient merely to keep careful measurements and records of the unfit and the fit, the impure and the pure, through the ERO. They needed

---

66. Harry Laughlin, who worked as superintendent of the ERO under Davenport, was the son of a minister in the Christian Church.

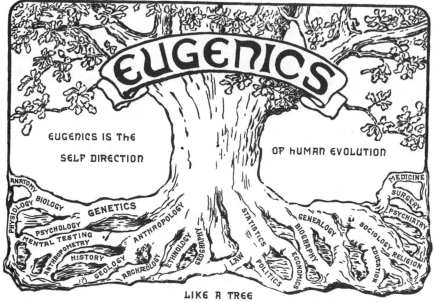

**Figure 3.14. "Eugenics is the self direction of human evolution." From Eugenics Record Office Records, courtesy of American Philosophical Society**

to capture the imaginations of the citizenry. Religion was perhaps the root closest to the ground, and the AES found there clergy eager to prove that they were on the modernist side of the modernist/fundamentalist rift. Through cooperation with the AES, the YMCA, and the ASHA, through thoughtful reviews and provocative sermons, clergy took up their calling in that "great field of usefulness" that supported Protestant eugenics.[67] The sociologist, the psychologist, the anthropologist, and the social worker were on the ascendancy, and mainline pastors throughout America were determined not to seem obsolete or, even worse, backward. As one reads the "modern" attempts

---

67. The reference is to Leland Foster Wood, "The Church and Education for the Family," *Religion in Life* 3 (1934): 420-31. Arguing for "pre-marital interviews" to promote emotional and social fitness, Wood declared: "As rapidly as the clergy can be trained for this work, they will enter into a great field of usefulness." Further: "While the psychiatrist, the social worker, the judge of the court of domestic relations, the family physician and others render a great service to families, the minister of religion, whose business it is to interpret life as a whole, has his own unique place of service" (p. 431).

to prove a bowing acquaintance with eugenics, it is not difficult to surmise why mainline laity were unable to resist the allure of proving their own families fit at the expense of others. Faced with the challenge of remaining relevant and seeming well educated in a modern world, many mainline Protestant clergy serving parishes and academe, in cities and in the country, did nothing less than capitulate.

In her meticulous treatment of the key religious players in the popularization of eugenics, Christine Rosen detects this as a "clear pattern": "The liberals and modernists in their respective faiths — those who challenged their churches to conform to modern circumstances — became the eugenics movement's most enthusiastic supporters."[68] Rosen's conclusion is irrefutable. To cite one contrast, the Roman Catholic Church — with marked consistency from the grass roots to the Vatican — resisted laws forcing sterilization as well as the mind-set behind the movement, while some of the most hearty supporters of the AES found happy soil in the Anglican and Episcopal Churches.[69] The cross-Atlantic links of the latter church allowed eugenic theologians like Canon Charles Kingsley to influence priests such as Karl Reiland (in New York City) and Walter Taylor Sumner (in Chicago), who were eager to prove themselves legitimate fruit of the *forward*-thinking branch of the apostolic church.

One article in the *Christian Century* from 1924 is telling. Reporting on a conference on the church and science held by the aptly named British Churchmen's Union for the Advancement of Liberal Religious Thought, the piece relates at length the words of Oxford University professor and lay Anglican J. S. Haldane. In the quotation Haldane insists that people of faith "cannot afford to be hampered by unintelligible beliefs which are mainly materialistic accretions of Christianity and which greatly weaken its influence on those who are worth influencing." Distinguishing "religion itself" from these accretions, Haldane warns that "any shirking of the questions involved or cowardly sheltering behind mere traditional authority is fatal."[70] The desire to remain in the good graces of "those who are worth influencing," namely, (apparently) those well-educated citizens who had made the scientific turn, was clearly a part of the story.

68. Rosen, *Preaching Eugenics*, p. 184.

69. See Sharon M. Leon, "'Hopelessly Entangled in Nordic Pre-suppositions': Catholic Participation in the American Eugenics Society in the 1920s," *Journal of the History of Medicine and Allied Sciences* 59 (2004): 3-49.

70. J. S. Haldane, cited in "Churchmen and Scientists Discuss Mutual Problems," *Christian Century*, September 25, 1924, pp. 1244, 1250, 1252. See also J. S. Haldane, *The Sciences and Philosophy* (Garden City, N.Y.: Doubleday, 1929); and Haldane, *The Philosophical Basis of Life* (Garden City, N.Y.: Doubleday, 1931).

Yet there are other salient patterns in Rosen's research. The "modern circumstances" to which eugenics enthusiasts compelled their brethren to conform were the "modern circumstances" of a significantly growing and noticeably changing populace — a populace that seemed out of ecclesial and civic reach. During a time when various "helping" professions were on the rise among middle-class Protestants, there were regions, neighborhoods, and families who seemed out of "charitable" control. Those who would not be assimilated into the organizational plans of progressives seemed not only extraneous but also dangerously chaotic. One popular facet of eugenics was its tidy promise to justify those margins. The right algorithms and tools helped those called to tend the boundaries of civic life to conceive of and perform their tasks. Variously unfit people played also, simultaneously, the necessary role of "the problem."

The sense that those gifted to do so should take up their civic duty to form a more perfect union was also pervasive. For many mainline Protestants, the call to be a "good citizen" was tied up with the active formation of civic order. This perhaps puts a different spin on Rosen's well-drawn conclusion. The Protestants most accustomed to their role as well-educated *citizens* had the fewest theological resources to resist the messages of eugenics. The oldest and most unquestionably *American* of the Protestant churches were the first to jump on the eugenics bandwagon.

### "Improving the Quality of the Race"

The least that must be demanded is a clean bill of health. That is why I have often praised clergymen for good citizenship who refuse to marry couples without such a clean bill of health.[71]

This quotation from *Fewer and Better Babies* reflects another facet of the eugenics movement — the push for only "health marriages." Those found to be tainted, who might "propagate epilepsy, idiocy, feeblemindedness and criminality," should not be permitted to "propagate their ailments"; indeed, any practice to the contrary "should be declared detrimental to the welfare of the commonwealth and punishable." As the ones to whom many couples turned when on the verge of marriage and, presumably, reproduction, clergy were in a key position to help ensure that "the future children of the nation" would be "prepared for competent and comfortable citizenship."[72]

71. A. Jacobi, in Robinson, *Fewer and Better Babies*.
72. A. Jacobi, introduction to *Fewer and Better Babies*, by Robinson, pp. 14-15, 18.

Several articles from the *New York Times* followed the efforts of the Very Reverend Walter Taylor Sumner, dean of the Protestant Episcopal Cathedral of Saints Peter and Paul in Chicago, to meet this call. Sumner declared in 1912 that neither he nor any other clergy at the cathedral would perform marriage services without a "'clean bill of health' signed by a reputable physician" for the prospective partners. A *Times* headline distills Sumner's message: "Must Be Normal and Well to Wed." His timing was striking. Sumner announced that his plan — to ensure that the certificates of marriage issued by the cathedral would represent "absolute purity" — was to begin on Easter Sunday. Beginning the day Protestant Episcopal congregants would celebrate the bodily resurrection of a crucified savior, the only people married in the cathedral would be those officially declared to be "normal physically and mentally." This move, Sumner hoped, would send a message that would reverberate throughout the city of Chicago, provoking a "deeper interest in the problem and a wider action on the part of fathers and mothers." While some of Sumner's fellow clergymen had concerns about the practicality of his plan, they agreed with his overall aim of "purifying the marriage ceremony," stating that "the principle is beneficent and ought to be upheld by all Christian people."[73] His hope evidently bore fruit. Several months later the *Times* announced that "the most striking result" of Sumner's "edict" was "the action taken last week by 200 clergymen of Chicago" who "adopted a resolution unanimously urging pastors to direct their energies toward creating public opinion indorsing [*sic*] Dean Sumner's plan."[74]

A year later the Reverend Dr. A. E. Keigwin led a group of clergy from the New York City area in a "platform meeting" on eugenics at his West End Presbyterian Church. Joining him in the effort to "push a eugenics campaign" was the Reverend Dr. Newell Dwight Hillis of Plymouth Church, Brooklyn. Keigwin believed that "much of our public difficulty and more of our public expense" were due to "dense ignorance" regarding marriage. He linked the growing movement of eugenics to the health of the country: "If we will deliver men and women from the shackles of ignorance concerning themselves we shall effect a reform that is vital to the whole human family, and especially to our own country." The entire Liberal Ministers' Association of New York was appointing a Eugenics Committee to consider making the movement for "health marriages" a part of its official platform. As a key participant in the

73. "Must Be Normal and Well to Wed," *New York Times*, March 25, 1912, p. 3. I am indebted to Christine Rosen for her reference in *Preaching Eugenics* to this series of articles.

74. "Should Ministers Marry the Physically Unfit? Distinguished Doctors and Divines Discuss the Edict of Dean Sumner of Chicago That No More Marriages Will Be Permitted in the Episcopal Cathedral without Health Certificates," *New York Times*, June 2, 1912, p. 4.

conversations, the Reverend Dr. John Haynes Holmes called his fellow clergymen to take up their "moral responsibility" to "perform nothing but health marriages." Suggesting that "Dean Sumner and the Chicago Cathedral have shown us the way," Holmes presumably found a hearing, given that both the Reverend Dr. Charles L. Slattery of Grace Church (Protestant Episcopal) and the Reverend Dr. William P. Merrill of Brick Presbyterian Church — two ministers among those in their day who, according to the *Times,* performed "the largest number of fashionable marriage ceremonies" — signed on to officiate only for certifiably healthy alliances.[75]

The progressive, liberal, and "fashionable" clergy of New York and Chicago were helping to counter what was seen as a reckless romanticism endangering the future of families in America. As figure 3.15 makes clear, the "abnormal" or "tainted" did not have the option of indulging in "chance" or "'blind' sentiment." The poster, circa 1929, was part of the American Eugenics Society's effort to strengthen the connection already present in George Napheys's advice on the "transmission of life." Shown in the Human Stock section of fairs, the message appealed to the presumed common sense of parents. A part of animal husbandry, it admonished, is being an aptly perspicacious parent.

On what may seem, at first glance, to be a lighter note, the *Journal of Social Hygiene* in 1927 described an extensive ASHA program to provide "a new interpretation of Valentine's Day." Asking "Beyond a frolic, does Valentine's Day mean anything?" the project attempted to convince clergy to use "the week of St. Valentine's Day" as "the occasion for a sermon and inspirational talks on the meaning of love and marriage as great social and moral forces." Through a letter sent to two thousand ministers, ASHA hoped to enlist clergy and laity in a concerted shift from the frivolity of the day to "the purpose of enriching, strengthening, and cleansing human life in its sex and family relations; the ultimate purpose of improving the quality of the race." As a part of this two-year project, ASHA also printed valentines "with greetings from the American Social Hygiene Association" to be used in place of the "hundreds of thousands" of meaningless cards usually sent out. The valentine drew on the inspirational text of David Starr Jordan, encouraging young people to keep themselves pure for the sake of their own and their children's futures.[76] The choice was apt for an endeavor to improve "the quality of the race," given that Jordan, who served at the helm of both Indiana and Stanford Universities,

---

75. "Pastors for Eugenics," *New York Times,* June 6, 1913, p. 10.

76. Editorial, "A New Interpretation of Valentine's Day," *Journal of Social Hygiene* 13 (December 1927): 535, 538, 537, 550.

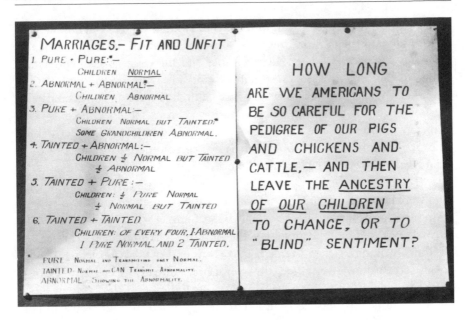

Figure 3.15. "Marriages — Fit and Unfit." Image from Fitter Families Collection, American Eugenics Society Records, courtesy of American Philosophical Society

was also the author of *The Blood of the Nation: A Study of the Decay of Races through the Survival of the Unfit* (1902) — a book that made him, according to Edwin Black, "America's first eminent eugenic theorist."[77]

### Is Christianity Dysgenic?

An active part of the eugenics conversation was the concern that Christianity itself was dysgenic, inasmuch as charitable giving took from the presumably productive and gave to the presumably parasitic. For those directly serving food and clothing, whether informally or professionally, the question was a practical one. To quote again McCulloch, who served many free hot meals through his Congregational parish in Indianapolis, the "benevolent public" insisted on merely "encouraging" those who lived an "idle, wandering" existence. For those asked indirectly to give, the question was practical in a different way. They had worked hard for their money, and it was part of Christian

---

77. Edwin Black, *War against the Weak: Eugenics and America's Campaign to Create a Master Race* (New York: Four Walls Eight Windows, 2003), p. 65.

stewardship to be responsible givers. *Eugenics: A Journal of Race Betterment* addressed the question head-on. "Is Christianity Dysgenic?" and "Is Christian Morality Harmful? Over-charitable to the Unfit?" included responses from one rabbi and three clergymen serving in New York City.[78] The answers of the three Christian clerics warrant careful reading, for each explicates differently the relationship between traditional faith and science to draw conclusions about Christianity and eugenics.

"Evolution is a term that applies to religion as well as biology," explained the Reverend Dr. Karl Reiland of St. George's Protestant Episcopal Church. The "early Christian concept that the world should be despised" is a "foot binding," a "drag on the progress of religious thought" that "keeps the church from 'stepping out.'" Those who were willing to embrace an aptly evolved religion would recognize that "the first and foremost salvation of man individually, collectively and universally is the here and now salvation of a healthy heritage." As Reiland read the relation between "science and religion," the more conventional form of salvation — of one's soul and body through a savior — is dependent on the securing of "sound, safe and sane human beings"; indeed, "the more we get of these salvations the more likely is any other, and the surer is the kind of religion that can help mankind." Reiland understood his challenge as a clerical spokesman for eugenics — "with inexorable certainty of perspective" — to be threefold: "to revive and accelerate progress along the higher levels of thinking; . . . to convince the religious conscience that whatever our creed, we are dealing with nature for the fundamental welfare of human nature; and lastly, to be prepared to discover that God was the God of biology before the Bible came on the scene."

Reiland did not directly answer the immediate, practical question posed by the journal. He went well beyond it, defining religion within the purview of human evolution and social utility. Situated in this way, Christianity could be cleared of the charge of practicing dysgenics. But what is more, Christianity, "whatever our creed," could be squarely in service to the eugenic aim "to produce sound, safe and sane human beings." Evolution applied to religion necessitated boldly taking one's place as a vanguard, eschewing when necessary both traditional doctrine and institutional polity in order to lead. As a final gesture of obeisance to the sponsors of the journal, Reiland suggested that evolved Christians concede the primary, revelatory power of biology.

It is in the implied conversation between Harry F. Ward and John A.

78. "Is Christian Morality Harmful? Over-charitable to the Unfit? Four Religious Leaders Discuss a Charge Sometimes Made," *Eugenics: A Journal of Race Betterment* 1 (December 1928): 20-21.

Ryan that Reiland's rather elastic theology found traction.[79] The two men held down parallel positions in their respective denominations — Ward a Methodist, Ryan a Catholic; each served as a professor at his church's premier institution of higher education and as a national spokesman for the progressive wing of his church. Yet their answers were strikingly different.

Ward argued that "the principles of Jesus" would not necessarily "weaken and destroy society" unless one was "short-sighted" in his interpretation of said principles. The true answer to the question posed by the journal would not overlook the "vital fact" that "the principles of Jesus" call for the "transformation" of the weak. "In seeking this goal," Ward argued, Christians with a properly broad vision would accept "the challenge of removing the causes that produce the weak, including the hereditary factor." And here Ward was blunt. The "aim" of proper Christianity is "a healthy society where all are strong." The faithful are thus not only allowed but also "compelled" to be "eugenic." A "social ethic based on the principles of Jesus" no less than requires "the elimination of the weak, not their perpetuation, and this it accomplishes by making them strong and by preventing their production, through both breeding and environment." By Ward's estimation, Christians had a crucial role to play in a "coordinated world-wide effort to control population" and "to [attain] the highest standards of health and development by all the population." While Reiland suggested that Christianity should be involved in securing "sound, safe and sane human beings," Ward cut to the chase. The true goal of Christianity, as Ward read it, was to perpetuate strength and eliminate weakness. That the elimination of weakness would involve the sterilization of the weak was but part of a larger project of forming a "healthy society."

With this trickled-down brew of Hegel, Darwin, and American progressivism, Ward defended Christianity against the charge that it coddles the weak. Between Reiland and Ward, the answer was clear: Christianity would not prevent the social body from vaccinating itself against the unsafe, the unsound, and the insane. Quite the contrary — the Christianity of their day was to participate in the process of inoculation.

It is John Ryan who most clearly complicates Christine Rosen's suggestion that progressivism and eugenics were inextricably linked. Here was a bona fide progressive, a tireless advocate for the working class and the unemployed poor who helped move his church to heed a radical strand of social thought all

79. Ward was professor of Christian ethics at Union Theological Seminary (1918-41) and was also a founder of the Methodist Federation for Social Service (1907). In 1928, Ryan was a professor of both political science and moral theology at the Catholic University of America and director of the National Catholic Welfare Council's Social Action Department.

but buried in the nineteenth century. Yet Ryan answered the question of the relation between eugenics and Christianity with two points that cut to the heart of the eugenic presumption. First, Ryan reminded his interlocutors that "society, apart from the human beings composing it, is a mere abstraction"— that is, the social body exists only in and through real, embodied human beings. "Therefore," Ryan patiently prodded, "to subordinate the weaker groups to the welfare of society means simply that some human beings are to be made instruments to the welfare of other human beings." This is all well and good, Ryan warned, for "one who believes that morality is identical with physical force." However, "one who does not identify right with might" will be unable to argue for "treating the weak as of less intrinsic worth than the strong, even though the former may be in the minority." Ryan left unspoken that the "one" who identified right with might and considered the weak to be of less intrinsic worth could hardly call himself or herself a Christian.

Then, with a rhetorical twist, Ryan reminded the eugenic readers, and presumably his fellow clergy, that they would do well to consider another, more practical problem. Reiland, Ward, and other like-minded Christians might hope to find a hearing now by proving their solidarity with the strong. But if the eugenic program succeeded, they might eventually find themselves on the receiving end: "The practical argument against this theory is that once society decides that the weak may rightfully be left to perish, it will extend the principle to all of the so-called inferior classes, so that in the end the 'welfare of society' will come to mean the welfare of a few supermen, namely those who have been powerful enough to get themselves accepted at their own valuation."

As Ryan saw the movement, eugenics was primarily about the power of the currently strong to use the apparently weak for securing something as nebulous as a "higher average welfare." Faced with the temptation of siding with the worthy against the unworthy, the other two clergy had succumbed. Sacrifice your faith, Ryan warned, and tomorrow you may find yourself counted among the weak.

### "Purge the Dross"

Many sermons inspired by the AES sermon contests reveal the tragically short-sighted tendency of Protestant clergy to align with the strong against the vulnerable. Three sermons published in 1929 in three different journals by men representing three different denominations may serve as characteristic examples.

Edwin Bishop preached "Eugenics and the Church" at Plymouth Congregational Church in Lansing, Michigan; like the dysgenic/eugenic debate, the sermon appeared in the official ERO publication from New Haven, *Eugenics: A Journal of Race Betterment.*[80] A second sermon, "The Refiner's Fire," appeared in the *Homiletic Review.* The Reverend Phillips Endecott Osgood, rector of St. Mark's Unitarian Church in Minneapolis, had won the 1926 AES Eugenics Sermon Contest with his rousing demand to purge "the dross" of humanity through eugenics, and the publishers of the ecumenical journal not only found the sermon worthy of print but also endorsed the AES contest, declaring with editorial authority: "Eugenics is an approved thing."[81] The third sermon, "Eugenics: A Lay Sermon," by George Huntington Donaldson, was chosen by the *Methodist Review.*[82]

The three sermons suggest that the popularizing efforts of the scientific eugenicists were quite effective. From an ERO journal to an ecumenical Protestant review to a focused, denominational publication, the message was taking hold. A Congregationalist in Michigan, a Unitarian in Minnesota, and a Methodist in New York City each took to the pulpit to affirm (quoting Donaldson) that "the strongest and best are selected for propagating the likeness of God and carrying on his work of improving the race."[83]

In an ironic use of anti-Catholic dialect, the Congregationalist in the group noted that the science of heredity was confirming "Irish Pat's sage dictum that 'a family tree is a foine thing if it ben't too shady.'" Science had proved that everything from "night blindness" to "a tendency to health and longevity" was "heritable," and, according to Edwin Bishop, it was through these scientific advances that God called humans to "participate with him in *conscious* evolution" (emphasis in original). Appealing, as did so many eugenicists, to old-fashioned animal husbandry, Bishop argued that "if we used as much intelligence in human mating as we use in breeding horses and cows," we could prevent "ills" and encourage "excellencies." Would not Jesus himself encourage "any program that would aid children to be physically well-born"? Again, in a characteristic eugenic move, Bishop referred to the rock-solid proof of numbers. A quantitative study had shown that "of 476 children born to 144 marriages among feeble-minded folk only six were normal," indicating that "native ability furnishes the bulk of the basis of achievement." Those who follow Jesus needed therefore to see eugenics as "a potential ally" in the holy pursuit of "racial self-fulfillment." "Through neglect of

80. Edwin Bishop, "Eugenics and the Church," *Eugenics: A Journal of Race Betterment* 2 (August 1929): 14-19.

81. Osgood, "The Refiner's Fire," pp. 406, 405.

82. George Huntington Donaldson, "Eugenics: A Lay Sermon," *Methodist Review* 112 (1929): 59-68.

83. Donaldson, "Eugenics," p. 60.

eugenic knowledge and practice," Bishop warned, "tares are sprouting widely through the wheat." By forming a prudent alliance with eugenics organizations, Christians could reverse the growing imbalance of the "well-born" and the "less favorably born" — a menacing imbalance proven by "carefully assembled data" (likely provided by the AES in their letter of invitation to the sermon contest).[84]

It is for very good reason that Christine Rosen begins *Preaching Eugenics* with Osgood's "The Refiner's Fire." His call, with which we began this chapter, to prove one's "bowing acquaintance" with the "larger truths" of eugenics was a rhetorically masterful use of his homiletic gifts.[85] Opening with Malachi 3:3, "He shall sit as a refiner and purifier of silver," Osgood called God the "Refiner of the generations," for whom Christians should "count themselves the agents of his purposes." Lest any of his hearers or readers ask inconvenient questions about Jesus and the meek or poor, Osgood reminded them: "Jesus sometimes said ruthless things" if "men deserved them." Such was the time again. Jesus "was superlatively concerned to better the qualities of human living" and testified that "grapes cannot be gathered from thorns nor figs from thistles." Citing each child's "inalienable right to life more abundant," Osgood asserted that Christians were to take up "the refining responsibility," recognize that "the future is in our hands," and secure by "creative forethought" the purity of future generations. Loath to limit himself to Scripture, the Unitarian clergyman reminded his hearers that "Xenophon, long ago, recommended that slaves should be allowed the reward of children for good conduct." "The recommendation," Osgood suggested, "has merit also for those not slaves."[86]

From sterilizing "the criminal" to stigmatizing the "victim of inheritable malady," Osgood argued with exegetical flourish for the basic tenet of eugenics — the excellent must prevent the propagation of the reprehensible and the pitiable. The present generation had a responsibility to act as the "redemptive helper of the next generation." If one but compared the Jukes family to the family of Jonathan Edwards (a move first made by A. E. Winship),[87] one might see that heredity is the "major factor" in "our cooperation with the Refiner's work."[88] Here Osgood played on the metallurgy metaphor in two ways. To determine who among the Refiner's creatures were called to do the cooperative refining, one needed primarily to look at heritage. To determine

84. Bishop, "Eugenics and the Church," pp. 16, 17.
85. Osgood, "The Refiner's Fire," p. 406.
86. Osgood, "The Refiner's Fire," pp. 405, 406.
87. Albert E. Winship, *Jukes — Edwards: A Study in Education and Heredity* (Harrisburg, Pa.: R. L. Myers, 1900).
88. Osgood, "The Refiner's Fire," pp. 406, 407.

the proper tools to be used by the refined, one needed only to look at the heredity studies. Osgood's conclusion is clear:

> God will provide his Spirit to our children's children; why handicap its incarnation? It will be the finer in its manifesting if it need not labor under handicap. The kingdom of God on earth is not an end of growth, but the beginning of true destiny. Until sin and weakness and disease and pain are done away, we are only starting to commence to get ready to enter into life as it may be. Until the impurities of dross and alloy are purified out of our silver it can not be taken in the hands of the craftsman for whom the refining was done. God the Refiner we know: do we yet dream of the skill or the beauty of purpose of God the Craftsman with his once purified silver? May the time soon come when in refined humanity he can see his own face, clear and unsullied.[89]

Invoking no less than "the name of God who is Love," Osgood suggested that the culmination of God's creation was dependent on the elimination of suffering. This involved not acts of mercy toward the sick and the poor but acts to secure a future free of those who would "handicap [the Spirit's] incarnation."[90] Twice referring to the *saecula saeculorum,* Osgood placed the "refining responsibility" within the Latin liturgy. The "forever and ever," "the ages of ages," becomes, in his sermon, a future dependent on eugenic resolve.[91]

From the husbandman to the blacksmith and, now, to the gardener: George Huntington Donaldson used a botany metaphor in his sermon to extol the virtues of Christian eugenics. He urged Methodists and fellow humanists to see the "beautiful and efficient answers" that emerge when one envisions God as akin to the nation's most beloved gardener, California plant breeder and eugenicist Luther Burbank. "When we contemplate this patient toiler in his wonderful garden, in fellowship with and conformity to that trinity of creative laws, namely: *heredity, variation,* and *selection,*" we may understand "the progressive creation of better life on this earth." By reading Genesis with eugenic science in view, one can see that "the whole creative process described [in the creation story] had been progressive." Using Unitarian poet William Herbert Carruth's line "Some call it Evolution, / And [others] call it God," Donaldson waxed poetic on the "third law" of creation. Through selection, God continues to use "the strongest and best" for "propagating the likeness of God and carrying on his work of improving the race." If one reads

89. Osgood, "The Refiner's Fire," p. 409.
90 Osgood, "The Refiner's Fire," pp. 408, 409.
91. Osgood, "The Refiner's Fire," pp. 405, 407.

Scripture carefully, one may detect a pattern: from the story of Joseph's rise over his "mongrel" brothers to the desert wandering (which "purged" the weak) to the "choicest souls" who followed Ezra and Nehemiah, "those who have been purified" are able to "see God."[92]

Exegetes, sociologists, biologists, and theologians heartily agreed on this point: "there is but one fixed and unchangeable thing, and that is heredity." To bring this point home to his congregation, the preacher sounded a liturgically resonant theme. For Methodists, hymnody was (and remains) a significant part of weekly worship. Donaldson's use of language from Matthew 7:24-25 played effectively upon echoes with the beloved Methodist hymn by Edward Mote, "My Hope Is Built." While the hymn intoned "My hope is built on nothing less than Jesus' blood and righteousness," Donaldson proclaimed, "Heredity is a rock on which we can build with unfailing certainty." By setting the initial creation within the story of evolution, Donaldson was able to set the new creation through Jesus within the larger story of "improving the race." Those who were baptized into Christ became partners in the work of selecting, yanking out, and cultivating. With "proper selections and combinations all good can be produced and all evil eliminated"; the one following Jesus needed to cut down the "crop of defectives" who "weaken and burden the race."[93]

Donaldson showed a characteristic familiarity with the big names of scientific eugenics. By alluding to the founder of British eugenics, Francis Galton, and quoting Henry Fairfield Osborn, president of the American Museum of Natural History in New York (1908-33) and of the Second Eugenics Congress (in 1921), he gave evidence of his own knowledge of the field and made obeisance to those who were developing the proper gardening tools. His sermon came back to holy horticulture, employing the Johannine Jesus' imagery of vine and branches to link God the Father with God the Selective Gardener: "So, returning to our Bible account, we read the words of Jesus, 'I am the vine, ye are the branches, and my Father is the gardener,' or husbandman. And just as at the beginning we saw Luther Burbank watching over his gardens, selecting here a fine strain, there another, and taking the pollen of one to unite with the egg cell of the other and so produce a finer fruit or flower, so in this wonderful book, God as Gardener has been watching over humanity."[94]

As the rousing conclusion of his sermon, Donaldson asked whether

92. Donaldson, "Eugenics," pp. 59, 60, 63, emphasis in original.
93. Donaldson, "Eugenics," pp. 63, 65.
94. Donaldson, "Eugenics," pp. 65-66.

Christians would have the courage to "Make democracy safe for the world" by ensuring "progressive betterment." In the hymn on which Donaldson relied for a potent echo, it was Jesus' blood that secured the future. Layering metaphor on metaphor, Donaldson suggested that those made "perfect" by Jesus' "death upon the cross" were called to make democracy safe by ensuring the "pure and undefiled" transmission of human blood "to the coming generations."[95] The Christian hope is thus *rebuilt* on nothing less than Jesus' blood and Galton's best.

The subtitle I have given to this subsection of the chapter, "Interpreting the Historic Faith in a Modern World," plays on the motto of the *Quarterly Review,* the United Methodist journal of "theological resources for ministry." Rather than a "modern world," the journal aims to interpret "the historic faith" in a "postmodern" one. The editors of the *Quarterly Review* at the turn of the twenty-first century also signaled the intention of the journal by way of a motto: "interpreting the historic faith in a postmodern world." In this quest, the articles emerge from "the context of a distinctively United Methodist and Wesleyan perspective — without ever becoming parochial or narrow-minded."[96]

This promise — to avoid parochialism and narrow-minded thought — seems to most mainline and liberal Protestants today to be a key ingredient of truly *relevant* theology. The editors of the *Methodist Review* issue of 1929 may very well have used that criterion in choosing Donaldson's sermon. Donaldson more than amply proved his allegiance to what the editors of the *Homiletic Review* called the "approved thing" of eugenics. Yet the editors of the current *Quarterly Review* also signal that essays "interpreting the historic faith in a postmodern world" should emerge from within the Wesleyan tradition. Presumably, the call to remain relevant, to attempt to eschew parochialism or narrow-minded thought, does not trump the call to remain within the range of Wesleyan thought represented by the various Methodist traditions.

Striking in the sermons above is the facility with which each of the preachers was able to bend Scripture to suit the eugenic project. Many mainline Protestants had come to believe that, as the pro-eugenics editor of the *Methodist Quarterly Review* put it, because "the Bible nowhere undertakes to give a detailed account of the process of creation . . . it leaves ample room for any theory to which careful scientific investigation may lead."[97] The scrip-

---

95. Donaldson, "Eugenics," pp. 67, 68.

96. Accessed 2003: www.quarterlyreview.org.

97. Gilbert T. Rowe, "Christianity and Evolution," *Methodist Quarterly Review* 75 (1926): 138.

tural story of salvation in the Old Testament all too swiftly became a story of God's refining, purifying, and selecting in order to produce a stronger, heartier stock of humans. Jesus' parables regarding the kingdom of God swiftly became parables for the eugenic separation of human wheat from human chaff. Osgood and Donaldson both also employed liturgical cues, setting the practices of sterilization and selective mating within the context of worship.

All three preachers were able to interpret "the historic faith" in a "modern" (i.e., Darwinian) way: defining Christians as cooperative agents in bringing to fruition God's purposes, which primarily meant the strengthening of the assumedly dominant race in the assumedly promised land of the United States. Having gone the way of the modernists in accepting evolutionary science, the mainline denominations represented in these published sermons were able to distinguish themselves from the "backward" Christian creationists. In the words of Gilbert T. Rowe, editor of the *Methodist Quarterly Review* (1921-28), mainline readers were particularly interested when they found a "thoroughly Christian" writer who could prove himself "no hard and fast dogmatist."[98] One who could so "thoroughly" narrate the tradition in a way consonant with evolution was a particularly reliable guide to the present and future. But in the process of renarration, these preachers and the theologians on whom they drew arguably left few theological barriers to the all-encompassing narrative of eugenics. And having accepted civic leadership as their primary duty, they arguably left few theological barriers to the racist nationalism of eugenics. Determined to think in modern, patriotic, and well-educated ways about the role of the faithful in America, these preachers attained their sophistication at the expense of the vulnerable. They leveraged the lives of others to establish their own strength.

### "Safeguarding the Future"

Another way to detect the theological moves made by mainline churches during the eugenic era is to read the distillation of eugenic thought in journals aimed at clergy and learned laity. Journals such as the *Methodist Quarterly Review* and *Religion in Life* printed essays about the church's engagement with theological as well as secular disciplines. The volumes of journals from the 1920s and 1930s apply evolutionary thought to Christian theology. In one *Methodist Quarterly Review* piece, Gilbert Rowe sought to sort through the implications of three books from three different authors, attempting to forge

98. Rowe, "Christianity and Evolution," p. 140.

a pathway to Christ through evolution and to make a new theological language that combined evolution and redemption.[99] *Religion in Life* reviewed *The Doctrine of Redemption in the Light of Modern Knowledge,* and in another piece, by the author of *Do the Ten Commandments Stand Today?* and *Evolution for Christians,* asked, "Has the concept of humanity a scientific basis?"[100] The journals gave a particularly Christian (and particularly mainline Protestant) interpretation of the biology and sociology filtering through the university classrooms and over the radio airwaves. Mainline clergy and laity across the country faced the task of thinking at the intersection of evolutionary biology and practical theology. Their efforts are important for understanding the sense that "Eugenics is an approved thing," again to quote the editors of the *Homiletic Review.*

One local pastor in Missouri, Rev. C. L. Dorris, wrote an extensive essay inspired by Philip Archibald Parsons's *Introduction to Modern Social Problems* for the *Methodist Quarterly Review* in 1926.[101] This young pastor was serving in the Methodist Episcopal Church, South in the small town of Milan, Missouri, when he felt compelled to write "The Impending Disaster," adding "his voice to the voices in the wilderness warning that unless something is done disaster will soon befall us." This, the last line of the essay, indicates the exigency of the effort. The sense of moral urgency, of peril and promise, registered even in a sleepy town of around two thousand people.[102]

The records of Dorris's training and travels do not indicate that he came to his conclusions after encountering the throngs of immigrants on either shore. Rather, they suggest that the message of eugenics came to him perhaps through his reading at the public library or through a teacher in his congregation. He, in turn, published an essay to be read by local Methodist ministers eager to bring the latest in sociological discernment to their parishes. In it, the ru-

---

99. Rowe, "Christianity and Evolution," pp. 138-41. The essay involves a review of *To Christ through Evolution,* by Prof. Louis Matthews Sweet (1925); *Nineteenth Century Evolution and After,* by Rev. Marshall Dawson (1923); and *Evolution and Redemption,* by Rev. John Gardner, D.D. (1925).

100. Ismar J. Peritz, "Christ and Evolution," review of *The Doctrine of Redemption in the Light of Modern Knowledge,* by George A. Barton, *Religion in Life* 4 (1935): 462-64; J. Parton Milum, "Has the Concept of Humanity a Scientific Basis?" *Religion in Life* 5 (1936): 52-63. Milum is also author of *Do the Ten Commandments Stand Today?* (London: Epworth, 1936), *Man and His Meaning* (London: Skeffington, 1945), and *Evolution for Christians* (London, 1933).

101. C. L. Dorris, "The Impending Disaster," *Methodist Quarterly Review* 75 (1926): 720-24, citing Philip Archibald Parsons, *An Introduction to Modern Social Problems* (New York: Knopf, 1924).

102. In 1920 the population of Milan was 2,395; in 1930 it was 2,002. Thanks to Jason D. Stratman at the Missouri Historical Society.

ral pastor took in a considerable amount of intellectual territory, borrowing clout from Englishman Henry Havelock Ellis (author of the six-volume *Studies in the Psychology of Sex*), Professor James Quayle Dealey (tenth president of the American Sociological Society), the Reverend Josiah Strong (prominent Congregational pastor and author of the anti-urban tract *Our Country*), professor and sociologist Charles A. Ellwood, and Harvard president Charles W. Eliot. The essay reads as an authoritative call to attention and action.

Beginning with the sin of sloth, Dorris admonished readers that "one of the gravest dangers" among Methodist congregants was "a lack of pride in providing capable offspring for future generations." Clearly, "too many physically, mentally, and morally defective" persons were gaining way in society, and Christians needed to relinquish "the individualistic theory of marriage for personal pleasure." Quite the contrary — marriages needed to be planned with "racial consequences" in view. Without such prudence, Dorris warned, "we are going to continue to produce a crop of defectives."

Here Dorris employed a practical strategy commonly enjoined in eugenic texts of the time — the sacrifice of romantic sentiment for the sake of society. Quoting Ellis's *Psychology of Sex,* Dorris affirmed that "the birth of a child is a social act" and that the "community," in being "invited to receive a new citizen," is "entitled to demand that that citizen shall be worthy of a place in its midst." Dorris repeated this crucial point: "We should demand that each child born is worthy a place in our midst." The demand required the full arsenal of "public sentiment in favor of safeguarding the future," for "public sentiment is one of the most powerful weapons of defense." In this way, Dorris defined the primary task of his clerical and lay readers: to bring the "American people" to "see the dangers threatening us," so that "they will demand the raising of proper safeguards."

A local pastor from rural Missouri gave an effective populist appeal for the work of eugenics, bringing the civic role of "safeguarding the future" down from New Haven and Cold Spring Harbor and Boston and Manhattan to the grass roots of the heartland. Methodists were to do their considerable part to enforce proper marital standards based on "the law of the survival of the fittest."[103]

There were many ways to avert "the disaster," ranging from the legal and institutional, to address the inferior, to the more nuanced propaganda necessary to encourage the "truly better elements of society" to see their civic duty to replenish "the stock."[104] Regarding the former, there were laws "to prohibit

103. Dorris, "The Impending Disaster," pp. 720, 721.
104. Dorris, "The Impending Disaster," pp. 722, 723.

the marriage of the unfit," intended to "eliminate the weaker stock" and "build up the race through its stronger elements." There was also the prospect of widespread sterilization. But Dorris argued that sterilization would be insufficient for the "hopeless types of defectives." The public should seek means for "permanent segregation" that would force these otherwise "expensive" individuals "to support themselves in properly conducted institutions and colonies."

Yet even with these concerted measures, leaders needed to be vigilant to encourage the reproduction of those representing "the higher forms of life." Quoting sociologist James Dealey, Dorris explained that only "when (society) frowns alike on the large family of the poor and the childless family of leisure" will "rapid advance" ensue. The "future civilization" depended as much on the breeding of the "leadership" class as it did on the institutionalization of the "defectives." And while he was on the topic, Dorris reminded the "leisure class" not to "confide their children to the care of ignorant and incapable servants."[105]

Again, this from a local pastor in Milan, Missouri. It is a testimony to the brilliance of those in the eugenics movement that they were able to direct the mainline Protestant desire for class superiority toward the popularization of such notions. Dorris's essay thus reveals a crucial part of the tale. Recall the AES Fitter Family poster warning that a mere 4 percent of Americans were born with the "ability to do creative work and be fit for leadership." The fact that the AES could display this sign at county fairs in Missouri, Michigan, and Minnesota without engendering moral outrage is at first glance unfathomable. While it makes some intuitive sense that a Charles Davenport could appeal to the vanity of railroad tycoon-widow Mrs. E. H. Harriman with such "AES calculations," the fact that the hoi polloi in places like rural Missouri found themselves in the 4 percent rather than the 96 percent begs for explanation. By writing of the "impending disaster" from his unassuming Methodist parsonage, Dorris left behind evidence — a vital clue to the eugenics puzzle. He assumed that he and the people who read the *Methodist Quarterly Review* had as central a role to play in civic leadership as did Mr. and Mrs. Rockefeller. Quoting Professor Charles A. Ellwood, Dorris explained that "the growing complexity of social life, as social evolution advances, calls for an ever-increasing means of control over individual character and conduct." As good Christian citizens, Methodists needed to address "the woes of the world" with "religion of the right kind" — a religion with proven influence "in elevating character, in diffusing peace and good will, in fitting men to la-

---

105. Dorris, "The Impending Disaster," pp. 721, 722.

bor and to endure," and indeed, "in lifting mankind to a higher sphere morally and spiritually." It was a critical time for the country, with aspirations as high as the sense of economic and demographic vulnerability. With progress, Dorris warned, also comes "degeneration," and the mainliners of the heartland had a role to play in safeguarding against it.[106]

And here Dorris was arguably dead-on. Religious and secular historians alike could have relegated the AES and ERO and the American Breeders Association to mad-scientist status if those organizations had not made such headway on everything from state sterilization laws to the popularization of eugenic aspirations among the middle class. The movement *won* with the considerable aid of men like Dorris and the women and men who heard his call to *"demand that each child born is worthy a place in our midst."*[107]

## The New Eugenics and the "Democratic" Calculus of Worth

### *"On the March towards 'the Good Life'"*

> A new eugenics has arisen, based upon the dramatic increase in our understanding of the biochemistry of heredity and our comprehension of the craft and means of evolution. . . . The old eugenics would have required a continual selection for breeding of the fit, and a culling of the unfit. The new eugenics would permit in principle the conversion of all of the unfit to the highest genetic level.[108]

By the mid-1930s, the eugenics and domestic hygiene movements were moving toward a supposedly race-neutral, scientifically impartial sequel to the Keeping Fit and Fitter Family campaigns. Frederick Henry Osborn, a man who became "the respectable face of eugenic research in the post-war period," began what was to be a decades-long effort to rid the eugenics movement of its "class snobbery, ancestor worship and race prejudice," promoting instead the cooperation of scientific eugenicists with the growing number of related programs in population and family studies.[109] The Rockefeller Foundation

---

106. Dorris, "The Impending Disaster," p. 723.

107. Dorris, "The Impending Disaster," p. 720.

108. Robert L. Sinsheimer, "The Prospect of Designed Genetic Change," *Engineering and Science* 32 (April 1969): 8, 13.

109. The characterization of Osborn (nephew of Henry Fairfield Osborn) as the "respectable face" of eugenics is from the American Philosophical Society background note to the Frederick Henry Osborn papers. Accessed 2003: www.amphilsoc.org. The second quotation is

(led by Raymond Fosdick) took a longer, more thoroughly scientific route toward the ultimate goal of what Fosdick called social "seemliness and dignity." Reminding fellow eugenicists that there was "no short cut to the Promised Land," Fosdick led the foundation to fund basic research in "psychobiology," a field that would produce a more thorough "Science of Man."[110] As science historian Lily Kay explains, "Precisely because the old eugenics had lost its scientific validity, a space was created for a new program that promised to place the study of human heredity and behavior on rigorous grounds."[111] This ambitious new program in science resulted in statistical calculations for conditions thought to be inherited and, by the 1950s, definitive genetic tests for conditions such as Down syndrome.

The AES, the Rockefeller Foundation, and various research centers on disability and heredity would again need field-workers to promulgate the knowledge. This niche would eventually attract a new generation of (largely female) workers eager to be both useful and scientifically relevant. With the opening in 1940 of the Heredity Clinic at the University of Michigan came the institutional birth of what was for some time called "genetic hygiene." The second institute to open its doors to students was the Dight Institute at the University of Minnesota, charged by its founder Charles F. Dight "to promote biological race betterment — betterment in human brain structure and mental endowment and therefore in behavior."[112] Sheldon Reed, the center's second director, was concerned that the term "hygiene" connoted personal care products; he changed the term to "counseling" — and the new field of "genetic counseling" was born.[113]

The ostensible message of the new, *voluntary* form of popular eugenics was more "democratic," and the new Methodist journal *Religion in Life* (first issue 1930) ran an essay in 1936 that reflected that shift. Declaring that "evolution is now part of our mentality," J. Parton Milum asked, "Has the Concept

---

from "Democracy and Eugenics," *New York Times*, May 16, 1937, p. 66, cited in Rosen, *Preaching Eugenics*, p. 167. I am indebted to Rosen for the idea that Osborn led the shift from coercive to purportedly voluntary eugenics.

110. Kay, *Molecular Vision of Life*, pp. 36-39, 8-9, quoting Raymond B. Fosdick, *The Old Savage in the New Civilization* (Garden City, N.Y.: Doubleday, 1929), pp. 184, 185.

111. Kay, *Molecular Vision of Life*, p. 9.

112. Charles F. Dight, will dated 1927, file 52043, Hennepin County Probate Court, Minneapolis, quoted in Daniel J. Kevles, *In the Name of Eugenics: Genetics and the Uses of Human Heredity* (Cambridge: Harvard University Press, 1999), p. 253.

113. Kevles, *Name of Eugenics*, p. 253. Edwin Black reports that Reed, in a letter to the AES in 1961, complained that the Holocaust had given eugenics a bad name. Reed argued: "As far as I can see, the motives behind the liquidation of the Jews were not eugenic, not genocide . . . but just plain homicidal robbery" (Black, *War against the Weak*, p. 424).

of Humanity a Scientific Basis?"[114] Milum criticized old-school eugenicists for their simple faith in evolution, advocating for "a better understanding of the limits of evolution" so that "the concept of humanity may find its revindication." What makes the human distinctly human, Milum argued, is "the social milieu, the culture or civilization." It is through the "utterly impartial" assessment of the "qualities we want in our population" that "a Christian civilization" may contribute to a better society.[115] In this "impartiality" was the critical shift denoting the change from old to new — the new science would take off race and class blinders to assess *all lineages* for their promise or peril. Noting that two of the "most evident departures from the normal human form," namely, "cretinism and mongolism," had been "traced to changes in the internal secretions," Milum proposed a de-racialized pursuit of eugenics. Those of *any* race or class who "come of a stock" likely to beget "feeble-mindedness" should prevent "the propagation of unsound stocks" by submitting to voluntary sterilization. "That such will refrain from parentage is not too much to expect," he reasoned. Through such "mutual adjustment of the various families of mankind," "the Christian ideal" might be met in civilized society.[116] Change the implied "white" in the phrase "for the sake of the race" to "human," and one had the new eugenics. But what about the "cretins" and "mongols"? Were they humans, or departures? The marks of the "unsound stocks" still overlapped with older, well-worn indicators of taint and impurity.

Part of the new effort involved the reformed, subtler dissemination of eugenic ideas to those on the verge of marriage. Although Reed worried over the bath-soap connotations of the term "hygiene," ASHA continued to advocate *hygienic* courtship. An editorial introducing the April 1950 issue of the *Journal of Social Hygiene,* "Sexual Behavior: How Shall We Define and Motivate What Is Acceptable?" commented on a 1948 symposium on sexual behavior. The new, ostensibly positive spin on the promise of good homes is obvious in a passage quoted from the symposium's *Proceedings:* "Human institutions by their consciously planned and directed efforts can hasten the evolutionary process. . . . If in the future, as in the present symposium, the American Social Hygiene Association is able, by bringing to bear the judgment of related fields of knowledge, to assist the process of evolution towards 'the good life,' it will, we believe, have served a useful purpose." Lauding the "progress" evident in recent discussions, the editorial described "mankind

114. Milum, "Has the Concept?" p. 52.
115. Milum, "Has the Concept?" pp. 55, 59, 61, 63, 60.
116. Milum, "Has the Concept?" pp. 54, 60, 63.

wanting and searching for his higher self, mankind looking towards far hori-zons," as "mankind in truth on the march towards 'the good life.'"[117]

The language of "evolution" and progress permeates the issue, adopted by editors, commentators, and essayists seeking to contribute to a concerted climb upward. The definition of the goal had much to do with the promotion of health marriages, but the wording is more delicate than that of the earlier ASHA campaigns.

At the dawn of the Atomic Age, eugenicists like Paul Popenoe found ready platforms for the message of prudent breeding. Popenoe, whose *Applied Eugenics* was key for the old eugenics, urged YMCA and YWCA readers to be prudent when "surveying the chances" of marriage in 1948. Popenoe's article, which appeared also in *Eugenical News,* noted that people "are marrying ear-lier than they used to," and "in larger numbers." This was, in itself, a healthful pattern, but, Popenoe warned, it could become problematic if "too large a pro-portion of the [resulting] babies are born in homes which can give them the worst start in every way." Promoting "farm families" as "more stable" and "happier," Popenoe admonished his newly mobile readers not to succumb to the allure of the city, "a destroyer of population." A "carefully planned popula-tion policy," he argued, was "indispensable for national survival."[118]

In an attached article, Helen Southard was even more explicit, stating: "There is no one family situation. Some want children and should not have them; some want and cannot have them; some don't want any and should have many; others just don't care, but keep on having and having them. From all this, stems conflict." Advocating carefully planned parenthood on campus, Southard suggested that "this is parental — and Christian — duty in our day."[119] To quote again the caption below the picture that opens this chapter, educated Christians agreed to ask, "How many; how healthy?"

### *"Manifest Domesticity"*

The shift to a subtler, voluntary, less explicitly racist understanding of repro-ductive responsibility may seem at first glance to answer the eugenic problem. To view *more critically* the transition into what Robert Sinsheimer called the

---

117. Editorial, "Problems of Sexual Behavior — and Their Solutions," *Journal of Social Hygiene* 36 (April 1950): 129. The editorial quotes Charles Walter Clarke, introduction to *Prob-lems of Sexual Behavior,* symposium proceedings, ASHA Annual Conference of Social Hygiene Executives (New York: American Social Hygiene Association, 1948), p. v.

118. Popenoe, "Surveying the Chances," pp. 9, 10.

119. Southard, "Planning Parenthood on Campus," pp. 10, 11.

"new eugenics," however, one must cultivate a suspicion toward domesticity in the twentieth century. In "Manifest Domesticity," Amy Kaplan suggests that the notion of "home" that developed among the cultural elite of the nineteenth century was "related to the imperial project of civilizing" — indeed, "the conditions of domesticity" often served as "markers" to "distinguish civilization from savagery." Kaplan continues: "Through the process of domestication, the home contains within itself those wild or foreign elements that must be tamed; domesticity not only monitors the borders between the civilized and the savage but also regulates traces of the savage within itself."[120]

Given the legacy of this narration, we may question the marketing of domesticity in the twentieth century as well as the methods for "civilizing" children and families. One must also break open the assumptions about the meaning of "voluntary" eugenics, particularly given the power of cultural norms and the real, economic consequences of supposed reproductive irresponsibility and presumed lack of procreative foresight. Many supposedly "private" decisions to have fewer and better babies were arguably rooted in messages that drove the old eugenics.

The promise of the "new eugenics" continued to perpetuate the logic that some human beings lived on the "highest genetic level" while others, "losers in that chromosomal lottery," floundered in a genetic backwater.[121] The new eugenics was purportedly more democratic, but the male leaders as well as the female foot soldiers continued to assume a genetic continuum of human life. The "unfit" were still a problem — albeit a more scientifically manageable one. With the burgeoning field of human genetics, different traits could be mapped at the chromosomal level, not merely "observed" over generations in rural Virginia. By midcentury, geneticists were able to bring statistical specificity to Charles Davenport's mere speculations and suspicions. The patrons, scientists, marketers, and recipients of this new set of scientific tools interpreted them in ways consonant with the growing market of middle-class domesticity.

As early as 1885, clergyman Henry Ward Beecher had declared Pears' Soap a "means of grace." After all, "Cleanliness is next to godliness." Through this "spokesman for a middle-class America,"[122] the advertisement linked "moral things" with middle-class respectability and mass-marketed hygiene. The residual logic of cacogenics and eugenics, of taint and purity, underwrote

---

120. Amy Kaplan, "Manifest Domesticity," *American Literature* 70 (1998): 586, 582.

121. Sinsheimer, "Designed Genetic Change," p. 13.

122. Clifford E. Clark, Jr., *Henry Ward Beecher: Spokesman for a Middle-Class America* (Urbana: University of Illinois Press, 1978).

much that passed for normative parenthood in the twentieth century. With the institutional hygiene movement itself, professional women were charged with bringing order to the otherwise chaotic domesticity of the rural poor and the urban immigrant — applying a generous layer of soap to the unwashed masses. At face value their choice of religious metaphors and their high ideals may now seem merely quaint, and arguably life saving. Given that children in North Carolina were dying of hookworm as a result of sewer seepage, it may seem churlish to question the ideology behind posters illustrating the difference between a "hygienic" and a "dirty" home.

But the effort to bring godly cleanliness to those not yet privy to the new privies was problematic. Those who lived in dirty homes became, in the process, "soiled." The rules of professionally controlled domesticity traded on a sense of menace that encompassed not only the parasites that preyed on the children of the working poor in North Carolina but also the children themselves. It was not only the kitchens of rural or tenement homes that seemed backward, inefficient, and ugly. The parents, grandparents, and children who gathered to eat in those kitchens became the *other* kind of family — the kind from which aspiring citizens hoped to distinguish themselves. This is a crucial point. With the new armies of professionals in social welfare came newer, cleaner outhouses, vaccinations, public awareness about child abuse and labor, and a myriad of other basic improvements in the lives of families and children. But the rhetoric relied in no small part on *shame*. Some families were put under threat of a new arsenal of scrutiny — judged by a set of seemingly scientific measurements of health and worth.

Dorris's cold assessment had arguably won the day by World War II. The responsible citizenry had a right to demand that each child born was worthy of "a place in our midst." The turn from overt, coercive eugenics to implicit, voluntary eugenics may be less a sign of the failure of eugenic ideology than a sign of its success. The "modern," Darwinian sense of a division between the "highest" and the "lowest" in humanity lent scientific legitimacy to the fears at play in the middle-class neighborhoods that began to flourish after World War II. There were some children meant to flourish and others whose lives were insufficiently ordered and wholesome. Distinguishing one group from the other was a whole set of signals — from the shoes on a little boy's feet to the number of braids in a girl's hair, from the marks on a second-grader's report card to, eventually, the Apgar score assigned to his newborn sister. This is not even to mention the clear, blatant, and often deadly markers of race. The same Methodists Dorris called upon to address the "impending disaster" of America's degeneration were ready to lead again by way of voluntary eugenics. Promoting the medical tools of "responsible parenthood," mainline Protestants endorsed family planning and orderly hygiene as practices integral to civic duty. Taking their cues from *Ladies' Home Journal* ("The Magazine Women Believe In"), many mainline Protestant mothers employed Ivory Soap and the principles of discriminating reproduction to make sure their offspring were legitimate inheritors of the promised land.

### *"The Christian Asks: How Many?"*

The author of *Fewer and Better Babies* anticipated in 1916 that working-class parents who produced more than two children would eventually be considered "anti-social, as criminal members of the community."[123] The distinction between perspicacious and "indiscriminate" fecundity was solidified by the late 1940s, when most mainline Protestant denominations had accepted (and some were actively promoting) contraception. The eugenicists of yesterday linked immigration with fitter marriages and better offspring — health certifications before marriage were as vital as those at immigrant entry points. The sense that a citizenry must judge which immigrants would make a "desirable acquisition," to quote Henry Cabot Lodge from 1891, was formally similar to the sense that certain mates would make for the production of a better-quality citizen.[124]

A *North American Review* article of 1879 called Irish Catholic immigrants "separate in blood, separate in religion, . . . little likely to merge in the old race of American Republicans" — a charge eerily similar to Samuel Huntington's charge that today's Latino Catholic immigrant families are resisting conformity to the Anglo-Protestant culture that is at the core of American identity.[125] The issue was a live one during the welfare reform debates in the early 1990s, as women on poverty-related public assistance were actively scrutinized over family size.[126] Although one may not be able politically to justify coerced sterilization in the current climate, one may gain political purchase

123. Robinson, *Fewer and Better Babies*, p. 26.

124. Henry Cabot Lodge, "The Restriction of Immigration," *North American Review* 152 (January 1891): 31. Lodge was quoting here the U.S. consul at Budapest (1886); quoted in Jacobson, *Whiteness*, p. 77.

125. James Anthony Froude, "Romanism and the Irish Race in the United States, Part I," *North American Review* 129 (December 1879): 523, quoted in Jacobson, *Whiteness*, p. 70; Samuel Huntington, *Who Are We? The Challenges to America's National Identity* (New York: Simon and Schuster, 2004).

126. Some states actually discussed incentives to encourage women to submit to Norplant. See *Skin Deep* (New York: Distributed by Women Make Movies, 1997), vidoerecording.

by pointing with concern to the high birth rates of Latino Catholic immigrants. Controlling the reproduction of the social body and individual bodies, controlling the quality and quantity of the next generation in order to form a more perfect union — these impulses remain a part of American culture.

Published in 2001, the *New Yorker Book of Kids Cartoons* features only three drawings with families of more than two children — one a family of fish, another a family of cats, and a third an obviously poor, white working-class family.[127] The third cartoon ran in the magazine in 1940, but it was published in the book without its date or historical context. In it a mother with a crookedly drawn face stands next to a wood-burning stove, eight children variously active around her. She has unevenly cut hair, sagging nylons, and shoes that are obviously too large. Several of the boys are wearing overalls. The room is lit by an oil lamp, and the walls have cracks. Various mismatched dishes are on a table with several mismatched chairs. The scene captures the moment when her husband arrives home from his job; he is wearing a work hat and a patched jacket and is carrying a lunch pail. She announces to him, "Boy, did I have an afternoon! The census man was here." The presence of two cats and a dog reinforces the implied link between large families and "animal-istic" breeding. The fact that the family is clearly white rather than Latino or African American presumably clears the *New Yorker* editors of ill judgment. The humor unquestionably draws on the old racism and classism apparent in the "white trash" studies of an earlier generation. Many of the other cartoons in the 2001 book lampoon the obsessive or negligent parenting of the privileged, latte-sipping, tennis-playing set. This is the only cartoon to imply that a family is less than human.

A beloved classic of American family life involves a brood of twelve. When Frank Gilbreth, Jr., and Ernestine Gilbreth Carey first published *Cheaper by the Dozen* in 1948, the matter of class and family size must still have been fluid enough to grant the story a hearing, perhaps owing in no small part to the clear intellectual superiority of the Gilbreth parents. But the politics of family planning are different today, as film critics noted in response to the 2003 rendition of the classic. Catherine Graham of the *Santa Cruz Sentinel* said the appeal of Steve Martin and Bonnie Hunt as movie parents could not "make the audience suspend disbelief and go along with the movie's central premise: That a *modern, educated, middle-class couple without apparent affiliations to the Mormon or Catholic churches* find themselves living

127. Robert Mankoff, ed., *The New Yorker Book of Kids Cartoons* (Princeton: Bloomberg, 2001).

with 12 offspring."[128] Ben Goldstein of *Maxim* was even more blunt: "All in all, it's a solid family comedy with a very important . . . message: Always, *always* use condoms."[129] The judgment apparent in Monty Python's (British, but also American) classic "Every Sperm Is Sacred" segment in *The Meaning of Life* is clearly open as a source for derisive humor. As John Cleese sings to a house full of children about Catholicism's unconditional acceptance, "modern, educated, middle-class" people "without apparent affiliations to the Mormon or Catholic churches" are encouraged to guffaw:

And the one thing they say about Catholics is:
They'll take you as soon as you're warm.
You don't have to be a six-footer.
You don't have to have a great brain.

The joke is not without political import. It was Margaret Sanger who first warned of the "indiscriminate fecundity" of the poor, arguing that charity only "encourages the healthier and more normal sections of the world to shoulder the burden of unthinking and indiscriminate fecundity of others; which brings with it . . . a dead weight of human waste."[130]

A senior analyst and professor at Harvard, Samuel Huntington answers the question posed by his book *Who Are We?* with a very similar warning. He explains that the United States was founded on "Anglo-Protestant culture," and it will thrive only inasmuch as it affirms this foundation. Forged by "dissenting Protestantism," the "American Creed" contributed the solvents to render potable the melting pot. The American belief that an individual should be judged according to her ability to contribute to society, the American virtues of "sobriety, thrift and initiative," and the Calvinist sense that Americans are a "chosen" nation make up the "Creed." This is the "American civil religion," the "Christianity without Christ" (as Huntington labels it, without apparent irony) that constitutes who *We* are.[131]

One could comment on much in this troubling book, but the resounding refrain involves the "Hispanization" of America. This Hispanization has

128. Catherine Graham, "'Cheaper' Is Fun, but Unnecessary," *Santa Cruz Sentinel*, December 24, 2003, Style section; emphasis added.

129. Ben Goldstein, review of *Cheaper by the Dozen* (20th Century Fox, 2003), *Maxim*. Accessed 2003: www.maximonline.com; emphasis in original.

130. From her chapter "The Cruelty of Charity," in *The Pivot of Civilization*, p. 133. There are other, similar statements, such as "[W]e are paying for and even submitting to the dictates of an ever increasing, unceasingly spawning class of human beings who never should have been born at all" (from the chapter "Dangers of Cradle Competition," p. 185).

131. Huntington, *Who Are We?* pp. 59, 97, 106.

several components, but the driving force is "higher fertility rates" combined with "slow assimilation" to the Anglo-Protestant culture. The challenge to American identity that most troubles Huntington is "the huge numbers of immigrants from Latin America and the Philippines, almost all of whom are Catholic and have high birth rates." Huntington predicts a growing subculture of Mexican immigrants, in particular, who sport what he deems an insufficiently entrepreneurial attitude and who make unfair use of social welfare programs. With graphs, charts, and (often bizarrely chosen) anecdotes, Huntington shows that Latino Catholics do not accept wholeheartedly the "common" sense that each individual should be judged by his or her economic contribution, that "thrift and initiative" are vital, and that the United States is a uniquely chosen nation. Because most "Mexicans marry Mexicans" and remain Roman Catholic, their cultural matrix presents a resilient Latino Catholic challenge to dominant, Protestant culture.[132]

The perceived social cost of being associated with the *wrong kind* of families is apparent in a recent "Lives" feature essay in the *New York Times Magazine* called "When One Is Enough."[133] As she tells her story, a thirty-four-year-old with a committed boyfriend of three years decided that the prospect of becoming a mother was less burdensome than the mood swings she was experiencing on the pill. She and her boyfriend decided that they would indeed bring to term any resulting pregnancy. She then became pregnant with triplets. After some time she decided to procure the "shot of potassium chloride to the heart of the fetus" that would result in selective termination. Her narrative is blunt, clear, and unapologetic. Her reasoning behind the decision is indicative. While she currently lives in the East Village, with a good job, she grew up under a "fear" that she could, any day, make a disastrous "slip" into a life defined by unplanned, ill-timed children rather than "country-club memberships and station wagons." She explains:

> I grew up in a working-class family in Pennsylvania not knowing my father. . . . Growing up with a single mother, I was always buying into the myth that I was going to be seduced in the back of a pickup truck and become pregnant when I was 16. I had friends when I was in school who were helping to rear nieces and nephews, because their siblings, who were not much older, were having babies. I had friends from all over the class spectrum: I saw the nieces and nephews on the one hand and country-

---

132. Huntington, *Who Are We?* pp. 227, 254, 100, 97, 240.
133. Amy Richards, as told to Amy Barrett, "When One Is Enough," *New York Times Magazine,* July 18, 2004, p. 58.

club memberships and station wagons on the other. I felt I was in the middle. I had this fear: What would it take for me to just slip?

Although her boyfriend had misgivings about her decision, she pursued the abortions. The sense of being on the verge of association with the friends on the *other* side of the class spectrum had returned when she discovered she was pregnant with three, and these fears were sufficient to warrant selective termination. "When I found out about the triplets, I felt like: It's not the back of a pickup at 16, but now I'm going to have to move to Staten Island. I'll never leave my house because I'll have to care for these children. I'll have to start shopping only at Costco and buying big jars of mayonnaise. Even in my moments of thinking about having three, I don't think that deep down I was ever considering it."

The class issues are not merely implicit in her decision. She feared moving out of a trendy, arts-class sort of disorder that is the East Village into a home and neighborhood in the more working-class Staten Island. The specter of being associated with the kind of people who stay at home to care for three children, shop at Costco, and eat mayonnaise was enough to tip her over the edge toward her choice to abort. The pregnancy to which she was open was not the type of pregnancy that could result in such a change of identity. The fact that this young woman did not confess a fear of moving to Harlem or the Bronx presumably, again, clears a major New York publication of ill judgment.

The East Village woman was arguably astute in her estimation of the social stakes involved in conspicuously deviant procreation. In her case the question was quantity; in others it is quality. The matter addressed in posters from the National Campaign to Prevent Teen Pregnancy is some implied combination of bad quantity, quality, and timing. The specter of the unplanned child, born to be a burden on the social body, is still a powerful tool in the propaganda of cultural assimilation. Americans who wish to have their children accepted do well to follow the cultural cues of worth and recognition.

This effort to prevent teen pregnancy makes the Keeping Fit campaign seem subtle. Pictures posted in high schools and featured in teen magazines from this new century show a Latina girl with "CHEAP" emblazoned across her body. The African American girl is labeled "REJECT" (fig. 3.16), the Asian girl "DIRTY," and the working-class white girl "NOBODY." The posters use brute shame to bring females from four subcultures into conformity on the question of teen pregnancy. The small print advocates condom use, but the advertisements all too effectively present the judgment that some mothers are

**Figure 3.16. From National Campaign to Prevent Teen Pregnancy**

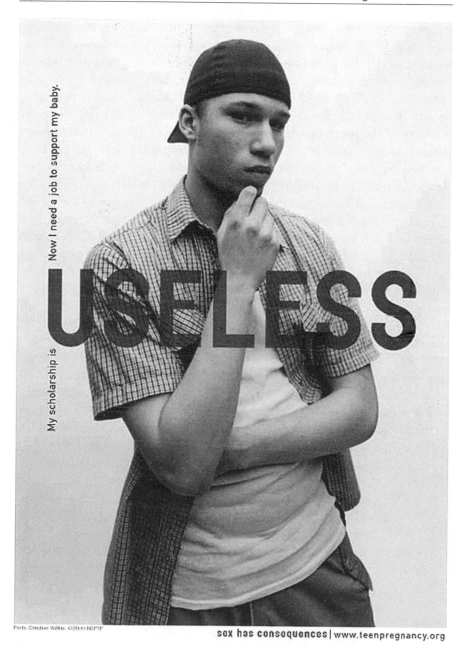

**Figure 3.17. From National Campaign to Prevent Teen Pregnancy**

cheap, dirty nobodies, social rejects with no future, and that there is little hope for their illegitimate children. The stark photos are reminiscent of the ASHA posters of the syphilitic boy and the girl blinded by gonorrhea, but the propagandists responsible for this series leave nothing to interpretation, labeling the girls clearly for the viewer, in order to cultivate a potent combination of disdain and fear. Each girl stands alone, judged. Possibly the most troubling of the posters features a white boy whose intimacy resulted in an unexpected pregnancy (fig. 3.17). The class prompts are clear. He has on a button-down and the ubiquitous backward baseball hat of a college student. He is labeled USELESS, and the fine print reads: "My scholarship is USELESS. Now I need a job to support my baby."

Taken together, the posters imply a deeply problematic message. The college boy who leaves school to take care of the CHEAP REJECT's baby is USELESS. If the girls are seen to represent the African American and Latina working class and working poor, and the boy is seen to represent the white, college-educated class, the relinquishing of individual, paternal responsibility is only one small part of the message. The poster series symbolically signals that a white, male-dominated society should hardly be responsible for the care of the indiscriminately bred babies of the women "beneath" them.[134]

The campaign's board of directors includes CEOs from major corporations and leaders from political parties right and left, representing a broad consensus across the United States. The agreement is arguably the culmination of a long American history of judging a pregnancy either USELESS or potentially useful. In a 1912 letter to the director of the Human Betterment Foundation, Dr. Lydia DeVilbiss assured: "*We have found we can get everybody to agree: Every child has the right to be well born.*"[135] As it turns out, she was not overly optimistic.


### "The Christian Asks: How Healthy?"

The Cold Spring Harbor Dolan DNA Learning Center feature for the seventy-fifth anniversary of Oliver Wendell Holmes's decision to advocate

---

134. The National Campaign to Prevent Teen Pregnancy. Accessed 2003: www.teenpregnancy.org. The Web site in 2007 includes thanks to the agency of Ogilvy and Mather for the creation of the images.

135. Dr. Lydia DeVilbiss, in a letter to the director of the Human Betterment Foundation, May 8, 1951, Gosney Papers, 7.6, California Institute of Technology, Pasadena, quoted in Kline, *Building a Better Race*, p. 64, emphasis added. DeVilbiss is credited with first proposing the name Planned Parenthood; see Linda Gordon, *Woman's Body, Woman's Right: Birth Control in America* (New York: Penguin Books, 1990), pp. 340, 528 n. 1.

sterilization had a Web link to Vivian Buck's report card. Presumably, this piece of evidence was included to speak against the accuracy of Charles Davenport's science and Wendell Holmes's wisdom. After all, Carrie Buck's baby daughter made the elementary school honor roll. Yet she died before she reached the second grade, succumbing to the measles.

What is a new generation of mainline Protestant readers to make of this? The *new eugenics* requires that Methodists, Episcopalians, and Congregationalists, so eager in the past to prove their relevance, answer some questions. What if Carrie had been able to predict that Vivian would die before reaching adulthood? What if little Vivian *had* been mentally limited? What if she *had* been, as geneticist James Watson so crassly put it, *stupid?* And what of now? Would Carrie be irresponsible *now* to give birth to an infant with cystic fibrosis or Down syndrome? Given the current availability of prenatal testing and the future availability of preimplantation genetic diagnosis, would Carrie be remiss if she did not voluntarily vaccinate the social body against the birth of such a child?

Researcher Edwin Black, having followed for four hundred pages the various eugenics organizations in the United States and Germany, concludes: "After Hitler, eugenics did not disappear. It renamed itself. What had thrived loudly as eugenics for decades quietly took postwar refuge under the labels *human genetics* and *genetic counseling*."[136] In 1926 William Van Duzer Lawrence founded what was to be a college to prepare fashionable young women for fashionable marriages. In 1968, the same Sarah Lawrence College (SLC) began the first master's program in genetic counseling. The program's 2005 Web site summarizes the history:

> In the years after James Watson and Francis Crick cracked the structure of DNA in 1953, scientists made great breakthroughs in identifying diseases with genetic origins. The expansion in knowledge presented a new challenge to the medical profession: how should physicians impart this information to patients? And how would patients use these new data?
>
> Melissa Richter, an SLC graduate who taught both psychology and biology before becoming director of SLC's Center for Continuing Education, saw a great opportunity in this challenge.
>
> Richter sensed the need for a new type of professional, one conversant with the manifestation of genetic diseases as well as techniques of psychological support. A trained caregiver, acting as an assistant to a physician, could "bridge the gap between the increasingly complex scientific knowl-

136. Black, *War against the Weak*, p. 411.

edge on human genetics and the severely inadequate services provided by most hospitals to physicians and to the patients at risk for or affected by these diseases."

SLC's Center for Continuing Education turned out to be a natural home for such a program. For as SLC President Esther Raushenbush later put it, genetic counseling is a "discipline that can affect the personal and family lives of women, and also provide a new career especially appropriate for women."[137]

As with the earlier call for young women to participate in the Eugenics Record Office studies, here women are considered particularly suited to "impart" genetic information to the public. As "trained caregivers," genetic counselors are able to fill a niche. According to the official Sarah Lawrence story, Richter met initially with medical male chauvinism until she received an unexpected miracle in the form of a March 2, 1969, *New York Times Magazine* cover article that asked, "Will the Baby Be Normal?" As the official Sarah Lawrence narration goes, with "the huge expansion of genetic knowledge — and with the advent of technology such as amniocentesis — doctors and other professionals were making strides in taking the guesswork out of predicting genetic risk for disease."[138]

What is left implicit in the Sarah Lawrence story is the changing tide, following the much-publicized Swedish abortion of *Romper Room* host "Miss Sherri" Finkbine in 1962, for the legalization of abortion for disability. Finkbine's fears, that the fetus she was carrying might have been affected by her use of thalidomide, were confirmed after the termination. *Time* magazine had run a similar article in 1960, opening with Richard III's lament: "Deformed, unfinished, sent before my time / Into this breathing world, scarce half made up, / And that so lamely and unfashionable / That dogs bark at me as I halt by them." The piece continued, "Every day, hundreds of thousands of U.S. women have in the back of their minds the nagging question, 'Will my baby be normal?'"[139] The new urgency of this question depended in part on the technology newly available to detect genetic difference. But the urgency also drew on echoes of past fears and eugenic efforts.

There are historians on both sides of the abortion debate who agree that the fear of the fetus with disability played a significant role in many states during the 1960s as doctors testified to the newly discovered dangers of tha-

137. Accessed 2003: www.slc.edu.
138. Accessed 2003: www.slc.edu.
139. "Will the Baby Be Normal?" *Time*, August 1, 1960.

lidomide and, following the outbreak in the mid-1960s of rubella (German measles), the obvious link between rubella and fetal disability.[140] Both discoveries led to preventive measures. Thalidomide was never approved for prenatal use by the FDA and was taken off the market for decades. By 1969, scientists had developed a vaccine for rubella.

Yet alongside the growth of the preventive measures was the increase in selective termination for disabilities. What one could not prevent, one could terminate. The current abortion rate for fetuses detected with Down syndrome (DS) is from 80 to 90 percent. The rate has climbed in spite of the considerable medical advances that allow people with DS to grow into adulthood. The hard questions about disability and normality persist.

The narrative running from eugenics to social hygiene to pre- and postnatal health to genetic testing is not a simple one. As with the earlier work of ASHA, the new public awareness of child and maternal health in the 1950s and 1960s yielded unquestionable benefits for children and women. Public interest in prenatal care and postnatal testing for fragile genetic conditions like phenylketonuria (PKU) resulted in unquestionable gains for infants and their mothers. The development, in 1959, of a postnatal test for PKU led to early intervention for children who would otherwise have suffered brain damage. From the early 1970s, scientists and social workers also eagerly promoted the use of folic acid for the sake of fetal health. But there was again a cost for the new knowledge — a cost related to a long-standing fear of irresponsible women, burdensome families, and inauspicious children. For the vast majority of conditions now screened through prenatal testing, there is no treatment. The choice parents face is simply for or against the termination of a pregnancy measured as genetically defective. To choose *for* such a pregnancy still involves a sense of social shame and isolation.

In her award-winning book *Testing Women, Testing the Fetus,* cultural anthropologist Rayna Rapp meticulously records conversations with parents in order to evaluate "The Social Impact of Amniocentesis in America" (the book's subtitle). It is a key textbook of bioethics and genetic counseling, used by many genetic counseling programs in the country. The first nine of the book's eleven chapters record primarily the reflections of parents — the ma-

---

140. According to the nonprofit organization Every Child by Two (ECBT: The Carter/ Bumpers Campaign for Early Immunization): "If a woman gets rubella in the early months of her pregnancy, her chance of giving birth to a deformed baby may be as high as 80%. These babies may be born deaf or blind. They may have damaged hearts or unusually small brains. Many are mentally retarded. . . . The last big rubella epidemic was in 1964. As a result of that epidemic about 20,000 babies were born with severe birth defects." Accessed 2004: www.ecbt.org.

jority in the study — who, having received a report of Down syndrome, gender ambiguity, or other condition, chose to terminate. All these chapters treat primarily the unexpected *fetus*.

In the tenth chapter Rapp turns to reflections of the minority of parents who gave birth to "the unexpected baby." The three quotations with which she opens the chapter set the tone. One woman reports that the doctor who delivered her baby girl with Down syndrome responded coldly to her question, "What should we *expect?*" with, "Don't expect much. Maybe she'll grow up to be an elevator operator. Don't expect much." Another mother reports that her doctor literally "yelled" at her for not having submitted to genetic tests earlier: "How could you let this happen?"[141] The third quotation is from Stephen Jay Gould, who writes: "In humans, the twenty-first chromosome suffers nondisjunction at a remarkably high frequency, with unfortunately rather tragic effects. . . . But at least it can be identified in utero by counting the chromosomes in fetal cells, providing an option for early abortion."[142] Precisely. The women who did not take this option report with searing uniformity the profoundly negative responses of the medical personnel around them. One doctor offered, unbidden, to turn the baby over as a ward of the state. Another "painted this gloomy terrible picture"; yet another consoled the mother: "The only blessing is that they don't tend to live very long."[143] This is not distant history. Rapp began her project in the 1980s.

Drawing on the language of "alienated kinship" and "a kinship of affliction," Rapp considers the "barriers — both subtle and overt — to normalizing kin ties with disabled children."[144] A doctor warned one mother that she had the "vague suspicion he doesn't look like he's related to anyone in this family," and another doctor worried: "If you had a lot of Irish moon faces in your family, I'd be happier about seeing this child."[145] Rapp seems unable or unwilling to question head-on this implied association of disability with a different "people" — a pattern with a long and menacing history. Perhaps because of her determination to maintain her nonjudgmental, "women-centered analysis," Rapp does not probe the class and race fears underlying the responses either from that majority of parents who do terminate or from

141. Rayna Rapp, *Testing Women, Testing the Fetus: The Social Impact of Amniocentesis in America* (New York: Routledge, 1999), p. 263.

142. Rapp, *Testing Women*, p. 263, quoting Stephen Jay Gould, "Dr. Down's Syndrome," in *The Panda's Thumb: More Reflections in Natural History* (New York: Norton, 1980), p. 161.

143. Rapp, *Testing Women*, p. 266.

144. Rapp, *Testing Women*, pp. 273-82.

145. Rapp, *Testing Women*, p. 274.

the medical professionals who deal with the minority who refuse termination. In what is at best a confusing move, Rapp relates the history of Down syndrome and racist, evolutionary terminology *not* for the sake of questioning those who choose to terminate but to "interrogate" the "religious notion of specialness and innocence" that some women, particularly "those raised as Catholics," use for their children.[146] Her "interrogation" would be more directly relevant to the overt dread of disorder, disability, and difference reflected in comments like the following:

> I had my abortion on June 30th, and I was a mess. I was weeping all the time, I was inconsolable, and we went away for the 4th of July, and I couldn't calm down at all. We were watching the parade on Main Street in Hamlet, at my in-laws' cottage, and a family with a kid with Down's was standing in front of me. Right there at the parade, honest to God, like a sign direct to me. And the thing was, I really looked at the kid, how she dripped her ice cream all over, how she couldn't be made to do what the other kids wanted. I looked at her and thought, "She doesn't belong in that family." She didn't look like them, she looked like someone else. Like a lot of someone elses, not quite from the same race, if you know what I mean. And it made me feel, well, that I'd done the right thing, that the one I aborted wasn't quite from my family, either. (Emily Lockhardt, 37, white antiques restorer)[147]

This reflection contains salient traces of the history of American eugenics. In the celebration of national pride and independence, a white woman of at least middle-class means (given that her in-laws owned a cottage in Hamlet) saw God's hand signaling to her that she had chosen rightly to terminate her pregnancy. Although she herself was "inconsolable" and unable to "calm down," the child who "dripped her ice cream all over" served as a clear signal of disorder and difference. She was an "honest to God" and "direct" signifier of the type of "someone elses" from whom this woman needed to distinguish herself to maintain her identity as *not* someone else. In her inability to "be made to do what the other kids wanted," the little girl became "not quite from the same race," associated with the "lot of someone elses" who signify unseemliness. In her testimony, this white antiques restorer both reflects and reinforces a fundamental distinction between those born to operate elevators and those who will go on to visit holiday cottages for the Fourth of July.

In 1999, Robert Edwards — who with Patrick Steptoe perfected the in

---

146. Rapp, *Testing Women*, pp. 3, 283.
147. Rapp, *Testing Women*, p. 274.

vitro fertilization procedure by which the first "test-tube baby" was conceived — reflected a growing public sentiment when he announced bluntly to an international gathering: "Soon it will be a sin of parents to have a child that carries the heavy burden of genetic disease. We are entering a world where we have to consider the quality of our children."[148] With the expansion of reproductive technology services in the United States, this usually implicit sense that the parents of a child with a detectable disability have made a moral mistake will likely only grow more definite in the future. The current University of Minnesota Health Careers Center Web site recommends genetic counseling as a promising field for the future: "The future looks excellent. . . . Projections indicate that current and anticipated genetic research into predisposition and adult disorders and new reproductive technologies will lead to a greater need for genetic counseling professionals in traditional and expanded medical settings. Genetic counselors are involved in teaching, research, and screening programs. Depending on geographic location and years of experience, the average starting salary for a genetic counselor is $35,000."[149]

In *The Future of the Disabled in Liberal Society,* Hans Reinders, Willem van den Bergh Professor of Ethics and Mental Disability at the Vrije Universiteit in Amsterdam, suggests that the future looks considerably less excellent for those who do not follow the expert advice of such counselors. Reinders's book is an extended moral reflection on genetics and disability, and it directly counters the usual argument that the overriding ethical concern attending prenatal testing is that of simple distributive justice. Indeed, Reinders suggests, the ever-widening distribution of such technologies may in fact weaken the already tenuous commitment of liberal nations to funding disability services: "Assuming that disabled people will always be among us, that the proliferation of genetic testing will strengthen the perception that the prevention of disability is a matter of responsible reproductive behavior, and that society is therefore entitled to hold people personally responsible for having a disabled child, it is not unlikely that political support for the provision of their special needs will erode."[150]

According to Reinders, the question of civic and social hospitality is key, but political liberalism is not ultimately capable of engendering and fostering hospitality toward people with overt, recalcitrant needs. The norms encir-

148. Robert Edwards, quoted by Lois Rogers, "Having Disabled Babies Will Be 'Sin,' Says Scientist," *Sunday Times* (London), July 4, 1999, Home News section.

149. The information is from the National Society of Genetic Counselors. Accessed 2003: www.healthcareers.umn.edu.

150. Hans Reinders, *The Future of the Disabled in Liberal Society: An Ethical Analysis* (Notre Dame, Ind.: University of Notre Dame Press, 2000), p. 14.

cling the liberal axis of individual autonomy cannot easily accommodate lives dedicated to the care of perpetually dependent individuals, or admit the intrinsic value of these individuals. Meticulously considering the policy implications of this tension, Reinders concludes that it is neither within the liberal purview nor within the limits of the practical to address it through legal restrictions on procreative technology and abortion. The predicament facing liberal society, then, is cultural, not political. "The benefits bestowed by love and friendship are consequential rather than conditional, which explains why human life that is constituted by these relationships is appropriately experienced as a gift. A society that accepts responsibility for dependent others such as the mentally disabled will do so because there are sufficient people who accept [this] account as true."[151]

The sense that a life may be rightly mapped on a grid of social use, productivity, or beauty begs for an account that can see life *otherwise*. Mainline Protestants in the United States too often failed to offer such an account in the past. The efficiently eugenic future now beckons.

151. Reinders, *Future of the Disabled,* p. 17.

# 4   For Domestic Security

## The Atomic Age and the
## Genomic Revolution

*This is my song, O God of all the nations,*
*A song of peace for lands afar and mine.*
*This is my home, the country where my heart is;*
*Here are my hopes, my dreams, my holy shrine;*
*But other hearts in other lands are beating*
*With hopes and dreams as true and high as mine.*

*My country's skies are bluer than the ocean,*
*And sunlight beams on clover-leaf and pine.*
*But other lands have sunlight too and clover,*
*And skies are everywhere as blue as mine.*
*Oh, hear my song, O God of all the nations,*
*A song of peace for their land and for mine.*

Lloyd Stone, 1934[1]

---

1. "This Is My Song," Lloyd Stone/Georgia Harkness © 1934, 1962 Lorenz Publishing Company. Stanza 3 by Georgia Harkness © 1964 LPC. Reprinted by kind permission of the publisher.

**Figure 4.1. "The first hamburgers ever cooked with atomic energy." General Electric announcement, 1955**

> *Truly the superpower which man has released from within the atom's heart is not one but many giants. . . . But all are within man's power, subject to his command.*[2]

The language of domestic fitness and the rhetoric of atomic progress are related through what seem, on first glance, to be some fairly bizarre examples. While certain readers of this book may recall firsthand images such as the one from a General Electric handout touting the domestic advantages of nuclear power (fig. 4.1),[3] I see such images as somewhat macabre. My generation held no illusions that the Civil Defense Department's "Duck and Cover"

2. *A Is for Atom,* General Electric/John Sutherland Productions, 1953.
3. General Electric announcement, 1955, cited in Thomas Hine, *Populuxe* (New York: Knopf, 1986), p. 134. In personal correspondence, Hine reports that this was a handout picture from General Electric, found in the archives of the *Philadelphia Inquirer.*

safety drill would save us from a nuclear attack, and a good number of my co-hort suspected that the adults running our country could not ensure that we would live into adulthood. The mixing of happy homemakers, hamburgers, and atomic energy seemed quite odd, at first look. The idea that the "super-power" released "from within the atom's heart" was "within man's power, subject to his command" — to quote the General Electric film *A Is for Atom* — was extraordinary. But what passed as ordinary sense during the Atomic Age was made up of images that intertwined national progress, orderly fami-lies, and the obedient atom, "subject" to human reason.

One example from chapter 3 may be helpful. Paul Popenoe's essay "Sur-veying the Chances" runs alongside Helen Southard's "Planning Parenthood on Campus" in the January 1948 issue of the YMCA/YWCA *Intercollegian*, both of which are linked to the picture of the two blond toddlers and the cap-tion "The Christian asks: how many; how healthy?" (fig. 3.1). Below that pic-ture is another intriguing juxtaposition — an excerpt from Hermann Hagedorn's book-length poem *The Bomb That Fell on America*:

"There is power in the human soul," said the Lord,
"When you break through and set it free,
Like the power of the atom,
More powerful than the atom,
It can control the atom,
The only thing in the world that can.
I told you that the atom is the greatest force in the world, save one.
That one is the human soul!"[4]

On the same page that Southard insists that "there is no disparity between the findings of modern psychiatry and the contributions of religion," Hagedorn's poem calls forth an existential faith in the "human soul" as the one "force in the world" capable of establishing "control" over the most recent modern sci-entific discovery.

Its summons is characteristic of an era. To paraphrase another section of the poem, the bombs that destroyed Hiroshima and Nagasaki threatened to destroy as well the reigning faith in human ingenuity and scientific prog-ress. The Atomic Age had begun, and a new generation of mainline Protes-tants — the *Intercollegian*'s target audience of future church and civic leaders — faced an interpretive task. Christians would need to determine again whether there was "no disparity" between the "findings" of a new scientific

4. Hermann Hagedorn, *The Bomb That Fell on America* (1946; reprint, New York: Associ-ated Press, 1948), p. 62, quoted in *Intercollegian*, January 1948, p. 11.

paradigm and "the contributions of religion." Peering inward, at the "power in the human soul," many mainline Protestants would discern what they judged as the moral strength sufficient to control the force unleashed at Los Alamos, New Mexico.

The Popenoe and Southard essays work as a prelude to Hagedorn's ode to the soul. Crucial for the atomic era in America was the promotion of the wholesome, modern, *nuclear* family. In a concerted effort between corporate science and federal planners, the atom came to signify not threat but promise for a better future for the American family. Through mainstream films, articles, speeches, and images, the various parties invested in the atomic project put an effective spin on the science of tomorrow. True, a rather large and potentially destructive genie was out of the bottle (to use a popular image of the time), but the genie was, quite happily, at the command of humans for the sake of a better tomorrow. He could irradiate produce that would not rot in the suburban kitchen. He could help measure the effectiveness of Vicks VapoRub for soothing stuffy-nosed kids in the suburban bedroom. He could provide energy to the cities and bounty to the Southwestern countryside, and he could propel a whole new breed of airplanes to link the modern, nuclear family with the grandparents back on the farm. And this is not even to mention what was undeniably the primary use of the atom. The enormous genie, emerging from a microscopic bottle, could dutifully protect the American family from the threat of Communism. He was, in short, an "Obedient Atom," to quote the title of a *National Geographic* article from 1958.[5]

In this chapter I will introduce some characteristic moves in the effort to domesticate the atom — moves carefully made to render a serviceable icon for scientific progress. This history has significance for the overall questions of the book in three ways. First, the birth of the Atomic Age helped solidify the norm of a relatively isolated, nuclear family, anchored by its use of consumer goods. Second, the marketing of the new atomic science involved a determined, amnesiac push beyond the horrific events of Hiroshima and Nagasaki. The speed with which the mainstream press offered a happy atomic future to replace an abhorrent past is, in retrospect, astounding. Finally, the effort to surmount the fear of past atrocities called for an unparalleled civic hope in scientific progress. While some voices perpetually called for historical memory and caution, they were quelled by the normative, mainstream media. Technological optimism was the order of the day, the perspective called for in the Atomic Age. The resulting consensus echoes still.

5. Allan C. Fisher, Jr., "You and the Obedient Atom," *National Geographic*, September 1958, pp. 303-53.

294

The icon for scientific progress and the family of tomorrow is no longer the atom. The atom now works as a marker of past science, the science of one's grandparents. The symbol for true knowledge and domestic progress at the beginning of the twenty-first century is the double helix. Featured at the center of the Genomic Revolution (the title of a national exhibit through the American Museum of Natural History), the double helix signals a stairway to a better future for those who will make the climb.

The cover of one book from a major mainline Protestant publishing house (and, in the interest of full disclosure, one to which I contributed an essay) is characteristic of how this new image is used in the theological publishing world. The worthwhile "paradigm for renewal" in the Methodist church, as depicted on the cover of the book, involves the multicolored double helix, emerging from a laboratory beaker. The virtual stairway toward the sky, perhaps inspired by the popular *Matrix* films, indicates the proper direction — ever upward. The effect is a kind of reconceived Jacob's ladder from the book of Genesis, providing the would-be reader with the clear message that this is a forward-thinking book, a book of essays by progressing men and women like myself. Thus *The Wesleyan Tradition: A Paradigm for Renewal,* published by Abingdon in 2002, signals the hopeful beginning of a new millennium.[6]

The Human Genome Project began in 1989 under the auspices of the Department of Energy (DOE), the cabinet-level agency that succeeded the Atomic Energy Commission (AEC) and the later Energy Research and Development Administration. The explicit link between the Atomic Age and the Human Genome Project involves the effects of radiation and, more generally, atomic energy on genetic structures. To determine genetic "mutations" resulting from atomic radiation, the DOE needed a baseline, or "reference sequence," optimally a map of an entire human genome.[7] Thus began the most recent revolution in applied science — the genomic revolution. Not known for her subtlety, *Nation* journalist Jacqueline Stevens has captured one aspect of the narrative: "The key event responsible for research aimed at delineating human DNA fragments was the bombing of Nagasaki and Hiroshima. Hence the institutional home of the Human Genome Project is actually the Manhattan Project."[8]

6. Paul Chilcote, ed., *The Wesleyan Tradition: A Paradigm for Renewal* (Nashville: Abingdon, 2002).

7. See "Why Is the Department of Energy (DOE) Involved in the Human Genome Project?" at http://genome.gsc.riken.go.jp/hgmis/project/whydoe.html.

8. Jacqueline Stevens, "From the Manhattan Project to the Human Genome Project," in "The Secret History of Jessie Gelsinger's Death," ed. Arthur Kroker and Marilouise Kroker, special issue, *Tech Flesh 9* (May 9, 2001). Accessed 2001: www.ctheory.net. See also Stevens, *Reproducing the State* (Princeton: Princeton University Press, 1999).

Stevens interprets the meeting that originated the project: "Rather than clean up the environment," eliminating the radioactivity already *known* to cause illness, "these scientists came up with the idea to clean *us* up"; the scientists agreed that the "correct object of intervention was the human body."

The story is more complicated, as Robert Cook-Deegan narrates (most pithily in his "Origins of the Human Genome Project").[9] Although Charles DeLisi, head of the DOE's Office of Health and Environmental Research, moved the idea of genome sequencing forward as a concerted program in 1986, Robert Sinsheimer had proposed the idea a year earlier, and several scientists had published proposed methods for the project a full decade earlier. What Stevens exploits is one part of the history, an evocative one, considering the currently powerful symbolism of genomic science. It does not seem far-fetched to suppose that in twenty to thirty years, the method for achieving the cleanliness that is *truly* next to godliness will no longer be the Pears' Soap advertised by Henry Ward Beecher in 1885. The field of human genomics proposes to decode *the definitive language of human normality itself.*

Thus, in addition to genetic hygiene and the production of *goods* using the "raw materials" of human genetic data, the genomic project promises, much more ambitiously, an account of who we are as human beings. According to the DOE booklet *To Know Ourselves: The U.S. Department of Energy and the Human Genome Project,* published in 1996, "The ultimate goal [of genomics] is to exploit those resources for a truly profound molecular-level understanding of how we develop from embryo to adult, what makes us work, and what causes things to go wrong." After enumerating the various medical goods "in the offing," the pamphlet quite explicitly raises the bar, to describe the full import of this new effort: the Human Genome Project offers "a new intellectual perspective on who we are and where we came from."[10] As with the Abingdon book cover, signaling renewal ever upward, the cover of the DOE booklet promises nothing short of a new kind of knowledge about who *we* are. In the face of such a promise, it seems worthwhile to take several steps back into history — to assess the patterns of marketing the science that make this effort to know ourselves seem plausible.

The materials, goods, and knowledge related to human genetics did not

---

9. Robert Mullan Cook-Deegan, "Origins of the Human Genome Project," *Risk: Health, Safety and Environment* 5, no. 97 (1994). Accessed 2003: www.piercelaw.edu.

10. Human Genome Project, *To Know Ourselves: The U.S. Department of Energy and the Human Genome Project* (U.S. Department of Energy, 1996). Accessed 2001: www.ornl.gov.

emerge in a hermetically sealed vacuum of "pure science" but grew out of a history directly related to domestic security in the Atomic Age. The "new intellectual perspective on who we are and where we came from" that constitutes genetic knowledge about "ourselves" involves a web of cultural assumptions established decades prior. By the mid–twentieth century the normative Protestant assumption was "how many; how healthy?" This consensus emerged precisely during what historian Thomas Hine calls the "Populuxe Era," an era of unprecedented expectations for consumer goods and domestic comfort. In Hine's words: "The decade from 1954 to 1964 was one of history's great shopping sprees, as many Americans went on a baroque bender and adorned their mass-produced houses, furniture and machines with accoutrements of the space age and of the American frontier." Indeed, "each householder was able to have his own little Versailles along a cul-de-sac."[11]

The "how many" assumed by an increasingly homogenized middle class depended on an algorithm of ever-expanding domestic consumption. Likewise, the "how healthy" depended on the ever-expanding consumption of biomedical products for detecting those differences that would not fit the increasingly homogenized norms of domesticity. The questions posed by a study of the family during the atomic era thus rise to the surface again when considering the new age of the genome. How are assumptions of *quantity control* at the beginning of the twenty-first century shaped by technological progress and patterns of consumption? How do the normative assumptions about the proper, wholesome, or even merely economically *viable* family at the beginning of the twenty-first century neglect, isolate, or abandon those who do not fit? How do assumptions of *quality control* function in the genomic revolution? To import the Bikini Atoll incident from the atomic era, who is voted off the island in order to further the biotechnological revolution?

The rhetoric of hope in genomic progress often squelches precisely such questions. This is exacerbated by the overall tendency within the field of medical ethics to localize each particular technology, assessing each advance apart from the historical trajectory in which it developed. Much as the catchphrases of the Atomic Age clued in viewers and readers to the proper stance toward atomic science, the new genomic science involves a weighted language of progress, hope, and virtually unfettered optimism. To be wary or in opposition is to be deemed *backward*. I hope to persuade some mainline Protestants that it is time to risk association with those who, in the past, made a case against progress.

11. Hine, *Populuxe*, p. 3.

## The Atomic Age

> [A defense] must get public support by being based on more durable motivations than fear or horror; it must offer a promise of better and more secure living; it must be made an effective part of our war deterrent; it must be built into our way of life.[12]

The marketing of "better and more secure living" through an atomic "way of life" required moving the mainstream public beyond the immediate, visceral fear of nuclear annihilation. The default conduits for scientific knowledge of the time reveal this shift, as do less obvious sources such as Walt Disney and the American lay Catholic movement the Christophers. From *National Geographic*, which lent its worldly, educated mystique to the living room coffee table, to *Life*'s all-American perspective on national identity, the magazines to which the postwar family turned interpreted the time as one of confidence. While this message of hope in atomic progress was not univocal, it was powerfully consonant with the broader cultural tendency toward technological optimism.

Although even the standard bomber's-eye view of atomic devastation was harrowing, the middle-class, magazine-subscribing public digested the news alongside advertisements like one that ran in *Life* in 1952 (fig. 4.2). Americans were thus sorting through the perils and promise of atomic science while being simultaneously assured that their new Black-Daylite TV would offer them wholesome, even prayerful, family entertainment — with "blacker blacks" and "whiter whites" — "anywhere, anyplace, anytime." The "greater power" offered through General Electric was craftily marketed as consonant with the good Christian family. Note that the father in the ad and Santa himself consult to bring a television into the Christmas scene, complete with two expectant children and a cross-topped Christmas tree. The televised image of the children in prayer settles the matter — here is a product to bring the family together, to reinforce domestic cohesion and familial piety. (It is left open for double meaning that the children might in fact be praying for a television.) If, for technology and comfort, "You can put your confidence in General Electric," what better source than GE to explain the ABCs of the Atomic Age? One year after the Christmas advertisement ran in *Life*, GE's film *A Is for Atom* ran as a short in theaters across the country, reassuring moviegoing families that atomic science was "A giant of limitless power, at man's command."

12. "Scientific Blueprint for Atomic Survival," *Life*, March 18, 1957, p. 154.

Figure 4.2. Advertisement for new GE Ultra-Vision TV. *Life*, 1952

But before interpreting closely the GE film (as well as "Atomic Energy as a Force for Good" — another Hollywood venture), one needs to step further back. Several articles during the immediate aftermath of Japanese surrender and the public revelation of the Manhattan Project may characterize the spinning required for adequate moral disorientation. Entire families had been obliterated using a new, apocalyptic form of weaponry, a form of weaponry that could eventually obliterate families at home. Spin was necessary if the American public was to take this revelation in stride. Using well-worn signifiers of strangeness only one year after atomic bombs annihilated two cities in Japan, *National Geographic* bid a perversely whimsical "farewell to Bikini" with photographs of Bikini Atoll families "waiting for the moving man" so that their homes could be used for testing atomic bombs.[13] A year later *National Geographic* writer M. A. Huberman employed powerful rhetoric to indicate that the "backwoods" Japanese had not been bombed back to the Stone Age but rather, quite felicitously, had been bombed forward into the Atomic Age.[14] That same year, in a series of articles exploring the relationship of "man and the atom," *Collier's* appropriated the image of the mushroom cloud as a signal of progress, with a man wearing a hospital gown rising out of the cloud, a now happily superfluous wheelchair in the background.[15]

The whimsy and hope conveyed in these documents display a well-crafted summons to forget the horrors wrought by atomic weaponry. The call to amnesia was largely effective. By 1955 Eisenhower's special assistant on disarmament, Harold E. Stassen, was promising the readers of *Ladies' Home Journal* "a world in which there is no disease . . . where hunger is unknown . . . where food never rots and crops never spoil," all brought to them by "atoms for peace."[16]

### "The Power That Lights the Stars"

In August 1945 the United States dropped atomic bombs that would kill approximately 140,000 people in Hiroshima and approximately 80,000 people

13. Carl Markwith, "Farewell to Bikini," *National Geographic*, July 1946, pp. 97-116.

14. M. A. Huberman, "Backwoods Japan during American Occupation," *National Geographic*, April 1947, pp. 491-518.

15. "Man and the Atom," *Collier's*, May 3, 1947, pp. 11-15, 38-44, 56-59, 82-85. The series' constituent articles were David E. Lilienthal, "The Atomic Adventure," pp. 12, 82-85; Lester Velie, "Inertia — U.S.A.," pp. 13, 38-42; Albert Q. Maisel, "Medical Dividend," pp. 14, 43-44; and Robert De Vore, "Passport to the Golden Age," pp. 15, 56-59. The wheelchair photograph is on p. 14.

16. Harold Stassen, "Atoms for Peace," *Ladies' Home Journal*, August 1955, pp. 48-49.

**Figure 4.3. "Atomized Hiroshima."** *National Geographic,* **February 1946**

in Nagasaki. A precise reckoning of those killed was elusive, in part because entire families were destroyed, with no surviving members to give an account of recent infants or visiting relatives. While it would be years before the numbers were sorted out — and years before photographs of strewn bodies and bleeding children were released for public view — the American public was privy to news reports such as one in *Life* that featured two facing pages dominated by the two mushroom clouds. The bold print announced "Hiroshima: Atom Bomb No. 1 Obliterated It" and "Nagasaki: Atom Bomb No. 2 Disemboweled It."[17]

Clearly, the United States had ushered in a new and terrifying era. If, as *Life* reported, servicemen had seen the blast from 250 miles away, the story on the ground — and the danger wrought by the "new weapon of terrible but virtually untried destructive power" — was beyond the imaginations of

17. "The War Ends: Burst of Atomic Bomb Brings Swift Surrender of Japanese," *Life,* August 20, 1945, pp. 26, 27.

Americans at home. "Man had unleashed atomic power on man," *Life* reported, and even the carefully distanced (and bizarrely elaborate) reports of postbomb cloud formations could not easily dispel the potential for cognitive disintegration.[18] Mainstream Americans had seen themselves as clearly, definitively the "good guys" in a fight for GOOD against EVIL. The fruits of the Manhattan Project threatened to call this account into profound question.

The crisp contrast between black and white that helped sell General Electric televisions was one obvious method of dealing with the news that the United States had not only developed a weapon of mass destruction exponentially more lethal than any before but had also used it, twice, on cities as full of children as of soldiers. This destruction had been a part of war, a war that had come to be perceived in the first instance as deeply just and necessary. In various ways, those purveying the news crafted the moral space to allow Hiroshima and Nagasaki to fit within this largely agreed-upon narrative. The production of elaborate images of the atomic cloud served to announce threat, but manageably, from a significant distance. In the *National Geographic* photographs of the B-29 "Superfortress" and "Atomized Hiroshima" — from a 1946 article entitled "Air Power for Peace" — the distant, bomber's-eye view arguably allowed people at home to retain a sense of moral pride (fig. 4.3). Images of on-the-ground devastation would not emerge in public for another eight years. The bomber's-eye view, shown in photographs of the immediate postwar era, may have allowed readers to maintain a semblance of observing *us* versus a foreign *them.*

Two *National Geographic* articles illustrate another distancing technique, providing their middle-class audience with a narrative that would build toward faith in atomic progress and national identity. In "Farewell to Bikini" (1946) and "Backwoods Japan during American Occupation" (1947), an American readership was given cues for narrating the role of an atomic America, past and future. The articles are not only representative but also arguably key components of the larger campaign to restore an almost limitless hope in technological progress.

A slogan originated by early National Geographic Society leader Alexander Graham Bell in 1900, to bring interested, aspiring Americans "the world and all that is in it," remains the unofficial motto of *National Geographic*. By 1918 the magazine had a readership of 500,000, making it easily "the most widely read source of general scientific information."[19] By 1950

18. "The War Ends," p. 26.

19. Philip J. Pauly, "The World and All That Is in It: The National Geographic Society, 1888-1918," *American Quarterly* 31 (1979): 517, 523.

subscriptions numbered 2 million, making the magazine the primary conduit of information on the role of American ingenuity in the postwar world. Its editors played a pivotal role in spinning the story of atomic progress, and its largely white, upper-middle-class, Anglo-Saxon Protestant readers were unquestionably the prime purveyors of "common sense" during the period.

Moving from the bomber's-eye view down to earth, the photographers and writers put the Bikini Atoll inhabitants and "the Japs" into perspective, rendering them as quaint, subtly subhuman, and overtly backward. In their *Reading National Geographic,* Catherine A. Lutz and Jane L. Collins suggest that through photography and careful narration, the magazine "helped white, upwardly mobile Americans to locate themselves in a changing world."[20] The location they sought was domestic security. The magazine thus served in the postwar era to reinforce what Lutz and Collins call a "defiant innocence." The "optimism, power, and . . . sense of invulnerability" characteristic of the postwar era were carefully shored up by the magazine that graced many a middle-class home.

In "Farewell to Bikini," Carl Markwith — a photographer's mate, third class, in the United States Navy "on leave from the National Geographic Society" — lent his name as author to what was likely a collaborative, artful tribute to the "natives of Bikini Atoll in the Ralik Chain of the Marshall Islands." The ostensibly independent authorial agency is misleading, given that Markwith was unquestionably writing as a member of the Navy photographic team, as noted (with no apparent disclaimer) in the report's first footnote. While the authorial voice takes on an amused but gently sympathetic tone, this is a particularly serviceable narration of the people whom "modern civilization suddenly overtook" in February 1946. The people in question are still, in a sense, perceived from above, from several levels up the scale of human evolution. "These brown people had progressed to using kerosene lanterns and a few imported steel hand tools, introduced by missionaries," the article explains, and although "a few could read and write their simple language," they "knew little about" the "outside world." Yet "almost overnight, the natives found themselves in the Atomic Age." And how did these "natives" take their introduction to an advanced culture and alternative future? Although the first paragraphs imply the potential for conflict between the "natives" and the Navy, the article quickly confirms that the "local chief," after conversation with Commodore Ben H. Wyatt, "signified that they would be happy to cooperate." In case readers of the magazine in Ohio, Georgia, or

20. Catherine A. Lutz and Jane L. Collins, *Reading National Geographic* (Chicago: University of Chicago Press, 1993), pp. 36-38.

Connecticut have residual qualms about compelling "simple" people to enter the Atomic Age, the article makes it clear: Wyatt sought to "gain their consent," and it was granted happily — a felicitous coincidence. This reassurance of consent is strangely intermingled with a simultaneous reassurance that these are a childlike people — primitive in needs and expectations.[21]

The impression that the islanders are essentially less evolved because of their isolation in the atoll is reinforced throughout, with subheadings such as "Hungry? Prospect the Cooking Pit," "Thirsty? Drink Coconut Milk," "A Monocle Creates a Sensation," "Islanders Clever with Their Hands," and "Here Clothes Are No Problem."[22] This last subheading is indicative of another method of separating reader from those read about. The named author presents the South Seas island as "idyllic," enduringly innocent, and unashamedly naked. Intertwined with the subtle placement of the Bikini islanders beneath the author and reader is the placement of the island itself outside reality. This take is executed both implicitly and explicitly. In what one could arguably read as a glimmer of morally inspired mischief by the photographer's mate charged with putting his name to this piece of propaganda, he narrates an exchange with a whaling sailor: "When I commented that the setting might have come out of Nordhoff and Hall's stories about the South Seas, one of the sailors in the whaleboat alongside said, 'Naw, you mean the *National Geographic.*'"[23] By referring to Nordhoff and Hall (authors of the romantic Bounty Trilogy and numerous other South Seas novels), the author perhaps both inserts his own ironic perspective and evokes the overall mystique of the South Seas reflected in their genre. The answering sailor makes explicit the link between the "scientific" source of "the world and all that is in it" and an operative form of romantic fiction.

Along with the narrated images of palm trees and coconut milk are photographs of the islanders, some deliberately staged (and noted as such) and others less formal. While the article brings to the fore the faces of the actual people inhabiting Bikini Atoll, the overall impression reinforces the messages of romantic distance and less-than-fully-evolved existence. In one of the first photographs, titled "Carrying the Message to Bikini! U.S. Navy Officers Tell of the Proposed Transfer of the Islanders to a New Home," the American officers stand or lean against palm trees, while the islanders sit on the sand, looking up at the military architects of their future.[24] In one of the last

---

21. Markwith, "Farewell to Bikini," p. 97.
22. Markwith, "Farewell to Bikini," pp. 99, 103, 106, 107.
23. Markwith, "Farewell to Bikini," p. 97.
24. Markwith, "Farewell to Bikini," p. 101.

photographs of life on Bikini, a man obviously struggles to open a box of K rations, and the caption reads, "In their haste to sample something new, some of the villagers lost the keys for opening the small containers. The boys solved that difficulty by unpeeling the tin ribbons with their teeth!" The caption continues: "Chief occupations among the men are fishing and loafing."[25] Both photographs set Navy personnel, author, and reader apart from native islander, drawing a sharp distinction between a world of planned authority and premeditated rations and one of casual, informal existence. Other photographs are more overtly romantic, trading on the Nordhoff and Hall fiction of a vulnerable but accessible island paradise. In one, a young woman leans over to drink from a bucket with a caption reading, "Bikini's 'Old Oaken Bucket' Is Made of Tin."[26] This reference places the islanders within the context of Samuel Woodworth's 1817 poem and the folk song that resulted, reminiscing about the simpler days of country childhood.

Another young woman is pictured throwing darts with a group of little boys (fig. 4.4). The caption reads, "The Belle of Bikini Forgets Coquetry to Play Darts," and continues with the commentary, "She made eyes at U.S. sailors and giggled and blushed when they spoke to her. Here she joins island boys in a game of marksmanship."[27]

The particular patterns of daily life on the doomed island are thus rendered merely picaresque. Given the circumstances, they are *poignant* caricatures, but caricatures nonetheless. The details of family life, courtship, and childhood are clearly meant to be viewed as inherently *informal and unplanned* rather than taken seriously as imminent casualties of the American atomic program. The culture of Bikini Atoll is not an intricate web of humanity, but a curiosity. In this way the article about the vanishing Bikini Atoll people flows smoothly into the article that immediately follows, "Mystery Mammals of the Twilight," which features text and photographs about the lives of bats. Rather than inviting repentance, or even grief, the Bikini piece declares almost with a sense of necessity, "farewell to Bikini." The narration and photographic commentary encourage the convenient perspective that these people are destined by the rules of history to be evicted from their prelapsarian existence in Eden. As the "pioneers sail for new home," the "friendly brown people, small in stature but beautifully formed," are bid good-bye, relocated to Rongerik.[28]

---

25. Markwith, "Farewell to Bikini," p. 112.
26. Markwith, "Farewell to Bikini," p. 109.
27. Markwith, "Farewell to Bikini," p. 106.
28. Markwith, "Farewell to Bikini," pp. 97, 99.

**Figure 4.4. "The Belle of Bikini Forgets Coquetry to Play Darts."** *National Geographic*, **February 1946**

The Belle of Bikini Forgets Coquetry to Play Darts

She made eyes at U. S. sailors and giggled and blushed when they spoke to her. Here she joins island boys in a game of marksmanship. Island youngsters developed surprising accuracy in tossing the feathered darts (page 102).

Islanders Turn the Tables on the Author, Inviting Him into the Family Circle for a Photograph

One girl primps, others deliberately pose. The hut is a combination of imported Jap-sawed lumber, island palm poles, and thatching. Much of the side thatching has been removed for transport to Rongerik.

**Figure 4.5. "Islanders Turn the Tables on the Author, Inviting Him into the Family Circle for a Photograph."** *National Geographic*, **February 1946**

Two photographs remain powerfully haunting, even from this narrated and now temporal distance. We can find in both, taken together, a small tear in the fabric of the overall narrative. I found in them a glimpse of hope for humanity in the midst of what may otherwise be read as an effort at dehumanization. In the first (fig. 4.5), the photographer himself poses, shirtless, below a household of women and children. The caption is candid: "Islanders Turn the Tables on the Author, Inviting Him into the Family Circle for a Photograph."

It is impossible to read with certainty the apparent informality of the photograph. It may have been very deliberately staged. But the photographer's pose, as well as his very existence as the now-photographed, is suggestive of another interpretation beyond the dominant, official story told by the Navy and *National Geographic*. The image suggests — and the caption states — that the mothers, sisters, and children invited the man charged with their narration into their "family circle." While "the author" must tell the story of these women and children at a carefully choreographed distance, they are depicted here as inviting him to be seen as "one of them." The fact that Carl Markwith has positioned himself at the lowest place in the photograph, at the feet of one of the girls and even below the children, may suggest his own perspective on the assignment. It is my wish to interpret the image in this way — as Markwith's insertion of an image that counters the overall tone of the piece. He has accepted the invitation to be in the image with those whose homeland will be destroyed.

This possible reading of invitation, humility, and proximity may stand in particular contrast with the photographs of supposedly cacogenic people in chapter 3. It is virtually impossible to imagine the ERO-trained field-workers stepping into their careful narration and documentation of cacogenic families. The foot soldiers of the eugenics movement are resolutely *not* in the pictures they take. It is almost impossible to imagine one of the "Investigators" in the cacogenic studies posing beneath, and as kin with, the people she is photographing. It is possible to read Markwith as involved in such a fragile grace.

The caption for the article's last photograph, "A Bikini Family Says Farewell at the Grave of a Loved One" (fig. 4.6), explains that the man at the far left had requested that the photographer take an extra photograph, one of his family at his sister's burial site. The placement of this photograph at the end of the article may subtly subvert the dominant themes of evolutionary and romantic dismissal. "Civilization and the Atomic Age had come to Bikini, and they had been in the way," the author closes, and his final image may stand as a testimony to the islanders' own grief.[29]

29. Markwith, "Farewell to Bikini," p. 116.

A Bikini Family Says Farewell at the Grave of a Loved One

Laiboei, left, helped the Navy photographers who filmed the village ceremonies in the cemetery (page 104). Upon its conclusion he asked the author to make this photograph of the burial place of his sister.

**Figure 4.6. "A Bikini Family Says Farewell at the Grave of a Loved One."** *National Geographic,* **February 1946**

Is this to refute in some small way the author's assigned task — to eliminate the need for the reader's own grief, for American repentance? The reader may, at the very least, take a cue from these conflicting signals. A story intended to rebut national guilt and reinforce geographic distance may thus crack open a different interpretation.

Not two years after Hiroshima and Nagasaki, *National Geographic* ran the story "Backwoods Japan during American Occupation." The piece is ostensibly about the Japanese area for which General MacArthur set up a Forestry Division in October of 1945, but the essay features a running commentary that associates the "backwoods Japs" with the presumably "backwoods" people living in wooded regions of the United States. Using various cultural cues, the narrator, himself an American forestry expert, takes readers on a tour of a people who "depend amazingly on their forests" in order "to build their wood and paper houses; to cook their food and keep themselves warm over their braziers; to ensure water for irrigating the valley rice fields."

The article opens by setting MacArthur as the industrious authority who brought in experts, such as the author, to "advise them on forest resources and forest products." Similar to the Bikini essay, it employs humor to signal the superiority of the readers to those interpreted. The chauffeur who drove the officials to one meeting "seemed to use only horn and accelerator. . . . I doubt that he ever needed to have his brakes relined." But even on the first page, the author quite explicitly notes for the reader the importance of maintaining a critical distance from the "backwoods" people who seem, at first glance, "hospitable and courteous." The author warns: "In traveling away from the densely populated, heavily bomb-damaged centers such as Tokyo, Yokohama, Osaka, and Nagoya there always was the danger of forgetting that the people we saw in the villages and in the hills were also warmaking Japs."[30] Using the war-propaganda epithet "Jap" interchangeably with "Japanese" throughout overtly signaled readers that these seemingly peaceful, "eager" people whom MacArthur's team was sent to assist represented the invading force to whom the United States was forced to respond with advanced weaponry. Later in the article the author tells of a trip down a mountain road with "an unsmiling Jap" who seemed intent on threatening their safety. "I could think only of *kamikaze* pilots. Surely this Jap wouldn't try deliberately to take several Americans with him to meet his ancestors by rolling the car over the brink!"[31]

This overt signal of moral superiority is interspersed with apparent indications of aesthetic and intellectual superiority. "No plant visit was complete without at least one cup of sugarless tea in a handleless cup. After such a tea party the host, with much bowing, would motion us to lead the way."[32] As the author and his team attempted to gather data, better to assist the "Japs" with their forest industry, they found that "questioning almost invariably produced divergent answers."[33] With bits of commentary on their interviews with personnel and management at the plants, the author brings the reader in on the joke, inviting families back home to chuckle and shake their heads at the frustration of dealing with such evasive strangers: "A time-consuming habit of the Japanese reminded us of a radio comedian's gag," and "It was dif-

---

30. Huberman, "Backwoods Japan," p. 491.
31. Huberman, "Backwoods Japan," p. 508.
32. Huberman, "Backwoods Japan," p. 491.
33. Huberman, "Backwoods Japan," p. 492.

ficult for us to keep our faces straight during such proceedings, but the Japs never seemed to think it funny." Again: "We were comically reminded of Gilbert and Sullivan's *The Mikado* by one mayor [identified by the subheading as one of the 'Pooh-Bahs of the Villages'] who was president of the local forestry association."[34] One picture, "By Their Saws You May Tell Yank and Japanese," is characteristic. The standing marine, with apparent patience, offers the superior tool to the primitive Japanese.[35]

The piece renders Japanese family life as a combination of Gilbert and Sullivan and (cartoon character) Snuffy Smith. The author encountered "a charcoal burner and his wife about lunchtime." The man "seemed to growl to his wife," and she, by turns, "giggled" and obeyed her husband's various commands.[36] The homes of those visited are described with meticulous attention to the supposed lack of furniture and decorative detail: "The family sat on the floor, ate off trays on the floor, and slept on a *futon,* or quilts placed on the floor." In another caption, the "backwoods" connection is blunt: "A Still in the Kyushu Backwoods Cooks, Not Sour Corn Mash, but Fragrant Camphor."[37] The depiction of the Japanese children as "runny-nosed, bright-eyed" beggars appealing to their occupiers for "Gummu" and "Chocolettu" lends to the narrated image of the "GI" as "a friendly gentleman" in the midst of little people. The mothers, "in response to the contagious grin of the big Americans," "smilingly allowed their babies to have the sweets."[38] The overall narration is clear: American occupation is a blessing to the people of "backwoods Japan."

The editors apparently intended to seal an even more disturbing interpretation by immediately following the article with the special color series "Operation Crossroads," with two Charles Bittinger paintings and eight color photographs from the Navy's Joint Task Force I depicting the first atomic blasts on Bikini Atoll. The page facing the conclusion to the "backwoods Japan" piece features *Dave's Dream,* the B-29 that brought Bikini's first atomic bomb, soaring through bright blue sky and fluffy white clouds. Another photograph bears the caption "Uranium Explodes with the Power That Lights the Stars." The last image announces: "An Atomic Volcano Sprays the Target Fleet with Invisible Poison and Sinks Three Capital Ships in One Blow."[39] While

34. Huberman, "Backwoods Japan," pp. 492, 493, 496, 497.
35. Huberman, "Backwoods Japan," p. 498.
36. Huberman, "Backwoods Japan," p. 499.
37. Huberman, "Backwoods Japan," pp. 504, 505.
38. Huberman, "Backwoods Japan," pp. 514, 515.
39. "Operation Crossroads (Bikini Atoll, Marshalls)," *National Geographic,* April 1947, pp. 519-30.

"backwoods Japan" has been in the woods of darkness, military planes have flown into the wild and beautiful blue yonder carrying the very power that lights the stars. Without American occupation and the American victory enabled by nuclear weaponry, these backwoods people would have had little hope of moving out of their simple existence and into the twentieth century.

One can look at the subjects of these *National Geographic* pieces on Bikini and Japan as recipients of a (macabre) form of American largesse. One important aspect is the way this tale of national identity, science, and progress is mirrored in one form of narration of Western, Christian missions in mainline Protestantism during the same era. Writers in *Together: The Midmonth Magazine for Methodist Families,* during its first decade, also tended to depict mission fields as receiving "civilization" through the work of American missionaries. Two examples are characteristic.

In 1960 *Together* ran a pictorial essay titled "Sarawak — Once Head-Hunter Land."[40] The opening text reads: "In this strategic, far-off tropical wilderness, primitive tribes descended from onetime pagan savages and 'wild men of Borneo' cast off superstition, fear, and force for the 'Strong Jesus' religion of missionaries."

Another 1960 essay focused on Japan: "When Civilization Came to Shimabuku."[41] Clarence W. Hall (a senior editor at *Reader's Digest*) opens his essay thus: "Whenever I think of the Bible's extraordinary power to transform men and society, I can't help remembering Shimabuku, a tiny village on the island of Okinawa." Hall describes the reaction of a group of American soldiers who came upon the Japanese village in 1945. "Huddled beneath its groves of banyan and twisted pine trees, this remote village of some 1,000 souls was in the path of American advance, and so received a severe shelling." Yet this advance was preceded by a different advance, one that made the ultimate difference in the fate of the "souls" alive there. "We were amazed at the spotlessly clean homes and streets, the poise and gentility of the villagers, their apparent high level of health and happiness." And what was the source of the apparent "transformation"? Through the mainline Protestant mission work from decades prior, the village had been given the tools to make itself "a diamond in a dung heap"; the town had "no jail, no brothel, no drunkenness, no divorce." Through the good work of an American Methodist missionary who had made "a pair of converts" and left them a Japanese translation of the Bible thirty years prior, Shimabukans had re-

---

40. "Sarawak: Once Head-Hunter Land," *Together,* January 1960, p. 37. Three years prior, *Together* had run a similar essay, "Converting Ex-Headhunters," *Together,* September 1957, p. 20.
41. Clarence W. Hall, "When Civilization Came to Shimabuku," *Together,* October 1960, pp. 45-46.

ceived "their ideas of human dignity, the rights and responsibilities of citizen-ship." When an older member of the town "bowed humbly" and apologized if they seemed "a backward people," the chaplain replied to the narrator, "*They* are backward?" The difference between being on the "dung heap" and being a "dia-mond," it seems, was the difference made by the influence of Christianity, brought to this people by a single Westerner eager to spread the gospel of Jesus. Hall goes on to contrast the "pure and simple society" present in Shimabuku with the "big and brawling boom town" of Koza. Thus, even the Japan that had been moved along by American occupation, to share in "modernity's more noi-some accompaniments," as Hall puts it, may stand as a contrast to the properly civilized Japan that was under the control of Christianized civilization. The way the narrative functioned in the postwar period, it seems that even those Japanese worthy of protecting in their "pure and simple" form were worthy of protection by virtue of their "strong faith" *seeded by the West.* In this way, Hall's conclusion — "Maybe we're using the wrong kind of weapons to make the world over!" — fails to address the core distinction between "civilized" and "uncivilized" hu-manity, a distinction working its way through the tale of atomic progress.

### *"America on the Move"*

As one reads through the *National Geographic* bound volume for 1945, the tran-sition from "Flying Our Wounded Veterans Home" (September) to "Your New World of Tomorrow" (October) seems surreal. Catherine Bell Palmer's detailed account of the effort to evacuate men wounded in battle is a whole world away from the fantastic descriptions of "the world of the future." But the *National Geographic* issues from the years 1945-47 are full of such seemingly unreal juxta-positions. In "Your New World of Tomorrow," the same airships that enabled the efficient evacuation of human beings wounded beyond recognition will lead to the ability to "send mail by rocket across the Atlantic Ocean." So prom-ised a "rocket research man" in the opening paragraph of F. Barrows Colton's tribute to the world of tomorrow. "Such transatlantic rockets won't come right away, but the mere fact that they're being talked about shows how science is re-making our world and scrambling our old ideas of geography."[42]

In a nation that had suffered military casualties but not war on its soil, the shift from technological victory to technological promise came quickly. The first subheading of Colton's essay is "The Age of Atomic Power," and the

---

42. F. Barrows Colton, "Your New World of Tomorrow," *National Geographic,* October 1945, p. 385.

**Figure 4.7. "New Vacationist, Honeymoon Couples, Mothers and Daughters Travel by Air."** *National Geographic,* **September 1946**

shift from "the first tremendous atomic bomb" to the hope for harnessing "the same almost inconceivable power that keeps the universe running, the same energy that has kept the sun and all the other stars burning and shining with terrific heat for millions of years," is immediate. Although the nuclear scientist quoted does caution that "we must learn to control atomic power," the message is clear — the "colossal energy of the universe" has been "unleashed" in a way that will issue forth in an "Age of Atomic Power."[43] The arti-

43. Colton, "Your New World," p. 385.

cle moves on to other technological wonders shining on the horizon — many, developed "under the urgent demands of war," now holding promise for civilian use, "offsetting somewhat war's terrible waste and destruction."[44]

And what might possibly tip that balance? The author offers a jarringly incongruous array: televised sports, theater, opera, and "window shopping" (commercials); FM radio without "static, fading, and station interference"; "quick trips to far places"; "an electronic housemaid" that "guards your home from dirt"; and a "home freezer" that will "keep your meat in cold storage." And, in case you want that meat thawed quickly, a photograph caption announces: "In 11 Seconds This Electronic Heater Thaws Three Pounds of Frozen Cherries."[45] The "New World" of the future was one of technological promise, and *National Geographic* easily narrated the continuity of military and domestic promise. Those who evicted the Bikini islanders and bombed the "Japs" into the twentieth century had every reason to place their families' hope in the scientists who had crafted modern warfare.

Yet the promise of a transformed family life, happily enhanced by television, frozen meat, and quickly thawed cherries, was particular. There were families clearly *not quite meant* to be transformed at all. There were children who did not fit within the narrative of imminent promise. In a *National Geographic* photo essay of September 1946, "America on the Move," the opening image shows a fashionably suited mother with her daughter, in shiny white shoes, approaching the stairs to board a DC-4 (fig. 4.7). They are clearly Americans "on the move," two of the two million domestic air travelers who, the caption reports, flew during the first three months of 1946. The next caption assures the magazine's readership that "Boxcars Will Bring You That New Radio, Washing Machine, Vacuum Cleaner," the happy train worker in the photo clearly enjoying his labors.[46] The piece moves on to show GI Bill recipients in a University of Wyoming trailer camp as well as "sheep on the move" across the Grand Coulee Dam, vacationers in upstate New York, and some of the "more than 110,000 passengers" who travel through Washington National Airport every month.[47] From GIs to sheep, America is a nation of movement, of progress. Even while at home, housewives are part of the movement, ordering up the appliances of progress, brought to them by cheerful trainmen.

In the middle of the photographic feature, a two-page spread signals the difference between families who are "on the move" and those who are *not*.

---

44. Colton, "Your New World," p. 387.
45. Colton, "Your New World," pp. 388, 393, 402, 407.
46. "America on the Move," *National Geographic,* September 1946, p. 358.
47. "America on the Move," pp. 360, 362, 363, 365.

Three children look forward, toward the horizon, pointing upward at their high-flying kite (fig. 4.8). The caption reads, "Chicagoans Enjoy High Winds and Soaring Kites on Outings to Sand Dunes at the Michigan Shore." Below are two children, separately photographed, with their heads touching the magazine's gutter — as the center divide is called. The caption on the right (fig. 4.10) reads, "This Tennessee Hill Boy's Traveling Days Will Come Later: Now, with food shortages world-wide, he is better off at home. Most ration tickets went unused among hill folk, for they grew nearly all their own food." In the commerce of limitless horizons, this boy is out of luck. His community, the "hill folk," was outside the realm of ration tickets, and now is outside the realm of an "America on the move." The caption for the other photograph leaves even less open for interpretation: "To a Deep South Farm Urchin, There's No Place Like Home: His world is where his short legs can carry him between meals. Some Sunday afternoon the two incipient fryers will go where the watermelon is going" (fig. 4.9).[48] The racism of the photograph is clear, with the child depicted, positioned, and named as caricature, and the association between the "Tennessee Hill Boy" and the "Deep South Farm Urchin" is marked. Both are outside the purview of the readership, and both are outside the glow of technological promise. Indeed, by one possible reading, each child symbolizes by his happy consumption that the readership is beyond reproach for turning merely a mirthful eye on their existence. They both have access to the basic necessities of watermelon, fryers, pickles, and potatoes. The parents of the "Hill Boy" did not even register their need for ration tickets.

But even beyond this obvious reading, there is a subtle implication. The Americans "on the move" were "on the move" precisely inasmuch as they were able to distinguish and distance themselves and their own progressing children from children like these. They were "on the move" inasmuch as they were evolving, through technology, toward a new existence. "The world and all that is in it" included those who had and those who did not have; as part of its skillful narration of the post-Hiroshima years, *National Geographic* helped readers interpret the distinction.

### *"Atom Bomb . . . Uncensored"; or, "What We May Face"*

In its September 29, 1952, issue, *Life* ran graphic images never before seen by the American public (fig. 4.12). The text of "When Atom Bomb Struck — Uncensored" explains that the photographs, taken by Japanese photographers

---

48. Images from "America on the Move," pp. 368-69.

Figure 4.8. "Chicagoans Enjoy High Winds and Soaring Kites on Outings to Sand Dunes at the Michigan Shore." *National Geographic*, September 1946

To a Deep South Farm Urchin, There's No Place Like Home
His world is where his short legs can carry him between meals. Some Sunday afternoon the two incipient fryers will go where the watermelon is going.

**Figure 4.9. "Deep South Farm Urchin."** *National Geographic,* September 1946

This Tennessee Hill Boy's Traveling Days Will Come Later
Now, with food shortages world-wide, he is better off at home. Most ration tickets went unused among hill folk, for they grew nearly all their own food.

**Figure 4.10. "Tennessee Hill Boy."** *National Geographic*, September 1946

immediately after the blast, had been "suppressed by jittery U.S. military censors through seven years of the Occupation." With the lifting of U.S. censorship in Japan according to the terms of the San Francisco Peace Treaty of 1951, Japanese publishers had already revealed the images to the Japanese public. In bringing the images to the American public eye, *Life* effectively recalled the horrendous stakes involved in America's nuclear program. The first page of the article drew on the impassioned plea of a teenage survivor for "peace at any price."[49] The article brought shockingly forward the cost of a victory and called into question the moral legitimacy of the nuclear threat. The placement of the advertisement for Glamorene (fig. 4.11), on the page opposite the story about Japan, seems somehow oddly apt. American ingenuity was producing "magic new cleaners" to eliminate stains of all kinds, leading housewives to leap in adulation. The sticky past, however, continued to complicate the picture of unfettered progress and wholly holy hygiene.

With the atomic bomb, America had introduced a completely unknown set of possibilities, some of them obviously horrific. In the January 1951 issue of the *Journal of Social Hygiene*, Charles Walter Clarke, M.D., executive director of the American Social Hygiene Association (ASHA) and clinical professor of public health practice at Harvard, brought a strong dose of controlled domesticity to bear on the era's potential nihilism. In the 1920s ASHA had participated actively in the movement to ensure cleanliness and encourage better breeding. As part of the effort to "make the difference between isolated effort and social order," ASHA had now joined similar organizations in supporting the United Defense Fund.[50] Clarke's piece — "VD Control in Atom-Bombed Areas" — presents one of ASHA's proposed contributions to the cause of national defense and social hygiene.[51]

The very title evokes bleakly comedic images of *Mad Max* meets *Sex in the City*, but redirecting through narration the fear evoked by the increasingly public images of nuclear annihilation was serious business. Peeking from behind the facade of the freshly washed family and the promise of domestic prosperity is the fear of the moral rupture that had occurred with the dawn of nuclear weaponry. Clarke's essay opened with a haunting image from inside the Urakami Cathedral in Nagasaki after the city's annihilation (fig. 4.13).[52]

49. "When Atom Bomb Struck — Uncensored," *Life*, September 29, 1952, p. 19.

50. Editorial, "Something New Has Been Added," *Journal of Social Hygiene* 37 (January 1951): 2.

51. Charles Walter Clarke, "VD Control in Atom-Bombed Areas," *Journal of Social Hygiene* 37 (January 1951): 3-7.

52. Verification that the photograph is of the Urakami Cathedral came through a letter from the Nagasaki Atomic Bomb Museum, Artifacts Section, Nagasaki, Japan.

Figure 4.11. Glamorene Carpet Cleaner advertisement. *Life*, September 29, 1952

Figure 4.12. "When Atom Bomb Struck — Uncensored." *Life*, September 29, 1952

America was responsible for bringing into the world a force that could destroy humanity itself. How to wash out *that* damned spot?

Announcing "What We May Face," Clarke explains that "In case of an atom bomb attack on an American city, gravest social hygiene problems will almost certainly arise." Yet it would be possible, with proper planning, to prevent "a state of great panic." While "immediately following an attack" there would likely be a grand exodus of people "striving desperately to escape from the bombed area and from the city," ASHA and related organizations could help establish some semblance of order. The maintenance of proper norms of domesticity was key to a way forward out of the chaos. In the "great overcrowding in temporary housing at refugee centers and of doubling-up of families . . . all sorts of people would be thrown intimately together." It would be imperative, should the unthinkable happen, that "clergymen, case workers, group workers and recreation leaders" cooperate to prevent the spread of "promiscuity" and its twin curses: "venereal disease" and "illegitimate births." Without adequate foresight, surviving areas would likely see "idle" and "uprooted" people, "youths" in particular, ready to rove and incite disorder. Because of the "grave long-range effects in the population" of "syphilis in pregnancy," it would be crucial not to overlook venereal disease in order to focus

319

Figure 4.13. "Nagasaki, Fall 1945." *Journal of Social Hygiene,* January 1951

only on other, seemingly more urgent matters, "for example, an epidemic of influenza." The proposed amoral spectacle is now bizarrely macabre: *as if* the long-range effects of syphilis were even in the same universe as the short-range or even long-range effects of a nuclear bomb; *as if* there would be roving bands of youths, with skin burned beyond recognition by radiation, seeking even the slightest physical contact. But Clarke was dead serious. The piece closes with two appeals to those who could maintain some proximity to normalcy should America suffer an atomic attack. There must be "strict policing," which would include "vigorous repression of prostitution and measures to discourage promiscuity, drunkenness and disorder." Finally, "social and religious services should be emphasized in such an area." Service workers and clergy would need to be on call, ready to travel to affected areas to "support or restore morale" and "safeguard morals."[53]

### "The Obedient Atom"

The restoration of the solid and safe nuclear family was the order of the day. A look at the period between Clarke's 1951 national call to ensure social hygiene and the 1959 "Kitchen Debate" between Vice President Richard Nixon and Soviet premier Nikita Khrushchev reveals a patterned coupling. The technologically revolutionary family was resolutely the normative and wholesome family. Atomic technology was also revolutionary — but "obedient," even nourishing. By ushering in the Atomic Age, the United States had not brought the world to the brink of utter, nihilistic destruction but had instead broken through to "a dream as old as man himself." The project that had incinerated homes was now a project for peace, for health, for healing, and, ultimately, for shoring up precisely what mattered most — comfortable domesticity. By 1962, three years after the vice president showed families of the world the superiority of technologically advanced consumerism, a zany but reassuringly familiar space-age family called the Jetsons would epitomize that pairing.

The birth of the Atomic Age thus helped solidify the norm of a newly mobile, nuclear family anchored by its use of comforting and entertaining consumer goods. The "boys" who returned home from the war were encouraged to new mobility not only through government subsidies but also through the marketing for a newly modern marriage and family. This was a family grounded not so much in the past or the land but by DuPont polyester ("Better Living through Chemistry"), Coca-Cola ("Where There's Coke

53. Clarke, "VD Control," pp. 3, 4, 6, 7.

There's Hospitality"), Johnson & Johnson, Minute Rice, and an ever-growing array of household appliances from the company in which you could "put your confidence" — General Electric. If the Progressive Era involved domestic development through social control and carefully administered charity, the Atomic Age involved domestic progress largely through the consumption of new and improved household products for Mother, Father, Dick, and Jane.

With the Cold War came a threat to this consumerist construal of the American family, which was in full swing by the turn from the forties to the fifties. The family that emerged during the early Cold War period had everything to do with purchasing power. As historian Elaine Tyler May recounts in *Homeward Bound: American Families in the Cold War Era*, the 1959 Kitchen Debate represented a fundamental aspect of the modern family in the early Cold War. At the American Exhibition in Moscow, Nixon indicated as obvious evidence of capitalist superiority the "model home," the car, and the television set — "each the newest and most modern of its type," and each available to the American family. When Khrushchev countered, accusing American builders of market-driven, intentional obsolescence, holding up in contrast the Soviet commitment to build not only for one's children but also for one's grandchildren, Nixon accepted the argument and turned it skillfully on its head. Nixon boldly explained that American engineers were producing better homes for each new generation, so that grandchildren would not *want* to live in the old-fashioned homes of their grandparents.[54] The nuclear family was moving forward, into a more secure and comfortable future, and that domestic security was brought to them in no small part by the Atomic Energy Commission (AEC).

One way to visualize what the purveyors of the atomic era had to overcome, and how far they were able to reach, is to contrast the photograph that appeared immediately above the title of Clarke's 1951 ASHA article on VD control and the full-color image featured in the 1958 *National Geographic* article "You and the Obedient Atom" (fig. 4.14). Although ASHA's executive director did not once in his article refer directly to the atrocities at Hiroshima and Nagasaki, speaking instead of "bombed cities of Europe," the haunting photograph of Nagasaki opens the piece. Taken from within the ruins of the Urakami Cathedral, looking out from the one remaining apse onto the devastation of Nagasaki, the photo has the simple caption "Nagasaki, Fall 1945." The photograph sharply signals what was at stake in postwar America — total moral disintegration wrought at the hands of military scientists and the federal government. But by 1958, as depicted beautifully in the *National Geographic* illustration, that im-

---

54. Elaine Tyler May, *Homeward Bound: American Families in the Cold War Era* (New York: Basic Books, 1999), pp. 145-46.

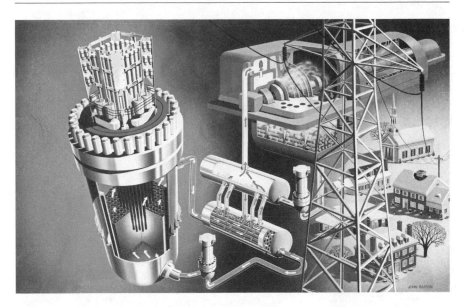

**Figure 4.14. "You and the Obedient Atom."** *National Geographic,* **September 1958**

age had been supplanted by the cumulative message of technological progress. Atomic power was now the benevolent force behind peaceful hamlets such as the one featured, complete with village church and reassuring steeple. The snow-covered roofs of homes and church lend a cozy ambiance to the imagined interiors, heated and illuminated by the domesticated atom.

### *"The Atomic Adventure"; or, "Atomic Energy as a Force for Good"*

As early as 1947, *Collier's* ran a four-essay argument in vivid prose and with full-color illustrations for the promising atomic future; one multiexposure photograph featured a maniacally smiling patient — presumably cured — emerging from the atomic mushroom cloud itself (fig. 4.16). The opening copy, from an essay by AEC chairman David E. Lilienthal, was vividly contextualized within a panorama of progress by advertising illustrator Frederick Siebel (fig. 4.15).[55] Siebel had served as the artist for at least one World War II poster, and this rendering is similarly unsubtle and potent in its message, displaying in bold ico-

55. Images and text from "Man and the Atom," *Collier's,* May 3, 1947. Text (from the image) is excerpted from Lilienthal's essay in the "Man and the Atom" series, "The Atomic Adventure," pp. 84, 85, emphasis added.

Figure 4.15. "Man and the Atom." *Collier's*, May 3, 1947

... CONTINUED ... MAN AND THE ATOM

MAN AND THE ATOM

## MEDICAL DIVIDEND

### BY ALBERT Q. MAISEL

The first benign results of atomic bomb research have been new tools for medical scientists which promise cures for hitherto incurable diseases. There have been failures, but the work is just starting and researchers generally are hopeful

THE facts are coming out slowly, in confusing little driblets, from a hundred different research laboratories and hospitals. Some of them seem to promise new medical wonders; some relate the bitter story of hope proved false. But all of them, put together, add up to the fact that man-made atomic energy—now the most destructive force ever known—is capable of saving human lives.

From the Oak Ridge laboratories that gave us the most painful problem of our age now flows a small but steady stream of radioactive isotopes. These strange by-products of atomic energy production may yet prove as important to mankind as the atomic bomb or the cheap atomic power that is still only a promise on the horizon.

For to scientists, radioactive isotopes are tools of power in the eternal fight against pain and death; they may be even a means of prying open the once tightly shut door to an understanding of the inner processes of life itself.

Already, here and there, one can find testimonials to the power of atomic medicine. There are a few people alive today who by every pre-Atomic Age rule of medicine should long since have been dead. One such is Mr. B. B., fifty-one, who can be found helping out in the Occupational Therapy Department of Montefiore Hospital in New York.

Mr. B's troubles began in 1923 when he developed a goiterous condition of his thyroid, the great shieldlike gland at the front of the neck that plays a major part in regulating the body's processes. Patient B went on the operating table and the swollen gland was removed—just in time, it then seemed, for under the microscope, the excised tissues were revealed to be cancerous.

Fifteen years went by with Mr. B in apparent good health. Then, in 1938, he became increasingly nervous. He lost weight rapidly and began to develop all of the alarming symptoms of an overactive thyroid. But, of all the ills of humankind, this was the last that would have been expected to befall Mr. B. For how could a long-since-removed thyroid gland start acting up?

Puzzled, his doctors went over him from hair to toes. At last, in the middle of his back, they found a small tumor. Again Mr. B was trundled to the operating room. When they removed and examined the tumor they discovered that the operation of 1923 had occurred too late to prevent the thyroid cancer from sending out "daughter cells." Wandering in the blood stream, these had at length produced a second cancerous tumor of wildly growing thyroid cells far from the site of the original cancer.

Even the removal of this back tumor did not "cure" Mr. B. For two years more, the doctors worked on their strange patient, but still the symptoms of thyroidism increased. X rays gradually disclosed a host of other "daughter" cancers, each flooding the man's body with thyroid secretions. But all resisted high-voltage X-ray treatment.

The rapidly weakening patient was transferred to Montefiore Hospital, and a new team of cancer specialists went to work on him. First they fed him Lugol's solution, an iodine product, which seemed for a time to moderate his *(Continued on page 43)*

PHOTOGRAPH FOR COLLIER'S BY BAUMAN–GREEN

Figure 4.16. "Medical Dividend." *Collier's*, May 3, 1947

nography what was at stake in the decision facing Americans of a potentially "great" generation. The cumulative effect of the *Collier's* piece was to reframe the question of domestic danger and paternal responsibility. A *great* people would rightly perceive that the true menace was *collective flaccidity*. A truly *great* people would not "slacken" in the face of the atomic adventure, stifling its promise, but would instead forge ahead, ready to climb the mountain, tower above others, demonstrate to all the world their "faith in knowledge" by supporting the work of Lilienthal's Atomic Energy Commission.

The hand of God dominates the illustration, with a lightning burst of energy issuing from the divine palm. The burst lights the corn and wheat — the bounty of atomic agriculture — as well as a crisscrossed field of green and amber. To the left of the field is a burgeoning city, fueled by an atomic reactor. To the right is a scene from the Southwest, with a shining adobe structure overlooking the bounteous fields. Below this vision of hope is "routine" personified, a parson with bolo tie, scowling around his oversized cigar and tangled in yards of conspicuous red tape. Below him is a greenish, dying figure who is riding an anthropomorphized snail. The snail is shriveled and looks on with stupefied alarm at the scene of a dying Southwest — with deteriorating adobe and a leafless stump of a tree, gray-black clouds rolling toward a misbegotten future. With the atomic adventure comes the chance to receive from the hand of God an opportunity not to be missed — an opportunity not only for new gadgetry but for life-giving knowledge that separates civilized from uncivilized humanity.

The illustration powerfully answers its own question. On which side will you find yourself? On the side of progress — or wrapped in yards of red tape? Will Lilienthal's readers, those middle-class mothers, fathers, and grandparents who subscribe to *Collier's*, grasp the opportunity, forging ahead toward a better future for their children and their children's children in the "New World" of the Atomic Age?

Two of the most rhetorically rich examples of marketing the "atomic adventure" appeared in cinematic form. This last notion regarding one's "children's children" closes a brilliant piece of cinematic rhetoric sponsored by General Electric in 1953 — a John Sutherland production entitled *A Is for Atom* (fig. 4.17). Over seven million children and parents were witness to its persuasive power in the first two years after its release, and it won artistic awards as well as recognition from *Scholastic Teacher* and the Freedoms Foundation.[56] Trained at Walt Disney Studios, Sutherland had worked on

56. Program note, *A Is for Atom,* Prelinger Internet Archive. Accessed 2002: www.archive.org.

*Bambi,* but he spent the remainder of his career winning awards from various patriotic, educational, and entrepreneurial groups as head of a company that produced industrial advertising aimed at middle-class consumers, young and old.

The second cinematic example is quite different in form but strikingly similar in argument. The Christophers was a mainstream, prototypically American lay Catholic group, also with significant Hollywood connections, organized to restore "divine truth and human integrity" to American civic life.[57] Its offering, "Atomic Energy as a Force for Good," appeared in living rooms across the country in 1955 as part of a television series instituted in 1952 to bring mainstream, Americanized Catholic thought to the public and to bring Catholic laity into the mainstream. Both films powerfully appeal to the civic hope that Americans might craft a deep and abiding *good* out of atomic science — an atomic adventure rather than an atomic atrocity.

The imagery in the Siebel illustration is magnified and extended narratively in both offerings. Each film is effective in conveying a contrast between a backward attitude of fear and the forward-thinking optimism that could characterize a better future for American families. Both assume Lilienthal's "faith in knowledge," linking this corporate- and military-driven science with the beneficent gifts of the Almighty. The Manhattan Project is christened as a divine fait accompli.

Writer True Boardman, fresh from work on the screenplay for a Lassie movie (*The Painted Hills,* 1951), wrote the story for the animated short *A Is for Atom,* the John Sutherland–General Electric venture aimed at convincing viewers of the goods of atomic science.[58] In a calm, pedagogically patient tone, the film's narrator leads viewers through what might otherwise be the difficult science of atomic physics and the difficult argument over America's nuclear program. The fatherly voice teaches in an overtly soothing tenor, allaying without ever needing to address head-on the fear of immediate atomic peril. The implication throughout is one of benign providence. Only at the end is there an explicit summons to responsibility, and by that time there seems hardly rhetorical room for dissent. Given the promise, given the dream, and given the source of the knowledge, one would be an irrational alarmist indeed not to find in the technology hope for a better tomorrow for one's grandchildren.

---

57. James Keller, "Explaining the Christophers: By Way of Introduction," in *You Can Change the World! The Christopher Approach* (New York: Longmans, Green, 1948), p. viii.

58. Boardman went on to write for *Perry Mason, Bonanza,* and *My Three Sons.* Carl Urbano, who directed the animation, would eventually direct episodes of *The Jetsons.*

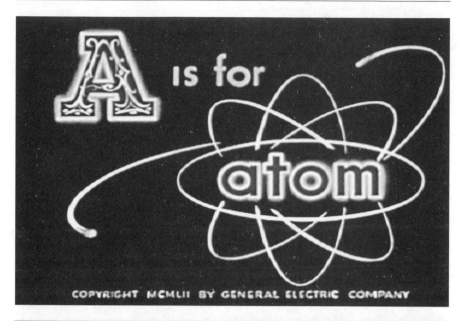

Figure 4.17. *A Is for Atom.* General Electric/John Sutherland Productions, 1953

The film begins with dramatic music quickly rising to a crescendo, but the narrator opens with a contrasting, matter-of-fact tone and a passive-voice appeal to providence: "The Atomic Age was born." After a pause, he continues, with apt emphasis: "There is no denying that since that moment, the shadow of the *atom bomb* has been across all our lives." As he summarizes the postwar decade in two sentences, a shadow spreads over a bomber's-eye view of town and field and then city, where the United Nations building comes into focus and the voiceover explains: "All men of goodwill earnestly hope that a realistic control of atomic weapons can and will be achieved. Meanwhile, good sense requires that all of us prepare for any eventuality." These words come as from elder citizen to less knowledgeable, younger citizens — creating a context of civil, gentlemanly agreement through the use of language such as "all our lives," "men of goodwill," and an appeal to "good sense" for "all of us."

Then the narrator gently takes the podium, explaining in a kindly tone that "wisdom demands *too* that we take time to *understand* this force, because here, *in fact*, is the answer to a dream as *old* as man himself." The dream? "A giant of limitless power, at man's command." Here, a stylized mushroom cloud morphs into an atomic giant, standing tall on the horizon, awaiting his command — a ghostly genie crossed with Mr. Clean (fig. 4.18). The narrator continues: "And where was it science found that giant? In the atom." The story takes an artfully whimsical turn at this point, as the narrator moves from facing the "in fact" to explaining the "tiny building blocks which make up everything in the world — ships and shoes and sealing wax [*pause*] and cabbages and kings." The animation smoothly shifts to focus on a sparkle on a pin in a red pincushion, moving on to a fanciful swirl of multicolored atomic structures, then a swirl of ships and shoes and sealing wax, and finally cabbages and self-important, red-robed cartoon kings.

The 1951 Disney production of *Alice in Wonderland* lends its nonsensical charm to the narration. The poetic reference to Lewis Carroll's "The Walrus and the Carpenter" (a section from *Through the Looking Glass*) sets a reassuring yet vaguely disorienting context for the rendition of atomic science. What seems menacing is wholesome. What seems complicated is simple. What seems like a military-corporate effort to capture your imagination is, well, a *very effective* military-corporate effort to capture your imagination.

The narrator explains that the "atom's binding force" is a kind of "cosmic glue," and as the Elmer's-like white stuff pours over the little circles marked positive and negative, the story shifts to appeal indirectly to the cosmic glue of postwar life — the peaceful household. The overall effort to domesticate the atom is given stylized clarity in the film's creation of "Element Town." Here,

**Figure 4.18.** *A Is for Atom.* General Electric/John Sutherland Productions, 1953

viewers are led by their beneficent narrator through the homes of the hydro-gen, oxygen, gold, and uranium families. Uranium appears with atom-headed wife and child. The child wears a sailor suit and holds a cherry-red lollipop. The ensuing explanation of radioactivity is brilliant. "Now, most atoms of most elements are content with their lot in life. We speak of them as being sta-ble." "But others," the narrator explains (with an intonation of "boys will be boys"), "are busy day and night, being what science calls radioactive." Here ra-dium dances frenetically to the wacky song on a phonograph, with tuxedo and cane. He jumps like a meteor from house to house until he "does become sta-ble, at last." With a "Home Sweet Home" cross-stitch framed above his bed, ra-dium turns out the light, pulls up the covers, and goes to sleep. The tune in the background is "Be it ever so humble, there's no place like home" (fig. 4.19). The "spontaneous changing of elements," or "natural transmutation," thus be-comes inherently controllable, and the narrator carries this meaning through into what follows: "Its discovery gave men of science an idea. If an atom could change itself, why couldn't man change an atom?"

    This kindly, curious, slightly amused "Why not try?" attitude (a ques-tion the narrator eventually asks explicitly) runs throughout the detailed de-scription of nuclear fission. This was "truly a discovery to change the world,"

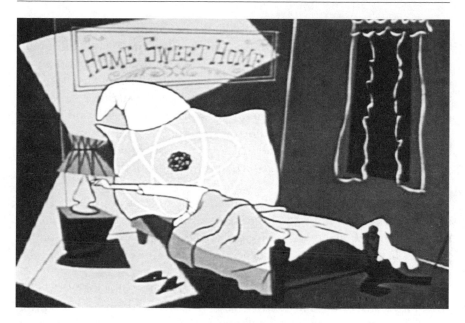

**Figure 4.19.** *A Is for Atom.* **General Electric/John Sutherland Productions, 1953**

a "double miracle of science." The same dramatic music with which the film began plays again, but in a major rather than minor key, and the "chain reaction" of "a million billion billion atoms exploding within two seconds" transmutes to the still green of a baseball field. "And the force? It would take Yankee stadium full of dynamite to equal the energy released in the complete fission of an amount of U-235 the size of a baseball."

Using the all-American pastime played on the field graced by Yogi Berra and Mickey Mantle, the narrator makes the birth of America's nuclear program seem downright homely in retrospect. What about the bomb? Well, given that "at the time the free world faced a war for survival," the narrator explains, with a patronizing tone, "it was little *wonder* the first thought was a weapon." By the conclusion of the film, however, the only reasonable interpretation is clear. Alternating between active and passive voice, the narrator tells a story of scientific ingenuity and inevitable progress. Various "all but impossible" projects proved "possible," and eventually "the superpower which man has released from within the atom's heart" became "not one, but many giants." Here the superpower-genie-giant-Mr. Clean is joined by five homologous giants — a "warrior," protecting homes with airplanes flying around his head; an "engineer," holding lines of electricity flowing down to the city; a "farmer," standing over a barren desert that morphs into a modern ranch-style house surrounded by green fields; a "healer," emerging from the hospital, medical shield in hand; and a "research worker," superimposed over a building clearly labeled "SCIENCE." The narrator explains the giants thus: "One is the warrior, the destroyer. Another is the engineer, seeking to provide vast quantities of energy to run the world's machines. Another is the farmer, helping to better feed tomorrow's world. Still another is the healer, helping to diagnose and cure the sick. And the last is the research worker, working on in the fields of *pure science*, to reveal more of the mysteries of the universe."

The conclusion simply states what has become obvious: "But all are within man's power, subject to his command." As the image of the atom becomes a spinning globe, we receive the verdict: "On man's wisdom, on his firmness in the use of that power, depends now the future of his children, and his children's children, in the New World of the Atomic Age."

Actor Paul Kelly's name appeared below that of a collie in *The Painted Hills*, the Lassie/cowboy movie written by True Boardman immediately prior to *A Is for Atom*. Two years later Kelly received top billing in the *Christopher Closeup* television series installment "Atomic Energy as a Force for Good" (fig. 4.20).[59] The episode is a masterful piece of religious propaganda set in the rugged Southwest, complete with Kelly again in cowboy hat and bolo tie. The film goes right to the center of the anti-atomic argument, directly countering the sentiment among some Roman Catholic leaders that the Manhattan Project had unleashed a force for human evil with which American Roman Catholics should not collude.

Kelly plays the trusted patriarch of a small town, a rancher named John Vernon, and the first half of the episode culminates in his speech against the AEC. Arguing that the people of the town should refuse the AEC's proposed plant because the moral cost would be quantitatively greater than the income accrued, Kelly eventually comes around, during the second half, to promote the goods of atomic science. Replete with rousing appeals to God, civic duty, and moral responsibility, the episode solidly sets the atomic project within the context of a truly *good* country.

Some background is crucial to understand the broader, religious context of this piece of cultural history. While the television series in which it was set has Roman Catholic roots, it fits well within the broader sweep of mainstream Protestant influence during the 1950s. The Christophers, or "Christ Bearers," movement had begun with Maryknoll Father James Keller's promise

---

59. Accessed 2002: www.archive.org.

**Figure 4.20. "Atomic Energy as a Force for Good," 1955**

to lay Catholics in America that they could "change the world!" In his book introducing the movement, entitled *You Can Change the World! The Christopher Approach,* Keller argued that the *responsible* Catholic in America would be engaged in mainstream culture: "Always striving to implant more firmly the fundamentals which others are trying to uproot, the Christopher emphasizes the normal rather than the abnormal."[60] His interpretation of "Christ's command" was to enter the public spheres of American society to shore up what the "perverse" Communists sought to undermine. His assumption about Catholic influence was quite in line with mainline Protestant arguments for daily discipleship in the halls of government and education. "Did you ever stop to think that the United States is being effectively undermined by less than *one percent* of the people of our country, of whom only a portion are Communists?" he asks in the very first sentence of the book.[61] Using their growing numbers as a contrasting sign of strength, Keller urges lay Catholics to count themselves among the "normal, decent citizens of America" willing

60. Keller, "Explaining the Christophers," p. viii.
61. Keller, "Explaining the Christophers," p. vii.

to "get into the mainstream of American life" and thus protect the country against "those with evil designs."

Under the supposed threat of infiltration by the Communist enemy, "the Christopher" should sow the good seeds of "divine truth and human integrity" in "the four influential spheres of activity which touch and sway the majority of the people: (1) education, (2) government, (3) labor-management, (4) writing (newspapers, magazines, books, radio, motion pictures, television)."[62] Father Keller was particularly adept with item 4, forming working relationships with Walt Disney, Bing Crosby, William Holden, and Bob Hope, and opening the Christophers television series in 1952 with an all-out tribute to American aspirations, called "You Can Change the World." Part of Keller's genius was weaving together patriotism, entertainment, and an accommodated version of Judeo-Christian faith. "Atomic Energy as a Force for Good" may today seem like a campy piece of Americana, but it served as an adept cinematic testimony to America's nuclear adventure. For our purposes, it goes further than the GE film, specifically naming atomic science as "one of the greatest blessings God has ever given us."

As with *A Is for Atom,* the story opens with a direct reference to the atom bomb. Driving his beautiful brunet daughter and his blonde, Shirley Temple–esque granddaughter home to his ranch, John Vernon comes upon a roadblock. A handsome, burly man tells them to wait in their car until allowed to move on, and explains: "You've got yourself a front seat to something you're not going to forget so quick. See that hill? You'll see it light up like you never saw light before. Any minute now they're going to test an atomic bomb."

Grandfather and daughter exchange startled looks. "Dad, let's turn back!" she urges.

The burly man replies, with a swagger, "Wouldn't get very far. Ought to go off any minute now." The message implied is hardly subtle — there is no turning back. The adults must face the present with steely resolve.

"But what about Vivian? She'll be terrified!" says the daughter.

The grandfather replies, with a sense of grim knowing, "It'll be just like *fireworks* for her. She doesn't know what it means. *We'll* be the ones who'll be frightened" (fig. 4.20b).

While *A Is for Atom* works by all but dismissing the menace of atomic weaponry, "Atomic Energy as a Force for Good" hits the argument for wariness head-on, and the countdown to the atomic blast goes on in excruciating detail. We see uniformed men adjusting knobs, speaking into radio transmit-

62. Keller, "Explaining the Christophers," p. viii.

**Figure 4.20b. Scene from "Atomic Energy as a Force for Good," 1955**

ters, peering at gauges, all in preparation for an atomic blast that erupts to ominous, surrealistic music. It is a scene of overt fear and destructive potential. While the girl with blonde curls watches from the back seat with bright-eyed curiosity, her mother and grandfather look on in horror.

The first half of the story maintains this perspective. John Vernon greets the visit of an AEC representative with a snarl: "The atomic bomb. Isn't there enough unhappiness in the world without that? And now they want to bring it here." The AEC wants to buy Vernon's ranch, and he is having none of it. Quite conspicuously in the background is Vernon's granddaughter, spending her last months with a brain tumor learning to ride a pony and enjoying the Southwest sunshine. This is the reason for the trip to see Grandfather. They had been in San Francisco, "hoping against hope that one day the doctors would come up with some miraculous cure"; now the mother has brought the little girl to the relatively remote desert town to find some happiness back at the ranch. This will lead, quite predictably, to the turning point of the story.

But before we learn that the AEC will produce just the medical miracle for which the mother has prayed, the various patriarchs of the town meet in the local general store to discuss the AEC's plans to take over the area. The shopkeeper/mayor, kindly doctor, and shrewd banker all give arguments for the public revenues, added medical facilities, and jobs that the project would bring. On the other side of the debate is the prototypical old coot, played by character actor Will H. Wright, and a World War II veteran, who seems at points to be on the verge of a nervous breakdown.

In farmer's hat and with taciturn scowl, the old coot insists, "I won't be goin' to sell! It's my *home*, Harry! It's where I was born and raised! It's where my *folks* settled when they came out here in covered wagons. And they looked *all* over before they picked *this* as the best spot." To the arguments that the plant might bring a better hospital and a decent water system, Wright's character retorts, "Looks like we got along without them so far!"

For his part, the veteran, face damp with perspiration, exclaims: "I was at *Hiroshima*, Doc, maybe eight or nine days after the bomb was dropped. I *saw* what was *left*. So they're going to make the atomic bomb here. Well, I'm selling my place and leaving town. I don't want any part of it."

After he storms out the door, the banker, mayor, and doctor exchange the requisite responses: "I can understand how he feels — after that kind of an experience, naturally he is afraid of the whole idea of the bomb"; and, "Let us be honest. We're all afraid. We're all terrified, and so are people all over the world"; and yet, "The fact of the matter is, the bomb is here. Now that it's been invented, we just can't stick our heads in the sand and pretend that it doesn't exist."

In the midst of this tangle of prudential and moral considerations, John Vernon sits listening, with cowboy hat respectfully in hand. The men now turn to him for his perspective, and Vernon gives the soliloquy that brings the first half of the episode to resolution:

> The bomb's been invented. There is nothing we can do about that. The point is, do we want it here? [*Pauses*] Harry says the plant will bring money into the town. That's fine, of course. We can all use a little more money. I know I can. [*With a wry smile at the others*] Farrell says it will give us new schools, and a hospital and so on. [*Countenance changes, and he continues with a somber tone*] But where will all this come from? From the atomic bomb. And the atomic bomb, no matter how thin you slice it, is simply a machine for killing people. [*Pauses*] My folks came here about the same time yours did, Tim. Maybe today it isn't as big a town as they'd dreamed it would be. Probably isn't as rich a town. All we did was grow our crops and raise our cattle. But at least we never tried to make any

money out of other people's unhappiness. [*Pauses*] Some of you are worrying that the town will change. I'm worrying about the people who live in this town. What sort of people we will be after we grow rich on the atomic bomb. With our schools and hospitals that we know one day will have to be paid for with other people's lives. [*Pauses*] That's the change I'm worrying about. I don't think it's worth it.

This speech convinces the other town leaders, and the town council votes to petition their representative in the U.S. Congress to refuse the AEC's proposal to build in their area.

The scene now shifts to Washington, where Congressman Maynard, concerned that his constituents do not know "the whole picture," recruits an atomic scientist, Professor Cullers, to help him educate the townspeople about the wide, beneficial uses of atomic energy. They arrange an immediate trip and call first on John Vernon, whom the congressman perceives as the driving force behind the resolution. Challenging the notion that atomic energy is "just the bomb," worthy of hatred, Professor Cullers explains:

That's mostly what you read about, I grant you that. It's mostly what it's been used for so far. That's the *tragedy* of nuclear energy. It had to begin at Hiroshima. No wonder the world is confused. Many of us are afraid. Mr. Vernon, think about primitive man thousands of years ago before he learned the use of fire. All fire meant to him was forest fire that might burn him to death; fire from volcanoes. He was afraid of it. He *hated* it. Naturally, he never thought that *fire* would become man's *servant* instead of his *master*. . . . In spite of Hiroshima, if we control [atomic energy] rightly, as fire has to be controlled rightly, it will be one of the greatest blessings we've ever received.

With a pointed appeal to reason and fairness, the congressman persuades Vernon that Cullers deserves a full hearing. The townspeople gather to hear him narrate a film, made in Washington, that will equip them with "all the facts." After demonstrating that "atomic energy [is] a force for good in industry and agriculture," the film goes on to show "a more dramatic use of this God-given force."

A young girl appears on-screen, one suffering from thyroid cancer, and the scientist tells the townspeople that "she has a chance" because of the radioactive iodine solution that will allow her doctors to pinpoint the location of her tumor. Going on, he explains that radiophosphorous is allowing doctors to detect "the exact location of brain tumors," leading to "revolutionary" surgical success in several cases "hitherto considered hopeless."

The film thus gives the local doctor an idea, and Vernon's daughter and granddaughter are soon flying off into the sunset to pursue this new hope, brought to them by the AEC. Vernon meets with the council to register his reversal on the issue: "Because of atomic research, there's a chance now for my granddaughter. What's even more important, there's a better chance for children like her in the future. That is, if we don't put obstacles in the way of atomic research."

This television special would be a decent piece of propaganda if it closed here. But it does not. It is a truly remarkable piece of propaganda because it revisits the moral question. Sure, there is new hope for Vernon's granddaughter, and future hope for children like her, but does this completely answer the townspeople's previous concerns about building the plant on their land? The last scene provides two shifts. The first is from a sense of wariness and even pessimism regarding the uses to which atomic science had been and likely would be put. The second shift is from the local authority of the town council to the wisdom of the congressman from Washington.

The troubled veteran again voices the word of pessimism. He and the old coot, the two previous skeptics, have the crucial exchange. Speaking first to the desperate grandfather, the veteran presses: "I understand how you feel, Mr. Vernon. But, as you say, we have to take the whole picture. Now is it worth it?"

Here the old coot, now dressed in bow tie rather than farmer's hat, speaks up: "As far as I'm concerned, that isn't the point. I voted against atomic energy because I thought it was the work of *the devil*. Now I know I was wrong. You see, *God* made the atom. I see that now. He made it *just as surely* as he made the *hills* and the *sea* and, and — and *life itself*. And God never made anything that was *of itself* evil."

The veteran, beginning to perspire, counters: "I can't argue that, Tim, but what about Hiroshima?"

The old coot shakes his head. "Oh, you can't blame the energy that God put in the atom for *that*," he says. "No, we've got *ourselves* to blame, *mankind*, for fighting wars and using what God has given us for — for *destruction*."

The veteran interrupts, now shouting: "Yes, but it happened! And maybe it'll happen again, and much worse next time! So is it worth it? [*Quieter, sweating, appearing to struggle for control*] Men being what they are, wouldn't it really have been better if this thing hadn't been invented?"

With this question, the second shift occurs. Which will it be, America? Perspiring pessimism or hopeful conversion? To whom will Americans turn in order to choose well the path forward? In his closing speech Congressman Maynard addresses the convened council, the watching townspeople — and television viewers across the country. It is worth quoting at length:

You know, I don't leave Washington every time a city council passes a resolution. But this is something about which every town in America has to think clearly. And, let's hope, every town in the world. Of course, you're right, Mr. Benson. The energy in the atom is the most destructive force the world has ever seen. But as Cullers has shown us, it can also be one of the greatest blessings God has ever given us. Which is it to be? Because on that depends the future of mankind.

Sure, we sometimes wish it hadn't been invented. We're afraid of the responsibility because the results will be so terrible if we misuse it. But it has been invented, and we have to take the responsibility. We can't just shut our eyes to it. You, Mr. Benson, you saw the destructive side in Hiroshima. And now all of you, with the hope that's been given to John Vernon, you've seen a little of the good it can bring, and its promise for the future of the world. That's how high the stakes are. For Good. Or for Evil. And that's the challenge you've accepted. To do your part in making atomic energy not a *curse*, but a *blessing* to mankind.

Of course, this is just one town, and there are only a few of us in this room. But all over America, and all over the whole world too [*here vaguely patriotic music begins to play in the background*], people must sooner or later face this *same* challenge, and I pray that they too make the right choice.

Oh, we've [*light chuckle*] — we've muddled and we've made mistakes. But this time God has entrusted us with a physical force bigger than we've ever had before. One that can destroy us, or can lead us on to new horizons. And with this choice before us, God willing, we shall not fail.

Carl Benton Reid, who plays Congressman Maynard, had recently played Clem Rogers, Will Rogers's father, in *The Story of Will Rogers*. He delivers this speech with a beautiful mix of gravitas and homespun optimism. By the end of the episode he has become the central interpreter of the future. Hiroshima and Nagasaki have become an instance of humans having "muddled" and "made mistakes." The moral task facing television viewers "in every town in America" has become a matter of sheer hope in their own capacity to move on to "new horizons." The episode begins with the atomic blast, and the voice of the veteran carries the memory of the "curse" of atomic weaponry. Perspiring, disheveled, virtually paralyzed by irrational fear, the veteran represents the past, the snail who will not be moved. Even the old coot is sufficiently nimble to keep up with the times, recognizing that he was wrong to think that the AEC was involved in the work of the devil. Viewers who were previously skeptical, even opposed, are to find themselves faced with a choice of perspective. On the one side is the war veteran, witness to the burned bodies and horrific, mass violence of atomic weaponry. On the other side is, well, "all of you," witnesses to "the hope that's been given to John Vernon." From this perspective the potential for life-saving medical therapies represents the more compelling choice "for the future of the world." Intertwined with this claim — that potential medical therapies hold "promise for the future of the world" — is the claim that Americans will effectively make the choice of Good over Evil by validating the Atomic Energy Commission's work. The initial scene, wherein it is apparent that the *primary* aim of the AEC is to develop atomic weaponry, is rhetorically eclipsed by the vision of little Vivian, once without hope and now with a future in the hands of medical researchers.

In the words of the now-converted old coot, "God made the atom," and the question evidently hanging in the balance is whether Americans will cower in sweaty fear with the veteran or step forward in faith. Here the providential, passive voice of *A Is for Atom* is made more explicit. The divine will and human "responsibility" virtually collapse. Recall that we began this chapter with Hermann Hagedorn's poem, which the *Intercollegian* ran adjacent to Popenoe's and Southard's odes to eugenics and planned parenthood. In 1948, it seemed apt to the editors to encourage among the YMCA/YWCA readers hope for the future, hope set firmly within the "power of the human soul." "More powerful than the atom," Hagedorn wrote — "It can control the atom, / The only thing in the world that can." Note that the editors ran this inspirational poem following an essay by a man who served as a key Protestant leader in the movement that resulted in the forced sterilization of tens of thousands of people in the United States. Confidence in the ability of *good* citizens to organize in order to secure *good* science is common in both the Progressive and the atomic eras. With the knowledge of the good that can be wrought from organized industry, government, and science, would Americans move past their fears of nuclear annihilation, forging forward into what AEC chairman Lilienthal named the "great adventure"? Only a "great people," with an almost unshakable faith in the "power of the human soul," would have the courage, or the hubris, to do so.

### "Yes, Atoms for Peace!"

Imagine a world in which there is no disease . . . where hunger is unknown . . . where food never rots and crops never spoil . . . where "dirt" is an old-fashioned word, and routine household tasks are just a matter of pressing a few buttons . . . a world where no one ever stokes a furnace or curses the smog, where the air everywhere is as fresh as on a mountaintop and the breeze from a factory as sweet as from a rose. . . . Imagine the world of the future . . . the world that nuclear energy can create for all of us.[63]

For Americans to accept the atom as a symbol of peace and abundance, there needed to be a bit of ironing, so to speak. The rhetoric had to be strong enough to smooth the wrinkles caused by the fear of nuclear annihilation. An advertisement for a new General Electric iron ran in the *Ladies' Home Journal (LHJ)* in August 1955 (fig. 4.21), espousing the difference that electric power could make in a woman's life. It was followed twenty pages later by an article making the case for atomic power. In addition to being a tireless champion for peace and international cooperation, Harold Stassen was chosen by President Eisenhower "to help the world end war." His name is on the piece telling readers how they might benefit from the atomic adventure.

The article brings together two themes of this chapter: the growth in consumption of domestic technology and the marketing of atomic science. This is the domesticated atom. To paraphrase the narrator of *A Is for Atom*, the Eisenhower administration attempted to persuade *LHJ* readers that here *in fact* was the answer to a dream as *old* as woman herself. The dream? A giant of limitless power, at woman's command. Radioisotopes become microscopic handymen in the piece, capable of tasks great and small. "The weird and wonderful things they do! They do grand tasks like fight cancer, destroy bacteria, make exact measurements, and odd jobs like helping to mix paint, check leaks and weldings, or grow larger peanuts and potatoes. And this is only the start." The essay promises that atomic science will be the engine forward into a better future for housewives everywhere. "From the odd-job list," the essay continues, "take a look at what [scientists] have done to improve one humble dishwasher." In this example, the text explains a research protocol that involved "atomic engineers" feeding radiophosphorous to hens, waiting for their eggs to emerge, cooking the eggs, washing the cooking implements in the dishwasher, then examining the implements, the water, and the appliance itself for traces of phosphorous. What a wonder! For "in this way, an exact knowledge of the effectiveness of the dishwasher was discovered."

This description, narrated in some detail, would have been satisfying to *LHJ* readers on at least two levels. First, atomic scientists were not involved in a project to destroy the planet. No, no, no. Scientists were involved in helping

---

63. Harold Stassen, "Atoms for Peace," *Ladies' Home Journal*, August 1955, pp. 48-49. Stassen was Special Assistant to the President on Disarmament.

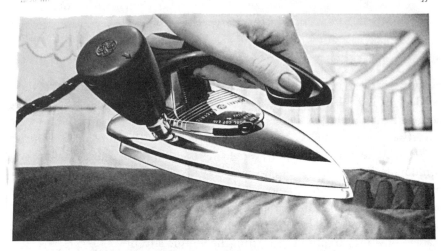

## New G-E Portable Steam Iron Weighs Only 1¾ Pounds...
## Does All Pressing Jobs Quickly, Easily!

Lightweight, <u>AC-DC</u> steam and automatic dry iron folds up for easy storage...costs only $14.95.*

**Never before** has there been an iron that weighs so little . . . and yet does such an efficient job!

Special ironing and pressing jobs like delicate ruffles . . . shirt sleeves . . . accordion pleats . . . can be done *in less time* with this new G-E!

No need to "bear down" to get out wrinkles. Heat and moisture, not weight, are what smooth out the most difficult wrinkles without effort. There's plenty of steam in this new portable to do a perfect job!

Without the bulb, it becomes a fine automatic dry iron. And it works on both AC and DC!

Keeping clothes always crisp and fresh looking is *easy* with the new G-E Portable Steam Iron.

General Electric Company, Small Appliance Division, Bridgeport 2, Connecticut.

*Manufacturer's recommended retail or Fair Trade price.*

*Progress Is Our Most Important Product*

## GENERAL ⒢ ELECTRIC

**OPEN HANDLE AND COMPACT DESIGN** let you do more jobs more easily. You save time and yet do a professional-looking job.

**SUCH A HELP IN SEWING** because it's the handiest of all irons for pressing seams, darts and tucks, steaming pleats, ironing out wrinkles as you go.

**IDEAL FOR TRAVELING** because it's so compact. Iron slips into its own carrying case. Takes up no more space than a pair of slippers.

Figure 4.21. Advertisement for General Electric iron. *Ladies' Home Journal*, August 1955

women make their homes more efficient and wholesome. The presumed "odd-job list" (or, as my mother called it, the "Honey-do list") lengthened daily for the white, middle-class women to whom *LHJ* appealed. The domestic magazine market encouraged its readers to form a running mental list of hoped-for items and fix-it-up tasks to make their kitchens, living rooms, and yards more like those advertised ubiquitously in *LHJ* and its competitors. This list was, according to the piece, precisely what the AEC also had on its mind, as the atomic engineers formulated new ways to perfect the household dishwasher.

Second, the mental vision of atomic scientists cooking eggs and washing dishes would have been satisfying on a whole different level. Here were men not afraid to become involved in the everyday work of cooking and washing — scientists who could *understand* their needs. Granted, the author admits, it is "not easy to switch over one's thinking on atomic energy." Most women, he explains, still think of the bomb when they hear the word "atomic." But "What a thrill it was when we in the National Security Council first began realizing that we were now strong enough to consider the possibilities of doing what everyone connected with atomic energy had so long wanted to do." Thus the necessity of this article. After all, "the women of America" will soon "come face to face with one or another of the wonders of this new age," and it will be crucial that they fully "understand" and "act intelligently" regarding the possibilities. Once adequately informed, they will come to understand "the reality of atomic energy and its very real, very great potential to ease drudgery and pain."

On the drudgery front, radioisotopes would help scientists produce "better tooth pastes," more efficient watch springs, and perfect household plumbing. The piece reports the story of "one lucky Texan" who serves as the prototypical "ordinary householder." When he moved into his "new, modern house," he discovered that his heating bills were exorbitant. Luckily, he was "scientifically shrewd" and "called in an expert in the handling of isotopes." The "expert" found the leak "without difficulty," saving the householder hundreds of dollars. From North Carolina tobacco to Long Island potatoes, the AEC was also intent on promoting "a whole program of direct radiation of seeds, plants and foods." The drudgery of work at home and on the farm would soon come to an end.

As for easing pain, the essay tells what feats radioisotopes will accomplish in "the world of medicine." The story illustrating the cooperation of the AEC with medical scientists is characteristic. Relating the case of "one seventeen-year-old boy," the essay says the malignant tumors in his lungs would have been virtually untreatable prior to the newly discovered efficacy of radioactive iodine. "Today his lungs are clear of all tumors, and he is a well boy."

Yet this is only part of the story. "Exciting as these steps are, too, they are only by-products of the major triumph of harnessing and controlling atomic energy to provide new power." The "revolution in power production" literally "defies the imagination," "to think about it all gets into the realm of the really fantastic." The possibilities! Here the AEC becomes almost a fount of every domestic-technological blessing. "You hear talk from electronic engineers about houses without any wiring, but with portable, cheap baby watchers, bedmakers, cordless irons, lamps and toasters, and light, thin, motorless TV sets, refrigerators and air conditioners."[64] The woman of tomorrow would have at her control "portable, cheap baby watchers" (just what did he mean here?) and "bedmakers" (ditto) — appliances large, small, and in between — all thanks to the AEC.

The essay anticipates the skeptical holdouts in two related ways. To doubtful interlocutors, the piece explains patiently: "Yes, these things are fantastic — and yet they are not. With low-cost, limitless power — and that's what atomic energy is potentially — all sorts of dreams can come true." This was a claim about which readers could hardly quibble. The audience was all too familiar with the growing array of electrical consumer goods. With the electrically powered mixers, irons, and hair dryers would also come higher electrical bills. The overall promise of technological ease, constituted by particular promises sold by the hundreds in each month's *Ladies' Home Journal*, would require advances in the production of technological power. If the American household was to become the epicenter of a better future, it would require "low-cost, limitless power."

And what about those "nervous" readers who maintained a sense of limitation, an instinctive "fear and dislike [of] industrial progress"? The piece gives them an ultimatum: If you are not *for* the overall work of the AEC, you might as well remove yourself from civilized society. Those Americans who retain a sense of wariness about the proposed technologically enhanced future should "try living in a primitive society without doctors, sewers, medicines and machinery of any but the most basic sort for about six weeks — and then see if they can still work up an argument against it."

It is with a recapitulation of this effective "So there" that the piece concludes, this time with direct reference to God's providence. Stassen, a lifelong Baptist, was a member of the Northern Baptist Convention and a vital participant in the National Council of Churches by the time he wrote this article.[65]

64. Stassen, "Atoms for Peace," p. 49.

65. "Biography of Harold E. Stassen," introductory notes to Harold Stassen Papers, Minnesota Historical Society. Accessed 2004: www.mnhs.org/library. The biography is helpful also for noting H. E. Stassen's extensive contributions to efforts for international peace and disarmament.

Perhaps the administration for whom Stassen worked assumed that many of those skeptical about the limitless power of atomic energy were Christian. They would unquestionably have known that the vast majority of *LHJ* readers were mainline Protestants.

The essay thus closes with a powerful appeal to divine providence. Readers learn of a conversation between two men. The first man held "a fundamental, unswerving belief in God" yet found it difficult to believe that "God had permitted the discovery of the atomic bomb." The second man, "who happened to be a scientist" and "no doubt had faced this problem himself," claimed that the "present sources of fuel" would eventually be depleted. Without atomic science, civilization would face not only a cessation of progress but a regression to a previous stage of existence. For "without fuel, dependent once again solely upon the energies of our hands and bodies, we would be threatened with a return to the primitive stages from which we developed." With the "discovery of nuclear energy" came the promise of "inexhaustible sources of power, thus once again assuring the progress of man." This providential promise of power, begotten through the Manhattan Project, would prevent a return to "dependent" existence.[66]

The man of faith questioned the wisdom of Providence, wondering at the destructive power of the atomic bomb. The man of science answered by resituating the AEC's originating project. The man of faith had been myopic, unable to see the grand narrative of the atomic adventure. The man of science could set Hiroshima and Nagasaki in proper perspective. Seen within the larger scope of human progress, the atomic bomb was merely a regrettably necessary step toward a world "in which there is no disease" and "where hunger is unknown." Those who thought otherwise should either get on board or go try their luck in a "primitive society." Providence is on the side of a particular kind of progress — technological progress involving comfortable consumer goods and limitless access to the power that fuels those goods. The domesticated atom requires a domesticated version of divine will as well — a God who may be serviceably interpreted within the confines of Lilienthal's atomic adventure and within the purview of the *Ladies' Home Journal* readership.

The use of the implied shame of "primitive" or uncivilized existence is crucial. The words of the day were "modern" and "advanced" and "improved." The *newer*, well-appointed homes were somehow also *homier*, more conducive to the flourishing of family life. Families without access to the new stuff were, by implication, not only backward but also less *wholesome*. This is

66. Stassen, "Atoms for Peace," p. 49.

a particularly masterful feature of the domesticity marketed in the fifteen years after World War II. Through modern technology, a consumer family could procure something akin to traditional notions of respectability. By embracing the *new revolution in domestic products,* a white, middle-class mother could more firmly establish her family as *civilized.*

In her brilliant book *A Consumers' Republic: The Politics of Mass Consumption in Postwar America,* historian Lizabeth Cohen discusses the photo essay "Family Status Must Improve," one characteristic commentary on consumption, from a *Life* issue of May 1947.[67] In the essay Ted and Jeanne Hemeke are shown with their children in a juxtaposition between old and new family life postwar. The text reveals the assumed connections between the responsibility to purchase consumer goods, broad economic growth, and *proper* domesticity. It was a civic duty — a *should* — to aspire to the "decency" standards represented by matching dishes and stationery: "The Twentieth Century Fund figured that to achieve a health and decency standard for everyone by 1960 each U.S. family should acquire, in addition to a pleasant roof over its head, a vacuum cleaner, washing machine, stove, electric iron, refrigerator, telephone, electric toaster and such miscellaneous household supplies as matching dishes, silverware, cooking utensils, tools, cleaning materials, stationery and postage stamps."[68]

The piece appeared as part of a longer essay entitled "The Price Problem," discussing the results of a report by the "highly respected Twentieth Century Fund," endowed — no big surprise here — by Edward A. Filene, head of William Filene's Sons (the pioneering Boston retailer).[69] The Hemekes are presented as a pictorial lesson in economically responsible domesticity. The "what *is*" and "what *should be*" pictures serve to accentuate the aesthetics of properly ordered and appointed family life.

On *one* side Ted Hemeke arrives home from work in well-worn clothing that bespeaks his working-class status, with the child at his side in shorts, a wrinkled shirt, and shoes with no socks (fig. 4.22). His wife stands at the doorway of their frankly "drab" home, a child in her arms; the other child sits

---

67. Lizabeth Cohen, *A Consumers' Republic: The Politics of Mass Consumption in Postwar America* (New York: Vintage, 2004), pp. 112-13, discussing "Family Status Must Improve: It Should Buy More for Itself to Better the Living of Others," *Life,* May 5, 1947, pp. 32-33.

68. "Family Status Must Improve," p. 33.

69. "U.S. Tackles the Price Problem," *Life,* May 5, 1947, pp. 27-33. Regarding Filene, Cohen recommends an unpublished paper by Meg Jacobs, "Edward Filene, the Twentieth Century Fund, and the New Science of Consumption: From Bargain Basement to Bargaining Table" (paper presented at colloquium, New York University, June 7, 1996); see Cohen, *A Consumers' Republic,* pp. 422-23 n. 81.

listlessly nearby on what appears to be a large log. The yard is unkempt, the pathway to the door strewn with sticks and dry, wayward grass. The other picture (fig. 4.24) shows Jeanne bending to shovel ashes from a "dirty" furnace. A child sits on the floor sucking her thumb as a shaggy dog and two kittens romp in the dusty mess.

On the *other* side, Ted arrives home in a business suit, holding the hand of a child with a knit hat, fashionable swing coat, and shiny shoes, with socks (fig. 4.23). The yard is manicured, the home clearly a modern, suburban ranch house. His wife stands at the door, the child in her arms now in puff-sleeved dress; the other cheerfully pedals a trike. In the interior photograph, Jeanne is no longer bent but dressed in flowered frock, nylons, and shiny high heels, using an electric mixer in a bright kitchen, which is all decked out with the latest appliances (fig. 4.25). The baby of the family sits in a high chair sucking on a clean plastic toy. Her bottle of milk awaits her on the tray.

As Cohen explains, the piece served as part of a federal and corporate effort to convince Americans that "mass consumption in postwar America would not be a personal indulgence, but rather a civic responsibility designed to provide 'full employment and improved living standards for the rest of the nation.'"[70] There is much to interrogate in the economics behind what Cohen terms "the consumers' republic." Even the explicit expectation that middle-class buying would lift all Americans into the realm of domestic consumerism proved to be illusive. But it is important also to note another assumption in the *Life* piece (and in many of the other sources cited by Cohen). The expectation that middle-class buying would *lift* previously *sub*standard families into a more *respectable* and *wholesome* existence underlay much of the thinking in formal and popular economics in the postwar period. The *Life* piece concludes: "But aside from gadgets there is a more promising aspect for American life. It is in the order, charm and added leisure that such surroundings and such conveniences should inspire and facilitate in our whole mode of living by 1960."[71]

The Hemekes' existence in a "drab" house with a "dirty" furnace represented a *problem* for the projected progress of modern existence in much the same way that the "backwoods Japanese" represented a *problem* in the *National Geographic* article discussed above. From their relatively dark abode, to their clothing, to their posture, these people represented the *atavistic*. They were insufficiently evolved, appearing on the wrong side of the divide of progress.

70. Cohen, *A Consumers' Republic*, p. 113.
71. "Family Status Must Improve," p. 33.

Figure 4.22. *Life*, May 5, 1947

Figure 4.23. *Life*, May 5, 1947

**Figure 4.24.** *Life*, May 5, 1947

**Figure 4.25.** *Life*, May 5, 1947

**Figure 4.26.** *Our Friend the Atom*, 1956

The coal and oil resources of our planet are dwindling, yet we need more and more power. The atomic Genie offers us an almost endless source of energy. For the growth of our civilization, therefore, our first wish shall be for: POWER![72]

To be up to the task of progress, Americans would need not only to pursue consumer goods but also to convey to their children the promise of technology. In his *Ladies' Home Journal* piece, Stassen advocated atomic education for public school children, praising the states that had already implemented programs to introduce the peaceful promises of atomic science. One effort aimed at schoolchildren across the country was a book and film produced by Walt Disney, the film in conjunction with the United States Navy

72. Heinz Haber, *The Walt Disney Story of Our Friend the Atom* (New York: Simon and Schuster, 1956), p. 137.

and General Dynamics and the book with Simon and Schuster. Both drew upon the expertise of Heinz Haber, a German physicist who had served under Adolf Hitler and later became chief science consultant at Disney Studios.[73] Haber also helped narrate the film, which aired as a "Tomorrowland" segment on the Disneyland television show.[74] Both productions worked as multicolored advertisements for the AEC and Disneyland itself, which, at least in Tomorrowland, was conceived as one big paean to the goods of corporate and military technology. The children of tomorrow would be told a story, setting the atomic adventure within the hope for a better, more efficient, comfortable, and entertaining tomorrow.

In his foreword to the book, Walt himself suggests that "Fiction often has a strange way of becoming fact." Referring to the "magical force" that propelled the submarine in *20,000 Leagues under the Sea*, Disney suggests that a "tale has come true."[75] That dreamed-of "magical force" has come through our friend the atom. "The atom is our future," Disney explains, "so important" that Walt Disney Studios had "embarked on several *atomic projects*." Within the Hall of Science in Tomorrowland would be an entire exhibit on the promises of atomic energy. The three-pronged educational effort — book, film, and exhibit — was to combine the best of science (hence Heinz Haber) and the best of Walt Disney storytelling. "Of course, we don't pretend to be scientists — we are story tellers. But we combine the tools of our trade with the knowledge of experts." Thus, "the story of the atom" becomes "a fascinating tale of human quest for knowledge, a story of scientific adventure and success." The "fruits" born of that adventure were the "work of many inspired men," a "kind of chain reaction" that began as a "positive, creative thought." Those "inspired men" who started the atomic adventure "created modern science with its many benefits to mankind." Therefore, Disney's book "tries to make it clear to you that we can indeed look upon the atom as our friend."[76]

The fiction that is to become a reality in *Our Friend the Atom* is quite similar to the ones told in Lilienthal's 1947 *Collier's* essay, in Stassen's 1955 promise to the housewives of America, and in the two films from General

---

73. Haber, *Our Friend the Atom*, p. 137.

74. Regarding Heinz Haber's participation in Nazi science, see Karl Heinz Roth, "Flying Bodies — Enforcing States: German Aviation Medical Research, 1920-1970, and the DFG" (presented at symposium "Man, Medicine and the State: The Human Body as an Object of Government Sponsored Research, 1920-1970," October 10, 2003). Regarding the film and book, see Mark Langer, "Disney's Atomic Fleet," *Animation World Magazine*, April 1, 1998, available online at http://mag.awn.com/?article_no=537.

75. Walt Disney, foreword to *Our Friend the Atom*, by Heinz Haber, p. 10.

76. Disney, foreword to *Our Friend the Atom*, p. 11, emphasis in original.

Electric and the Christophers. Although "the story of the military atom" is well known, "the story is not yet finished." The call to good children, would-be citizens, is to "give the story a happy ending." By understanding properly the hope of the atom, the next generation could "make a hero out of a villain." With this "simple moral," Haber encourages his young readers to consider the *Arabian Nights* story "The Fisherman and the Genie" (fig. 4.26).[77] "We ourselves are like that fisherman," able to realize the "age-old wish of man to be the master of a mighty servant that does his bidding." Using the same "what would happen if . . ." tone as General Electric in the narration of *A Is for Atom,* Haber explains: "Like the fisherman, man marveled at his strange find and examined it closely for its value. He pried it open — split it in two."[78]

This is quite brilliant, rhetorically, in that the scientists working on the first atomic weapons become like the surprised fisherman. The atom's energy, at the beginning of the narrative, has a "force of nature" quality — beyond our control and machinations. It is, to paraphrase the old coot in "Atomic Energy as a Force for Good," something simply in *nature* that *God* made, as full of potential for good as "the hills and the sea and . . . life itself!"

Yet at the end of the narrative we see a shift, making clear that this force of nature is capable of doing man's "bidding." Thus, chapter titles such as "Atoms Everywhere," "Atoms at Work," and — especially — "The Atom Splits," with the atom itself as the subject-agent, work well to suggest that the atomic adventure started with an inevitable discovery in creation. The final three chapters, on the "three wishes" of "Power," "Food and Health," and "Peace," present the genie at man's command. The narration of the story is serviceable: "When these scientists created their theories and made their discoveries, they perhaps hardly foresaw that there would ever be widespread application of their work. *They simply marveled at the world around them and deeply desired to know about Nature and her ways.*"[79] Simply by studying "Nature and her ways," those who "marveled" made possible not only the atomic bomb but also a force to "grant the gifts of modern technology to even the most remote areas." As the story closes, its young readers are to foresee a future in which atomic science will "give more food, better health — the many benefits of science — to everyone."[80] The last illustration of the book makes this point in pyrotechnic form. The city of tomorrow floats amid a multi-colored whirl of microscopic structures.

77. Haber, *Our Friend the Atom,* p. 13.
78. Haber, *Our Friend the Atom,* p. 20.
79. Haber, *Our Friend the Atom,* p. 160, emphasis added.
80. Haber, *Our Friend the Atom,* p. 160.

This city set upon the hill of human creation, a new heaven created on a new earth, was often given explicitly postmillennial, Christian narration. By one reading of the Atoms for Peace campaign, the era revolved around inspired human choice: choice for life abundant or choice for life lived in an "economy of scarcity," as William L. Laurence puts it in his 1958 essay for *Together*, "Yes, Atoms for Peace!"[81] In "Atomic Energy as a Force for Good," Congressman Maynard named "this choice before us," with the confident prayer, "God willing, we shall not fail." These intertwined emphases of human choice, divine providence, and a radical new, scientifically discovered source of plenty seem consistent throughout the Atoms for Peace materials. As Laurence writes for Methodist families in *Together*, "man" was about to emerge from a "world of nightmares" and enter a world wherein "peace, prosperity" would be "made to order by his own creative efforts."[82]

Through the "vast power of the atom," man would be able to transform "the world's great wastelands" into sources of myriad gain. All sources of suffering and conflict — from water and food shortages to cancer to infectious diseases to the common cold — would be rectified through the initiative of man, through "the creative forces inside of him." (Not incidentally, in an inset to the piece, Laurence hails the future use of atomic blasts to expand oil drilling in Alaska.)

Crucial to this transformation was the triumph of "the spirit of man," a spirit that "is always trying to rise toward a heaven of its own conception." Put succinctly in this Methodist magazine piece is precisely this key point. With Atoms for Peace, man himself (gender specificity in the original) would create a new heaven on a new earth: "We shall have a world in which *science will have forced man everywhere to accept the concept of freedom. And that is the greatest contribution that science will make.*" With the "practically unlimited source of energy" released in the atom, poverty would be eliminated, and thus war would be no more.[83]

The eschatological claim of the essay — the claim about the time present and the time to come — was that the United States during the Atomic Age represented the creation of *abundance* itself: "In this, the 16th year of the Atomic Age, mankind stands on the threshold of the greatest industrial, social, and economic revolution in the million years of his existence on this earth. . . . From a civilization limited and controlled by an economy of scarcity, man is about to enter into a civilization built on plenty." The rhetorical

---

81. William L. Laurence, "Yes, Atoms for Peace!" *Together*, October 1958, pp. 12-14.
82. Laurence, "Yes! Atoms for Peace," p. 12.
83. Laurence, "Yes! Atoms for Peace," p. 13, emphasis added.

power of this claim is palpable. Americans might mistake the limitlessness of atomic power as precisely its danger. Being a force beyond reckoning might render it, in the civic imagination, a source of incalculable menace. But here, in the premier Methodist periodical, a "two-time Pulitzer Prize winner" and "*New York Times* science editor" reassures mainline Protestants that it is precisely the unquantifiable aspect of atomic power that makes it a source of boundless promise.[84] Tomorrow would see "a world in which the forces of good must triumph over the forces of evil."[85]

An icon is an icon inasmuch as it beckons the reader's eye beyond the image itself, to see the glory of God, the author of goodness. Here in *Together,* the atom is depicted as a kind of icon. Readers are presented with atomic science as the source of abundance, goodness, and life without poverty or suffering. Beyond the atom is the promise of an eschaton. What might have otherwise been perceived as a symbol of death and destruction becomes an icon of hope and new life. What might have been otherwise perceived as a symbol of a war in which scarcity and struggle were the ruling assumptions, becomes an icon of abundance and peace. In what the Methodist editors note was a "science-minded age," even the storytellers at Disney could not have told a better story.

### "Let's Look Ahead 20 Years . . ."

Science has wonderful things in store for us. . . . The tireless electron runs refrigerator, washing machine, kitchen gadgets — even guards the house like a faithful watchdog. . . . In the America of 1977, products of the electronic-atomic age will pour in a steady stream from assembly lines run by machines which think, take notes of what they are doing, and correct what they do wrong. . . . Life 20 years from now will revolve, as it always has, around the home and the family. The instinct to build a home and rear a family will be unchanged.[86]

Hope in the Atomic Age and mainstream domesticity converges explicitly with Protestant progress in a feature essay from the fourth issue of *Together.* The two-page essay "How We'll Live in '77" is framed by large color-toned drawings depicting the world toward which postwar Americans were progressing (fig. 4.27). On the left side is a towering cityscape, skyscrapers ris-

84. Laurence's credentials run along the top of the essay's opening pages as a highlighted editor's note, "Chronicler of the Atomic Age," pp. 12-13.

85. Laurence, "Yes, Atoms for Peace!" p. 14.

86. From Leo Cherne, "How We'll Live in '77," *Together,* January 1957, pp. 20-23.

**Figure 4.27.
Detail from
"How We'll
Live in '77."**
*Together,* January 1957

ing into a starry night encircled by superhighways and adjoined with a domestic scene of a glass-domed house. A helicopter whirling between the city center and the suburb indicates the new means of commuting between the two. The suburban yard, not shown in the panel, is kept tidy with an efficient robot disk that cuts the grass. Father sits with a newspaper on a lawn chair. Mother (having not yet been replaced by a machine) approaches with a tray of snacks. Junior runs out to join the two on the smooth lawn.

The illustrations on the right side of the feature portray some of the particular advances likely for the Methodists of the future. At the center of the fourfold sequence is a large, white male hand, with index finger extending upward and outward to press the uppermost of three toggle buttons. At the top of the collage, three jet planes soar upward in formation, tracing three white lines through a starry sky. The large profile of a fourth airplane moves into view. Between the white finger and the night sky is an image of a sleeping child. The mother views the image of her blonde child on a video screen. In a crisp shirtdress with cinched waist, the mother looks toward the screen with a blissful smile, her hand adjusting the image with a dial. Below the male hand's index finger is a scene of a male visitor (presumably, the author) arriving on the suburban lawn. In this scene, the father rises from his lawn chair to greet the guest.

With these four images, each aligned above the other, the artist has layered the symbolism. If one moves directly up the middle of the collage, the vertical line bisects the father on his lawn, the tip of the male index finger pressing the button, the mother's small hand adjusting the child's screen, and, at the top, the technology-filled night sky. Moving upward from the man of industry resting on his Sabbath, to his finger pressed on the pulse of an electronic future, to his beloved wife and child, upward into the stars, the sky is apparently the limit. Yet the home is still the center (albeit reconfigured by the relationship of mother to video screen). The illustration is stylistically streamlined, and the only two faces that appear in detail are those of the mother and her child. Their size relative to the master-hand is quite small. The mother's entire figure is roughly the same length as the male hand's index finger. Yet their drawn particularity — with the child's sweet, sleeping eyes beneath twinkling stars and the mother's relaxed smile and pert nose — accentuates to the viewer the reassuring import of Leo Cherne's *Together* essay: "Science has wonderful things in store for us," and "the instinct to build a home and rear a family will be unchanged."

This *Together* essay serves well to answer the "still, small voice" of the 1956 Ad Council poster we encountered in chapter 1, the voice that asks the nuclear family: "Where do I fit into the Atomic Age?" The nuclear family in the *Together* essay is portrayed as the direct beneficiary of all that is in store. The text conveys this in detail, beginning with a congenial invitation to the reader: "Let's look ahead 20 years — at the America of 1977 . . . and let's think of the day of our visit as sunny and the sky as blue."

On this sunny day in the future, today's "youngster" next door will be a father himself, reading the paper on his lawn, rising to greet guests, extending his index finger to activate the home of the future. To enter the home twenty years hence is to encounter a myriad of hygienic improvements — "spic and span, amazingly efficient and convenient, full of electronic marvels." Here is a home wherein all those little "Lessons in Spiritual Efficiency" (to reference a regular feature in *Together*) have yielded a future of amazing convenience and cleanliness. The time traveler will experience these changes smoothly, without jarring shifts.

This is the tomorrow toward which today naturally inclines. The lights in the living room are "shadowless," casting a "soft" glow that complements the "rich and warm" colors on the "picture-thin" television screen. The program under way "in full color" in the living room need not be interrupted. Mother merely "pushes a button beside a small television screen" and is able to see "the face of a sleeping child." The description of this device follows the reassurance arguably at issue in the entire piece. The little one sleeping beneath the starry sky is safe; the "tireless electron" is acting as a "faithful watchdog." The early Cold War symbolism here is intertwined with that of an older war — the one against germs: "Dust and extremes of temperature are banished — even germs practically eliminated by sterilizing rays." The work of the "tireless electron" is even responsible for a perfect meal: "Foods purchased months before have been sterilized by atomic radiation and will keep indefinitely without refrigeration." With the "fabulous energy released by atomic fission," the family of tomorrow will inhabit a domicile free of extremes, germs, toil, and interruption.

There is no structure marked obviously as a house of worship in the large, framing montage. There is no cross, however futuristic, sitting atop a building in the city center. There is no Christian imagery of any kind hidden in the crevices of the illustrations for "How We'll Live in '77." Yet, just as the text is careful to point out that, in spite of sterilizing radiation, future homes will still need refrigerators, the author suggests that, in spite of being "surrounded by comfort and convenience," "man . . . will remain troubled within," seeking "divine help more than he has since the Industrial Revolution began." The author even predicts the coming of a "great religious revival."

This tension between the essay's prediction of a "technological Garden of Eden" and the ostensible reason for *Together*'s being is also at play in a sidebar essay. The illustration highlighting "Homecoming 1977: A Family Forecast" is drawn in a different style, with a sketch of a burgeoning city on the horizon.[87] In the foreground is a large church spire, pointing heavenward.

87. Herman B. Teeter, "Homecoming 1977: A Family Forecast," *Together*, January 1957, p. 22.

Between the distant city and the church are a long, sleek monorail and an adjacent "superhighway," both bisected by the spire. The vertical image of the spire contrasts with the streamlined, horizontal movement of train and "groundcars."

The sidebar itself is a short vignette about a Reverend Paul Smith and his family, who are moving along the superhighway, taking in the vista of the future as they travel back to Pastor Smith's boyhood church. The words "sleek," "new," and "super-fab" set a tone of futuristic wonder, contrasting with the now apparently outdated bad colds (eliminated by "anti-tabs") and "old-fashioned hamburgers" (rendered obsolete by "vita-burgers"). To Pastor Smith, "The world of 1957 seemed far away," perhaps long since left behind by the "slim, rocket shape" monorail, a vehicle whose 150 mile per hour speed makes their 90 mile per hour "radar-controlled groundcar" seem slow. It is this sense of obsolescence that the story is apparently to address, with the spire remaining at the center and the pastor's household still intent on a "homecoming." Yet the same progress that has eliminated the "slums" in favor of a "green, sunny, antiseptic" vista with "smokeless buildings of glass and steel" has also made Pastor Smith's home church seem "not new and pretty," to quote little Bobby Smith. The First Methodist Church built only twenty years prior (in the reader's present) appears to the children to be thoroughly outdated in its climbing ivy and red brick. The story closes as Pastor Smith and his wife chuckle at Bobby's request to eschew the family car for the ride home after their visit. Bobby plans to take the monorail.

Leo Cherne ends his essay on life in 1977 with a reassurance of sorts. Churches will not become obsolete: "For man will return to religion as he discovers he cannot explain life without it. Men and women of 1977 will not find real happiness in the technological wonders around them. They must seek it elsewhere." The monorail, picture-thin television screen, helicopter, robot lawn mower, and such will not replace the church, with its spire reaching heavenward. Yet something rings quite hollow in this reassurance, and not only because life twenty-five years past 1977 suggests otherwise. The thrust of the featured future is toward life described as "spic and span," "amazingly efficient and convenient." The cumulative momentum of *Together*'s photography and advice is toward a form of domesticity that will eventually banish suffering, inconvenience, even dirt itself. Using Cherne's own language, the telos toward which *Together* often seems to tend is indeed a "technological Garden of Eden." Family life on the covers of the *Midmonth Magazine for Methodist Families* is presented as seamless and portrait-ready. The home toward which the present naturally inclines is thus a home ready at the press of a button — a domicile purged of the extraneous difficulties of life. This is not at all to suggest that *To-*

*gether* was uniformly, monolithically dedicated to technological progress in America. It offered its readers other ideas and themes as well. But there is a significant gulf between the sort of life portrayed as normative — portrayed as approaching "real happiness" — and life portrayed as merely, well . . . life.

Two years after *Together* ran its prediction, Walt Disney began collaboration with General Electric to create Progressland, a state-of-the-technological-art exhibit for the New York World's Fair of 1964-65. The "space age" themes for the fair were "Man in a Shrinking Globe in an Expanding Universe," "Peace through Understanding," and "A Millennium of Progress," among others. General Electric and Walt Disney were significant sponsors for the fair as a whole, but Progressland was the pinnacle of their participation, inviting viewers quite literally to enter the world of the future, a world made possible by the limitless resources of nuclear power.

The image of a family entering Progressland (fig. 4.28) is taken from a commemorative brochure on Progressland, produced by Disney Studios.[88] The family life of tomorrow would be entertained and enhanced through the marvels of domestic technology, appliances, and such brought to them by General Electric, fueled by the nation's projected reliance on a previously unfathomable source of immeasurable power. The central exhibit in the pavilion of Progressland, the heart of "progress" itself, was the virtual nuclear reactor, from which would emerge periodically a brilliant light show. The brochure called this the "climax" of the exhibit, and the term seems quite apt. Disney and General Electric produced for fairgoers a full-blown technological utopia — a powerful summons to a Technicolor life, realized through the collaboration of what GE called "pure science" and industry.

The projection of a more wholesome, happier, nuclear family was unquestionably a crucial piece of this narrative. If the center of progress was nuclear power, the central recipients of that progress were the normatively beautiful and configured families who could afford to attend the fair. The pictures situate the new, leaner, modern family as the focus of the viewer's eye. The father, in business suit, beckons his fashionably dressed wife forward. Their two children enter the world of tomorrow, thanks to Mr. Disney.

Consider one of the images from the brochure, of a young couple looking down at the nuclear reactor as the imagined midpoint for concentric circles of reference, the outermost ring being the limitless universe, which was welcoming the "space age." An intermediate circle is the globe itself, the image

---

88. Image from *Progressland Commemorative Brochure*, Walt Disney Company. Thanks to Bill Young, Webmaster. Accessed 2004: www.nywf64.com. See also Steven Watts, *The Magic Kingdom: Walt Disney and the American Way of Life* (Boston: Houghton Mifflin, 1997).

**Figure 4.28. Cover of Progressland brochure. General Electric and Walt Disney, New York World's Fair, 1964-65**

of the world's people united through the promise of scientific understanding. The center of the circle — the nuclear couple empowered for their newly enhanced domestic life by the nuclear reactor — makes a difference for the ways the fairgoing public would perceive the nation, the globe, and the beckoning universe. The resulting renarration of the role of the United States in the world is quite effective. No longer is the United States the nation that brought the atomic menace to the world stage, threatening to obliterate humanity from the planet. The United States is instead responsible for bringing unfettered atomic progress to every continent on the globe, allowing universal, even limitless possibilities for domestic happiness.

Many of the New York World's Fair materials featured the Unisphere, a large steel globe encircled by rings that make up the atomic icon (fig. 4.29). The rings serve many purposes. They may represent aspirations in space — as orbits of imagined space vehicles — as well as the promise of atomic peace enabled by universal, technological prosperity. Later resituated at Disneyland, the Progressland exhibit became the Carousel of Progress. Its theme song, by Disney songwriters Richard M. and Robert B. Sherman, lent a jaunty, *Mary Poppins* air to the hope awaiting the Disney target audience:

> There's a great big beautiful tomorrow
> shining at the end of every day.
> There's a great big beautiful tomorrow,
> and tomorrow's just a dream away.[89]

Those families that stepped inside the carousel of technological progress were merely a dream away from bliss. With the proper *story*teller, the sky was the limit. With that, let's look ahead twenty years . . . to the great big beautiful tomorrow of today.

## The Genomic Revolution

An image of a genetic unisphere greets visitors at the Health Adventure, a delightful children's museum in Asheville, North Carolina (fig. 4.30).[90] The

---

89. "There's a Great Big Beautiful Tomorrow," words and music by Richard M. Sherman and Robert B. Sherman (Wonderland Music, 1963).

90. Figure 4.30 is from a mural by artist Jim Stewart at the Health Adventure Museum, Asheville, North Carolina. Information courtesy of Jim Taylor, the museum's director of programming. Copyright 2007 by The Health Adventure, Asheville, North Carolina. Used by the kind permission of The Health Adventure.

**Figure 4.29. Unisphere Postcard, 1964-1965**

children and parents who climb the stairs to the second floor of exhibits see a mural that spans three walls and lays out the biotechnological aspirations of North Carolina. Front and center is the image of the earth itself, wrapped in the double helix. All the world's peoples, from all inhabited continents, are bound up together with the double helix structure. To the left of the helixed globe is a collage of animals — wolf, squirrel, and frog — representing, presumably, the nonhuman animal world. To the right, running along the lower part of the mural, are more animals, along with sketches of people sitting and playing in the outdoors.

The dominant images in the collage are, to the right of the globe, a couple with a baby carriage, looking somewhat amused. Around and above them are various characters: what seems to be a clergywoman (or perhaps a teacher) reading to a child; a man with a hard hat and architectural plans; and a man in a business suit. The buildings rise above these characters, with a residential area above the smiling couple and carriage, and a much larger industrial complex above the three vocational characters. The artist captures well the mix that characterizes much of western North Carolina — a love of the outdoors, the influx of new parents and new housing, and the growth of "New South" industry.

While a child would likely focus on his or her favorite animal running along at child's-eye level, the combination of images, when considered to-

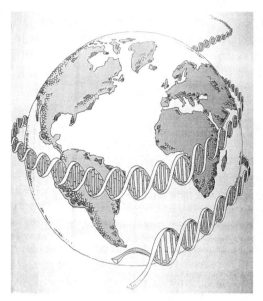

**Figure 4.30. Health Adventure Museum, Asheville, North Carolina**

gether, seems to convey a particular perspective on the future. With the double-helixed globe as its center, the depiction suggests the larger implications of a specific industry, that of genetic biotechnology. While the globe might have been surrounded by healthy vegetables and fruits, it is surrounded by a ribbon of the double helix structure. The museum is focused on health, and the growth industry rising above the right-hand side of the mural may arguably be read to represent one of the many new centers of biotechnology in North Carolina.

The Health Adventure Museum features an admirable (and entertaining) mix of well-crafted exhibits to convey health advice to children and their families. Children learn about shopping for a broad range of food groups, drinking plenty of water, avoiding foods that contribute to clogged arteries, and using their seat belts. My own children have enjoyed hours upon hours at the museum, and I have quite happily exposed them to the messages conveyed by its exhibits.

But the mural itself cues museum visitors that the future contribution of North Carolina to the wider world is focused around medical — in particular, *genetic* — technology. The globe is wrapped in the current icon of scientific progress. The man of industry who tops off the vocational characters is notably in a suit, not a hard hat or, what would have been more likely in the past, a farmer's hat. The relation of North Carolina's past with North

363

Carolina's future is accentuated by one other contrast. Across a small bridge, tucked way off, literally in the corner, is a farmhouse. It is not an afterthought but quite clearly, particularly, *situated* across a bridge, set perilously on a cliff, notably below the industrial complex. It is barely visible from the stairway. To give some sense of the scale, the entire farmhouse is smaller than the businessman's attaché case. The farm functions in a slightly less overt way than does the dying Southwest running below Lilienthal's remarks in *Collier's* on the atomic adventure. Recall that the artist for that piece accentuated the contrast between a dying Southwest and one that is rejuvenated through atomic technology. The message here is more subtle, but it seems to serve a similar purpose. The farm is the North Carolina of the past, separated by a barely bridgeable gap. The *future* of the region is in genomics.

This is just one of many ways the promise of genomics infiltrates the popular, museumgoing imagination in the United States. To paraphrase Congressman Maynard, from "Atomic Energy as a Force for Good": "Of course, Asheville, North Carolina, is just one town, and relatively few families of the world pass through the stairwell of the Health Adventure. But all over America, and all over the whole world too, people must face the challenge of interpreting the genomic revolution." The patterns of rhetorical persuasion in much of the material presented to the public resemble those of the era of atomic promise.

The "Genomic Revolution" is the title of one multimillion-dollar exhibit of the American Museum of Natural History in New York. Financed through federal, state, local, and pharmaceutical sources, the exhibit went on international tour, appearing first in the epicenter of the biotechnological New South, a region known as the Triangle. Visitors to the North Carolina Museum of Natural Sciences in Raleigh could, for a small fee, introduce their children to the future — a future in which "A Midlife Crisis Will Start at 75" and "Suddenly, the Question 'Are You a Man or a Mouse?' Actually Requires Some Thought." This is how two posters announced the exhibit, the first featuring a hipster, gray-haired couple in black leather, with the woman in the driver's seat, riding through the desert Southwest on what appears to be a Harley-Davidson. No stay-at-home, free-babysitting grandmother here. The future looks bright for those who hope, in retirement, to get their motors running and head out on the highway, looking for a biotechnologically enabled adventure. "In the next 20 years, the human life span could increase by 50 percent," the brochure beckons. The exhibit "explores how our application of [genetic] knowledge forecasts a dramatically different future for you and your children."[91]

91. "The Genomic Revolution," *North Carolina Naturalist,* Spring/Summer 2002, p. 3.

*"What Makes You You"*

The messages of the exhibit are not subtle, but they are varied, acknowledging different target audiences and potential naysayers. "We're all related in a way because we all have DNA," reads *The Gene Scene,* the brochure given to school-age visitors to the museum.[92] Most likely taking its cue from early reports that the public was generally wary about the perils of genetic discrimination, the exhibit reiterates throughout that human beings share 99.9 percent of their genes. Walking something of a tricky line, the museum planners seem intent on conveying that genetics is responsible for not only "what makes you *you*" and "what makes me *me*" but also what makes us *us,* by virtue of our common genetic heritage. In fact, as one multicolored part of the exhibit explains: "Scientists have confirmed, as they long suspected, that there is no genetic or biological basis for race" — "THE ONLY RACE IS THE HUMAN RACE."[93] Through genetics, we are many but one. This is told one final time in the epilogue to the exhibit, which reminds viewers that genetics proves the "fundamental unity of all life."[94]

Simultaneous with allaying fears about the potential for discrimination, the exhibit offers the hope of genetic therapy. In the "Changing Our Genes" display the board reads, "You may be born with your genes, but that doesn't mean you can't change them. Fixing genetic malfunctions by repairing 'flaws' in the DNA code — using a technique called gene therapy — is no longer science fiction." The Web site for the exhibit features an introductory page with a loop of various promises, all beginning with "In the near future . . .":

> "In the near future . . . genetic enhancement may make us better looking and more athletic."
> "In the near future . . . most surgery will become obsolete."
> "In the near future . . . parents may have the option to choose traits for their children, such as hair and eye color."
> "In the near future . . . nearly all violent criminal cases can be decided on the basis of genetic information — the ultimate fingerprint — left at the crime scene."
> "In the near future . . . human life span can be increased to 150 years."

92. Jordan Brown, *The Gene Scene* (New York: American Museum of Natural History and the National Center for Science Literacy, Education, and Technology, 2001), p. 3.

93. American Museum of Natural History. Accessed 2004: www.amnh.org.

94. American Museum of Natural History. Accessed 2004: www.amnh.org.

> "In the near future . . . super foods may be genetically programmed for maximum nutrition and maximum appeal."[95]

Enhanced health, more choice, foolproof safety, perpetual youth, and more nutritious and appealing food — all brought to you, me, and us by genomics.

The projections of the genomic adventure resemble the promises of the Atomic Age. Enhanced life, domestic security, and a more enjoyable future, all within our reach, at man's command, subject to our control. The museum writers sound a note of caution, by indicating the need for ethical discernment, but these reminders of sobriety are resoundingly overpowered by the overall message of the exhibit.

When I visited the exhibit, this was made palpable by a humorous exchange I had with the docents. The first installation — after a big screen conveying promises like the ones above — featured a double helix of little television screens, with various noted bioethicists giving sound bites about the importance of considered discernment on the future of genomics. However, one could hardly hear their voices, because the attached stereo speakers were apparently malfunctioning. I asked the young docents at the entryway whether the volume had been turned down at that particular installation. "Yeah," one of them said. "Otherwise, the voices just get so annoying, droning on and on." Indeed. One wouldn't want one's experience soured by the droning voices of bioethicists. The epilogue at the exhibit subtly, but effectively, makes this same point, telling the narrative in a way that makes clear how one is to leave the hallway of conveyed knowledge and enter the outside world: "The genomic revolution holds great promise — and raises many questions. As individuals and societies, we now must come to terms with how to use our newfound knowledge. In a sense, this is only the beginning."[96] There's a great big beautiful tomorrow . . .

The location for the national premier of the "Genomic Revolution" was well chosen. North Carolinians are unabashed in their candor about the need for biotechnological training. State leaders have few qualms about the "urgent need to inspire students and educators" to embrace new forms of the natural sciences. Betsy Bennett, director of the North Carolina Museum of Natural Sciences, makes this call for inspiration in the museum's brochure for the inaugural exhibit, pointing to a piece in the brochure written by then University of North Carolina president Molly Broad. Appealing to "our competitiveness in the marketplace," Director Bennett joins her voice with President

95. American Museum of Natural History. Accessed 2004: www.amnh.org.
96. American Museum of Natural History. Accessed 2004: www.amnh.org.

Broad's, who insists that "Genomics and biotechnology are indeed revolutionizing North Carolina industries that range from health care to agribusiness to pharmaceuticals."[97]

Of the six "major sponsors" of the exhibit, three were directly biotechnological. Along with Eisai and GlaxoSmithKline, the North Carolina Biotechnology Center helped ensure that Raleigh would host the exhibit first. The Center's mission is to move "biotechnology from the mind to the marketplace."[98] Two of the other three sponsors spending top dollar were SAS Institute, the leader in software to manage biotechnological trials and implementation, and the University of North Carolina System, whose links to the biotechnological Research Triangle are well traveled. The director of the museum raves that the key players in biotechnology are "excited about the potential of the exhibit to connect visitors with their work in genomics." The "scientists, business people, bioethicists, and specialists in bioinformatics . . . urgently want to relay the message that genomics is changing how we think about nature."[99]

I intentionally visited the exhibit on a Sunday afternoon. During my hours there, I spent time not only reading the materials but also trying to interpret those who were reading the materials. Most of the visitors that day were in their "Sunday best," dressed in a way that highly suggested (in this otherwise fairly informal region) that they had come to the museum after church. I was interested in finding out how parents were sorting through the information and sifting it for their children. As I sat at the entrance to this special exhibit, I overheard several adults trying to answer children's queries. The questions that ran along the lines of "What is this about?" or "What is that thing?" (pointing at one double helix structure made with phone books) were answered similarly: "This is about what makes you who you are," or, alternatively, "That thing is the shape of the stuff that makes you who you are." Sitting at the exit, I watched as children and their parents or other adult relatives tried to explain a large screen that showed the outline of each person standing in front of it with multicolored As, Ts, Cs, and Gs. This was perhaps the most highly symbolic part of the exhibit, as children walked across the front of the screen, their shadows made up of the letters identifying the four bases of DNA, and shouted, "Hey! That's me there!" or "Look! There I am!" This form of departure from the exhibit seemed to reinforce

97. Betsy Bennett, "Director's Report," *North Carolina Naturalist*, Spring/Summer 2002, inside cover; Molly Broad, "Genomics and Our Schools," *North Carolina Naturalist*, Spring/Summer 2002, p. 10.

98. North Carolina Biotechnology Center. Accessed 2005: www.ncbiotech.org.

99. Bennett, "Director's Report."

one of the key takeaway messages of the "Genomic Revolution." The overall intended impression regarding genetics and human identity seemed to be this: Genetics provides *the* knowledge to explain what makes you *you* and what makes me *me*.

### "Not — Quite — Destiny"

This message about genetic identity is reiterated in cover story after cover story in the mainstream media. A *Life* magazine cover from April 1998 asks, "Were You Born That Way?" The smaller print continues: "Personality, temperament, even life choices. New studies show it's mostly in your genes." A multicolored double helix winds its way upward beside the text, and various words appear in fainter print, repeated in a string that runs throughout the page. "Aggression." "Obesity." "Addiction." "Anxiety." Although the article inside gives a somewhat more nuanced answer to "Were you born that way?" the general message of the piece is yes.

The article's photographs show various children, in indicative postures. One represents shyness, as she peeks around the leg of her mother.[100] Two little boys wrestling in what appears to be a boxing ring represent aggression. The sidebar beside that photograph is on genes and violence. In it psychologist David Lykken announces his proposal to deal with violent crime: parental licensing. "We wouldn't let a crack addict, a teenager or a criminal adopt a child," he says. "Why not make the same minimal requirements for people having children biologically?" The sidebar talks about the complicated mix of "high heritability" and "environment," and even references (negatively) sterilization laws in the past, but it gives an overall impression that there is a serious link between, as the title reads in all capitals, "GENES AND VIOLENCE." Quoting Lykken as an authority, the magazine gives credence to his suggestion that "the place to fight crime is in the cradle," predicting by looking at a detailed parental (even grandparental) pedigree whether an individual is fit to care for his or her child.[101]

The photographs of adults in the article simply underscore the genetic identity issue. A twenty-eight-year-old stuntman, shown literally alight, explains that he has been "happily falling out of trees since early childhood." The title of the page reads "Thrill-Seeking." There is no mention of the well-

---

100. George Howe Colt (text) and Anne Hollister (reporting), "Were You Born That Way?" *Life,* April 1998, p. 38.

101. Colt, "Were You Born?" p. 44.

documented effects on children of precisely the kinds of films the stuntman works on. Another sidebar photograph and caption show a twenty-six-year-old woman who weighs 265 pounds. The title reads, again in all capitals, "OBESITY," and the text explains that her grandmother "reached 650 pounds." There is no mention of the well-documented connections between the multimillion-dollar fast-food industry, poverty, and morbid obesity. Still another photograph shows a man smoking and drinking a martini. The title line reads, "ADDICTION," and the man explains that he "started smoking at fifteen, mostly to be cool." While there might have been plenty of fodder in this one small confession for a sidebar piece on the considerable history of tobacco advertising to children and teens, the text instead interprets his situation thus: "Powers comes from a long line of smokers and drinkers; twin studies bear out a genetic influence on addiction."[102]

As is the case with the "Genomic Revolution" exhibit, this piece makes a requisite nod to the history of eugenics, specifically the eugenic plans of the Third Reich and of (Darwin's cousin) Francis Galton from the United Kingdom. But the piece moves quickly past these distant, foreign examples, quickly concluding, with journalist William Wright, that thus to reject behavioral genetics as a field "makes as much sense as rejecting electricity because of daytime television."[103]

The *Life* piece resoundingly reinforces two presuppositions behind the eugenics movement in the United States. First, it assumes throughout that biology, or genetics, is almost completely destiny. A line repeated twice in the article is that "genes are not — quite — destiny."[104] The "quite" here functions only minimally. The overall impression of the text, interspersed with stark images of human beings representing such ills as obesity and addiction and peppered with expert testimony and scientific statistics, is one of almost complete genetic determinism. At the very least, if read with a strong dose of salt, the piece conveys a kind of titillating interest in the *possibility* of genetic determinism — of determining, through the new knowledge of genetics, not only who *I* am and who *my* child will become but also, quite importantly, who that *other person* is and who that *other person's* child will become.

Related to this is another assumption — that there is a *continuum of worth* along which each human life falls. The author muses: "Before my wife and I had our daughter, genetic counselors were able to tell us whether she

---

102. Colt, "Were You Born?" pp. 41, 42, 48.
103. Colt, "Were You Born?" p. 48.
104. Colt, "Were You Born?" pp. 39, 44.

had the genes for Down syndrome or Tay-Sachs disease. By the time she is ready to be a mother, genetic counselors will be able to tell her whether *her* fetus is genetically inclined toward depression or addiction."[105] The author here assumes a continuum running from Tay-Sachs and Down syndrome through, somewhat further along, genetic inclination toward depression. This assumption about the evaluation of human life should give pause, regardless of specific traits named. But, after a full stop, one may note another assumption embedded in this larger one. While Tay-Sachs is a quickly and painfully fatal genetic condition, Down syndrome is most often neither chronically painful nor fatal (thanks in no small part to medical advances in cardiology).

The author's conflation of the two conditions is typical — Tay-Sachs and Down syndrome are often mentioned in the same breath (along with cystic fibrosis). A life with Down syndrome (now, predictably, lasting well into middle age) is considered on a par with the excruciatingly painful, certain, early-childhood death from Tay-Sachs. While the question of selective fetal termination, to which the author is here referring, is arguably replete with tragedy when considering a prenatal diagnosis of Tay-Sachs, it is quite arguably different for a diagnosis of Down syndrome.

The article later, at a crucial juncture, underscores the conclusion that a projected, measurable contribution to society matters when citizens and parents evaluate the future uses of human genetics. "Caution is needed," the author allows. "Weighed against the potential benefits — might we end war by getting rid of aggressive genes? — is a Pandora's box of misuse." After a short reference to the eugenics movement, framed in terms of foreigners and fanatics, he notes the more recent calls of "religious fundamentalists" to correct the "genetic defect" of homosexuality and then asks, with medical ethicist Ronald Green: "Are we going to be wise enough to do it [that is, 'do' eugenics] well, in such a way that we don't impoverish the future? In trying to avoid a Ted Kaczynski, might we destroy an Einstein?"[106] This reasoning assumes that there are people *worth destroying* and people *worth keeping,* in order to enrich the future.

One crucial question to ask any vanguard proposing a "revolution" is, "Who is going to be first in line to the guillotine?" The thought that any one of us could be "wise enough" to determine who is and is not worth "avoiding" or "destroying" is brought up explicitly in the "Genomic Revolution" exhibit. If we are all 99.9 percent the same, what about the currently most obvious,

---

105. Colt, "Were You Born?" p. 46, emphasis in original.
106. Colt, "Were You Born?" pp. 48-49.

detectable genetic predispositions? What about Down syndrome, or cystic fibrosis, or even Tay-Sachs? "We're all related in a way because we all have DNA," the bright, multicultural brochure for children sings. But what if *your* DNA is quite obviously . . . well . . . *different?*

One panel of the "Genomic Revolution" shows an aesthetically normative (blonde and relatively thin, fashionably dressed) mother holding her little boy, who, even at first glance, seems subtly different. His bright smile seems perhaps a bit too large. His gaze up at his mother seems somewhat unfocused. The message about the child is clear from the bold text above his picture. This panel is about "getting the right tests." The story, told from the mother's perspective, explains that her physicians failed to offer her a newly available prenatal test for the syndrome that the child carries. She is now an advocate for prenatal testing. "[This mother] wants to get the word out: genetic testing should be widely publicized and readily available to everyone."[107] A smaller picture shows the child with his father, the caption explaining that the couple has divorced.

There is no treatment for the genetically detectable condition the child has. The only recourse a parent will have in the future, should she heed this mother's advice, is to terminate the pregnancy. Perhaps even more stark is the fact that the path the featured mother wishes had been offered to her would have terminated the child she now holds in her arms. In the middle of the genomic revolution, this child serves quite obviously as a specter — the image of a child the revolution will help parents and society at large to avoid.

### "To Know Ourselves"

In addition to the promise of answering questions of individual identity, the rhetorical power of human genomics involves questions of *corporate* identity. With genetics, we are apparently on the verge of being able *to know ourselves* — the title of the 1996 U.S. Department of Energy booklet that explains to the public the Human Genome Project. This sense that humanity is on the verge of a qualitative leap in self-understanding is alive in remarks made by Bill Clinton at the June 2000 White House news conference marking the completion of the project.

First, Clinton referred to the map produced by explorer Meriwether Lewis, a map that "defined the contours and forever expanded the frontiers of

107. "Getting the Right Tests," at www.amnh.org. Accessed 2005.

our continent and our imagination." With the Human Genome Project, the world could "celebrate the completion of the first survey of the entire human genome," a map Clinton declared to be "the most important, most wondrous map ever produced by humankind." The discovery of the "miraculous genetic code" is "an epoch-making triumph of science and reason." In fact, Clinton said, the researchers in the Human Genome Project have discovered "the language in which God created life." The "profound new knowledge" gives humans access to the intricacies of human existence, promoting a sense of "wonder" before "God's most divine and sacred gift." Clinton concluded by pointing to humans' remarkable genetic likeness as "one of the great truths" to emerge from this research: "Modern science has confirmed what we first learned from ancient faiths. The most important fact of life on this earth is our common humanity." If guided by this "incandescent truth," the Human Genome Project will lead to "the greatest age of discovery ever known." Francis Collins, head of the project — also a Protestant — spoke in similar terms, describing the milestone as "the first glimpse of our own instruction book, previously known only to God."[108]

Writing in *Nature Biotechnology*, Leigh Turner suggests that genetics now carries "all the social power of a belief system or surrogate religion."[109] This metaphor helps explain some of the fervor around this new celebration of science. Many of the depictions of race and genomics promise a sort of genetic Galatians 3:28 — a kind of synthetic, genetic redemption by which all the peoples of the world come to perceive themselves as *One*.

An image of a race clock-face served as the cover of the December 2003 issue of *Scientific American*. Differently hued faces revolve around the question "Does Race Exist?" The faces appear structurally identical, save for subtle changes that presumably indicate different racial identities.

In a side box, "About the Photoillustrations," we learn about artist Nancy Burson's invention, "the Human Race Machine," which generated the images. "The machine takes a photograph of an individual — in this case, a white woman — and adds and subtracts various outward features of racial identity to show what a person might look like if he or she were a member of another race. Burson says she seeks to use her work to underscore the commonality of humanity."[110] For the cover illustration she chose as the basic

108. White House news conference, June 26, 2000, transcribed by the *New York Times* in "Reading the Book of Life; White House Remarks on Decoding of Genome," *New York Times*, June 27, 2000, Science Desk section.

109. Leigh Turner, "Biotechnology as Religion," *Nature Biotechnology* 22 (2004): 659.

110. Michael J. Bamshad and Steve E. Olson, "Does Race Exist? About the Photoillustrations," *Scientific American*, December 2003, p. 84.

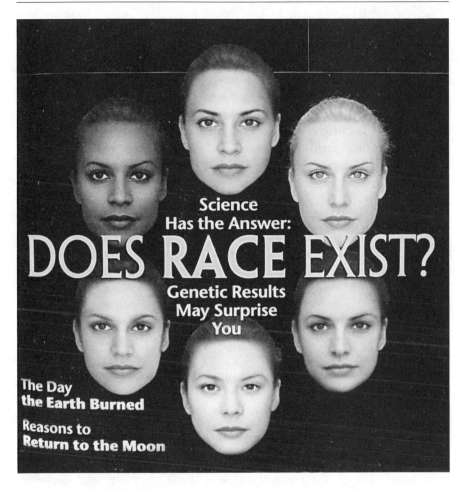

**Figure 4.31. Cover of *Scientific American*, December 2003**

template for all the races a woman configured racially as white. That genetics will "underscore the commonality of humanity" is one of the promises of unity through science alive in the genomic revolution. Collins and Clinton both made use of the rhetorical power of the unifying story in their news conference remarks of 2000. By glimpsing "our own instruction book," we may come to perceive that all humans are somehow in this together. By learning the code of life, we may better understand the way to emerge as a "common humanity." The headline announcing yet another museum exhibit, this one sponsored by the Baylor College of Medicine and the Houston Museum of Natural Science, sums up the hope: "The Secret of Life Revealed in New

Exhibition."[111] In this, genomics offers a primal story about human origins and human endings.

Writing this book from the region supposedly "too busy to hate" (to quote Atlanta's motto for the New South), I am, quite frankly, suspicious of this promise of unity through this genetic reconfiguration of identity. The land on which my home institution was built is still crossed with laws and customs and gated neighborhoods and school districts and private clubs configured to preclude an interpretation of Christian liturgy that makes "humanity" of one blood and of one body. Jim Crow laws were nothing if not the careful mapping of Christian congregations as segregated by different sorts of blood. The idea that genetic information about our common identity will be more powerfully persuasive than is the liturgy of Baptism, whereby Christians are no longer slave or free, or more potent than is the liturgy of Communion, whereby Christians become of one blood with one another, seems to underestimate gravely the enduring salience of racialized, social sin in American society.

The template of "commonality" in Burson's cover photo arguably did not just *happen* to be white. I suspect the image was chosen because whiteness continues to carry the mark of universality — the mark of what is normal in America. Christians in America privy to the promises of the genomic revolution should remember that we supposedly *already* know through the basic liturgy our churches share that we are of one blood and one race. We are supposedly *already* called to embody the holy miscegenation enacted when God became man, born in a manger, attended by shepherds and livestock. Will the "facts" of genetic science, displayed on the cover of an Advent issue of *Scientific American,* accomplish with more power what God has accomplished through the incarnation? Will indeed the laity and clergy of Southern congregations arise anew on Christmas Day, after hearing the summons of Francis Collins, to see one another as kin? This is one of the implicit promises of the current revolution. Even professional Christians, those who pastor churches and teach in seminaries, are not very likely to send their children to a public school with many free-lunch children. Even professional Christians are not very likely to adopt children with disabilities. Have Christian geneticists been made more likely, by their study of the double helix and its promises of universal kinship, to undertake such radical acts of hospitality? I hazard not.

111. Press release, Human Genome Sequencing Center, Baylor College of Medicine, April 2, 2003. Accessed 2003: www.hgsc.bcm.tmc.edu. The exhibit ran from April 23 to December 31, 2003, and was entitled "The Living Genome."

Many "ethical" conversations about genomics revolve around one or another particular technology. Is this or that procedure licit or illicit? An accurate assessment of the technology, however, requires a deeper look at the marketing of scientific or technological hope. At the very least, the story of the Atomic Age should give pause as we assess the claims of the genomic revolution. Some of the localized hypotheses about atomic technology turned out to be true — even, arguably, miraculous. Others turned out to be ridiculous — even, arguably, demonic. But the overall sense that mankind was on the verge of a giant leap forward into a realm of sheer abundance seems, in retrospect, at the very least quaint, and possibly heretical. The sense that mankind was on the verge of a giant leap forward into a future without suffering required a committed, concerted amnesia regarding the origins of nuclear technology. The sense of hope required a collective, willed ignorance about the people whose lives had been deemed expendable.

General Electric's motto during part of this period is telling: "Progress is our most important product." The *idea* of progress — of seeming modern and new and, to quote the *National Geographic* article, "On the Move" — was intrinsic to the hype and hope around atomic technology. Through advertising and essays, the would-be-with-it family learned that they could and should purchase domestic respectability. The allure of the new dishwasher, the new range, and the new electric mixer was in no small part a product of their association with the idea of progress. The details of this history point to a pattern helpful when assessing the marketed claims of genomics. The promises of a nuclear utopia assumed a particular snapshot of domestic bliss. Simultaneous with the period of "Atoms for Peace" was the emergence of the newly configured nuclear family, brought to you by General Electric and other major purveyors of household appliances. Concurrent with the "Atomic Adventure" sold in *Collier's* was an unprecedented emphasis on the relatively isolated, comfortable, and entertained family. As in the Eisenhower administration's *Ladies' Home Journal* piece, the promises of atomic progress seem inextricably intertwined with a growing division between the technologically enhanced and the primitive, between the civilized and the uncivilized. This division between evolved and atavistic had a direct bearing on the allure of genomic progress.

In 1997 Burson-Marsteller, the world's largest public relations firm, advised in a memorandum to a consortium of global biotechnological giants (including Pfizer and Eli Lilly) that "in order to effect the desired changes in public perceptions and attitudes, the bioindustries must stop trying to be their own advocates." Rather, corporations should seek to change people's imaginations by way of more generally shared "symbols eliciting hope, satisfaction, caring and self-esteem."[112] According to other reports on the leaked document, Burson-Marsteller further suggested that the industry concentrate on the creation of "good stories" that may "go around the world in minutes."[113]

Genomics is a story of human origins and human endings, but it also offers an account of redemption. Most redemption stories assume that there are particular barriers to the presumed goal — roadblocks to progress. One way to sort through the promises of the genomic revolution is to ask about the assumed barriers. Is the problem to be surmounted a lack of reliable, verifiable self-knowledge? Do I not know myself until I know my genetic code? Is the problem a lack of reliable, verifiable *corporate* knowledge? Do we not know ourselves as *one* body, as a "common humanity," without recourse to the Human Genome Project? These are important questions in and of themselves, but they take on a particular urgency if one considers them in light of what seem to be the working assumptions about the barriers to individual and corporate identity — that is, disability and difference. Much of the funding for the revolution goes into potentially marketable products for detecting traits that the dominant culture deems markers of disability. While there is some potential, eventually, to *cure* some conditions through genomics, the first-line use of human genetics is *detection*.

If the goal of biotechnological medicine were primarily to alleviate human suffering, taken in some broad, utilitarian sense, the universities would be building enormous, well-funded centers to educate the public about the already documented, basic barriers to human health. Bioethicists would pad their pockets with honorariums to speak about the need for lead abatement in low-income housing; for nutritious, low-fat meals in public schools; and for potable water in the two-thirds world, to name only three obvious examples.

But the goal of biotechnological medicine, at this point, seems to be more about *novel* possibilities for marketable pharmaceuticals. The applied practice of genetic medicine at the beginning of the twenty-first century seems to be most directly the practice of determining *who* is likely to be in some way disabled or different, and what proportion of that difference or disability is inherent in that person's genetic code.

Regardless of Clinton's hope and Collins's faith, physicians and con-

112. Jackie Stevens, "PR for the 'Book of Life,'" *Nation*, November 26, 2001. Accessed 2002: www.thenation.com. See also John Vidal and George Monbiot, "The PR Strategy — the Charm Offensive," *Guardian*, December 16, 1997, p. 4.

113. "EuropaBio: Manipulating Consent," *Corporate Europe Observer*, October 1997. Accessed 2002: www.corporateeurope.org.

sumers are using genetic detection to rid themselves of lives that do not fit. When considered at the level of *corporate* identity, this pursuit — of detecting potential disability, burden, and difference — may make for a society that is even less hospitable toward disability and difference than it is at present. Note that the *Life* article treats even "thrill-seeking," "obesity," and "addiction" as matters of genetics. This may allow the decision-making class in the United States — those who plan for social programs and public schooling and such — to see "problem" children and "risky" teenagers as matters of genetic testing and targeting. At the very least, the arguments for programs that provide broader behavioral, educational, and societal solutions to address risk taking, obesity, and addiction cannot but suffer in an "It's in the genes" culture.

This possibility for the future seems particularly menacing given another salient pattern of the past. The assessment of the progressive versus the regressive family involved the presence of a certain kind of wealth, productivity, and convenience. The nuclear family that served as *the* marketing tool for the atomic adventure was a family able to afford an unprecedented array of newly "necessary" domestic goods. The sense that some kinds of children would result in a drag on family progress, and that some families would add drag to a national economy, comes to bear as families supposedly "choose" freely whether to terminate for disability or to keep their family size to a "responsible" level. As genomics provides more and more of a sense of who *we* are, it is a very real possibility that *we* will become a society ever more intent on — and adept at — eliminating *others* and, when necessary, leaving those deemed less genetically "fit" to their own devices.

### *"Archetypal Helices" and a Hole in the Wall*

One contrast may illustrate two quite different responses to the question of genetically influenced disease or disability. To put the matter starkly, these divergent responses may represent two ways that society may in the future deal with the child who, in the genomic revolution, symbolizes the need for universal and expanding access to prenatal genetic testing. Allow him to serve as a canary, and we may consider which mine shaft to enter. For as he fares, so may other children with detectable difference — children with ADHD or autism or obesity or who seem prone to addiction. What kind of setting will we provide? How will society perceive our responsibility toward such children? How will the "best and brightest" at schools like Duke University choose to use their intellectual gifts and relative wealth if they perceive the call to be a part of a revolution in health care? Which path will the next generation of scientists choose? More to the point, how will those who profess Jesus as their savior perceive their role?

Appearing in late 2004 on the Cold Spring Harbor Web site was an invitation to visit DNA Stuff, a retail site with products inspired by the promise of genetics.[114] One may purchase clothing from the It's in the Genes, Jeans denim line. Or jewelry fashioned in the shape of the double helix from the Strands of Life or New Beginnings collections. "Joyful snippets of DNA" grace a pocket handkerchief. Why would one choose to adorn oneself in the icon of the double helix? Prominent during early 2005 was a bright cherry-red box with a paragraph narrating the power of this line of products. "Archetypal Helices," read the title: "Your Inner Self, Revealed." The paragraph explained: "Certain shapes seem to speak to our innermost beings. They inspire an almost visceral response in us. In a kind of self-recognition, we connect to their images at the most fundamental, unconscious level, as if driven by our DNA."

This description manages to promote the double helix as the archetype, as well as to suggest implicitly that an appreciation for other "archetypal" shapes is "driven by our DNA." The We Are One line of jewelry reinforces this message, with various charms representing world religions set on a bracelet with two charms of the unifying double helix. Perusing the photographs of young Cold Spring Harbor interns dressed in It's in the Genes, Jeans, viewers are apparently to find themselves caught up in a "visceral response" of recognition. (All but one of the dozen or so models are Anglo.) One photograph shows two young female interns standing with their It's in the Genes, Jeans backsides to the camera, one on either side of geneticist James Watson, codiscoverer of the double helix structure (who has also, not incidentally, argued for genetically improving female beauty). Another shows a young woman and young man in romantic embrace, she wearing double helix bracelet, necklace, and earrings, and he a golden bow tie decorated with blue double helices. The image seems intended to resemble an upscale wedding photograph. The site is, at the very least, eerie, particularly when one considers that Cold Spring Harbor was the home of the Eugenics Record Office.

The charity to which the profits from DNA Stuff go is Cold Spring Harbor's genetics laboratory. One DNA Stuff Web page displays a series of gold and silver Genetic Solutions lapel pins, small disks embossed with words and crossed through with diagonal lines representing "NO," as in "NO Breast Cancer," "NO AIDS," "NO Parkinson's," "NO Cystic Fibrosis," "NO Alzheimer's." "Shop with a conscience," viewers are urged. The explicit message of this product line is that its sales will help eliminate these devastating diseases.

114. Accessed 2004-2005: www.dnastuff.com.

But a secondary, implicit message — given the surrounding context of genetics, the history of Cold Spring Harbor, and the normatively attractive models — is more problematic. It is hard not to take away the impression that the proceeds will at the same time help eliminate the future *existence* of people with these diseases. At least for cystic fibrosis, the most immediate application of genetic research at the time of this writing is in preimplantation genetic diagnosis — to determine which embryos should be discarded because of the presence of genetic markers for the condition. It is hard to fathom a person with one of these conditions wearing an It's in the Genes baseball cap or a New Beginnings double helix necklace. By the definition of the archetypal helix, someone with one of these conditions carries the blueprint of the *problem*. If, indeed, "It's in the Genes," and if, indeed, I am identified with my DNA, and if, indeed, my DNA is in some way aberrant, then perhaps the "visceral response" I feel when viewing the site will be less than favorable. One would hope that the reaction of a parent with a child with cystic fibrosis would indeed be unfavorable.

According to the Web site, the founder of DNA Stuff was inspired by Paul Newman, in particular his model of using after-tax profits from a line of food products to fund charitable organizations.[115] This link begs for comparison. As explained on the official Newman's Own Web site, the charitable organization most explicitly identified with Paul Newman is the Hole in the Wall Gang Camp.[116] This camp, along with nine others in the Association of Hole in the Wall Camps, serves children from around the world who have been diagnosed with cancer, sickle-cell anemia, HIV/AIDS, and other serious illnesses.[117] Children who otherwise would be logistically (and often financially) unable to attend summer camp are able to participate in these camps, free of charge. With a full team of medical personnel, the staff is able to offer full health care in settings where children can play, swim, canoe, make lanyards and pottery, and play tricks on one another. These camps are an expensive endeavor. To set up places where children with such significant medical needs may be cared for while having a true "summer camp experience" is not a simple matter. It takes funding, countless volunteer hours, and an ever-broadening web of people whose lives have been graced by the work to pull off the yearly events. The Hole in the Wall Gang's online photo gallery speaks to the blessing this consciously crafted setting is for the participants.[118]

115. Accessed 2004: www.dnastuff.com.
116. Accessed 2005: www.newmansown.com.
117. The Hole in the Wall Gang Camp mission statement. Accessed 2005: www.hole-inthewallgang.org.
118. Photo galleries accessed 2005: www.newmansown.com.

The Hole in the Wall folks would almost certainly agree with the need for biotechnological research into the causes of and cures for childhood cancer, sickle-cell anemia, and HIV/AIDS. There would be no overt disagreement on the need for biotechnological science. But the difference in emphasis is significant, particularly the different faces put forward to the public. On the one Web site, children without hair, with bodies bloated from the effects of treatment, are featured as proud participants, one showing off her home-made painting, another holding up a fish just caught. On the other site, children wear It's in the Genes, Jeans in front of a shining silver double helix sculpture. The children with diseases at the Hole in the Wall camps are, by current genetic terms, lost. They are incurable. Thus, to enhance the quality of their lives, to put effort into their *care,* is to reject the notion that their lives are identifiable with their prospects for immediate *cure.* The Hole in the Wall camps may be best interpreted as one resounding NO to the sense that a child is merely a sum of his or her genetic predispositions or medical maladies. The originator of DNA Stuff quite missed the point when she found supposed inspiration through Paul Newman's system of giving. Newman's giving led to a different sort of NO than crossing through the names of conditions to be eliminated through the genomic revolution.

Might this comparison simply set up a false, zero-sum game? Could not a geneticist at Cold Spring Harbor also volunteer at a Hole in the Wall camp? Certainly. The search for a cure need not preclude the call to care. But rhetoric matters. The language and images that shape people's imaginations influence what we perceive as possible, and as worthy of our time and effort. To work at a Hole in the Wall camp is to understand *hope* in a way that is not progressive — in a way that does not necessarily lead to any quantifiable movement forward along a measurable continuum of strength or normative health. These children do not meet the "baseline" of physical normality, and work with them requires, in a real sense, setting aside the expectation that they may be "saved" by medical expertise. Crafting a present for these children requires seeing them as worth a great deal of work and planning and attention even though, by any plotting on a graph of "promise for contribution" or "prospect for recovery," they will not appear to amount to much. The Hole in the Wall camps are an example of one way to perceive the claim that a child who is diseased, disabled, or at risk makes on our resources and time. To care well may mean setting aside the standard measurements, in particular those measurements that are increasingly presented as tools for crafting a genetically promising future.

One T-shirt sold in 2005 at the North Carolina Museum of Life and Science in Durham reads "DNA is LIFE — The rest is just details." This message bluntly proposes passing all endeavors and ideas through the sieve of genetic science. If the marketing of the Atomic Age can teach us anything about the marketing of the genomic revolution, the lesson should be that we must pay attention to the overall narrative in which scientific promises are set. Those purporting to convey simply scientific knowledge are also selling a complex web of meaning and, not incidentally, an industrial complex on whose future our hope is supposed to depend. The probing of human DNA is ostensibly poised to usher in a new era of science and self-knowledge, a new era of LIFE. It seems crucial, on the verge of this revolution, to ask whose lives the proposed measures will render "accidental" or "aberrant." Whose lives will seem less worthy of attention as we continue the genomic "adventure"?

## A Philosophy of Life

As I complete this book, the United Methodist Church (UMC) has convened a task force to consider the intersection of genomics and faith, in particular the question of prenatal genetic testing and selective termination for disability. The reflections of the cochair of the UMC task force are worth noting:

> Decisions on termination are very difficult. These decisions are influenced by the seriousness of the genetic abnormality, the size of the family, financial circumstances, the availability of health care, and the couple's views on the societal implications of choosing which fetuses will be allowed to be born.
>
> Some people are concerned about the message being sent to people with disabilities when we chose [sic] to abort an embryo with a genetic disorder. They fear that we are implying that persons living with those disorders are inferior or unworthy. Some also believe that we need people with disabilities in order to maintain diversity in our society. As people of faith we are committed to caring for all people regardless of their disabilities. For most people, this does not mean that we will not try to prevent or treat infirmities for the sake of maintaining diversity. Jesus went about healing and apparently believed that people should be as free of infirmity as possible. When he healed the epileptic, he apparently did not consider that act disparaging to other persons with epilepsy (Matthew 17:14-22). Later in the same chapter, Jesus implies that he condones the use of our ability to change creation when he says "If you have faith the size of a mustard seed nothing will be impossible for you."
>
> These choices are extremely difficult to make but we can always be cer-

tain that, no matter what we chose [*sic*], God will always be with us as we seek to understand God's universe.[119]

The configuration of human diversity, illness, disparity, and occlusion in the material we have considered up to this point warrants pause. As a people of faith, mainline Protestants in the United States have not always been "committed to caring for all people regardless of their disabilities." In the best-case scenario, we have struggled in the last century to include within the ecclesial imagination the consanguinity of people across the divide of class, of overt disability, of construed race, and of racialized violence. In the default-case scenario, many mainline middle-class Protestant congregations accepted occlusion of or distanced pity toward people who were variously considered on the other side of kinship. In the worst-case scenario, mainline Protestants in America sought to implement a sort of "Christian 'Marshall Plan'" (to employ Karl Barth's term) to eradicate the sorts of people who simply would not conform with attempts to secure humanity against all suffering. To ignore the latter two scenarios may be to threaten considerably the first. In the face of willed amnesia, it is my hope to encourage the hard, contextual work of memory.

There are analogues in the Atomic Age, even in the *Midmonth Magazine for Methodist Families*. While *Together* was running "How We'll Live in '77" and "Yes, Atoms for Peace!" it was also running an essay by Dr. Martin Kawano entitled "Why Did I Survive the Atom Bomb?"[120] His piece gave readers likely eager to push forward out of the morass of nuclear fear and into an atomically fueled utopia reason to sit in silence, and to lament, and to sit again in silence. As Kawano describes in painstaking detail, atomic weaponry had incinerated people in mere moments, leaving behind their trace shadows on walls, but it had also ushered forth a horrifying holocaust during which people screamed for aid from others who could barely move. As he made his way slowly past buildings full of such dismaying terror, Kawano stopped to pick up a crying child; the child's mother was caught under the rubble of her own house and could not save him. On the hillside, watching the burning city, the author saw Urakami Cathedral lose another side of its facade. The presence of the church in that city prompted him to dwell on Psalm 91, and he ends his essay with a testimony to a future held only by a God to whom his life is indentured: "I don't know the future. But I know the same providence will

119. "A Guide for Discernment — Genetic Technologies and the United Methodist Church" (unpublished paper, February 2006), pp. 4-5.

120. Martin Kawano, "Why Did I Survive the Atom Bomb?" *Together*, August 1957, pp. 10-12.

lead me and make my life give glory to him. And I know that 'all things work together for good to them that love God.' But I did not love him first. It was he who loved me and sought me and saved my soul."

A sidebar on Dr. Kawano, "At Nagasaki He Lost All — but His Faith!" may be read as an editor's attempt to shore up the fragile theme of "providence" on which Kawano ends his essay. The exclamation point serves much the same purpose as the one in Laurence's 1958 *Together* essay on man's ingenuity and the abolition of suffering.[121] Reading Kawano's life as saved for the sake of "working," the editor seems to have missed the subtle point of Kawano's narration of survival. "To him the meaning was clear. Where thousands had died, he had lived. His life must have been spared for a purpose."[122] So edified, Methodist readers moved on to the next essay, "Can Coaches Be Christian?" The sidebar offered purpose-driven clarity whereas Dr. Kawano had registered continued lament, along with a precarious, tenacious hope in God's inscrutable purpose.

In chapter 1 we discussed the 1956 Ad Council poster promoting religion in American life, "Faith and the Atomic Age" (fig. 1.21), featuring the church-going, nuclear family. The text and image queried the "fit" of the faithful individual and the middle-class family in the Atomic Age. The question of contextualization in the atomic era begged for an answer about human tragedy and divine responsibility. By one reading, the faithful, strong, progressing nuclear family was the answer — the way God's blessing of a nation would proceed. Yet American Christians faced a particular challenge when presented with the narratives of other faithful Christians who had suffered incalculably through our nation's ingenuity. How to configure the mother crushed by her own home, left trapped as her child pitiably cried for her? How to configure the many people who died as Dr. Kawano watched helplessly on the hillside above Nagasaki? One way to read the American construal of such Japanese Christians is to read both charitably and probingly two essays about a group of women presented as "the Hiroshima Maidens." In this reading, Methodists may consider the ecclesial possibilities for self-delusion and for consanguinity.

We begin with the second essay, "The Hiroshima Maidens — 15 Years Later," written as a "happy sequel to Hiroshima" (as described on the essay's first page).[123] Norman Cousins, editor of *Saturday Review,* had written an earlier piece for *Together,* "The Hiroshima Maidens Go Home," published

---

121. "Yes, Atoms for Peace!"

122. "At Nagasaki He Lost All — but His Faith!" *Together,* August 1957, p. 12.

123. Norman Cousins, "The Hiroshima Maidens — 15 Years Later," *Together,* August 1960, pp. 14-17.

eleven years after the bomb obliterated Hiroshima.[124] The update in 1960 came in the thick of the Cold War, a year after the "Kitchen Debate" between Nixon and Khrushchev, and as America was gearing up further its nuclear arsenal. The story of these "23 girls," as they are called, seems constructed rather stiffly to portray confidence in the ability of Hiroshima to have a "happy sequel." The symbolic function of the twenty-three women may be read even in the title repeatedly given to them by the author. Cousins calls these grown, married women "maidens," even "girls," throughout the essay. By one plausible reading, the essay uses the "success" of the "maidens" to redeem the nation that most directly caused their disfigurement. The editors summarize the story thus: "The distinguished editor of *Saturday Review,* one of the first Americans to publicize the plight of the Hiroshima Maidens, . . . now brings *Together* readers up to date on the moving story of these victims of the first atomic attack. Thanks to surgery they received and skills they learned in the U.S., he reveals, the girls now lead happy, useful lives. And the example they've set has been an inspiration to others — on both sides of the Pacific."

Readers learn that, in addition to receiving reconstructive surgery on their burned and twisted limbs and faces, "the girls had availed themselves of every opportunity for education." Cousins evidently judges of particular interest to *Together* readers the success of Toyoko Minowa, whose fashion designs appear on models in a large photograph, and Suzue Oshima, pictured with her husband and baby girl, who owns a beauty shop in Japan named after her host town, Darien, Connecticut (fig. 4.32a). As signaled by the teaser text that runs above the title — "From Japan comes this heart-warming report on 23 girls whose sorrow has turned to joy" — the essay seeks to narrate American largesse as the source of salvation for the "maidens."[125]

But what of those who had not traveled to receive surgery and education in the United States? Quakers in Bucks County, Pennsylvania, had graciously connected with others in Hiroshima, offering "Christmas and birthday gifts, and in some instances providing financial assistance for scholarships."[126] Yet the original "maidens" had an impact beyond "many elaborate official projects." The essay ends with the assurance that the citizens of Hiroshima extend now a warm welcome to visitors from the United States, owing to the witness of these "ambassadors of friendship."

This essay from 1960 offers a "happy sequel to Hiroshima," but it also

---

124. Norman Cousins, "The Hiroshima Maidens Go Home," *Together,* October 1956, pp. 30-33.

125. Cousins, "Hiroshima Maidens — 15 Years Later," p. 14.

126. Cousins, "Hiroshima Maidens — 15 Years Later," p. 17.

**Figure 4.32a. Suzue Oshima and family, one of the "Hiroshima Maidens."** *Together,*
**August 1960**

elides a small truth of the story itself. Cousins writes in the fourth paragraph:
"It was after this one-year treatment that, in November of 1956, the Hiroshima Maidens had returned to Japan — all except Shigeko Niimoto and
Toyoko Minowa, who decided to remain in this country to study nursing and
fashion design, respectively, and Mitsuko Kuramoto, who was married in California." Yet on the third page, after writing that "All are standing on their
own feet," Cousins notes that "there are two who will always be missed:
Tomoko Nakabayashi, who died after surgery in New York, and Hideko
Hirata, who lost her life to cancer following her return home."[127] In this, an
almost parenthetical aside, Cousins has traced two important cracks in the
happy ending version of this "heart-warming report."

Alongside the final page of the essay runs another piece, by Alice W.
Pryor, "Sadako and the Paper Cranes" (fig. 4.32b).[128] Like Hideko Hirata,
Sadako had died of a form of cancer, and Pryor names her death of leukemia,

127. Cousins, "Hiroshima Maidens — 15 Years Later," p. 16.
128. Alice W. Pryor, "Sadako and the Paper Cranes," *Together,* August 1960, p. 17.

385

**Figure 4.32b. Doll symbolizing the "real" Sadako.** *Together,* **August 1960**

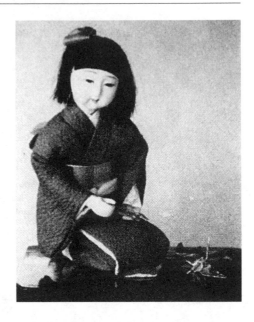

traceable to radiation exposure, as part of the legacy of "the atomic age." The image above Pryor's text is of a doll, a reminder of "the real Sadako," as Pryor calls her, a child whose story she feels compelled to tell. The ending of the story is different from the ending of Cousins's essay. Pryor's ending, of birds made of paper by children who themselves bear "the devil's claw marks," intimates the fragility of hope in a century creased by unspeakable death.

The other "maiden" from Japan "who will always be missed" is Tomoko Nakabayashi, a young woman whose story Cousins has told in his first essay, "The Hiroshima Maidens Go Home." While this earlier story tends at points toward sanguine Americanism (the Japanese pastor who accompanies the young women states that "The American people have been just and generous to Japan in defeat"), the narration of Tomoko's story bears the marks. As he does in the later essay, Cousins goes out of his way to describe the young women's improved appearance, noting frequently their interest in American norms of clothing and beauty. After two operations to bring her body toward normalcy, Tomoko submitted to a third, in an attempt to remove "an unimportant white scar high up on the inside of her right forearm."[129] But she died in surgery of heart failure. Cousins relates that, in informing the other young women of the death, "I had come to console them but it was they who did the

129. Cousins, "Hiroshima Maidens Go Home," p. 33.

consoling." In the next line, the author asks a question that winds its way in and out of both essays on "the maidens": "Why were we really doing this?" Was it out of guilt? as Tomoko herself asked before she died. The interpreter for the group, Helen Yokoyama, gave a different answer:

> "Suppose," Mrs. Yokoyama said, "that some people have a philosophy of life which enables them to regard all human beings as belonging to a single family. Even though they might not actually know each other, even though they might live thousands of miles apart, they might still believe in their closeness and in their duty to one another. The same love that members of a family feel for one another can be felt by those people for all others, especially for those who are terribly in need of help. Is this not possible?"[130]

Helen Yokoyama's answer in this postwar essay in *Together* may be read as cloyingly precious, as artificial as the little doll that represented a child who died of radiation and as flimsy as the paper cranes "the real Sadako" was said to have inspired. Yet it may be one small, tenacious answer in the midst of a new century and a new era intent on ushering in a scientific revolution to end all suffering.

When posed with a "philosophy of life" that offers to unlock the secrets of *genetic* consanguinity, Methodists may recall that we already have a story of incarnate consanguinity, albeit one that itself resides in mere flesh scarred by the sins of man. The challenge, I would suggest, is to live into such a life, to live into such a kinship. Such a "philosophy of life" and such a kinship may rely on a cruciform icon, a cruciform story, a cruciform hope for the end of time and the gift of existence itself.

## "A Small Light Indeed"

Writing for the *Nation* in 1957, Dan Wakefield crystallized his denunciation of "slick-paper Christianity" in a summary of the "full color eight-page feature" on portraits of Jesus with which "*Together* flamed forth" in its first issue.[131] The series of portraits in *Together* concludes with an image of Jesus that Wakefield characterizes as "the most happy fella imaginable — and more handsome than any man who ever played the role in a Cecil B. DeMille production." This Jesus, Wakefield suggests, appears quite amenable to shaving his

130. Cousins, "Hiroshima Maidens Go Home," p. 33.

131. Dan Wakefield, "Slick-Paper Christianity," *Nation,* January 19, 1957, p. 57. For a recent book on the "quest for the cultural Jesus," see Stephen Prothero, *American Jesus: How the Son of God Became a National Icon* (New York: Farrar, Straus and Giroux, 2003).

beard, donning a "grey flannel suit," and joining Dr. Norman Vincent Peale "in the good doctor's annual (paid) tour of large department stores at the holiday season to instill the employees with 'The Christmas Spirit.'" By Wakefield's interpretation, the Methodist church had rendered a Jesus with whom its readers could easily connect. The "Christmas Spirit" displayed in the pages of *Together* was more intent on conveying a sentiment akin to Peale's *Power of Positive Thinking* than living out the scandal of God, born in a manger — a Jewish baby born to a precarious Jewish mother in first-century Palestine.

This is in part what Wakefield also found so offensive in the *Together* story of the Hiroshima Maidens. By this story Methodists had tried to turn an atrocity into a means for hope. They had tried to apply a positive spin to tragedy. To use an artistic metaphor consistent with Wakefield's read of Jesus, they had taken a story of embodied horror and exacted aesthetic surgery to present the Hiroshima Maidens, healed and successful, fashioning new designer dresses and styling women's hair.

> If that is presented to warm the hearts of Methodists or anyone else, then the immorality of our times is so grotesque that we had all better weep for our souls. *A small light indeed is the healing of twenty-five girls beside the glare of an atomic bomb that was dropped on a Japanese city.* An ordinary human being might imagine that we'd have the morality to hide this pale flicker under a bushel instead of displaying it across the slick pages of a popular magazine to the greater glory of a Protestant sect.
>
> But glory and reward on earth and the message of success are repeated on page after page of *Together* in the most up-to-date magazine style.[132]

To present the story of Hiroshima with such a "happy" ending, as the editors later describe it, is very possibly to conceal the abiding marks on the body of Christ.

Wakefield's call to lament is crucial. But between the lines of the text, in the wounds that show in spite of concealer, is the possibility of a veritable, sober hope in the midst of weeping. The witness in *Together* is indeed a small light. As such, it is not a newly resilient, left-leaning Christian "Marshall Plan" to replace the resilient, right-leaning Christian "Marshall Plan." I would submit that the calling to be a "small light" is a calling that must reform mainline Protestants in the United States. It is a calling that is different from the calling to be the "Deciders." We are not called so much to be those who are rightly to determine "who should own the moon." We may be called instead to witness to the one in whose kinship we find our hope.

132. Wakefield, "Slick-Paper Christianity," pp. 58-59, emphasis added.

## CONCLUSION:
# Reconceiving Parenthood

## The Holy Spirit of Procreation

*And can it be, that I should gain*
*An interest in the Saviour's blood?*
*Died He for me, who caused His pain*
*For me, who Him to death pursued?*
*Amazing love! how can it be*
*That Thou, my God, shouldst die for me?*

*'Tis mystery all! The Immortal dies:*
*Who can explore His strange design?*
*In vain the first-born seraph tries*
*To sound the depths of love divine.*
*'Tis mercy all! let earth adore,*
*Let angel minds inquire no more.*

Charles Wesley, 1738

**Figure 5.1. Fifth-Place Winners of the National Typical American Family Contest, New York World's Fair, 1939-40**

ADMIRING FRIEND:
"My, that's a beautiful baby you have there!"

MOTHER:
"Oh, that's nothing — you should see his photograph."

Daniel Boorstin, *The Image*, 1961

The family portrait is intended to be *admired*. In a sense, it is even intended to be inspirational. The representation of a cleaned-up baby, child, and family — well tended, dressed, and coiffed — may have become during the twentieth century a kind of *anti*-icon. A truly *holy* icon leads the viewer past the image itself, on toward the gracious maker of life. One's own life becomes taken up into the blessing of God's gift of grace. The produced icons of family holiness in slick-paper imagery may produce a different sort of space between viewer and image viewed. Rather than leading the viewer past the image, on toward a gracious God, the perfected portrait may reverberate back in aesthetic judgment on the viewer.[1]

1. I am grateful to Hans Ulrich for helping to prompt this understanding of the simulated image as anti-icon, during discussion of my work. See Hans Belting, *Likeness and Presence:*

I think there may be a judgmental reverberation back and forth in the space between image and viewer. There may be between the magazine reader and the image on the cover an echo of judgment, moving back and forth between portrait and viewer. One danger of this reverberation from anti-iconic image to viewer is that she may subsequently try, again and again, to arrange her own home and her family as worth viewing by another human viewer. This is what I like to call the *Good Housekeeping* Panopticon: it is the sense a woman carries with her that she, and her home and family, are surrounded by and being scrutinized by the images of perfect domesticity they find in the pages of popular magazines.[2] She may try, again and again, to employ holy hygiene, prefer the corporate breast, gauge her offspring for fitness, and streamline her family to move forward in the genomic era. Daniel Boorstin's comical observation (above) about the viewer admiring a baby thus has a bite to it. The beauty of a mother's baby is "nothing" compared to the beauty of the image of his portrait, captured and still, ready for the adjudicating viewer.

The illustrated Rockwell image that begins my own book, with its haloed, hygienic family, may be read as an anti-icon from a eugenic era. While the haloed family is to inspire healthy living, it is possible that the frozen, ideal quality of family life in the poster is actually less holy than are images of untidy, creaturely, incarnate family life drawn by a more mature Norman Rockwell.[3] Inasmuch as the haloed family on the cover of this book became the ideal, those who did not fit were the ones to be avoided — whether through overt or covert segregation, sterilization, or shame.

Even the most staged picture is not necessarily what it seems. There are fissures between the stories and the idealized images from the chapters in this

---

A *History of the Image before the Era of Art*, trans. Edmund Jephcott (Chicago: University of Chicago Press, 1997), and Jean Baudrillard, *Simulacra and Simulation*, trans. Sheila Faria Glaser (Ann Arbor: University of Michigan Press, 1994).

2. See as relevant here, from a historical perspective, Colleen McDannell, *The Christian Home in Victorian America, 1840-1900* (1986; reprint, Bloomington: Indiana University Press, 1994): "Running alongside of denominational religion in America is a domestic religion, as well as a civil religion. This domestic religion shares both the symbols of individual traditions — Protestantism, Catholicism, Judaism — and the symbols of American domesticity. By combining traditional religious symbols with a set of middle-class domestic values, the Victorians rooted their home virtues in the eternal and allowed the more abstract traditional symbols to assume a real presence in everyday life. Domestic religion, in its uniquely religious and generally cultural forms, bound together what was truly meaningful in Victorian society" (p. 151). Thanks to Sarah Johnson for this reference.

3. Norman Rockwell's later images of exhausted, soiled, tattered families in America were a lovely form of American iconography.

book. There is indeed evidence of holy resistance in the in-between-space of domestic image and maternal viewer. There are cracks in the portraits, so to speak, differences between the messages *intended* by the advertisers and the internalized imaginative uses to which viewers put the images.[4] This may be read around the edges of *Together.* The cracks may be read in what was to be a straightforward piece of propaganda in *National Geographic,* as the "island-ers" turned the tables on the hired propagandist. By their inviting him to en-ter the family circle, and by his acceptance of the invitation, the scene is changed. The reader may catch a glimpse of an image bearing hope. It is pos-sible that women themselves did and may still take the DuPont perfection through chemistry sold to them and laugh, play, or own the material as their particular tools for survival. What might appear to be a family intent on proper portraiture may, with further conversation and attention, become more complicated, and more hopeful.

The image above the ironic quotation from Boorstin is just such a por-trait (fig. 5.1).[5] The picture is the official photograph of the fifth-place winners in the National Typical American Family Contest, held at the New York World's Fair of 1939-40. To paraphrase Boorstin, "If you think the image is beautiful, you should hear the real story." The fragment of a story I received from this family is more inspiring than the aspiration to be judged to be typical.

If you've come this far in my book suspecting that there *must be* stories of resistance in the periods covered, you'll enjoy this story. If you think I have overdetermined, or overinterpreted, the impact of images and rhetoric on mainline families in the United States, this story is also for you. There should indeed be a suspicion that there are stories of hope occluded by my own, al-most relentless, narration of enforced normality. This picture from 1939 may serve as a prompt for further probing, and for further conversation with kith and kin and congregant. If indeed my interpretation of the material in chap-ters 1–4 seems overly dour and insufficiently open to the possibilities of joy and life in the midst of a particular form of normalcy, the story behind the Typical American Family Contest may stand as a testimony to the kind of complicated *atypical* family that was and still is possible. Appearances of nor-

---

4. Condensed in this section is a set of arguments within cultural theory; these argu-ments are ripe for Christian analysis regarding the powerful forces of illusion and the resistant mischief of the Holy Spirit. See, in particular, conversation among scholars engaging the work of Stewart and Elizabeth Ewen. Stewart Ewen, *Captains of Consciousness: Advertising and the So-cial Roots of the Consumer Culture* (New York: Basic Books, 2001), and Stewart Ewen and Eliza-beth Ewen, *Channels of Desire: Mass Images and the Shaping of American Consciousness* (Minne-apolis: University of Minnesota Press, 1992).

5. Personal collection, Patty Roberts; used with permission.

mality can indeed be deceiving, thanks be to God. It is my prayer that the *type* of atypical for which we may hope is in the form of the story behind the portrait of the Typical American Family Contest. After a theological diversion, we will end the book with the story behind and beyond the image of the Typical American Family of 1939-40.

## "A Risky Thing"

In her reflections on "hospitality, dignity, and the power of recognition," Christine Pohl suggests that "when the larger society disregards or dishonors certain persons, small acts of respect and welcome are potent far beyond themselves." Such acts of receptivity to unbidden or unexpected guests "point to a different system of valuing and an alternative model of relationships."[6] Thus a small but tenacious light in the tradition of Protestantism in the United States may show us a way into this "different system of valuing" and this strange kind of kinship. Yet such small acts will require the courage to crisscross boundaries of normative domesticity, national progress, and what has come to be known as "responsible parenthood" in the mainline churches. It is also my conviction that such resistance and boundary crossing involve more than being an individual "agent for change" (to quote one evangelical college's motto for its graduates). Such boundary crossing and hope involve alliances and friendships and a multifaceted posse accountable for keeping tenacious hope alive. Here I will risk autobiography through a reading of adoption, one formal way of reflecting within the family the malleability of kinship.

"You just never know who you might end up with." Parents in the United States who embark on the work of hospitality through adoption almost invariably have stories to tell about receiving this particular caution, shared with remarkable liberality by friends, family, colleagues (yes, even theologians), and well-meaning people in the grocery store.[7] In my own family, we have come to call this the Rachel Lynde response, for Mrs. Lynde's words to Marilla in Lucy Maud Montgomery's 1908 novel *Anne of Green Gables:* "I'll just tell you plain that I think you're doing a mighty foolish thing — a risky thing, that's what. You don't know what you're getting. You're bringing

---

6. Christine Pohl, *Making Room: Recovering Hospitality as a Christian Tradition* (Grand Rapids: Eerdmans, 1999), p. 61.

7. These stories reside at the place of family identity and strangeness, much like the stories of families who otherwise do not fit the supposed "norm" due to race, class, and disability.

a strange child into your house and home and you don't know a single thing about him nor what his disposition is like nor what sort of parents he had nor how he's likely to turn out."

Although the technologically tested and meticulously planned adoption practiced by many upper-class Americans may no longer seem exactly a *"foolish* thing" to mainline Americans, adoption itself continues to be perceived as a "risky thing." As historian Barbara Melosh explains in *Strangers and Kin: The American Way of Adoption,* the sense of risk and inheritance from earlier eras continues to resound.[8]

The Rachel Lynde response begs for theological analysis. I will here name only three possible points. First, to suggest that an adoptive parent doesn't "know what" she is getting challenges the doctrine of creation. Christians can be certain that by adopting a human child they will be adopting a creature bearing the *imago Dei.* At least this would be the orthodox narration of divine creation.

Second, while adoption is a "foolish" and "risky" thing, it is true in a way that may be precisely the point of Christian soteriology. A strand of Protestant theology affirms that Christians are saved inasmuch as we are indeed ourselves adopted. Adoption is the form of salvation — a form that was and is for God quite foolish and risky. Fundamental to many articulations of salvation in Protestant hymns, liturgies, and sermons is the idea that adoption is the mode by which we ourselves become children of God. The way mainline Protestants think about adoption, therefore, may be a sort of test case for two doctrines of Protestant theology.

Finally, Rachel Lynde's warning that one never knows how an adopted child is "likely to turn out" is an error of eschatology. It is a wrong reading of history, if God is the author of history. Whether by a Calvinist reading of predestination or a Methodist hope for universal salvation, the idea that one's genetic parentage is an indication of one's place in God's salvation history is heresy. By my own Methodist tradition, I am to affirm the hope that this child, and each child, is "likely to turn out" at the heavenly banquet — in spite of the quite original ways each child is capable of sinning before the age of twelve. This eschatological way of reading parenthood requires a recalibration of mainline American thought about time. The past, present, and future of each and every life may be read as narrated by the moment when God created the world out of nothingness. History itself may be read as narrated

8. Barbara Melosh, *Strangers and Kin: The American Way of Adoption* (Cambridge: Harvard University Press, 2002). See in particular chapter 2, "Families by Design: 'Fitness' and 'Fit' in the Creation of Kin," pp. 51-104.

by the moment when Christ became for the world our salvation. The narrative of Anne, and of Rachel Lynde, brings the past, present, and future together, blessedly, in God's own palm.

Here an old book from my archival digging — a book that provides a counterpoint to Napheys's *Transmission of Life* discussed in chapter 3 — may be of use. The Reverend M. T. Lamb's *Heredity,* published twenty-seven years after Napheys's text on inheritance, offers a more theologically astute voice on the true transmission of life. The work is billed as "the second in a Series of four Booklets on CHILD SAVING."[9] As the superintendent of the New Jersey Children's Home Society, Lamb was apparently intent on persuading Christians to contribute toward the "unfortunate ones" who came from "such lowly and depraved beginnings" as those who ended up in the Home Society (p. 5).

With an apology from the outset for "discussing so bluntly and freely such delicate matters as prenatal influence," Lamb takes on the question most often posed to him in his appeals for hospitality on behalf of children (p. 4). He names the subject of the book — heredity — as the greatest barrier to hospitality facing the boys and girls for whom he is responsible: "The Society with which the writer is connected, in common with all similar child-saving agencies, finds this the one great, insuperable obstacle to its work in the minds of many of the best families of the country" (p. 7). Lamb accentuates the correlation between inhospitality and the ostensible means for extending such: "As a matter of fact, the objection grows stronger as you ascend the social scale."

Lamb's *Heredity* is a vibrant work of apologetics. Using statistics, anecdotal evidence, homiletic and photographic images, Lamb sets out to convince even "the best families of the country" that the children waiting at the Home Society "measure well up to the average" (p. 8). Given the expense of printing photographs in 1898, Lamb's extensive use of photography is worth attention. The book features portraits of children dressed in their Victorian finest with incongruous captions such as "Children Whose Fathers Drank" (fig. 5.2). The text describing one image reads: "Let now my readers who are skilled in 'Nature reading' scan the faces of these children, and see if you can discover any traces whatever of the drunkard's brand, either physically or morally" (p. 55). And again, "If you could pick two of the noblest parents on earth, father and mother both of royal nature and character, you could hardly look from such a union for a boy with a nobler countenance or more promising appearance" (p. 56).

Lamb's use of the photographic image may be read as a crafty piece of

9. M. T. Lamb, *Heredity* (Trenton, N.J.: Naar, Day and Naar, 1898), title page. Page references to this work have been placed in the text.

**Figure 5.2. "Children Whose Fathers Drank." From *Heredity*, by M. T. Lamb**

Children Whose Fathers Drank.

holy mischief, for he uses the tools of those who at this same time were determined to erect all possible obstacles to his form of "child saving." Sir Francis Galton's 1869 publication *Hereditary Genius* had years earlier been received with enthusiasm in the United States. An early enthusiast in the use of photography, Galton had begun using a method he termed "composite photography" as a rhetorical tool five years before he coined the term "eugenics."[10] Through photographic images, Galton had hoped to encourage others in the United States and the United Kingdom to perform a kind of "psychological inquiry." As one modern curator explains, "Galton experimented until the end of his life with a variety of techniques for making composites, including placing strips of mirrors at different angles to images and viewing the results through a telescope, . . . compounding photos with a copy-camera of his design."[11] A new form of knowledge had lent scientific legitimacy to the older "common sense" regarding class, race, and inherited "impurity," and the visual image of people considered on either end of the eugenic-to-cacogenic spectrum was a persuasive tool.[12]

10. Carol Squiers, *Perfecting Mankind: Eugenics and Photography,* exhibition brochure (New York: International Center of Photography, January 11–March 18, 2001), p. 6; available online at http://museum.icp.org/museum/exhibitions/eugenics/intro1.html.

11. Squiers, *Perfecting Mankind,* p. 8.

12. Squiers, *Perfecting Mankind,* p. 5.

The first chapter of Lamb's *Heredity* directly addresses the implications of Galton's text: "I have purposely multiplied illustrations strong, clear and apparently convincing, so that the warmest advocates of the certainties and the almost omnipotent power of hereditary laws cannot accuse me of unfairness."[13] Lamb then chips away at the idea of heredity. Arguing that "some of the brightest children we have ever received" have come from almshouses, Lamb dispels "inherited poverty" (pp. 34-35). Pointing to "some of the great geniuses, the mighty intellects that have sprung from the common herd," Lamb counters inherited feeblemindedness (p. 84). Insisting that "even if the immediate relatives were bad, there have been some good people back somewhere," Lamb resists the obsession with maternal influence (p. 44). Addressing head-on "the facts so clearly stated by Mr. Dugdale" regarding the "Juke family" (referring to *The Jukes: A Study in Crime, Pauperism, Disease, and Heredity* [1875]), Lamb argues that Scripture attests to the complicated nature of inheritance — after all, David's "very large family of children seem nearly all to have gone to the bad" (pp. 96, 99).

All the while, Lamb intersperses the visual rhetoric of photographed portraiture, as in the case of "Freddie": "Look at Freddie's face. There is certainly nobility there, royal blood from some source" (p. 78) (fig. 5.3). This pattern is indicative of Lamb's underlying theme of otherwise unrecognized worth, his first line of defense against the "insuperable obstacle" of an "unknown pedigree." His readers, Lamb says, would surely agree with his "almost instantaneous conclusion after seeing [Freddie]: 'I'll take my chances on such a face as that'" (p. 75).

This method of argumentation brings Lamb's case to an impasse, however. Lamb's use of portraiture and statistics is ultimately problematic, as he seems quite clearly aware. What if a child had inherited a strong dose of taint? What if the child were not white (as were all the children photographed), not fine featured (ditto), and not dressed in Victorian finery? What about a child whose physical countenance did not clearly "fit" in the eyes of the perspicacious readers of *Heredity?*

After having appealed to the visible confirmation of goodness and the calculable estimation of worth, Lamb shifts gears. It is this shift that I wish to underscore as essential for readers today. Lamb's answer to what he calls the "Conceit of 'Our Blood'" is worth quoting at length:

> The major portion of the objections urged by good Christian people against receiving into their homes and hearts certain children with supposed unfortunate antecedents is the offspring of conceit, pure conceit in

---

13. Lamb, *Heredity*, p. 31. Page references have again been placed in the text.

**Figure 5.3. "Freddie." From**
***Heredity,* by M. T. Lamb**

HEREDITY. 75

"Freddie is a lovely boy. We think a great deal of him. He is in our estimation a handsome bit of boyhood; full of life and mischievous, of course, but free, we think, from all bad traits. It was a mercy he was rescued. He is doing well in a Methodist preacher's home, and nothing would please your humble servant more than to have him grow up to be also a preacher of the gospel."

Freddie.

I think the majority of my readers will agree with my almost instantaneous conclusion, after seeing him: "I'll take my chances on such a face as that." Nor would you stop to inquire very particularly about his antecedents. Our notions of heredity all go to the winds in the presence of such a face.

the quality of our blood. "We and our children are A No. 1. The blood that flows through our veins is first-class blood; heredities all good. Thank the Lord we are not as other men; that Publican over there in the slums or carrying the coal-hod is low down, 'submerged'; his children are born with 'unfortunate antecedents,' and we need to be careful what privileges are accorded them." This is simple, simon-pure conceit. (p. 68)

After countering point by point the eugenic case on heredity, Lamb turns to "The 'New Heredity' or Regeneration" (p. 108). Here Lamb takes on the fundamental presumption he faces in his work with those who have the obvious economic resources to take in children variously orphaned by a death-dealing world. The entire matter of inherited taint and supposed nobility, he asserts, should hardly be of issue to Christians. For, with original sin, "all that is best and noblest in us is trampled in the dust and spoiled" (p. 109). Only through divine grace is *any* child granted "restoration." Clearly addressing the supposedly "finer" people to whom he has attended in his appeal, Lamb calls his hearers to recognize that such a meritocracy is contrary to grace. All pretensions are exposed: "God, in His infinite love for our fallen race, has thus planned our complete rescue and deliverance from the slavery of heredity" (p. 113).

Lamb's booklet is but a small light, but it answers in rather succinct form much that is covered in my own small book.

## "Fallen Buttons"

I would thus suggest two points to ponder. Resisting the norms of meticulously planned parenthood requires tackling head-on two facets of mainline Protestant life in the United States. First, resistance involves faith in a future secured, neither through scientific progress nor by way of the march of children to advance the race, but through the inscrutable birth of one child — the Word made flesh in an inauspicious manger surrounded by livestock. Second, and this is for me the trickiest part, resistance involves eschewing the various means by which I am to distinguish my own daughters from children who seem vaguely "backward," from those who are considered "at risk," from neighborhoods that seem forsaken by God and from schools deemed by quantified percentages to be subpar. Resistance means not only following the Word born in Bethlehem but also bringing one's own children along, to identify with and live among those considered to be the least of these.

Aspiring women like myself, eager to be of use to our children, our neighbors, our generation, and our country, are the target audience of *Together*, General Electric, "Atomic Energy as a Force for Good," and the American Medical Association's guides for prenatal testing. We are to be inspired to live into the echoes reverberating from image to life, from technological hope to messy present, from domestic order to family reality. Such women are the target audience for this book in another way. It is the white, middle-to-upper-middle-class womb on which the state and the market draw their sights. Our bodies have become the targets of quality control.

I hope my book encourages women like myself to be an audience to a very different story of fragility and life. This sort of life is not *progressive,* moving forward into a great big beautiful tomorrow crafted by Disney, the American military, or even the well-funded theological academy. This sort of life, as I read it, is more about apparently nonproductive repetition than about discernible progression. The story told in the hymns interspersed in this book is not so much a story of cleaning up and getting better and going on toward a brighter, American tomorrow, but a story of daily patience and vulnerability. It is the work of discipleship to string beads onto yarn with no clear knot on the end. I believe that seeing one's own nuclear family as set within a cyclical, liturgical repetition of vulnerability, joy, and lament —

through Christ's birth, death, and resurrection — may free anxious white mothers like myself from our clawed climb to normalcy. I thus wish to encourage women configured as progressive to recognize that Christian faith is, in an important sense, a call to accept into our lives children who will not "get better," learn to read, or make a name for themselves in the local or national paper. The call to be a Christian has become, for me, a call to risk seeming like just the sort of backward, crazy, Holy Spirit–inspired white girl that my grandmothers hoped I would progress beyond.

In the midst of trying to live up to the quality testing — from prenatal to preschool to precollege testing — our aspirations involve at least implicitly our desire to climb well above those other mothers who make mistakes, breed indiscriminately, risk shame, and cause a drag on the economy. I do indeed, in this way, target for moral interrogation women like myself for our complicity in the narrations that render other women's wombs as prodigal. While this estimation of my sisters may sound harsh, please hear also how eager I am to be proven wrong. Please, dear target audience, prove me wrong. It is my hope that a few white women reading this book will enter those areas, neighborhoods, and schools considered to be retrograde, and find that the Holy Spirit is already at work.

Those who hope to practice such resistance may pull on a small but still resilient thread through the mainline Protestant history in the United States. The early Wesleyan deaconesses in Chicago, for example, went forth unassumingly to offer what they could to those very same people whom eugenicists deemed contaminated.[14] There is also the embodied testimony of the women inspired by Jane Addams, whom *Together* magazine names as one

---

14. I am grateful to Abby Kocher for pointing out in a seminar the direct relevance of Professor Laceye Warner's work on the deaconesses to my own project. See in particular on the deaconess ministry to immigrant populations Laceye Warner, "'Toward the Light': Lucy Rider Meyer and the Chicago Training School." Accessed 2004: www.garrett.edu. One relevant quotation reads: "Immigrants were often captive to the systemic poverty within treacherously overpopulated urban neighborhoods throughout Chicago. M.E. Deaconesses offered ministries of compassion to immigrants through visiting, nursing, employment counseling, resource groups for mothers, English language training, social reform advocacy, as well as industrial schools and Sunday schools for children. At times subtexts of fear and prejudice, even among M.E. Deaconesses, contributed to negative stereotypes and the manipulation of evangelization into Americanization. For the most part, however, the M.E. Deaconesses' ministries dismantled barriers of class, race, and gender reshaping the Wesleyan theme of new creation on the background provided by the theological context of the time." See also Laceye Warner, "Offer Them Christ: Characteristics of a Wesleyan Paradigm for Evangelism," in *The Wesleyan Tradition: A Paradigm for Renewal*, ed. Paul Chilcote (Nashville: Abingdon, 2002), and Laceye Warner, *Saving Women* (Waco: Baylor University Press, 2007).

of its own in a 1957 essay titled simply "Jane Addams of Hull House."[15] In the same city that Lucy Rider Meyer trained deaconesses as part of the Chicago Training School, Addams matured to resist both the comfortable sentimentality of her age and the various eugenic schemes for justifying the margins of lives that did not fit. Addams arrived at her most mature thought when she recognized that she had much to learn from the very immigrant mothers she had deemed previously to be her projects. There are other small but vital stories, narratives known in families, congregations, neighborhoods, and families that attest to the *otherwise*. It is my hope that readers, in conversation with others who know their stories, will be inspired to holy mischief that is beyond my current reckoning.

Here, let me pause in the crescendo of authorial hope. It is all too easy for a perpetually distant father or grandfather in the theological academy to say a hearty "Amen!" to what I have written in this book. (After all, there was and is little public expectation that they will organize the children's sock drawers or keep the toilets clean or braid hair in time for the school bus.) It is entirely another thing for a woman changing Pampers or Depends to find the faith not to give up and throw out babies, elders, and the bathwater they are in. While I have narrated the ways that domesticity in America can be death dealing, I wish also here on the last pages to note that the bits of twig and twine with which many mothers patch together nests for our children and for those who come through our doors are not extraneous to the work of discipleship. The Good Samaritan receives plenty of credit throughout the Christian ages, but it was the innkeeper who cleaned the wounds and changed the bandages and held the recurring nightmares at bay. It is in part because these tasks are incarnate and holy that I wish to decompress the setting of scrupulously choosy motherhood.

One way to decompress is indeed through a deep consideration of sacramental life. I hope in my next book to write on the way of hope wrought in the blood and body of the Eucharist. But for now, I will risk one reference to Baptism. The repetitive work of caring for real bodies may be set within a strange narrative of God's repetitive work of drowning us, and raising us again to new life. Marilynne Robinson, in her novel *Housekeeping,* describes the texture of postbaptismal life incarnate more beautifully than I can. In the extended passage, the main character, Ruthie, is musing about the possibilities of her aunt Molly's work as a missionary. As it turns out, Aunt Molly

---

15. Karl Detzer, "Jane Addams of Hull House," *Together,* January 1957, pp. 14-16. See also Jean Bethke Elshtain, *Jane Addams and the Dream of American Democracy: A Life* (New York: Basic Books, 2002).

worked a desk job, but Ruthie (and the reader) here catches a glimpse of what it might mean to live with a kind of eschatological, hopeful realism in our homes and even in our most blighted regions.

> Even now I always imagine her leaning from the low side of some small boat, dropping her net though the spumy billows of the upper air. Her net would sweep the turning world unremarked as a wind in the grass, and when she began to pull it in, perhaps in a pell-mell ascension of formal gentlemen and thin pigs and old women and odd socks that would astonish this lower world, she would gather the net, so easily, until the very burden itself lay all in a heap just under the surface. . . .
>
> Such a net, such a harvesting, would put an end to all anomaly. If it swept the whole floor of heaven, it must, finally, sweep the black floor of Fingerbone, too. . . . There would be a general reclaiming of fallen buttons and misplaced spectacles, of neighbors and kin, till time and error and accident were undone, and the world became comprehensible and whole.[16]

For Robinson, the task of gathering all twine and twig is not our own. The task of making our children's world comprehensible and whole is not our own. This job has been taken. She will be back, and all that has been lost will be brought near.

## "'Tis Mercy All"

Hubris is the occupational hazard of moral theology. There have been times, during my research project, when I have succumbed to the notion that I must narrate truthfully and with prophetic witness every single bit of research on domestic marketing. I have been tempted, in short, to bring to every reader a coherent and compelling witness to life. In my zeal to document the American version of justification by responsible procreation, I have found myself determined to *save the day*. It was during just such a time in my own work, when I was so very weary from the task of trying to save the day, that I received an unexpected reminder that the job of saving the day, and saving the world, has already been taken.

I was searching the Internet for images from the National Typical American Family Contest, held as a part of the New York World's Fair of 1939-40 and sponsored by the Federal Housing Administration, the Fair trustees,

---

16. Marilynne Robinson, *Housekeeping: A Novel* (1980; reprint, New York: Picador, 2004), pp. 91-92.

and the Ford Motor Company. The questionnaires and qualifications for the contest closely resembled those of the Fitter Families for Future Firesides contest of the American Eugenics Society.

In my search I came across a culturally rich (and delightful) set of images posted by a woman named Patty Roberts. A grandmother, Patty has chronicled much of her own history online for her family's enjoyment. She has provided details about her childhood home in Sudbury, Massachusetts, pictures of her and her brothers in a Tom Thumb wedding, and a photograph of their First Congregational Church. Patty has included several pictures from her family's participation in the Typical American Family Contest, including both the official and unofficial portraits of the family, who won fifth place. In the unofficial photograph, Patty stands with a smirk and a Band-Aid on her knee. In another photograph the family sits together, looking a bit weary, listening to a prerecorded narration of progress in the General Electric building (fig. 5.4).

The photographs were irresistible. I summoned up my courage and wrote to the address posted on the site. Given that Patty grew up in the Congregationalist stronghold of Massachusetts, I worried that she would be offended by my project. (Many women had been in the past.) There was a good chance that she would get a sense of the potentially pro-life undertow of my work and send me a message of dismissal or even admonishment. So I wrote a fairly guarded, vague description of my project. Patty wrote back immediately, wanting to know more. So, summoning up more courage, I wrote back with a very clear description of my research and a bit of my own story as an adoptive mother.

I learned next that the Holy Spirit works in ways that I had not mapped and could not map as a scholar, theologian, or pastor. Her letter reminded me that my project on the American family is based on a truth about which I can only, with gratitude, testify. I learned that indeed there are stories of resistance and hope written into even the official portrait of a family that actually *won* by the rules of what counted as "typical" during the period I had been covering. This stranger from the Internet brought me a word of clear hope, from the history I had been covering and from the present I hoped to help ensure. Patty responded with a letter, included (with her permission) below. She relates the blessed reality that was the complicated family life that led them to the fair in the first place, and that led them to be a family that is atypically hopeful.

I sat at the computer and, honestly, wept tears of gratitude. In the midst of my lament for sterilized, incarcerated, incinerated, terminated, and discarded bodies, I had almost lost sight of the one to whom I was to lament. Lament, after all, presupposes one who will listen, and receive our mourning and rage. Through the message from Patty Roberts, I was reminded in an

**Figure 5.4.** Patty Roberts (second from left) and family. Fifth-place winners in the Typical American Family Contest, New York World's Fair, 1939-40

aptly idiosyncratic way that God was already up to the mischief of the Holy Spirit, working in and between the bits of eugenic and domestic culture I had been bringing together in my research. It is my closing prayer that families who read this book will find it possible to receive with a tenacious joy what is not typically depicted on the covers of magazines or in the statistics on selective termination or in the patterns of carefully segregated children.

I thus close my own narrative with Patty's testimony to another kind of "worth." If it is the case that the fairs to progress and the domestic magazines and the other conduits of popular family media in the United States are not the whole story of conceiving parenthood in America, it is my hope that the other, contravening stories may be formally similar to dear Patty's story. To employ one recent reading of consumer culture, if it is possible that the consumer may take over the tools given her by the dominant biotech market and own them in creative, life-affirming ways, then Patty's story must not be viewed as beyond the realm of reality. My question to those who say consumer culture may be taken over by the forces for life, asked with hope and in prayer, is: "Is it possible that these malleable tools might be used in ways akin to Patty's own family?" Like the hymns that intersperse the chapters of this book, Patty's letter may be a testimony to the complicated *otherwise* that is faithful life together.

Dear Laura,

Thank you so much for clarifying my questions. Your response was very enlightening and I did get a few chuckles from parts of it. My Dad only entered the contest so that we all could go to the World's Fair as there wasn't any financial way that we could have. We also had the reunion party at our place as we were the ones who had the space for that many people. We didn't pay for the party and I don't know who actually did but I would presume that the sponsors of the contest could have.

Dad entered many contests in his life, the World's Fair being the second, as when he and Mum got married, they were married in the Boston Home Gardens, 1932, in front of 16,000 people from a contest he won. Along the way coming from MA to CA in 1949, we were on the "Welcome Travelers" radio show in Chicago with Tommy Bartlett and the list goes on.

My Mum and Dad kept me clothed in Shirley Temple style due to the fact she had found a lady who purchased the clothes for her daughter and Mum bought them from her really inexpensively after the daughter had outgrown them. So I guess you could say, I wore second hand clothes! [smile] I didn't mind as they were so pretty and nice. We weren't putting on any pretence to look like what we weren't, as clothes were clothes to us and Shirley Temple was in vogue at that time. In fact, clothing me that way was cheaper than buying them in a store and nicer.

You mentioned that you have an adopted child; our son has four, one from Korea, one from Mexico, one Peruvian/German and one from Africa. Some of them came with medical issues that required attention but they couldn't have more love than if they were born naturally to them as who is to say that their own wouldn't have been ill also? They are smart kids in school and have many abilities.

Then our oldest daughter has a ten year old adopted son who has Duchenne's MD [muscular dystrophy], Autism, C.P., is hearing impaired, non verbal and non ambulatory and he's incontinent. He was the product of incest. She adopted him when he was eighteen months old. She already had two sons by birth. Her life has been totally involved with caring for special handicapped children and one point in time she fostered two young girls for quite a few years. Neither could talk nor walk and had to have all of their food blended. At that time she had the three children in wheel chairs and each of them had to have complete care. They all looked like they just stepped out of a band wagon as they were clean and [had] well kept hair and nice stylish clothes. The only time she could have to herself was her very limited respite care for the children. Now in her life, she cares for disabled adults and goes to their homes to care for them, working within her own schedule of her son. The other two sons are already out of school and gone from the home. She has been single for the past three-four years. She is quite a lady and the most Christ like person I have ever met and I am so very proud of her.

I really would hate to think that any of my 13 grandchildren and almost three g[reat]-grandchildren could or would have been terminated before birth as they have brought such joy to our families. Hard for the parents at times, yes, but very worth it for the love given and received. My oldest daughter's son, who is now ten years old, has been a joy to be around. Not when he gets into his screaming rages but when he cuddles next to you (licking you) and his arms around your neck and you get a big hug. The twinkle in his eyes melts your heart when he does something that he knows he shouldn't, even though he has pretty serious developmental disabilities as well. The doctors have told her that he is writing his own book as he has accomplished things they never thought he could nor would. We like to think that it was because of the unlimited love and wonderful care that he has gotten that has made the difference. When he is on the floor rolling around, he will go over to the bookcase where she has put family pictures on the bottom shelf for him. He will reach behind some of them to find Grandpa's picture, grab it and put it to his face and just slobber it. (His way of loving) There are spirits inside those disabled bodies so who can rightfully take their lives away? We feel that, somehow, they understand, even if only in their own way.

I guess I have rattled enough here about my family but knowing that you have an adopted child just pushed my button for me to tell you about ours.

Yes, you may use what you need to make your point for your book. I am proud of who I am and how I got to this point in my life. Trials, errors and life experience have a lot to do with who I am and as like a lot of folks, not much of it has been easy. I like a saying I once saw that was on a picture of Christ: "I never said it would be easy, but it will be worth it."

Warmly,
Patty Roberts

# Acknowledgments

The only danger in saying that this book is a group effort is to risk the supposition that people named here are in agreement with my choice and interpretation of the material. I will, nonetheless, risk saying that I could not have sustained this book without the support, the prayers, the arguments, the news snippets, and the many, many stories of hope and resistance that I received along the way.

In November of 2006, as I was completing the last edits of the manuscript, Lauren Winner sent to me a link to a news item. The presiding bishop of the Episcopal Church in the United States granted an interview to the *New York Times Magazine*. In response to a question regarding the Episcopal Church's diminishing numbers, the bishop made a distinction between the congregants of the Episcopal Church and those of the Roman Catholic and Mormon churches:

Q: How many members of the Episcopal Church are there in this country?
A: About 2.2 million. It used to be larger percentagewise, but Episcopalians tend to be better-educated and tend to reproduce at lower rates than some other denominations. Roman Catholics and Mormons both have theological reasons for producing lots of children.

Q: Episcopalians aren't interested in replenishing their ranks by having children?
A: No. It's probably the opposite. We encourage people to pay attention to the stewardship of the earth and not use more than their portion.

My students, colleagues, friends, and family could plausibly be divided up between those who think this statement just goes to prove all that is wrong with the Episcopal Church and those who would respond to the bishop with a resounding "Hear, Hear!" Both groups could also likely predict how I would interpret the bishop's remarks within the history of her (indeed, quite select and wealthy) mainline church in the United States. (I would encourage them to compare the percentage per person of square footage of air-conditioned and heated space taken up by Episcopalians in the city of Durham, North Carolina, with that taken up by Latino Catholics. Or to compare the dollars per person spent on clothing, on food, on automobiles, on gasoline. . . . Indeed, environmentalism comes in many forms.) I have subjected many, many dear people to my cultural-historical readings of class distinction, family planning, and constructions of words like "stewardship" and "the earth," and just what constitutes a "portion" for a particular community of faith in the United States.

As I droned on at potluck dinners, taught in congregations, lectured at secular institutions, and discussed the material for this book with students across the country and in Europe, the web of people sending me news snips about conceiving parenthood spread, and so did the web of people subjected, in turn, to my cultural analysis of news snips. Many such people responded to me in some form, pushing back against my interpretations and concerns or pushing even further than I had gone in one direction or another. This book thus reflects a crisscrossing map of face-to-face, phone, and epistolary conversation with scholars, parents, children, congregants, and scientists, some of whom love what I have written (and shudder at the bishop's remarks) and others of whom are quite grateful to God that I am not the presiding bishop of any church.

The scholarly and pedagogical acknowledgments for this book must go back to my undergraduate days studying sociology, politics, and cultural history at Emory. My sneaking suspicion that biotechnology, race, and class are intertwined in the United States grew through a myriad of readings and encounters. A course at Emory entitled "Southern Women, Black and White" with Professor Elizabeth Fox-Genovese formed me indelibly. As we sat there, many of us indeed women from the South and thus women configured racially on either side of a still-unbridgeable divide, we read (among other books) *Iola Leroy, The Private Mary Chesnut, Strange Fruit,* and *The Bluest Eye.* It was in this course that I began to try to articulate the intractable differences across racialized gender, as well as my hope in sober solidarity. After hearing bell hooks at Emory, I read *Feminist Theory: From Margin to Center,* which resituated for me every question posed by mainstream white feminism. Around this same time I attended a lecture by Marian Wright Edelman on the

Children's Defense Fund (CDF). Many of the liberal white participants (my own kind) were right on board with the efforts of the CDF, but only as long as their contributions could be made from a safe distance, keeping their *own* children securely segregated in gated communities and high-performing schools in Atlanta, the "city too busy to hate."

It was at this same time that I read, with Professor Nancy Ammerman, Max Weber's *The Protestant Ethic and the Spirit of Capitalism* (1905). If the culturally dominant Protestantism of the nineteenth century was characterized by efficient, productive, seemly labor, how might the culturally dominant Protestantism of the twentieth century help one interpret that century's women's labor? I began to suspect that what "everyone" in the academy knew about the South — that race and class had everything to do with whether a woman's body, baby, and kitchen were considered providential or accidental — might also be applicable to other regions. To paraphrase bell hooks, the holy mystique of *better* families may depend on a divide between *those* children and *ours*.

Friends who know me as a theologian have asked how in the world I came to write this book after having written a book on the writings of a dead white Danish man. One way to answer this question is with a story. In 1999 Thomas Murray, president of the Hastings Center for bioethics research, came to Yale to talk about his recent book *The Worth of a Child*. His lecture and the discussion afterward revolved around biotechnology and parenting — in particular, the growing array of prenatal testing and the emergence of childhood enhancement therapies. I was at the time a doctoral candidate in the last stages of completing my dissertation on Søren Kierkegaard. I was also a new mother and a newly ordained minister. I was serving as director of Christian education for children at an amazing church, First and Summerfield United Methodist Church. This work of holy mischief is an interracial, downtown congregation that reflects one formal church merger and many intricate fissures along race, class, and kinship lines. While Murray lectured on parenthood, children, and biotechnology, I kept a running set of threads going in my head regarding my ministry, motherhood, and the texts of Kierkegaard.

I had spent countless hours that year with Kierkegaard's *Works of Love*, in particular his suggestion that only infinite debt can give breath to veritable love; for Kierkegaard, finite appraisal and critical comparison suffocate love. Murray's reflections on the incalculable quality of childhood seemed to run right alongside these Kierkegaardian insights. Hearing Murray describe the temptation to perfect procreation through biotechnology, I heard as well echoes of Kierkegaard's pseudonymous musings on the near sacrifice of Isaac in

*Fear and Trembling.* I found myself newly questioning my frightening, fierce delight in my firstborn, and my pastoral, perhaps near-maternal possessiveness about the children struggling toward fellowship at First and Summerfield.

These thoughts emerged in a quite inchoate question I posed to Murray regarding love, baptism, biotechnology, and the quest for "better children." With characteristic grace, Murray tried to reword my question in a way that he hoped would make sense to me and to his audience. Was I asking him about the limits of genetically modifying human embryos, perhaps? Was I trying to discern the morality of using human growth hormone on children who are not hGH-deficient?

No, I replied (less graciously). I was asking an altogether different set of questions. I wished to trouble the working distinction between *my* child and an *other* woman's child. I wanted to trouble the way that aspiring, white mothers live through our children as if their accomplishments were our, and their, justification. I sought to probe a culture of "choosy" mothers. I wished to ask how baptism might upturn everything women like myself had been taught by middle-class Protestantism regarding "responsible parenthood" (which is the heading of the section in the *United Methodist Book of Resolutions* regarding family planning).

"Well, then," Murray rejoined with a laugh. "It seems that you are not only criticizing biotechnology. You apparently want to do away with piano lessons!" This book acknowledges the legitimacy of Thomas Murray's charge.

I am thus grateful to Thomas Murray, who helped me initially to name the strangeness of my questions, and to the congregation at First and Summerfield UMC, whose holy strangeness helped me to see what was at stake for communities of faith if we see children economically rather than through Baptism and Communion. Professors Margaret Farley and Gene Outka allowed me to struggle through the intersection of reproductive bioethics and Kierkegaardian faith in many conversations during my time at Yale. Reading Barbara Katz Rothman's book *The Tentative Pregnancy: How Amniocentesis Changes the Experience of Motherhood* was also crucial at this period of my formation. She has remained a gracious interlocutor. A. N. Williams, David Clough, Chris Steck, and Lauris Kaldjian each pressed me to name what was at stake in prenatal testing and selective termination. It was in friendship with each of them that I was able to begin to consider myself as a *pro-life* feminist. Jennifer Beste, Shannon Craigo-Snell, Lillian Daniel, and Karen Peterson-Iyer each pressed me, in different ways, to consider what it might mean to be a pro-life *feminist.* I will be grateful if each of these friends finds something of use in this book, for their agreements and disagreements were of incalculable worth to me as a scholar and mother.

I believe that it was Eric Gregory who first recommended that I read a little book by Oliver O'Donovan called *Begotten or Made?* In his evaluation of reproductive technology in the mid-1980s, O'Donovan put the matter in terms of practiced inefficiency: "Inefficiency is the worship [we] pay to the *humanum*, the human person and personal relationships, objects which cannot be subject to the laws which govern productive efficiency" (p. 73). What O'Donovan named regarding the field of reproductive technology and the pursuit of "productive efficiency" summarized the concern that has only grown for many in moral theology in the United States and the United Kingdom. I am grateful to Professor O'Donovan for this book, and for the many bioethics scholars who struggled through with me the implications of his work. Here I should name in particular the hospitality offered by the Society for the Study of Christian Ethics, whose members graciously allowed me to present my own reflections at two different meetings and on numerous occasions at various institutions in the United Kingdom: Brian Brock and John Swinton at Aberdeen, Esther Reed at St. Andrews, Bernd Wannenwetsch at Oxford, Celia Deane-Drummond at the University of Chester, Jolyon Mitchell and Michael Northcott at Edinburgh, and Sam and Jo Bailey Wells and Janet Soskice at Cambridge. Our dear friends Dan and Martina Holder offered hospitality and astute theological commentary a stone's throw from Safenwil.

Dean Greg Jones knew that I wanted eventually to critique the "medical industrial complex" (Barbara Ehrenreich's term), but he hired me nonetheless, for a position in the "City of Medicine," at a divinity school funded in part by biotech dollars. I am grateful for his courage. He suggested early on that I concentrate on a theology of baptism as the underpinning for my work in reproductive bioethics, and I hope that he will find his suggestion reflected in the book. Dean Willie Jennings convinced me to take a position at Duke in the first place, with his faith and joy in the work of the Holy Spirit in spite of human failings. Whenever I fell into a rough patch institutionally (and there were a few), he would say with a great laugh, "Amy Laura, you know your problem? You believe in Jesus!" I pray that readers find me guilty as charged. Dean Laceye Warner has been my colleague and friend for a decade. She is herself a true historian, and her suggestion, that I just "tell the story as I see it," was an abiding gift. Her work on the deaconess movement as a model for evangelism continues as a beacon.

Bishop Peter Storey and Bishop Ken Carder prayed for me and cajoled me not to give up on Methodism. Warren Smith and Steve Chapman came by to remind me to leave my desk and go to weekly worship. Teresa Berger, Thea Portier-Young, Tammy Williams, Susan Eastman, Cheryl Brown, Connie Shelton, Ellen Davis, and Mary McClintock Fulkerson each, in their own way, taught me when to testify and when to keep quiet. I did not always heed their advice, and their advice did indeed sometimes conflict, but I am grateful to have been on faculty with women who are engaged in a fruitful, blessed argument with and for one another. Richard Hays asked me while we were at Yale to reconsider the repercussions of a pro-choice ethic. My most trying questions to him, while we have been at Duke, have involved the repercussions of a seriously unconditional life ethic. He and Reinhard Hütter both encouraged me to pursue these questions, even as the questions became more than merely academic.

J. Kameron Carter arrived at Duke as I was beginning this project. I predict that his writing will reshape theology in the United States. He certainly shaped this book. When I first read an essay by Stanley Hauerwas, it was for a course at Yale with Margaret Farley. She suggested that I consider just how time-consuming and risky it is to care in the ways that Stanley has called Methodists to care. The Roman Catholic Church had leaned heavily on religious women to do the work of embodied hospitality; who was going to do this if Methodists were to take up a radical ethic of life? This book may be read in part as my hope that there is within even America's most mainstream church the ability to live up to the best that Stanley has written on disability. The fact that mainstream Methodism has not done so has to do in part with race and class fears. It is my prayer that Duke Divinity School may be an incarnate witness against those fears, lest others know we are Christian (only) by our books . . . by our books. . . . Grant Wacker invited me to fall in love again with cultural history, and his student, Sarah Johnson, spent more hours with me walking, talking, laughing, weeping, and praying about this project than any friend could expect. Sarah and also beloved Lauren Winner both read long portions of the book, with patience and prudence. Theologian Margaret Adam not only read a theology of hope to me, but read *Go, Dog. Go!* so many times to our youngest, Emily, that it became a kind of refrain as I tried to complete the project.

Colleagues in other departments at Duke have graciously lent me their ear and their perspective. Members of a working group on science and culture, led by Priscilla Wald, were particularly helpful. I am also grateful to Karla Holloway, who early on read the proposal and encouraged the work. Elizabeth Kiss, former director of the Kenan Center for Ethics, asked probing questions at vital points. Jeffrey Baker discussed the project from the beginning, in particular the role of technology in neonatal care. From philosophical ethicists to cultural anthropologists, there were colleagues across the humanities who offered aid and sometimes apt discouragement. In the sciences, Robert Cook-Degan suggested perspective on the origins of the Human Genome Project. Huntington Willard offered hospitality through the Institute on Genome Sciences and Policy (IGSP), asking me often to bring my research to the IGSP and also to teach in the elite FOCUS program in Trinity College. Scientists and students in the IGSP asked hard questions, offered apt skepticism, and continue to push my work in new ways.

My students at Duke Divinity School have been a delight. I am struck each semester by the work that the Holy Spirit is up to through their receptivity to the call to ministry. I would be remiss not to name in particular the members of one seminar focused explicitly on the material for this book. The hearty band of intrepid learners had to retool in cultural history while also catching signs of hope along the way. I pray that they find their influence here in these pages. As I was drawing the book to a close, I also taught an undergraduate course for first-semester students, incorporating material on national identity and progress. Their lively engagement with the questions taught me much about the ways that this material can be useful beyond my own narration. I hope that a few more students will take one of the many underdeveloped threads in the book and trace it back into the archives of their library. So much more is to be written. My students in the Trinitarian Class at Trinity United Methodist Church told me stories contemporaneous with my grandparents. They adopted me and my family as their own, and told me many stories of pain and hope amidst Jim Crow. Students in the Continuing Education Program at Duke Divinity School committed to consider radical hospitality in their congregations and city agencies. They transformed the Duke Alumni Memorial Common Room, with its rather stiff formality, into a place of vulnerable honesty and prayer.

Regarding congregational conversations, I must offer only an incomplete list of congregations and communities who engaged my work: Sierra Vista UMC, San Angelo; First UMC, Austin; Tarrytown UMC, Austin; First and Summerfield UMC, New Haven; St. Thomas More Roman Catholic Church, Chapel Hill; Immaculate Conception Catholic Church, Durham; Congregation Judea Reform, Durham; Blacknall Presbyterian, Durham; the Rutba House Community, Durham; the Isaiah House, Durham; our current parish, Trinity UMC, Durham; and the Anglican Congregation at Hawarden, Wales, who offered us gracious hospitality beyond measure. Within these communities, I must thank in particular the Knight family, Joan and Jean Link, Sarah Mustillo, Wendy Baucom, and Margot Hausmann (Proverbs 31), Jonathan Wilson-Hartgrove, Sarah Jobe, Jim Ayers, Joan Pepper, and Lauren Crowell. My two sisters, Rebecca and Laura Lee, linked up the stories of the book with the complicated stories of our lives. My brother, Bob, offered poignant humor and chaos Eucharist when that was most needed. Nana and Granddad Utz offered cookies, eggnog, and the blessings of Oak Grove UMC.

I am grateful to the Association of Theological Schools (ATS) for administering two grants that helped make this book possible — through the Lilly Foundation and the Luce Foundation. ATS facilitates as well conversation among scholars working across the range of disciplines, and these were invaluable. Ted Smith early on suggested that my reading of race and class in the eugenics material was applicable throughout. Brian Brock encouraged me to find the strands of resistance and hope in the very material that was also, by my reading, encouraging conformity and fear. The alternation of hymnody and narrative grew out of their prayers and the persistence of J. Kameron Carter. Dennis Durst, Sharon Leon, and Christine Rosen all very graciously shared their work on eugenics with me, and participated in a conference panel that helped me to sort through the historiography of eugenics. Stephen Ray was the respondent for that panel, and his suggestion that there is a working "conditional life ethic" at play in the United States crystallized for me what I wished to say in this book. I am very grateful for his work and friendship. Christina Cogdell's book and subsequent conversation were crucial. The editors at *Christianity Today,* in particular John Wilson, and at *Christian Century* offered me thorough questions from different spots along the Protestant spectrum. I am indebted to these editors for putting my work forward for two different readerships. To those readers who wrote to me, thank you. I received many helpful, prayerful, and thoughtful messages from pastors and laity through these essays related to the project. My thoughts were also shaped early on by gracious and probing conversations with Joel Shuman, Brian Volck, Margaret Bendroth, Christina Bieber-Lake, Jean Bethke-Elshtain, William Werpehowski, John Wall, Hans Reinders, Marcia Bunge, Gilbert Meilaender, John Witte, Don Browning, Paul Steven Miller, Karin Eschemann Ulrich, and Hans Ulrich. This is to leave out dozens of other scholars who have responded with assistance and advice.

The form of the project started while preparing for an invited lecture to the American Theological Library Association (ATLA). I am grateful for the invitation that came from Roger Lloyd and Andy Keck, both of whom have been supportive of this project with logistical and moral support. Early on, Andy became a gracious partner in research and documentation. The librarians who attended that lecture sent me archival sites and suggestions that sent the work rolling. I thus have many, many librarians to thank, from ATLA schools and non-ATLA schools. I hope that something in this book will send readers to dusty archives in corners of their blessed, blessed libraries. Fred Guyette at Erskine Seminary sent me information regarding the eugenics movement in the United States. Charles Bellinger, Charles Willard, and Martha Smalley each encouraged the digitizing of the images relevant to the project through a grant written by Andy Keck from ATLA. I hope people will make use of the database in their own teaching. Martha first introduced me to archival work when I was at Yale, and I hope to work further with her in the future. Both Robert Phillips and Holly Alyce Phillips offered me hospitality on a very snowy day at Roberts Library at Southwestern Baptist Theological Seminary. Holly Alyce was so very helpful to introduce me to a wonderful American Baptist periodical called *Hearthstone*. Bill Taylor of that same library facilitated our extended loan of *Hearthstone*. John Finley helped me learn about Milan, Missouri, and also allowed me the gift of learning with his daughter, Jennifer Finley. Crystal Smith at the National Library of Medicine helped me to follow a lead from NPR to the ASHA archivist, David Klaassen, at the Elmer Andersen Library of the University of Minnesota. David was consistent in his encouragement, commentary, and correction. I hope that I have not missed a historical nuance regarding the complicated sponsorship of the poster series. If I have, it was not due to lack of David's effort! Linnea M. Anderson of the Elmer Andersen Library very helpfully put me onto archival material for yet another project drawing on their archives, and Ahn Na Brodie provided technical assistance. Tracey A. Adams was the director of Community Outreach and Media Relations for the American Social Health Association when I began the project, and her move to the Divinity School allowed me the blessing of her commentary on the work. Gary N. Pattillo at UNC helped with verifying dates for publications. Denise Anderson at the University of Iowa Libraries helped to verify the dates of Walter Taylor Sumner's ministry at Saints Peter and Paul in Chicago. A blessed stranger at the Nagasaki Atomic Bomb Museum, Artifacts Section, confirmed the photograph of the Urakami Cathedral in Nagasaki.

The librarians in Special Collections at Duke University were untiring in their help with this project. Laura Micham, director of the Sallie Bingham Center, talked for hours about my work, and then sent me items of interest for years. The women with whom she works in Special Collections went digging for relevant advertisements, and even purchased new archival items on the Internet when possible. Here I must thank in particular Jacqueline Reid, director of the Hartman Center, for being an amazing sleuth. Lynn Eaton would not give up until she found the perfect Lysol advertisement for me, and Janie Morris corrected at least one error in dating. There were countless other occasions of conversation and digging. I would not have even known about the advertising council's images of the (literally) nuclear family if it were not for a member of that staff.

Then there were many lay archivists who befriended me along the way, sending me helpful links and information. Linda M. Young provided me with a synopsis of the Lassie movie, *The Painted Hills*. Kurt A. Sanftleben of Read'em Again Books helped me track down the reference for the Gold Dust Twins. James G. Mundie assisted with information about Ripley's Odditorium. Candi Griffin from *Carolina Parent* helped me track down the relevant citation. Thomas Hine, prolific author and commentator on popular culture, provided the terrific image of the mother cooking the nuclear-powered hamburger. Jim Taylor at the Health Adventure in Asheville, along with many other staff members of that terrific place, offered aid in various ways. Harry Finley helped me convince others that I was not making this stuff up. Elizabeth Baker put me on to the archived film site and to the importance of *A Is for Atom*. She also took her own time to help me figure out how to use a digital camera to begin taking my first digital photos of archived magazines.

I received generous grants from the Lilly Foundation, the Josiah Charles Trent Memorial Foundation, the Child in Religion and Ethics Project (directed by Professor Marcia Bunge at Valparaiso), the American Theological Library Association, and the Luce Foundation. Such gracious funding allowed me to pay for interested students to go with me into dusty archives, dig through back volumes, looking for the images that are represented here and on the ATLA digitizing Web site. These former students should not be held directly responsible for the politics or theology in this book. At times they wondered what in the world would become of my wacky ideas. On occasion they understood my project better than did I. Where indicated in the prose, these students collaborated by bringing me particularly compelling examples of ideas they had heard me sort through in class and elsewhere. Brian Madison offered me technical assistance before I had a penny of grant money, and before I knew what a scanner was. Bryan Langlands found the wonderful image from *Populuxe*, along with several others from the atomic era. Doug Johnson helped me sort through the postwar *National Geographic* issues, and I hope he will eventually write on the items I did not use. Plenty can still be written on the formation of national identity over and against Japan. Dan Rhodes found the particularly salient cover regarding the Columbine tragedy, and went through the manuscript to formalize the citations. Sarah Sours digitized every item for the ATLA project, and wrote up the metadata for future researchers on the Web. She and Jodie Boyer offered running commentary as we went through magazines from the 1920s to the 1950s, comparing them to their own memories and current realities of family life. Jennifer Mackenzie brought me the Disney short that summed up so perfectly one aspect of the book's argument. James St. Peter went digging through hymnals to make sure we were printing versions sung by congregants at the time covered and helped me to collect digitized images from last-minute finds. Sean Larsen and Craig Heilmann assisted in the final editing. Rebekah Eklund is responsible for the brilliant index. Without the help of Duke Legal Counsel and The Fair Use Project at Stanford Law School, this book would not be in print. I am grateful in particular for Kevin Smith and Anthony Falzone. AKM Adam introduced me to the Stanford project when I was ready to give up.

Carol Shoun was my writing mentor from the beginning of this project. As a faithful congregant and as an editor, she has shaped this book. She helped me to move from scholar to writer, and, many times, from despair to hope. Her patience with my prose was remarkable. I am grateful beyond chocolate. Joy-Elizabeth Lawrence read the entire manuscript and helped me to cull the images to the point where my grandmother's Sunday school class might actually be able to purchase it. Her sense of humor, inquisitiveness, and perspective were a gift, here at the end of this very long project. Tom Raabe took this final product, edited by all three of us, and moved it toward its final form, hopefully with all obscure metaphors and academic posturing thoroughly removed. If not, it is still my fault. Finally, Jon Pott stuck with this project from the point when it was a simple little book on bioethics to its present form. His faithfulness as a father, grandfather, and congregant, and the form of that faithfulness told during gracious lunches to discuss work and life, explains why it made sense for me to stick with Eerdmans, even as this project became a fairly complicated, big sort of book. I am grateful for fidelity.

I dedicated my first book, on the treachery of love, to John Fredric Utz. The words there will grow in relevance each passing year. As he has put it at times, "She writes the checks, and I have to cover them." While I have been digging into archives and capturing one story of death, he has been living into the truly difficult, daily work of life in a neighborhood, school, and family in need. The grind toward tenure at Duke was nothing in comparison to what many families around the world endure with grace each day. It seems almost obscene to complain. But it was unpleasant much of the time. Although union colleagues died on the picket lines to ensure a forty-hour workweek, faculty workers at Duke are expected willingly to submit to at least seventy. I am not proud of the weeks that I betrayed unionists and my family by trying to keep up. I am grateful, beyond words, for the minute and grand ways that John helped to hold us together. Rachel and Emily are so very blessed to have him as a daddy. Their friends in our neighborhood are blessed to have him as a host. The school children in their public school classes delight in his frequent work as a volunteer. Considering the cumulative work of the last seven years, I am amazed still to have him as my loving husband.

At least as important as any particular text or adult experience was my experience growing up in West Texas in Methodist parsonages, churches, and public schools. We moved often as my father itinerated, and there were two constants — my father's commitment to care for each and every congregant in even the trickiest parish, and my mother's abiding commitment to teach each and every student in even the most recalcitrant public school class. My mother's mother and father were also public school teachers in West Texas, teaching and counseling children, middle-class as well as working-class, Latino, African American, and Anglo, and seeking to be of use in the raising of offspring not biologically their own. They found food for that journey at First United Methodist, San Angelo, a congregation in a town marked by a brand-new high school, a military base, and the seasonal fragility of growing maize and raising sheep on semiarid land. My father's mother and father each grew up in the region around Palo Pinto County, settling eventually in a town marked by a huge WELCOME sign on a hill, a military base, and a nineteenth-century hotel that attracted out-of-towners for baths in mineral water. First United Methodist Church in Mineral Wells helped my formerly Baptist grand-mother prepare for a woman preacher in the family, and helped my grandfa-ther negotiate his role as a civic leader in the tumultuous 1960s. Both grand-mothers survived the task of raising children while their husbands served in World War II. Both grandfathers acquired the smoking habit with free ciga-rettes in boyhood, and each died from the results. Their stories and lives tra-verse the material I have typed up here in the North Carolina postindustrial town that was formerly known as Tobacco City. My daughters, Rachel and Em-ily, have the memories of generations etched into our daily lives as a family in the Texas diaspora. They will negotiate these memories and their future with the gifts and challenges received at Trinity United Methodist Church in Dur-ham. It is to my grandparents, parents, and children that I dedicate this book. The ways that this project has helped me to understand the pressures and blessings of the past may, I pray, be of some use to other people's children. I pray that the book may also be of some use to the parents and grandparents and congregations who try to conceive, and reconceive, the gift of each and ev-ery new life in our midst.

# Bibliography

Addams, Jane. *Twenty Years at Hull-House*. With autobiographical notes. New York: Penguin Books, 1961.

*A Is for Atom*. General Electric and Sutherland Productions, 1953. Film.

Alexander, Brian. *Rapture: How Biotech Became the New Religion*. New York: Basic Books, 2003.

American Academy of Pediatrics. "Television and the Family." http://www.aap.org/family/tv1.htm.

American Academy of Pediatrics Committee on Communications. "Media Violence." *Pediatrics* 95 (June 1995).

"America on the Move." *National Geographic*, September 1946.

Andrews, Lori B. *The Clone Age: Adventures in the New World of Reproductive Technology*. With a new afterword. New York: Henry Holt, 1999.

———. *Future Perfect: Confronting Decisions about Genetics*. New York: Columbia University Press, 2001.

Apple, Rima D. *Mothers and Medicine: A Social History of Infant Feeding, 1890-1950*. Madison: University of Wisconsin Press, 1987.

Arnold, H. H. "Air Power for Peace." *National Geographic*, February 1946.

"Art Gallery in a Church." *Together*, January 1957.

"At Nagasaki He Lost All — but His Faith!" *Together*, August 1957.

*Atomic Energy as a Force for Good*. The Christophers, 1955. Film.

Baker, Jeffrey P. *The Machine in the Nursery: Incubator Technology and the Origins of Newborn Intensive Care*. Baltimore: Johns Hopkins University Press, 1996.

Baldwin, Marian Park. "A Wardrobe for the College Girl." *Parents'*, September 1929.

Bamshad, Michael J., and Steve E. Olson. "Does Race Exist? About the Photo-illustrations." *Scientific American*, December 2003, p. 84.

Barney, Sandra Lee. *Authorized to Heal: Gender, Class, and the Transformation of Medicine in Appalachia, 1880-1930*. Chapel Hill and London: University of North Carolina Press, 2000.

Barrett, Amy. "When One Is Enough." *New York Times Magazine*, July 18, 2004.

Bartholet, Elizabeth. *Family Bonds: Adoption, Infertility, and the New World of Child Production.* With a new preface. Boston: Beacon Press, 1999.

Baudrillard, Jean. *Simulacra and Simulation.* Translated by Sheila Faria Glaser. Ann Arbor: University of Michigan Press, 1994.

—————. *The Vital Illusion.* Edited by Julia Witwer. New York: Columbia University Press, 2000.

Baumann, Zygmunt. *Liquid Modernity.* Cambridge, U.K.: Polity Press, 2000.

Baynton, Douglas. *Forbidden Signs: American Culture and the Campaign against Sign Language.* Chicago: University of Chicago Press, 1996.

Beck, Martha. *Expecting Adam: A True Story of Birth, Rebirth, and Everyday Magic.* New York: Times Books, 1999.

Belting, Hans. *Likeness and Presence: A History of the Image before the Era of Art.* Translated by Edmund Jephcott. Chicago: University of Chicago Press, 1997.

Bendroth, Margaret Lamberts. *Growing Up Protestant: Parents, Children, and Mainline Churches.* New Brunswick, N.J.: Rutgers University Press, 2002.

Bennett, Betsy. "Director's Report." *North Carolina Naturalist,* Spring/Summer 2002.

Berry, Wendell. *Life Is a Miracle: An Essay against Modern Superstition.* Washington, D.C.: Counterpoint, 2000.

Bérubé, Michael. *Life as We Know It: A Father, a Family, and an Exceptional Child.* New York: Vintage, 1996.

"Biography of Harold E. Stassen." Introductory notes to Harold Stassen Paper, Minnesota Historical Society.

"Birth Control Peril to Race, Says Osborn." *New York Times,* August 23, 1932.

Bishop, Edwin. "Eugenics and the Church." *Eugenics: A Journal of Race Betterment* 2 (August 1929): 14-19.

Biskind, Peter. *Seeing Is Believing: How Hollywood Taught Us to Stop Worrying and Love the Fifties.* New York: Pantheon Books, 1983.

Black, Edwin. *War against the Weak: Eugenics and America's Campaign to Create a Master Race.* New York: Four Walls Eight Windows, 2003.

Blackmar, Frank. "The Smoky Pilgrims." *American Journal of Sociology* 2 (January 1897): 485-500.

Bloch, Harry. "Thomas Morgan Rotch (1849-1914), America's First Full Professor of Pediatrics: His Contribution to the Emergence of Pediatrics as a Specialty." *Pediatrics* 50 (July 1972): 112-17.

Blumin, Stuart M. *The Emergence of the Middle Class: Social Experience in the American City, 1760-1900.* Cambridge: Cambridge University Press, 1989.

Boorstin, Daniel J. *The Image: A Guide to Pseudo-Events in America.* New York: Vintage, 1992.

Boyatzis, Chris J., and Gina M. Matillo. "Effects of 'The Mighty Morphin Power Rangers' on Children's Aggression with Peers." *Child Study Journal* 25 (1995): 45-56.

Boyer, Paul. *Urban Masses and Moral Order in America, 1820-1920.* Cambridge, Mass., and London: Harvard University Press, 1978.

———. *By the Bomb's Early Light: American Thought and Culture at the Dawn of the Atomic Age.* New York: Pantheon Books, 1985.

*Brain, Child: The Magazine for Thinking Mothers,* Summer 2003.

"Breast-Fed and Bottle-Fed Babies." *JAMA,* April 11, 1931.

Broad, Molly. "Genomics and Our Schools." *North Carolina Naturalist,* Spring/Summer 2002.

Bromley, Dorothy Dunbar. "Birth Control and the Depression." *Harper's Monthly Magazine,* October 1934.

Brown, Jordan. *The Gene Scene.* New York: American Museum of Natural History and the National Center for Science Literacy, Education, and Technology, 2001.

Bruinius, Harry. *Better for All the World: The Secret History of Forced Sterilization and America's Quest for Racial Purity.* New York: Knopf, 2006.

Brush, Edward F. "How to Produce Milk for Infant Feeding." *JAMA* 43 (1904): 1385.

Buchanan, Allen, Dan W. Brock, Norman Daniels, and Daniel Wilker. *From Chance to Choice: Genetics and Justice.* Cambridge: Cambridge University Press, 2000.

Butler, Jon. *Becoming America: The Revolution before 1776.* Cambridge: Harvard University Press, 2000.

Cameron, Nigel M. de S., Scott E. Daniels, and Barbara J. White. *BioEngagement.* Grand Rapids: Eerdmans, 2000.

Carlson, Elof Axel. *The Unfit: A History of a Bad Idea.* Cold Spring Harbor, N.Y.: Cold Spring Harbor Laboratory, 2001.

Cassidy, Anne. *Parents Who Think Too Much: Why We Do It, How to Stop.* New York: Dell, 1998.

Centers for Disease Control and Prevention. "Achievements in Public Health: 1900-1999: Healthier Mothers and Babies." *Morbidity and Morality Weekly,* October 1, 1999.

Chaplin, Joyce E. *Subject Matter: Technology, the Body, and Science on the Anglo-American Frontier, 1500-1676.* Cambridge, Mass., and London: Harvard University Press, 2001.

Cherne, Leo. "How We'll Live in '77." *Together,* January 1957.

Chilcote, Paul, ed. *The Wesleyan Tradition: A Paradigm for Renewal.* Nashville: Abingdon, 2002.

*Childcraft. In Fifteen Volumes.* Vol. 15, *Your Child in Today's World.* Chicago: Field Enterprises, 1954.

Chopp, Rebecca S., and Sheila Greeve Davaney, eds. *Horizons in Feminist Theology: Identity, Tradition, and Norms.* Minneapolis: Fortress, 1997.

Clark, Clifford E., Jr. *Henry Ward Beecher: Spokesman for a Middle-Class America.* Urbana: University of Illinois Press, 1978.

Clarke, Charles Walter. *Problems of Sexual Behavior.* Symposium proceedings, ASHA Annual Conference of Social Hygiene Executives. New York: American Social Hygiene Association, 1948.

———. "VD Control in Atom-Bombed Areas." *Journal of Social Hygiene* 37 (January 1951): 3-7.

*Cleanliness Brings Health.* Walt Disney, 1945. Film.

Cleveland, C. "The Wet-Nurse vs. the Bottle." *Archives of Pediatrics* 1 (1884): 346.

Coakley, Sarah. *Powers and Submissions: Spirituality, Philosophy, and Gender.* Challenges in Contemporary Theology. Oxford: Blackwell, 2002.

Cocks, Dorothy. "Look Your Best." *Parents',* October 1930.

Cogdell, Christina. *Eugenic Design: Streamlining America in the 1930s.* Philadelphia: University of Pennsylvania Press, 2004.

Cohen, Lizabeth. *A Consumers' Republic: The Politics of Mass Consumption in Postwar America.* New York: Vintage, 2004.

Collins, Ace. *Stories behind the Hymns That Inspire America.* Grand Rapids: Zondervan, 2003.

Collins, Patricia Hill. *Black Sexual Politics: African Americans and the New Racism.* New York and London: Routledge, 2005.

Colt, George Howe (text), and Anne Hollister (reporting). "Were You Born That Way?" *Life,* April 1998.

Colton, F. Barrows. "Your New World of Tomorrow." *National Geographic,* October 1945.

"Converting Ex-Headhunters." *Together,* September 1957.

Cook, William H. *Woman's Handbook of Health: A Guide for the Wife, Mother, and Nurse.* 5th ed. Cincinnati: W. H. Cook, 1866.

Cook-Deegan, Robert Mullan. "Origins of the Human Genome Project." *Risk: Health, Safety and Environment,* no. 97 (1994).

Coontz, Stephanie. *The Way We Never Were: American Families and the Nostalgia Trap.* New York: Basic Books, 2000.

Corea, Gena, Renate Duelli Klein, Jalna Hanmer, et al. *Man Made Women: How New Reproductive Technologies Affect Women.* Bloomington and Indianapolis: Indiana University Press, 1987.

Cousins, Norman. "The Hiroshima Maidens Go Home." *Together,* October 1956.

―――. "The Hiroshima Maidens — 15 Years Later." *Together,* August 1960.

Critchlow, Donald T. *Intended Consequences: Birth Control, Abortion, and the Federal Government in Modern America.* New York and Oxford: Oxford University Press, 1999.

Cunningham, Bert. *Heredity.* Ann Arbor: Edwards Brothers, 1926.

Currie, Elliott. *The Road to Whatever: Middle-Class Culture and the Crisis of Adolescence.* New York: Metropolitan, 2004.

Danielson, Florence H., and Charles Davenport. *The Hill Folk: Report on a Rural Community of Hereditary Defectives.* ERO Memoir Series, no. 1. Cold Spring Harbor, N.Y.: Press of the New Era, 1912.

Darwin, Charles. *The Descent of Man and Selection in Relation to Sex.* London: J. Murray, 1871.

Davenport, Gertrude. "Hereditary Crime." *American Journal of Sociology* 13 (November 1907): 402-9.

Dawn, Marva. *Is It a Lost Cause? Having the Heart of God for the Church's Children.* Grand Rapids: Eerdmans, 1997.

DeGrandpre, Richard. *Ritalin Nation: Rapid-Fire Culture and the Transformation of Human Consciousness.* New York: Norton, 2000.

Delbanco, Andrew. *The Death of Satan: How Americans Have Lost the Sense of Evil.* New York: Farrar, Straus and Giroux, 1995.

Detzer, Karl. "Jane Addams of Hull House." *Together,* January 1957.

De Vore, Robert. "Passport to the Golden Age." *Collier's,* May 3, 1947.

Donaldson, George Huntington. "Eugenics: A Lay Sermon." *Methodist Review* 112 (1929): 59-68.

Dorfman, Ariel. *The Empire's Old Clothes: What the Lone Ranger, Babar, and Other Innocent Heroes Do to Our Minds.* New York: Pantheon Books, 1983.

Dorris, C. L. "The Impending Disaster." *Methodist Quarterly Review* 75 (1926): 720-24.

Dower, John W. *War without Mercy: Race and Power in the Pacific War.* New York: Pantheon Books, 1986.

Downing, Elliot R. *Elementary Eugenics: A Revision of "The Third and Fourth Generation."* Chicago: University of Chicago Press, 1928.

Dunlap, Knight. *Personal Beauty and Racial Betterment.* St. Louis: C. V. Mosby, 1920.

Duster, Troy. *Backdoor to Eugenics.* With a foreword by Pierre Bourdieu. 2nd ed. New York and London: Routledge, 2003.

Ehrenreich, Barbara, and Arlie Russell Hochschild, eds. *Global Woman: Nannies, Maids, and Sex Workers in the New Economy.* New York: Metropolitan, 2002.

Eipper, Paul. *Animal Children.* New York: Viking Press, 1930.

_____. *Human Children.* New York: Viking Press, 1930.

Eiesland, Nancy L. *The Disabled God: Toward a Liberatory Theology of Disability.* Nashville: Abingdon, 1994.

Ely, Melvin Patrick. *The Adventures of Amos 'n Andy: A Social History of an American Phenomenon.* New York: Free Press, 1991.

England, Richard, ed. *Design after Darwin, 1860-1900.* Vol. 2, *Remaking the Watchmaker: Orthodox and Unorthodox Design Arguments.* Bristol, U.K.: Thoemmes Continuum, 2003.

English, Daylanne K. *Unnatural Selections: Eugenics in American Modernism and the Harlem Renaissance.* Chapel Hill and London: University of North Carolina Press, 2004.

Engs, Ruth Clifford. *Clean Living Movements: American Cycles of Health Reform.* Westport, Conn.: Praeger, 2000.

———. *The Progressive Era's Health Reform Movement: A Historical Dictionary.* Westport, Conn.: Praeger, 2003.

Estabrook, Arthur H. *The Jukes in 1915.* Washington, D.C.: Carnegie Institution of Washington, 1916.

Ewen, Elizabeth. *Immigrant Women in the Land of Dollars: Life and Culture on the Lower East Side, 1890-1925.* New York: Monthly Review, 1985.

Ewen, Stuart. *Captains of Consciousness: Advertising and the Social Roots of the Consumer Culture*. New York: McGraw-Hill, 1976.

Ewen, Stuart, and Elizabeth Ewen. *Channels of Desire: Mass Images and the Shaping of American Consciousness*. Minneapolis: University of Minnesota Press, 1992.

"Family Status Must Improve: It Should Buy More for Itself to Better the Living of Others." *Life*, May 5, 1947.

Fancher, Robert T. *Cultures of Healing: Correcting the Image of American Mental Health Care*. New York: Freeman, 1995.

Fisher, Allan C., Jr. "You and the Obedient Atom." *National Geographic*, September 1958.

Ford, Ian N. "Socio-educational and Biomedical Models in the Treatment of Attention Deficit/Hyperactivity Disorder and Related Neurobehavioural Disorders in Childhood and Adolescence, and Their Implications for Adult Mental Health." *Child and Adolescent Psychiatry Online*, 1996. http://www.priory.com/psych/iford.htm.

Ford, Norman M. *The Prenatal Person: Ethics from Conception to Birth*. Oxford: Blackwell, 2002.

Fosdick, Harry Emerson. *Christianity and Progress*. New York: Revell, 1922.

Fosdick, Raymond B. *The Old Savage in the New Civilization*. Garden City, N.Y.: Doubleday, 1929.

Fox, Richard Wightman, and T. J. Jackson Lears, eds. *The Culture of Consumption: Critical Essays in American History, 1880-1980*. New York: Pantheon Books, 1983.

Franklin, Donna L. *Ensuring Inequality: The Structural Transformation of the African-American Family*. New York and Oxford: Oxford University Press, 1997.

Franklin, Sarah. *Embodied Progress: A Cultural Account of Assisted Conception*. London and New York: Routledge, 1997.

Freeman, Ira M. *All about the Atom*. Illustrated by George Wilde. New York: Random House, 1955.

Froude, James Anthony. "Romanism and the Irish Race in the United States, Part I." *North American Review* 129 (December 1879): 523.

Fukuyama, Francis. *Our Posthuman Future: Consequences of the Biotechnology Revolution*. New York: Picador, 2002.

Funkenstein, Amos. *Theology and the Scientific Imagination from the Middle Ages to the Seventeenth Century*. Princeton: Princeton University Press, 1986.

Furedi, Frank. *Population and Development: A Critical Introduction*. New York: St. Martin's Press, 1997.

———. *Therapy Culture: Cultivating Vulnerability in an Uncertain Age*. London and New York: Routledge, 2004.

Geis, Sally B., and Donald E. Messer. *The Befuddled Stork: Helping Persons of Faith Debate Beginning-of-Life Issues*. Nashville: Abingdon, 2000.

General Electric Company. *Progressland a Walt Disney Presentation, 1964-65 New York World's Fair*. New York: General Electric, 1965.

"The Genomic Revolution." *North Carolina Naturalist*, Spring/Summer 2002.

Gilbert, James. *Redeeming Culture: American Religion in an Age of Science.* Chicago and London: University of Chicago Press, 1997.

Gilbreth, Frank B., Jr., and Ernestine Gilbreth Carey. *Cheaper by the Dozen.* 1948. Reprint, New York: Perennial, 2002.

Gilbreth, Lillian M. *Living with Our Children.* New York: Norton, 1928.

Gill, Theodore A. "General Conference: Cont'd." *Christian Century,* May 23, 1956.

Gillis, John R. *A World of Their Own Making: Myth, Ritual, and the Quest for Family Values.* Cambridge: Harvard University Press, 1996.

Giroux, Henry. *The Mouse That Roared: Disney and the End of Innocence.* Lanham, Md.: Rowman and Littlefield, 1999.

Gleisten, Samantha. *Chicago's 1933-34 World's Fair: A Century of Progress in Vintage Postcards.* Chicago: Arcadia, 2002.

Glimm, Zella Van Ornum. "Setting-Up Exercises for the Baby." *Parents',* October 1930.

Goddard, Henry H. *Our Children in the Atomic Age.* Mellott, Ind.: Hopkins Syndicate, 1948.

Golden, Janet. *A Social History of Wet Nursing in America.* Cambridge: Cambridge University Press, 1996.

Goldstein, Ben. Review of *Cheaper by the Dozen* (Twentieth Century-Fox movie, 2003). *Maxim.* http://www.maximonline.com/entertainment/reviews/review_movies_6714.html. Accessed 2003. Site now discontinued.

Goode, Erica. "Pills and Children (University of Maryland Report on Increase in Psychiatric Drug Usage)." *New York Times,* January 19, 2003.

Goodman, Alan H., Deborah Heath, and M. Susan Lindee, eds. *Genetic Nature/Culture: Anthropology and Science beyond the Two Culture Divide.* Berkeley: University of California Press, 2003.

Gordon, Linda. *Woman's Body, Woman's Right: Birth Control in America.* New York: Penguin Books, 1990.

Gosden, Roger. *Designing Babies: The Brave New World of Reproductive Technology.* New York: Freeman, 1999.

Graebner, William S. *The Age of Doubt: American Thought and Culture in the 1940s.* Boston: Twayne, 1991.

Graham, Catherine. "'Cheaper' Is Fun, but Unnecessary." *Santa Cruz Sentinel,* December 24, 2003, Style section.

Grant, Julie. *Raising Baby by the Book: The Education of American Mothers.* New Haven: Yale University Press, 1998.

Grant, Nicole J. *The Spelling of Contraception: The Dalkon Shield Case, Sexuality, and Women's Autonomy.* Columbus: Ohio State University Press, 1992.

Greenspan, Stanley J., M.D., with Jacqueline Salmon. *The Four-Thirds Solution: Solving the Child-Care Crisis in America Today.* Cambridge, Mass.: Perseus, 2001.

"A Guide for Discernment — Genetic Technologies and the United Methodist Church." Unpublished paper, February 2006.

Haber, Heinz. *The Walt Disney Story of Our Friend the Atom.* New York: Simon and Schuster, 1956.

Haeckel, Ernst. *Riddle of the Universe at the Close of the Nineteenth Century.* 1899. Reprint, New York: Harper and Row, 1905.

——. *The History of Creation.* New York: D. Appleton, 1925.

Hagedorn, Hermann. *The Bomb That Fell on America.* 1946. Reprint, New York: Associated Press, 1948.

Haldane, J. S. *The Sciences and Philosophy.* Garden City, N.Y.: Doubleday, 1929.

——. *The Philosophical Basis of Life.* Garden City, N.Y.: Doubleday, 1931.

Hall, Amy Laura. "Public Bioethics and the Gratuity of Life: Joanna Jepson's Witness against Negative Eugenics." *Studies in Christian Ethics* 18 (2005): 15-31.

Hall, Clarence W. "When Civilization Came to Shimabuku." *Together,* October 1960.

Hall, Stuart. *The Hard Road to Renewal: Thatcherism and the Crisis of the Left.* London: Verso, 1988.

Haraway, Donna, ed. *Simians, Cyborgs, and Women: The Reinvention of Nature.* New York: Routledge, 1991.

Harper, Francis E. W. *Iola Leroy, or Shadows Uplifted.* 1892. Reprint, Oxford: Oxford University Press, 1988.

Harris, John. *Clones, Genes, and Immortality: Ethics and the Genetic Revolution.* Oxford: Oxford University Press, 1998.

Hatch, Nathan. *The Democratization of American Christianity.* New Haven: Yale University Press, 1989.

Hays, Sharon. *The Cultural Contradictions of Motherhood.* New Haven and London: Yale University Press, 1996.

Heald, Phyllis W. "The Luxury of Being 50." *Together,* July 1957.

Henderson, Mark. "Let's Cure Stupidity, Says DNA Pioneer." *Times* (London), February 28, 2003, Home News section.

Heyrman, Christine. *The Southern Cross: The Beginnings of the Bible Belt.* New York: Knopf, 1997.

Hine, Thomas. *Populuxe.* New York: Knopf, 1986.

——. *The Total Package: The Evolution and Secret Meanings of Boxes, Bottles, Cans, and Tubes.* Boston: Little, Brown, 1995.

——. *I Want That: How We All Became Shoppers.* New York: HarperCollins, 2002.

Hinman, Helen R., and William I. Battin, Jr. *Population Pressure, War, and Poverty.* Newark, N.J.: Arthur W. Cross, 1945.

Hochschild, Arlie Russell. *The Commercialization of Intimate Life: Notes from Home and Work.* Berkeley: University of California Press, 2003.

Hofstadter, Richard. *Social Darwinism in American Thought.* New York: Braziller, 1959.

Hollinger, David A. *Postethnic America: Beyond Multiculturalism.* New York: Basic Books, 1995.

Holmes, Helen Bequaert, ed. *Issues in Reproductive Technology: An Anthology.* Grand

Reference Library of the Social Sciences, no. 729. New York and London: Garland, 1992.

hooks, bell. *Feminist Theory: From Margin to Center.* Boston: South End Press, 1984.

Huberman, M. A. "Backwoods Japan during American Occupation." *National Geographic,* April 1947.

Hudson, Winthrop S., ed. *Nationalism and Religion in America: Concepts of American Identity and Mission.* New York: Harper and Row, 1970.

Hulbert, Ann. *Raising America: Experts, Parents, and a Century of Advice about Children.* New York: Knopf, 2003.

————. "The Prodigy Puzzle." *New York Times Magazine,* November 20, 2005.

Human Genome Project. *To Know Ourselves: The U.S. Department of Energy and the Human Genome Project.* U.S. Department of Energy, 1996.

Huntington, Ellsworth, Eugene Robinson, Ray Erwin Baber, and Maurice R. Davie. "Wanted: Better Babies: How Shall We Get Them?" *People,* April 1931.

Huntington, Samuel. *Who Are We? The Challenges to America's National Identity.* New York: Simon and Schuster, 2004.

Hutchison, William R. *Religious Pluralism in America.* New Haven: Yale University Press, 2003.

"Is Christian Morality Harmful? Over-charitable to the Unfit? Four Religious Leaders Discuss a Charge Sometimes Made." *Eugenics: A Journal of Race Betterment* 1 (December 1928).

Jackson, Kenneth T. *Crabgrass Frontier: The Suburbanization of the United States.* New York and Oxford: Oxford University Press, 1985.

Jacobson, Matthew Frye. *Whiteness of a Different Color: European Immigrants and the Alchemy of Race.* Cambridge: Harvard University Press, 1998.

Jordan, John M. *Machine Age Ideology: Social Engineering and American Liberalism, 1911-1939.* Chapel Hill and London: University of North Carolina Press, 1994.

*Journal for the Society of Christian Ethics* 24, no. 1 (Spring/Summer 2004).

*Journal of Religion, Disability, and Health* 6, nos. 2/3 (2002).

Kahn, Susan Martha. *Reproducing Jews: A Cultural Account of Assisted Conception in Israel.* Durham, N.C., and London: Duke University Press, 2000.

Kaplan, Amy. "Manifest Domesticity." *American Literature* 70 (1998): 581-606.

Kaplan, E. Ann, and Susan Squier, eds. *Playing Dolly: Technocultural Formations, Fantasies, and Fictions of Assisted Reproduction.* New Brunswick, N.J., and London: Rutgers University Press, 1999.

Kaufmann, Helen L. "Should We Hand-pick Our Children's Friends?" *Parents',* August 1929.

Kawano, Martin. "Why Did I Survive the Atom Bomb?" *Together,* August 1957.

Kay, Lily E. *The Molecular Vision of Life: Caltech, the Rockefeller Foundation, and the Rise of the New Biology.* New York: Oxford University Press, 1993.

Keller, Evelyn Fox. *The Century of the Gene.* Cambridge, Mass., and London: Harvard University Press, 2000.

Keller, James. *You Can Change the World! The Christopher Approach.* New York: Longmans, Green, 1948.

Kevles, Daniel J. *In the Name of Eugenics: Genetics and the Uses of Human Heredity.* With a new preface by the author. Cambridge: Harvard University Press, 1999.

Kierkegaard, Søren. *Works of Love.* Edited and translated by Howard V. Hong and Edna H. Hong, with introduction and notes. Princeton: Princeton University Press, 1995.

Kilner, John F., Paige C. Cunningham, and W. David Hager, eds. *The Reproduction Revolution: A Christian Appraisal of Sexuality, Reproductive Technologies, and the Family.* Grand Rapids: Eerdmans, 2000.

Kilner, John F., Rebecca D. Pentz, and Frank E. Young, eds. *Genetic Ethics: Do the Ends Justify the Means?* Grand Rapids: Eerdmans, 1997.

Kingsley, Charles. "The Natural Theology of the Future." *Macmillan's Magazine* 23 (1871).

———. *The Water Babies.* New York: Dodd, Mead and Co., 1916.

Kite, Elizabeth. "The 'Pineys.'" *Survey: A Journal of Constructive Philanthropy* 21 (October 4, 1913).

Klaassen, David. "Social Hygiene Poster Campaigns in the 1920s." Social Hygiene Poster Series, Social Welfare History Archives, University of Minnesota. http://special.lib.umn.edu/swha/exhibits/hygiene/essay.htm.

Kline, Wendy. *Building a Better Race: Gender, Sexuality, and Eugenics from the Turn of the Century to the Baby Boom.* Berkeley: University of California Press, 2001.

Kozol, Jonathan. *Savage Inequalities: Children in America's Schools.* 1991. Reprint, New York: HarperCollins, 1992.

———. "The Details of Life." *Nation,* May 22, 2000.

Krakauer, Eric L. *The Disposition of the Subject: Reading Adorno's Dialectic of Technology.* Evanston, Ill.: Northwestern University Press, 1998.

Kristol, William. *The Future Is Now: America Confronts the New Eugenics.* Lanham, Md.: Rowman and Littlefield, 2002.

Kunzel, Regina G. *Fallen Women, Problem Girls: Unmarried Mothers and the Professionalization of Social Work, 1890-1945.* New Haven and London: Yale University Press, 1993.

Lamb, M. T. *Heredity.* Trenton, N.J.: Naar, Day and Naar, 1898.

Langer, Mark. "Disney's Atomic Fleet." *Animation World Magazine,* April 1, 1998.

Laurence, William L. "Yes, Atoms for Peace!" *Together,* October 1958.

Lemann, Nicholas. *The Promised Land: The Great Black Migration and How It Changed America.* New York: Knopf, 1991.

Leon, Sharon M. "'Hopelessly Entangled in Nordic Pre-suppositions': Catholic Participation in the American Eugenics Society in the 1920s." *Journal of the History of Medicine and Allied Sciences* 59 (2004): 3-49.

Leuchtenburg, William E. *The Perils of Prosperity, 1914-32.* 2nd ed. Chicago: University of Chicago Press, 1993.

Levine, Robert J. *Ethics and the Regulation of Clinical Research.* 2nd ed. New Haven and London: Yale University Press, 1988.

Lilienthal, David E. "The Atomic Adventure." *Collier's,* May 3, 1947.

Lodge, Henry Cabot. "The Restriction of Immigration." *North American Review* 152 (January 1891): 31.

Lopate, Phillip. *Being with Children.* New York: Poseidon, 1975.

Love, I. N. "The Problem of Infant Feeding — Intestinal Diseases of Children and Cholera Infantum." *Archives of Pediatrics* 6 (1889): 585.

Lukacs, Georg. *History and Class Consciousness: Studies in Marxist Dialectics.* Translated by Rodney Livingstone. Cambridge: MIT Press, 1971.

Luker, Kristen. "Sex, Social Hygiene, and the State: The Double-Edged Sword of Social Reform." *Theory and Society* 27 (1998): 609-10.

Lutz, Catherine A., and Jane L. Collins. *Reading National Geographic.* Chicago: University of Chicago Press, 1993.

Lynn, Richard. *Eugenics: A Reassessment.* Human Evolution, Behavior, and Intelligence. Westport, Conn.: Praeger, 2001.

MacIntyre, Alasdair. *Marxism and Christianity.* Notre Dame, Ind.: University of Notre Dame Press, 1984.

———. *Dependent Rational Animals: Why Human Beings Need the Virtues.* Paul Carus Lectures 20. Chicago and La Salle, Ill.: Open Court, 1999.

Maisel, Albert Q. "Medical Dividend." *Collier's,* May 3, 1947.

"Man and the Atom." *Collier's,* May 3, 1947.

Mankoff, Robert, ed. *The New Yorker Book of Kids Cartoons.* Princeton: Bloomberg, 2001.

Maranto, Gina. *Quest for Perfection: The Drive to Breed Better Human Beings.* Lincoln, Neb.: iUniverse.com, 2000.

Markwith, Carl. "Farewell to Bikini." *National Geographic,* July 1946.

Marsden, George M. *Fundamentalism and American Culture: The Shaping of Twentieth-Century Evangelicalism, 1870-1925.* Oxford: Oxford University Press, 1980.

———. *Understanding Fundamentalism and Evangelicalism.* Grand Rapids: Eerdmans, 1991.

Martin, Emily. *The Woman in the Body: A Cultural Analysis of Reproduction.* Boston: Beacon Press, 1992.

Marty, Martin E. "Inclusive Church — Inclusive Theology: The Hennepin Avenue Methodist Church, Minneapolis, Minnesota." *Christian Century,* February 27, 1957.

———. *A Nation of Behavers.* Chicago and London: University of Chicago Press, 1976.

Mathews, Donald G. *Religion in the Old South.* Chicago: University of Chicago Press, 1977.

Matt, Susan J. *Keeping Up with the Joneses: Envy in American Consumer Society, 1890-1930.* Philadelphia: University of Pennsylvania Press, 2003.

May, Elaine Tyler. *Homeward Bound: American Families in the Cold War Era*. New York: Basic Books, 1999.

Mayo, Leonard W. "A Healthy Personality for Every Child." In *Childcraft* (Chicago: Field Enterprises, 1954), 15:167-74.

McCulloch, Oscar C. "The Tribe of Ishmael: A Study in Social Degradation." *Proceedings of the National Conference of Charities and Correction* 15 (1888): 154-59.

McDannell, Colleen. *The Christian Home in Victorian America, 1840-1900*. 1986. Reprint, Bloomington: Indiana University Press, 1994.

McDermott, William F. "Tenement Manger: A True Story." *Together*, December 1956.

McFadden, Elizabeth. "Dey's All Got Debbils!" *Parents'*, October 1929.

McKibben, Bill. *Enough: Staying Human in an Engineered Age*. New York: Henry Holt, 2003.

McLuhan, Marshall. *The Mechanical Bride: Folklore of Industrial Man*. Corte Madera, Calif.: Gingko Press, 2002.

Mead, Margaret. "South Sea Hints on Bringing Up Children." *Parents'*, September 1929.

———. "Water Babies of the South Seas." *Parents'*, September 1930.

"The Meaning of Easter: An Editorial Message." *Parents'*, April 1929.

Melosh, Barbara. *Strangers and Kin: The American Way of Adoption*. Cambridge: Harvard University Press, 2002.

Mercogliano, Chris. *Teaching the Restless: One School's Remarkable No-Ritalin Approach to Helping Children Learn and Succeed*. Boston: Beacon Press, 2003.

Meyer, Edith Patterson. "Looking for Good Children's Books?" *Together*, November 1956.

Miller, Robert Moats. *Bishop G. Bromley Oxnam: Paladin of Liberal Protestantism*. Nashville: Abingdon, 1990.

Milum, J. Parton. *Evolution for Christians*. London, 1933.

———. *Do the Ten Commandments Stand Today?* London: Epworth, 1936.

———. "Has the Concept of Humanity a Scientific Basis?" *Religion in Life* 5 (1936): 52-63.

Mintz, Susan, and Susan Kellogg. *Domestic Resolutions: A Social History of American Family Life*. New York: Free Press, 1988.

Mohrmann, Margaret E. *Attending Children: A Doctor's Education*. Washington, D.C.: Georgetown University Press, 2004.

"The Monsters Next Door: A Special Report on the Colorado School Massacre." *Time*, May 3, 1999.

Montgomery, James. "What Is Prayer?" *Together*, May 1958.

Moore, R. Laurence. *Religious Outsiders and the Making of Americans*. New York and Oxford: Oxford University Press, 1986.

Morrison, Toni. *The Bluest Eye*. 1970. Reprint, New York: Penguin Books, 1994.

Mott, Frank Luther. *American Journalism: A History of Newspapers in the United States through 260 Years: 1690 to 1950*. Rev. ed. New York: Macmillan, 1950.

Murray, Thomas A. *The Worth of a Child.* Berkeley: University of California Press, 1996.

Murray, Thomas A., Mark A. Rothstein, and Robert F. Murray, Jr. *The Human Genome Project and the Future of Health Care.* Bloomington and Indianapolis: Indiana University Press, 1996.

Mussen, Charles, as told to Katherine J. Pitkin. "How Donald Learned to Say 'Okay.'" *Together,* October 1956.

"Must Be Normal to and Well to Wed." *New York Times,* March 25, 1912.

Napheys, George Henry. *The Physical Life of Woman: Advice to the Maiden, Wife, and Mother.* Toronto: MacLear, 1871.

———. *The Transmission of Life: Counsels on the Nature and Hygiene of the Masculine Function.* Philadelphia: J. G. Fergus, 1871.

Narodny, Ivan. *American Artists.* Introduction by Nicholas Roerich. New York: Roerich Museum Press, 1930.

"A New Interpretation of Valentines Day." *Journal of Social Hygiene* 13 (December 1927).

Nichols, Nell B. "Noiseless Housekeeping." *Parents',* October 1929.

Noll, Mark, ed. *Religion and American Politics: From the Colonial Period to the 1980s.* New York and Oxford: Oxford University Press, 1990.

Noll, Steven, and James W. Trent, eds. *Mental Retardation in America: A Historical Reader.* New York: New York University Press, 2004.

O'Donovan, Oliver. *Begotten or Made?* Oxford: Clarendon, 1984.

*Official Guide Book of the Fair, 1933.* Chicago: A Century of Progress, 1933.

*Official Guide Book of the Fair, 1933, with 1934 Supplement.* Chicago: Cueo Press, 1933.

*The Official Pictures of A Century of Progress Exposition, Chicago, 1933-34.* New York: Encyclopedia Britannica, 1933.

O'Grady, Kathleen, Ann L. Gilroy, and Janette Gray, eds. *Bodies, Lives, Voices: Gender in Theology.* Sheffield: Sheffield Academic, 1998.

O'Halloran, Elspeth MacDuffie. "Holy-Day." *Parents',* December 1930.

"One Hundred Years in India: Methodists Look to Future." *Together,* December 1956.

"Operation Crossroads (Bikini Atoll, Marshalls)." *National Geographic,* April 1947.

Osborn, Henry F. "Models of Extinct Vertebrates." *Science* 7 (June 24, 1898): 841-45.

Osgood, Phillips E. "The Refiner's Fire." *Homiletic Review* 97 (May 1929): 405-9.

Oxnam, Bishop G. Bromley. "The Christian Family, the Hope of the World." In *Report: The Christian Home — the Hope of the World,* pp. 3-6. Nashville: Board of Education, 1954.

Parens, Erik, and Adrienne Asch. *Prenatal Testing and Disability Rights.* Washington, D.C.: Georgetown University Press, 2000.

"Pastors for Eugenics." *New York Times,* June 6, 1913.

Patton, Edwin F. "Baby's Second Summer." *Parents',* July 1929.

Paul, Diane B. *The Politics of Heredity: Essays on Eugenics, Biomedicine, and the Nature-Nurture Debate.* Albany: State University of New York Press, 1998.

Pauly, Philip J. "The World and All That Is in It: The National Geographic Society, 1888-1918." *American Quarterly* 31 (1979): 517, 523.

Peril, Lynn. *Pink Think: Becoming a Woman in Many Uneasy Lessons.* New York: Norton, 2002.

Peritz, Ismar J. "Christ and Evolution." Review of *The Doctrine of Redemption in the Light of Modern Knowledge,* by George A. Barton. *Religion in Life* 4 (1935): 462-64.

Pernick, Martin S. *The Black Stork: Eugenics and the Death of "Defective" Babies in American Medicine and Motion Pictures Since 1915.* New York and Oxford: Oxford University Press, 1996.

Pierce, Anne. "Old Christmases for New: An Editorial Message." *Parents',* December 1929.

Pierce, Lovick, and J. Edgar Washabaugh. Editorial. *Together,* October 1956.

Pohl, Christine. *Making Room: Recovering Hospitality as a Christian Tradition.* Grand Rapids: Eerdmans, 1999.

Pollitt, Katha. "Betty Friedan, 1921-2006." *Nation,* February 27, 2006.

Popenoe, Paul. "Surveying the Chances." *Intercollegian,* January 1948, pp. 9-11.

"Problems of Sexual Behavior — and Their Solutions." *Journal of Social Hygiene* 36 (April 1950).

*Proceedings of the Third Race Betterment Conference, January 2-6, 1928.* Battle Creek, Mich.: Race Betterment Foundation, 1928.

Prothero, Stephen. *American Jesus: How the Son of God Became a National Icon.* New York: Farrar, Straus and Giroux, 2003.

Pryor, Alice W. "Sadako and the Paper Cranes." *Together,* August 1960.

Rafter, Nicole Hahn. *White Trash: The Eugenic Family Studies, 1877-1919.* Boston: Northeastern University Press, 1988.

Ramsey, Paul. *The Patient as Person: Explorations in Medical Ethics.* 2nd ed. New Haven and London: Yale University Press, 2002.

Rapp, Rayna. *Testing Women, Testing the Fetus: The Social Impact of Amniocentesis in America.* New York: Routledge, 1999.

Rauschenbusch, Walter. *Christianizing the Social Order.* New York: Macmillan, 1912.

———. *A Theology for the Social Gospel.* New York: Macmillan, 1919.

"Reading the Book of Life; White House Remarks on Decoding of Genome." *New York Times,* June 27, 2000, Science Desk section.

Reardon, Jenny. *Race to the Finish: Identity and Governance in an Age of Genomics.* Princeton and Oxford: Princeton University Press, 2005.

Reinders, Hans. *The Future of the Disabled in Liberal Society: An Ethical Analysis.* Notre Dame, Ind.: University of Notre Dame Press, 2000.

*Report: The Christian Home — the Hope of the World: Second National Conference on Family Life of the Methodist Church.* Nashville: National Conference on Family Life, 1954.

Riis, Jacob A. *How the Other Half Lives.* With 100 photographs from the Riis Collection. New York: Dover, 1971.

Robert, Dana L. *American Women in Mission: A Social History of Their Thought and Practice*. Macon, Ga.: Mercer University Press, 1997.

Roberts, Dorothy. *Killing the Black Body: Race, Reproduction, and the Meaning of Liberty*. New York: Vintage, 1997.

Robinson, Marilynne. *Housekeeping: A Novel*. 1980. Reprint, New York: Picador, 2004.

Robinson, William J. *Fewer and Better Babies: Birth Control; or, The Limitation of Offspring by the Prevention of Conception*. 35th ed. 1915. Reprint, New York: Eugenics Publishing, 1929.

Rodgers, Daniel T. *The Work Ethic in Industrial America, 1850-1920*. 1974. Reprint, Chicago and London: University of Chicago Press, 1978.

Roediger, David R. *The Wages of Whiteness: Race and the Making of the American Working Class*. London: Verso, 1991.

Rogers, Lois. "Having Disabled Babies Will Be 'Sin,' Says Scientist." *Sunday Times* (London), July 4, 1999, Home News section.

Roosevelt, Franklin D. "Fundamentals: An Editorial Message," *Parents'*, August 1929.

"Rosemary Goes to the Hospital." *Together*, October 1956.

Rosen, Christine. *Preaching Eugenics: Religious Leaders and the American Eugenics Movement*. Oxford: Oxford University Press, 2004.

Rotch, Thomas Morgan. "The General Principles Underlying All Good Methods of Infant Feeding." *Boston Medical and Surgical Journal* 129 (1893): 505.

Roth, Karl Heinz. "Flying Bodies — Enforcing States: German Aviation Medical Research, 1920-1970, and the DFT." Paper presented at symposium "Man, Medicine and the State: The Human Body as an Object of Government Sponsored Research, 1920-1970," October 10, 2003.

Rothblatt, Martine. *Unzipped Genes: Taking Charge of Baby-Making in the New Millennium*. Philadelphia: Temple University Press, 1997.

Rothenberg, Karen H., and Elizabeth J. Thompson. *Women and Prenatal Testing: Facing the Challenges of Genetic Technology*. Columbus: Ohio State University Press, 1994.

Rothman, Barbara Katz. *Parental Diagnosis and the Future of Motherhood*. New York: Viking Press, 1986.

———. *The Tentative Pregnancy: How Amniocentesis Changes the Experience of Motherhood*. 1986. Reprint, New York: Norton, 1993.

———. *Genetic Maps and Human Imaginations: The Limits of Science in Understanding Who We Are*. New York: Norton, 1998.

Rowe, Gilbert T. "Christianity and Evolution." *Methodist Quarterly Review* 75 (1926): 138.

———. *The Meaning of Methodism: A Study in Christian Religion*. Training Courses for Leadership. Nashville: Cokesbury, 1926.

Ryan, Mary P. *Cradle of the Middle Class: The Family in Oneida County, New York, 1790-1865*. Interdisciplinary Perspectives on Modern History. Cambridge: Cambridge University Press, 1981.

Rydell, Robert W. *All the World's a Fair: Visions of Empire at American International Expositions, 1876-1916.* Chicago: University of Chicago Press, 1984.

Rydell, Robert W., John E. Findling, and Kimberly D. Pelle. *Fair America: World's Fairs in the United States.* Washington, D.C.: Smithsonian Institution Press, 2000.

Sandel, Michael. "The Case against Perfection." *Atlantic Monthly,* April 2004, pp. 51-62.

Sanger, Margaret. *Woman and the New Race.* With a preface by Havelock Ellis. New York: Brentano's, 1920.

————. "Too Many People." *Together,* September 1957.

————. *The Pivot of Civilization.* 1922. Reprint, Amherst, N.Y.: Prometheus Books, Humanity Books, 2003.

Sapin, Ruth. "For Better or Worse — Servants Influence Children." *Parents',* January 1929.

"Sarawak: Once Head-Hunter Land." *Together,* January 1960.

Scanlon, Jennifer. *Inarticulate Longings: The Ladies' Home Journal, Gender, and the Promises of Consumer Culture.* New York: Routledge, 1995.

Schumacher, Michelle M., ed. *Women in Christ: Toward a New Feminism.* Grand Rapids: Eerdmans, 2004.

"Scientific Blueprint for Atomic Survival." *Life,* March 18, 1957.

Selbert, Norma. "Train Your Baby to Regularity." *Parents',* January 1929.

Shannon, A. H. *Racial Integrity: Other Features of the Negro Problem.* South Nashville, Tenn., and Dallas: Publishing House of the M.E. Church, 1907.

Shannon, Thomas A. *Made in Whose Image? Genetic Engineering and Christian Ethics.* Amherst, N.Y.: Humanity, 2000.

"Should Ministers Marry the Physically Unfit? Distinguished Doctors and Divines Discuss the Edict of Dean Sumner of Chicago That No More Marriages Will Be Permitted in the Episcopal Cathedral without Health Certificates." *New York Times,* June 2, 1912.

Shuman, Joel James. *The Body of Compassion: Ethics, Medicine, and the Church.* Boulder, Colo.: Westview, 1999.

Shuman, Joel, and Brian Volck, M.D. *Reclaiming the Body: Christians and the Faithful Use of Modern Medicine.* Grand Rapids: Brazos, 2006.

Shuman, Joel James, and Keith G. Meador. *Heal Thyself: Spirituality, Medicine, and the Distortion of Christianity.* Oxford: Oxford University Press, 2003.

Sigg, Ferdinand. "Karl Barth: Theology for a World in Crisis." *Together,* August 1963.

Sinsheimer, Robert L. "The Prospect of Designed Genetic Change." *Engineering and Science* 32 (April 1969): 8, 13.

*Skin Deep.* New York: Women Make Movies, 1997. film.

Slaten, A. Wakefield. Sermon 25. American Eugenics Society Papers. American Philosophical Society, Philadelphia, 1927.

Sloan, William David. *Media and Religion in American History.* Northport, Ala.: Vision, 2000.

Small, S., G. Eastman, and S. Cornelius. "Adolescent Autonomy and Parental Stress." *Journal of Youth and Adolescence* 17 (1988): 377-91.

Smith, Lillian. *Strange Fruit.* New York: New American Library, 1944.

———. *Killers of the Dream.* With a new introduction by Margaret Rose Gladney. 1949. Reprint, New York: Norton, 1994.

Smith, Roy L. "Herods and Shepherds, Little Lessons in Spiritual Efficiency." *Together,* December 1956.

Smith, Shawn Michelle. *Photography on the Color Line: W. E. B. Du Bois, Race, and Visual Culture.* Durham, N.C., and London: Duke University Press, 2004.

Smith, Wesley J. *Culture of Death: The Assault on Medical Ethics in America.* San Francisco: Encounter Books, 2000.

Solinger, Rickie. *Beggars and Choosers: How the Politics of Choice Shapes Adoption, Abortion, and Welfare in the United States.* New York: Hill and Wang, 2001.

"Something New Has Been Added." *Journal of Social Hygiene* 37 (January 1951).

Southard, Helen F. "Planning Parenthood on Campus." *Intercollegian,* January 1948, pp. 9-11.

"Special Report: Massacre in Colorado." *Newsweek,* May 3, 1999.

Spencer, Herbert. *On Social Evolution.* Edited with an introduction by J. D. Y. Peel. Midway Reprint. Chicago and London: University of Chicago Press, 1972.

Spigel, Lynn. *Make Room for TV: Television and the Family Ideal in Postwar America.* Chicago: University of Chicago Press, 1992.

———. *Welcome to the Dreamhouse: Popular Media and Postwar Suburbs.* Durham, N.C., and London: Duke University Press, 2001.

Squier, Susan Merrill. *Babies in Bottles: Twentieth-Century Visions of Reproductive Technology.* New Brunswick, N.J.: Rutgers University Press, 1994.

Squiers, Carol. *Perfecting Mankind: Eugenics and Photography.* Exhibition brochure. New York: International Center of Photography, January 11–March 18, 2001.

Stassen, Harold. "Atoms for Peace." *Ladies' Home Journal,* August 1955, pp. 48-49.

Steinberg, Deborah Lynn. *Bodies in Glass: Genetics, Eugenics, Embryo Ethics.* Manchester and New York: Manchester University Press, 1997.

Stephenson, Patricia, and Marsden G. Wagner, eds. *Tough Choices: In Vitro Fertilization and the Reproductive Technologies.* Philadelphia: Temple University Press, 1993.

Stevens, Jacqueline. *Reproducing the State.* Princeton: Princeton University Press, 1999.

———. "From the Manhattan Project to the Human Genome Project." In "The Secret History of Jessie Gelsinger's Death," ed. Arthur Kroker and Marilouise Kroker. *Tech Flesh* 9, special issue, May 9, 2001.

———. "PR for the 'Book of Life.'" *Nation,* November 26, 2001. Web only, http://www.thenation.com/doc/20011203/stevens20011121.

Still, George F. "The Goulstonian Lectures on Some Abnormal Psychical Conditions in Children." *Lancet* 159, no. 4104 (April 26, 1902): 1163-68.

Stolberg, Sheryl Gay. "Preschool Meds." *New York Times,* November 17, 2002.

Stuart-Macadam, Patricia, and Katherine A. Dettwyler, eds. *Breastfeeding: Biocultural Perspectives.* New York: Aldine De Gruyter, 1995.

Talmey, Bernard S., M.D. *Love: A Treatise on the Science of Sex-Attraction.* 10th ed. New York: Eugenics, 1937.

Teeter, Herman B. *The General Periodicals of Methodism.* Park Ridge, Ill.: United Methodist Publishing House, 1975.

———. "Homecoming 1977: A Family Forecast." *Together,* January 1957.

*Theology Today* 59, no. 1 (April 2002).

Thompson, E. P. *The Making of the English Working Class.* New York: Pantheon Books, 1964.

Tone, Andrea. "Contraceptive Consumers: Gender and the Political Economy of Birth Control in the 1930s." *Journal of Social History* 29 (1996): 485-506.

Towns, Emilie M. *Breaking the Fine Rain of Death: African-American Health Issues and a Womanist Ethic of Care.* New York: Continuum, 2001.

Trachtenberg, Alan. *The Incorporation of America: Culture and Society in the Gilded Age.* New York: Hill and Wang, 1982.

Turner, Leigh. "Biotechnology as Religion." *Nature Biotechnology* 22 (2004): 659.

Tweed, Thomas A., ed. *Retelling U.S. History.* Berkeley: University of California Press, 1997.

Ursel, Jane. *Private Lives, Public Policy: One Hundred Years of State Intervention in the Family.* Toronto: Women's Press, 1992.

"U.S. Tackles the Price Problem." *Life,* May 5, 1947.

Veblen, Thorstein. *The Theory of the Leisure Class.* New York: Dover, 1994.

Velie, Lester. "Intertia—U.S.A." *Collier's,* May 3, 1947.

Verhey, Allen. *Reading the Bible in the Strange World of Medicine.* Grand Rapids: Eerdmans, 2003.

Vernon, Walter Newton, Jr. *The United Methodist Publishing House: A History.* Vol. 2. Nashville: Abingdon, 1989.

Vidal, John, and George Monbiot. "The PR Strategy — the Charm Offensive." *Guardian,* December 16, 1997.

Wakefield, Dan. "Slick-Paper Christianity." *Nation,* January 19, 1957.

Ward, Jule DeJager. *La Leche League: At the Crossroads of Medicine, Feminism, and Religion.* Chapel Hill and London: University of North Carolina Press, 2000.

Ware, Susan. *Holding Their Own: American Women in the 1930s.* Boston: Twayne, 1982.

"The War Ends: Burst of Atomic Bomb Brings Swift Surrender of Japanese." *Life,* August 20, 1945.

Warner, Laceye. "Offer Them Christ: Characteristics of a Wesleyan Paradigm for Evangelism." In *The Wesleyan Tradition: A Paradigm for Renewal,* edited by Paul Chilcote. Nashville: Abingdon, 2002.

———. *Saving Women.* Waco: Baylor University Press, 2007.

———. Warner, Laceye. " 'Toward the Light': Lucy Rider Meyer and the Chicago Training School." http://www.garrett.edu/content.asp?A=9&C=2--36&bhcp=1.

Warshofsky, Fred. *The Twenty-First Century: The Control of Life.* New York: Viking Press, 1967.

Waters, C. Kenneth, and Albert Van Helden, eds. *Julian Huxley: Biologist and Statesman of Science.* Proceedings of a conference held at Rice University, September 25-27, 1987. Houston: Rice University, 1992.

Watson, J. A. S. *Heredity.* London: T. C. & E. C. Jack, n.d.

Watson, Rosalie Rayner. "I Am the Mother of a Behaviorist's Sons." *Parents',* December 1930.

Watts, Steven. *The Magic Kingdom: Walt Disney and the American Way of Life.* Boston: Houghton Mifflin, 1997.

Weber, Max. *The Protestant Ethic and the Spirit of Capitalism.* Translated by Talcott Parsons. 1930. Reprint, London: Routledge, 1992.

Weikart, Richard. *From Darwin to Hitler: Evolutionary Ethics, Eugenics, and Racism in Germany.* New York: Palgrave Macmillan, 2004.

Weinstein, Miriam. *The Surprising Power of Family Meals: How Eating Together Makes Us Smarter, Stronger, Healthier, and Happier.* Hanover, N.H.: Steerforth Press, 2005.

Werner, Hazen G., and Edward Staples. "The National Conference on Family Life: Opening Address." In *Report: The Christian Home — the Hope of the World.* Nashville: National Conference on Family Life, 1954.

————. "Report of the National Family Life Committee: For the Quadrennium of 1952-56." *Journal of the 1956 General Conference of the Methodist Church,* 1956, p. 1855.

Wexler, Philip, ed. *Critical Theory Now.* London: Falmer Press, 1991.

"When Atom Bomb Struck — Uncensored." *Life,* September 29, 1952.

Whitton, Mary Ormsbee. "So Early Monday Morning." *Parents',* November 1930.

Wiebe, Robert H. *The Search for Order, 1877-1920.* New York: Hill and Wang, 1967.

Wigger, John H. *Taking Heaven by Storm: Methodism and the Rise of Popular Christianity in America.* New York: Oxford University Press, 1998.

Williams, Peter. *America's Religions: From Their Origins to the Twenty-First Century.* Urbana: University of Illinois Press, 2002.

"Will the Baby Be Normal?" *Time,* August 1, 1960.

Winn, Marie. *The Plug-In Drug: Television, Children, and the Family.* Rev. ed. New York: Penguin Books, 1985.

Winship, Albert E. *Jukes — Edwards: A Study in Education and Heredity.* Harrisburg, Pa.: R. L. Myers, 1900.

Wood, Leland Foster. "The Church and Education for the Family." *Religion in Life* 3 (1934): 420-31.

Woodhouse, Chase Going. "Mother: General Manager of the Plant." *Parents',* February 1929.

Woodward, C. Vann, and Elisabeth Muhlenfeld. *The Private Mary Chesnut: The Unpublished Civil War Diaries.* New York: Oxford University Press, 1984.

World Health Organization. *Global Strategy for Infant and Young Child Feeding.* World Health Assembly, 2002. Geneva: World Health Organization, 2003.

Yates, Dorothy L. "We Put Christ in Our Christmas Cards." *Together,* October 1956.

Zelizer, Viviana A. *Pricing the Priceless Child: The Changing Social Value of Children.* Princeton: Princeton University Press, 1985.

Zenderland, Leila. *Measuring Minds: Henry Herbert Goddard and the Origins of American Intelligence Testing.* Cambridge: Cambridge University Press, 1998.

Zimmerman, Rachel. "Drug Makers Find a Windfall Testing Adult Drugs on Kids." *Wall Street Journal,* February 5, 2001.

Zito, Julie Magno. "Trends in the Prescribing of Psychotropic Medications to Preschoolers." *JAMA* 283 (February 23, 2000): 1025-30.

# Credits

## Introduction

Hymn     "HOPE OF THE WORLD," Words: Georgia Harkness, Words © 1954, ren. 1982 The Hymn Society (admin. Hope Publishing Company, Carol Stream, IL 60188). All rights reserved. Used by permission.

Fig. 0.3     Public domain.

Fig. 0.4     Reprinted by permission of the General Commission on Archives and History, the United Methodist Church.

## Chapter 1

Fig. 1.1     Used by permission of the Social Welfare History Archives, University of Minnesota Libraries.

Fig. 1.2     Creation of images was facilitated by the American Theological Library Association's Cooperative Digital Resources Initiative.

Fig. 1.4     Creation of images was facilitated by the American Theological Library Association's Cooperative Digital Resources Initiative.

Fig. 1.5     Creation of images was facilitated by the American Theological Library Association's Cooperative Digital Resources Initiative.

Fig. 1.7     Creation of images was facilitated by the American Theological Library Association's Cooperative Digital Resources Initiative.

Fig. 1.8     Creation of images was facilitated by the American Theological Library Association's Cooperative Digital Resources Initiative.

Fig. 1.13     Creation of images was facilitated by the American Theological Library Association's Cooperative Digital Resources Initiative. Courtesy of Special Collections, Duke University.

Fig. 1.18     Creation of images was facilitated by the American Theological Library Association's Cooperative Digital Resources Initiative.

Fig. 1.19    Creation of images was facilitated by the American Theological
             Library Association's Cooperative Digital Resources Initiative.
Fig. 1.20    Creation of images was facilitated by the American Theological
             Library Association's Cooperative Digital Resources Initiative.
Fig. 1.21    Creation of images was facilitated by the American Theological
             Library Association's Cooperative Digital Resources Initiative.
Fig. 1.24    Creation of images was facilitated by the American Theological
             Library Association's Cooperative Digital Resources Initiative.
Fig. 1.27    Public domain.
Fig. 1.28    Public domain.
Fig. 1.29    Public domain.
Fig. 1.30    Public domain.
Fig. 1.31    Public domain.
Fig. 1.32    Creation of images was facilitated by the American Theological
             Library Association's Cooperative Digital Resources Initiative.
Fig. 1.33    Creation of images was facilitated by the American Theological
             Library Association's Cooperative Digital Resources Initiative.
Fig. 1.34    Creation of images was facilitated by the American Theological
             Library Association's Cooperative Digital Resources Initiative.
Fig. 1.35    Creation of images was facilitated by the American Theological
             Library Association's Cooperative Digital Resources Initiative.
Fig. 1.36    Creation of images was facilitated by the American Theological
             Library Association's Cooperative Digital Resources Initiative.
Fig. 1.37    Creation of images was facilitated by the American Theological
             Library Association's Cooperative Digital Resources Initiative.
Fig. 1.38    Creation of images was facilitated by the American Theological
             Library Association's Cooperative Digital Resources Initiative.

## Chapter 2

Fig. 2.4     Creation of images was facilitated by the American Theological
             Library Association's Cooperative Digital Resources Initiative.
Fig. 2.5     Used by the kind permission of Mead Johnson.
Fig. 2.9     Creation of images was facilitated by the American Theological
             Library Association's Cooperative Digital Resources Initiative.
Fig. 2.10    Creation of images was facilitated by the American Theological
             Library Association's Cooperative Digital Resources Initiative.
Fig. 2.11    Creation of images was facilitated by the American Theological
             Library Association's Cooperative Digital Resources Initiative.
Fig. 2.13    Reprinted with permission of R. H. Donnelley.
Fig. 2.14    Reprinted with permission of R. H. Donnelley.
Fig. 2.15    Reprinted with permission of R. H. Donnelley.

Fig. 2.16     © 2007 Ripley Entertainment Inc.

Fig. 2.17     Reprinted with permission of R. H. Donnelley.

Fig. 2.18     Reprinted with permission of R. H. Donnelley.

Fig. 2.19     Official poster for Chicago World's Fair by George B. Petty, 1933, Chicago History Museum (Chi-06172).

Fig. 2.21     Reprinted with permission of R. H. Donnelley.

Fig. 2.22     Creation of images was facilitated by the American Theological Library Association's Cooperative Digital Resources Initiative.

Fig. 2.24     Creation of images was facilitated by the American Theological Library Association's Cooperative Digital Resources Initiative.

Fig. 2.25     Creation of images was facilitated by the American Theological Library Association's Cooperative Digital Resources Initiative.

Fig. 2.27     Creation of images was facilitated by the American Theological Library Association's Cooperative Digital Resources Initiative.

Fig. 2.28     Courtesy of Dupont. Creation of image was facilitated by the American Theological Library Association's Cooperative Digital Resources Initiative.

Fig. 2.29     Creation of images was facilitated by the American Theological Library Association's Cooperative Digital Resources Initiative.

Fig. 2.30     Creation of images was facilitated by the American Theological Library Association's Cooperative Digital Resources Initiative.

Fig. 2.31     Creation of images was facilitated by the American Theological Library Association's Cooperative Digital Resources Initiative.

Fig. 2.34     Creation of images was facilitated by the American Theological Library Association's Cooperative Digital Resources Initiative.

Fig. 2.35     Creation of images was facilitated by the American Theological Library Association's Cooperative Digital Resources Initiative.

Fig. 2.36     Creation of images was facilitated by the American Theological Library Association's Cooperative Digital Resources Initiative.

Fig. 2.37     Creation of images was facilitated by the American Theological Library Association's Cooperative Digital Resources Initiative.

Fig. 2.40     Used by the kind permission of Mead Johnson.

Fig. 2.41     Used by the kind permission of Mead Johnson.


## Chapter 3

Fig. 3.2      Reprinted by permission of the American Philosophical Society.

Fig. 3.3      Used by permission of the Social Welfare History Archives, University of Minnesota Libraries.

Fig. 3.4      Used by permission of the Social Welfare History Archives, University of Minnesota Libraries.

Fig. 3.5        Used by permission of the Social Welfare History Archives, University of Minnesota Libraries.

Fig. 3.6        Used by permission of the Social Welfare History Archives, University of Minnesota Libraries.

Fig. 3.7        Courtesy of Cold Spring Harbor Laboratory Archives.

Fig. 3.8        Reprinted by permission of the M. E. Grenander Department of Special Collections and Archives, University of Albany Libraries.

Fig. 3.9        Reprinted by permission of the M. E. Grenander Department of Special Collections and Archives, University of Albany Libraries.

Fig. 3.10       Reprinted by permission of the M. E. Grenander Department of Special Collections and Archives, University of Albany Libraries.

Fig. 3.11       Reprinted by permission of the American Philosophical Society.

Fig. 3.12       Reprinted by permission of the American Philosophical Society.

Fig. 3.13       Reprinted by permission of the American Philosophical Society.

Fig. 3.14       Reprinted by permission of the American Philosophical Society.

Fig. 3.15       Reprinted by permission of the American Philosophical Society.

## Chapter 4

Hymn          "This Is My Song." Lloyd Stone/Georgia Harkness © 1934, 1962 Lorenz Publishing Company Stanza 3 by Georgia Harkness © 1964 LPC. Reprinted by kind permission of the publisher.

Fig. 4.13       Used by permission of the Social Welfare History Archives, University of Minnesota Libraries.

Fig. 4.29       By artists Rapuano and Clarke.

Fig. 4.30       Copyright 2007 by The Health Adventure, Asheville, North Carolina. Used by the kind permission of The Health Adventure.

Fig. 4.31       Reprinted with permission of the artist, Nancy Burson.

## Conclusion

Fig. 5.1        Reprinted by the kind permission of Patty Roberts, www.pattyroberts.com.

Fig. 5.4        Reprinted by the kind permission of Patty Roberts, www.pattyroberts.com.

# Index of Subjects and Names